The publication of this book was made possible through a gift by SIDNEY NEUMANN, of Philadelphia, in memory of his parents, ABRAHAM and EMMA NEUMANN.

Pathways
Through
The
Bible

דְּרָכֶיהָ דַרְכֵי נֹעַם וְכָל נְתִיבוֹתֶיהָ שָׁלוֹם

"Its ways are ways of pleasantness
And all its paths are peace."

Proverbs 3.17

Pathways Through The Bible

By

MORTIMER J. COHEN

Illustrations by

ARTHUR SZYK

PHILADELPHIA

THE JEWISH PUBLICATION SOCIETY OF AMERICA

Dedicated
to the memory of
my mother, Rachel,
who was as gentle as her biblical namesake,
and
my father, Joseph,
who in his way was also a man of dreams.

Dedication

In March 1943 my beloved seventy-year-old mother, EUGENIA SZYK, was taken from the ghetto of Lodz to the Nazi furnaces of Maidanek. With her, voluntarily went her faithful servant, the good Christian, JOSEFA, a Polish peasant. Together, hand in hand, they were burned alive. In memory of the two noble martyrs I dedicate my pictures of the Bible as an eternal Kaddish for these great souls.

ARTHUR SZYK

New Canaan, Conn.

FOREWORD

ABOUT six years ago, the Jewish Publication Society of America launched the project of a simplified version of *The Holy Scriptures* which would be readable, easy to comprehend and even enjoyable. *Pathways Through the Bible* seeks to encompass and realize these goals. While this book is intended primarily for the young, it is believed that adults also will find in it interest, instruction and enjoyment.

A special committee advised with the author in planning this volume. It consisted of Mr. Bernard L. Frankel, Chairman; Mr. J. Solis-Cohen, Jr., President of The Society; Judge Louis E. Levinthal, Chairman of its Publication Committee; and Mr. Philip W. Amram. The following rabbis, scholars and educators were appointed as an editorial committee to represent various national institutions and organizations interested in the Bible and concerned with spreading knowledge and appreciation of it among the Jewish people: representing the Aleph Zadik Aleph of B'nai B'rith — Dr. Sidney Glazer and Rabbi Michael Alper; the Central Conference of American Rabbis — Dr. Solomon B. Freehof; the Hebrew Union College — Dr. Abraham N. Franzblau; the Jewish Theological Seminary of America — Rabbi Milton Steinberg; the National Council for Jewish Education — Mr. Nathan Brilliant and Dr. Samuel Dinin; the Rabbinical Assembly of America — Rabbi Alter F. Landesman. In addition to these, the following read all or portions of the manuscript: Dr. Sheldon H. Blank, Professor of Bible at the Hebrew Union College; Dr. Louis Finkelstein, President of the Jewish Theological Seminary of America; Dr. Jacob S. Golub, Librarian-Consultant of the Jewish Education Committee of New York; Dr. Isaac Landman, Editor-in-Chief of the *Universal Jewish Encyclopedia*; and Dr. David de Sola Pool, President of the Union of Sephardic Congregations.

Objectives and Methods

Pathways Through the Bible has been planned to give the reader a broad acquaintance with the contents of the Bible. It embodies such literary and pedagogical devices as will make for better understanding and richer appreciation of *The Holy Scriptures*. The general reader, as well as the teacher, will find here those classic passages of *The Holy Scriptures* which combine both literary beauty and the enduring ethical and religious values of Judaism. These readings are presented in chapters, each one of which contains a thought-unit.

While the Jewish Publication Society translation of the Bible has been used as the basic text, liberty has been taken occasionally to modernize that text by eliminating difficult words, obscure phrases and archaic expressions, or by substituting modern equivalents for old English words. Sometimes, too, verses have been transposed or rearranged in order to make the reading smooth and unobstructed, and the thought clear. The selections from the Book of Psalms, however, are given in the accepted version. Certain passages like the Ten Commandments, "And thou shalt love the Lord thy God," and a few others, have also been kept in their original English because they are met with in the Prayer Book and are often used for responsive readings in Synagogue services.

So far as possible, the biblical selections have been presented in chronological order, especially in the case of the prophets; and each prophetic book has been set forth as a modern writer would arrange his volume. Because of the abundance and variety of their contents, the selected readings from the Book of Psalms and the Book of Proverbs have been organized about a few large, general and important ideas. The Book of Job is presented as a modern reader would expect a drama to appear. The Books of Chronicles have been omitted as books, but selections from them have been woven into the corresponding portions of the Books of Kings. Certain of the Minor Prophets, too, have been left out; others are represented in their proper historical backgrounds by characteristic selections.

The form and structure of *Pathways Through the Bible* parallel, with minor exceptions, *The Holy Scriptures* in order to familiarize the reader with the latter's form and structure. The Hebrew names and titles have been retained also to help to make him aware of the parallel arrangement.

The purpose of the introduction to each book in *Pathways Through the Bible* is to arouse the curiosity of the reader, to enable him to discover the relevancy of the book's message to the present or to his personal interests, and to direct his attention to the main ideas of the book; and, also, to provide, where necessary, such historical and explanatory material as will assist him to understand better what he reads. The brief paragraph at the head of each selection likewise has its purpose: to prepare the reader to comprehend the specific selection by means of interpretation or rabbinical explanation, thus enabling him the more readily to grasp its significance; and, also, to serve as connective tissue binding the selections together into a continuous narrative.

It cannot be sufficiently emphasized that *Pathways Through the Bible* is not intended to replace *The Holy Scriptures* in the reading experience of young or adult readers; it is rather to be regarded as preparatory to the reading of the Bible itself. Its very title reveals its dominant intention. It seeks to hew out pathways through the richly luxuriant and forestlike complexities of the Bible literature, so that the unskilled traveller may find his way through it with ease and with pleasure. Having a kind of road-map, he is prepared to discover for himself the religious truths, the spiritual insights, and the inspiring literary beauties that lurk on every page and in every line and word of Israel's masterpiece.

If *Pathways Through the Bible* awakens the interest of its readers sufficiently to make them want to read *The Holy Scriptures* — the complete Bible of the Jewish people — then it may be truly said that the primary purpose of the Jewish Publication Society of America and the intention of the author have been fully realized.

In Appreciation

To the committee and the others who cooperated with me, I wish to express my profound appreciation and thanks for reading the manuscript in whole or in part, and for their helpful criticisms and suggestions. While I have profited greatly by their advice, they are not to be held responsible for any interpretations or conclusions expressed in this book.

I am deeply grateful to my teacher and friend, Professor Solomon Zeitlin, who kindly read the galley proofs and offered many helpful suggestions; and to my beloved uncle, Mr. Samuel W. Levine, whose critical appreciation of literature helped to improve the literary style of the book.

Above all, I wish to voice my sincere thanks to Dr. Solomon Grayzel who, as Editor of the Jewish Publication Society and as personal friend, gave freely of his time and knowledge towards the making of this book, offered many valuable suggestions towards its improvement and prepared the manuscript for the press. And to my good friend, Mr. Maurice Jacobs, Executive Vice-President of the Society, I am wholeheartedly grateful for his continuous encouragement and personal interest, and for his expert advice in determining the format and appearance of the volume.

I should, indeed, be utterly remiss, if I were to fail to mention my great indebtedness to my wife, Helen, whose kind patience, limitless sacrifices and ever protecting presence, enabled me to write this book in the midst of a crowded and exacting ministry, the responsibilities of which were greatly increased by the tragedy of World War II and the heartbreaking sorrows of Jewish persecution.

I humbly thank Almighty God for His sustaining spirit during the dark and fearful days of trial and suffering of the past few years. May He receive this book as an offering of thanksgiving and as an act of faith in His holy word. May it enable those who read it to walk its pathways joyfully into His presence.

MORTIMER J. COHEN

Philadelphia, Pennsylvania
January 1946
Tebet 5706

TABLE OF CONTENTS

THE LAW—תּוֹרָה

GENESIS — בְּרֵאשִׁית

EXODUS — שְׁמוֹת

LEVITICUS — וַיִּקְרָא

CONTENTS

AMOS — עָמוֹס

HOSEA — הוֹשֵׁעַ

ISAIAH — יְשַׁעְיָה

ISAIAH OF THE EXILE

JEREMIAH — יִרְמְיָה

EZEKIEL — יְחֶזְקֵאל

JONAH — יוֹנָה

THE WRITINGS—כְּתוּבִים

PSALMS — תְּהִלִּים

PROVERBS — מִשְׁלֵי

JOB — אִיּוֹב

THE SONG OF SONGS — שִׁיר הַשִּׁירִים

CONTENTS

LIST OF ILLUSTRATIONS

ARCHEOLOGICAL ILLUSTRATIONS

(FOLLOWING PAGE 548)

1. THE STELE OF MERNEPTAH
2. THE CODE OF HAMMURABI
3. KING SOLOMON'S STABLES
4. KING SOLOMON'S MINES
5. THE SITE OF KING SOLOMON'S MINES
6. THE MESHA STONE
7. BLACK OBELISK OF SHALMANESER
8. SEAL SIGNET RING OF JOTHAM, KING OF JUDAH
9. THE SILOAM INSCRIPTION
10. THE GEZER CALENDAR

MAPS

YOUR BIBLE

YOU have heard of the Bible. You know it is a sacred book, and that it has been highly esteemed by all mankind throughout the ages. You may have even tried to read it. You probably found it hard to read or become interested in, at least in those copies of the Bible you have seen. You may, indeed, have become discouraged about understanding the Bible, and have made up your mind that, like other classics, it is a book to be praised but not really to be read.

Here is the Bible especially prepared for you. It gives you almost all that the Bible contains, in simple, clear and direct language. Its purpose is to open for you pathways into the magic realm of the greatest literature ever written by men. It should enable you to read the Bible with understanding and genuine enjoyment.

What is the Bible?

Now, briefly, what is the Bible? The Bible tells the most wonderful story that has ever been told; it is a story of which men can never grow tired. It tells of men's search for the meaning of our existence in this vast world in which we live, and of all that it contains; and it describes how a small, but gifted people — the Jewish people — found that meaning in a universal God. Consequently, the Jews considered themselves a chosen people, not to master the world and its peoples, but to teach mankind to know God and what He wants of men, and so to contribute to mankind's understanding of the meaning of the universe, and of how they can make the most of their lives.

The Bible tells about the origins of this people and the beginnings of their religion. Since Judaism is the mother religion of both Christianity and Mohammedanism, the followers of those great faiths consider the Bible to be part of their religious possessions. Thus, the Bible has become the spiritual inheritance of a large part of humanity. Yet, though the Bible has become the possession of all the universal religions, it is a Jewish book, created by Jews, recording the life and spiritual adventures of the Jewish people.

Is the Bible one Book?

Is the Bible one book? The name "Bible" comes from the Greek word *biblos* which means a "book." However, it was specifically applied, from earliest times, to the Jewish scriptures as *The* Book. To be sure, we speak of the Bible as if it were one book, for we usually find it printed and bound in one volume. But, it is really more than one book. It is a collection of many volumes. It is, in truth, a library consisting of twenty-four books written over many centuries, in different countries, and by many men.

In a deeper sense, of course, the Bible does possess an inner unity. Running through all these varied books and unifying them is the inspiring theme of how God revealed Himself to the Jewish people, and through them to all mankind; how Israel's religious geniuses came to know God better and better; and how the Jewish people sought to live their lives, as individuals and as a people, in the light of what they believed God wanted them to do. Like the variations of a single melody, the books of the Bible, each different from the other, record this great and noble theme.

A living, exciting World

Unfortunately, the Bible is most often dressed in gloomy black. This misleads us into believing that the Bible is a sad and dismal book. Nothing could be further from the truth. On the contrary, its pages shine with the valiant and ofttimes thrilling deeds of daring men and brave women. It teaches wisdom for daily living. It sings of love and adventure. It records great sacrifice and noble faith. It is filled with beautiful and tender poetry. It is rich with stirring drama. It contains majestic and eloquent oratory. It describes battles and campaigns of swift-moving, shrewd military leaders. It recounts how the Jews conquered a land for themselves, built a glorious kingdom there, and played their role in the international world of that age. Across its pages march those inspired men — the Hebrew prophets — whose words still ring through the centuries, proclaiming that God wants men to live righteously and act justly.

The Bible also exposes all the evil deeds men do that make life dark and sad with pain and sorrow. It does not hide the sins of the great. It does not excuse the mistakes of Israel. It records everything. The Bible is the story of a living, exciting world, teeming with life and struggle, good and evil, defeat and triumph. This story the Bible tells with all its varied lights and shadows. Truly, it should be bound in the golden colors of the sun.

Almost the entire Bible was written originally in Hebrew; a few parts were written in Aramaic. It was translated into all the languages of the world. In this way its message spread everywhere. It became the universal treasure of mankind; and it helped men to discover the value and sacredness of life.

The Bible's three Divisions

The Bible is divided into three large parts. The first is "The Law" (in Hebrew, *Torah*), sometimes spoken of as the Pentateuch, the Five Books of Moses; the second is "The Prophets" (in Hebrew, *Nebi'im*); and the third is called "The Writings" (in Hebrew, *Ketubim*).

ARCHAEOLOGY AND THE BIBLE

"Truth springeth out of the earth."

(Psalms 85.11)

What is Biblical Archaeology?

ARCHAEOLOGY opens pathways into the distant past. And archaeologists are guides into ancient lands and civilizations that have disappeared but whose remains — towns and cities, houses, monuments, tools, pottery, and cemeteries — may be found covered up by the dust and sand of centuries.

The special branch of archaeology that deals with the lands and peoples mentioned in our Bible — Palestine, Syria, Babylonia, Assyria, and Egypt — and their civilizations, is called Biblical Archaeology. It is not very old, about a hundred years. Within this century, however, it has brought us a wealth of new information about biblical times and has helped us to a better understanding of our Bible.

Do We Need Archaeology to Prove the Bible is True?

Important as its discoveries are, archaeology cannot prove or disprove what our Bible teaches us about the great and eternal beliefs of the Jewish religion. It brings us, however, a larger understanding of the backgrounds of the biblical world, and a keener appreciation of the Bible's ideas and teachings in contrast with those of the world out of which it came.

A biblical scholar wisely said, "We can now see that though the Bible arose in the ancient world, it was not entirely of it; though its history and people resemble those of the surrounding nations, yet it radiates an atmosphere, a spirit, a faith, far more profound and radically different from any other ancient literature."

How does Biblical Archaeology help us to a better understanding and appreciation of our Bible?

Daily Life of Ancient Peoples

In the first place, it provides us with the actual details of the daily life of ancient peoples. We now know how they made their tents and built their houses; the kinds of clothes they wore; how they earned their livings and conducted their businesses, trades, and professions; their creative arts and crafts, their science and amusements; what their schools were like; how they worshiped their gods; and how they buried their dead.

We meet biblical names in use among the ancients, such as Terah, Nahor, Haran, Abraham, Jacob-el, and Benjamin. These do not refer to biblical characters, but reflect a common cultural background.

Such extra-biblical sources strengthen our acceptance of the reliability of our Bible and enrich our feelings about the reality of our ancestors.

Pushing Back the Frontiers

On a moving-picture screen, when the camera's eye expands and views the whole scene surrounding the main character, we see him standing not alone, as we thought, but on a crowded highway with jostling throngs swirling about him.

When the Bible was our only lens into antiquity, the stage of history seemed shallow in depth and narrow in breadth. Israel appeared to stand alone in a vast, almost empty world. With Biblical Archaeology pushing back the frontiers of the ancient world, we see the Bible in grander perspective.

We now see Abraham raised in the midst of the great Sumerian civilization whose history can be traced back at least 1500 years before his time. History really began with the Sumerians. Their inventions and literary accomplishments amaze us. They devised the first practical and effective system of writing called cuneiform (wedge-shaped).

Sumerian ideas, literature, philosophy, and religion were undoubtedly part of Abraham's education and thinking as well as of the little group that left Ur of the Chaldees with him and his father for Haran and the Promised Land beyond.

Expanding the Ancient World

Biblical Archaeology has revealed a world that moves deeper into time and has discovered a larger and broader world of space with more peoples and cultures than had previously been known.

Monuments and pictures on the walls of temples and royal palaces, and thousands of clay and stone tablets, record historical events and preserve codes of law and fascinating tales by peoples whose names alone survive in our Bible — the Hittites, the Hurrians (called Horites), and others. Only recently the remains of the people of Ugarit, living to the immediate north of Israel, have been discovered. Their language, so much like biblical Hebrew, has been used by scholars to ascertain more exactly the meaning of Hebrew words in our Bible.

For long centuries these peoples have slept unknown in the graveyard of history. The archaeologists have resurrected them. And a rich harvest of new knowledge now sets our Bible within a crowded, teeming, and struggling world of clashing peoples and warring empires.

Out of that now dead world, Israel only has survived.

Israel in the Mainstream of History

Biblical Archaeology has illuminated the perilous course of the Jewish people in the turbulent stream of world history. Our Bible implies the many contacts that existed between Israel and the surrounding nations. But only through archaeology have these relationships been exposed as being so widespread and intricate.

The earliest reference to Israel outside the Bible is found on a monument set up by a boastful Egyptian Pharaoh. Moab also celebrated its successful revolt against Israel on a monument. The very first pictures of a Jewish king and of Israelites were chiseled on an obelisk of an Assyrian emperor. Sargon II proclaims, "I besieged and conquered Samaria." Nebuchadnezzar tells how he seized Jerusalem, captured her king, and set up another king to his own liking. And another monument describes how a king of Judah in far off Babylonia lived on the bounty of the Royal Court.

These and other extra-biblical records witness to the events described in our Bible and help us to realize how deeply Israel was involved in the power politics and international events of ancient times.

Languages and Customs

Biblical Archaeologists faced enormous difficulties in unlocking the secrets of the past because the languages and the symbols in which they were written — cuneiform, hieroglyphic and others — were unknown. They enlisted the aid of linguists and philologists (experts in languages) to decipher these strange tongues. How these mysteries were unlocked is one of the most thrilling achievements of the human mind.

Archaeology has definitely established the wide dissemination of the writing skill in antiquity. It has refuted the arguments of some scholars that the patriarchs and Moses and the people of Bible times could not have written the Bible, nor were there sufficient numbers who could read what was written. Now we know that writing was already in use in the year 3000 B.C.E.

Biblical Archaeology has thus made possible more accurate translations from the Hebrew. It has cast new light on obscure passages in the Bible. It has enabled us through newly acquired literatures to trace the cultural development of some Jewish ideas, customs, and laws.

One example among many of how archaeology throws light on strange behavior in the Bible may be seen in the case of Rachel who took the household gods of her father Laban without his knowledge. Hurrian law and custom inform us that these figurines symbolized her title to her share of Laban's possessions. By taking them Rachel sought to protect her own and her husband's rights.

These then are some of the more important ways in which Biblical Archaeology has opened new pathways of understanding and appreciation of *The Holy Scriptures*.

On Using the Notes about Archaeology and the Bible

The reader's attention is directed by the downward-pointing arrow to the bottom of the page where he will be referred to a numbered item at the end of this book.

We include here only a few of the more interesting and valuable contributions of Biblical Archaeology. For fuller accounts and more numerous examples consult the Bibliography.

Pathways
Through
The
Bible

תּוֹרָה

THE LAW

בְּרֵאשִׁית

GENESIS

HOW did the world begin? Why is there evil in the world, that brings pain and suffering? Why do men have to work so hard to make a living? How did murder come into the world? What was the origin of clothes? How did the arts and crafts of civilization begin?

Men have always asked these questions. They have often wondered why there are so many nations, and why men speak different languages. They have marvelled at the mysteries of nature — its rainbow in the storm-clouds, its loathsome creeping things, its floods and earthquakes that destroy cities and peoples.

Our Jewish ancestors asked these questions, too, and many others. They were also curious about themselves and their origins. It was amazing to them how the Jewish people, small and weak, and buffeted about by mighty kings and powerful empires, managed to survive. Did they possess some secret power mightier than the sword? What was that power? Why was Abraham chosen to found the Jewish people, and why did God enter into a covenant, a kind of agreement, with him? What was the nature of this covenant? How did Canaan (now called Palestine) become the Land of Israel?

The Book of Genesis is concerned with these and many other matters. Of course, men in ancient times had different ideas from those that modern science teaches us of how the world and mankind were brought into being. But this need not confuse us.

The Bible speaks in "the ordinary language of men." Therefore, it used the ideas men had at the time it was written to enable them to understand more readily the great spiritual teachings of the Jewish religion. Although our ideas of the world have changed and, with increasing knowledge, may further change,

3

these great beliefs are unaffected by them, and will remain unaffected forever.

The real purpose of the Book of Genesis, like that of the rest of the Bible, is not to teach us scientific facts, but to tell us how God wants men to live in the world He created for them; and how the highest beliefs of the Jewish religion can help men to bring out the best within themselves and achieve a happy and worth-while life.

Genesis is the first of the Books of Moses, as well as of the Bible. Its Hebrew name is *Bereshith* and is taken from its first word which means "In the beginning."

I.

CREATING A GOOD WORLD

God had a great plan. He wished to bring into being a good world which could become man's home. Our sages,* who interpreted the Bible, said that God had created other worlds before this one, but they were not satisfactory, so He destroyed them. Then God made this one, fit for men to live in. Here they could find everything that would sustain them and enable them to achieve a happy and worth-while life, provided men used the abundant goodness of the world humanely and justly. To show that God wanted this kind of a world, the Bible states after each thing He created that God saw that it was good, and when the whole creation was completed God saw that the world was "very good" for men to live in.

IN THE beginning God created the heaven and the earth. The earth had no form, and darkness covered the waters; and the spirit of God hovered over the waters. And God said:

"Let there be light!"

And there was light. God saw that the light was good, and He separated the light from the darkness. God called the light Day, and the darkness He called Night. And there was evening and there was morning, one day.

Then God said:

"Let there be a firmament between the waters, dividing them!"

And God made the firmament, dividing the waters under the firmament from the waters above the firmament, and God called the firmament Heaven. And there was evening and there was morning, a second day.

Then God said:

"Let the waters under the heaven be gathered into one place, and let the dry land appear!"

And it was so. God called the dry land Earth, and the gathered waters Seas. And God saw that it was good.

*Our sages were the great and learned rabbis and teachers of Israel. They loved the Bible and studied it, and commented on almost every word in it. They explained what the Bible meant to them. Their explanations were written down later, and may now be found in many books, especially in *The Midrash* and *The Talmud*.

And God said:

"Let the earth bring forth grass, plants yielding seed, and trees bearing fruit of every kind, with its seed in it!"

And it was so. The earth brought forth grass, plants bearing seed of every kind and trees yielding fruit of every kind, fruit with its seed in it. And God saw that it was good. And there was evening and there was morning, a third day.

Then God said:

"Let there be lights in the heavens to separate day from night! Let them be for signs to mark out the seasons, the days, and the years! Let them shine in heaven to give light upon the earth!"

And it was so. God made the two great lights, the sun and the moon, the greater light to rule the day, and the lesser light to rule the night; and the stars. God set them in the heavens to give light upon the earth, to rule the day and the night, and to separate the light from the darkness. And God saw that it was good. And there was evening and there was morning, a fourth day.

Then God said:

"Let the waters swarm with living creatures, and let birds fly above the earth under the heavens!"

God created the great sea-beasts, and every kind of living creature with which the waters swarm, and also every kind of winged bird. God saw that it was good, and God blessed them, saying:

"Be fruitful, and multiply, and fill the waters of the seas; and let the birds multiply on the earth!"

And there was evening and there was morning, a fifth day.

Then God said:

"Let the earth bring forth all kinds of living creatures, cattle, reptiles, and wild beasts!"

And it was so. God made every kind of wild beast, every kind of animal, and every kind of reptile; and God saw that it was good.

Then God said:

"Let us make man in our image, after our likeness, and let him have mastery over the fish of the sea, the birds of the air, the animals, every wild beast of the earth, and every reptile that creeps on the earth!"

GOD'S GOOD WORLD

"... male and female created He them." *(Genesis 1.27)*

see page 6

ABRAHAM CALLED FROM UR
OF THE CHALDEES

"Leave your country, your kindred, and your father's
home for the land that I will show you." (*Genesis 12.1*)

see page 19

And the Lord God formed man of the dust of the ground, and breathed into his nostrils the breath of life; and man became a living being. So God created man in His own image.

Then God blessed man, and said:

"Be fruitful, and multiply, and fill the earth, and subdue it; and have mastery over the fish of the sea, the birds of the air, and every living creature that creeps on the earth!"

And God also said:

"Behold, I give you every plant yielding seed, all over the earth, and every tree bearing seed in its fruit; let that be your food. To every wild beast on the earth, and to every bird of the air, and to every living creature that creeps on the earth, I give all the green growth for food."

And it was so. God saw everything that He had made, and behold, it was very good. And there was evening and there was morning, the sixth day.

The Sabbath — A Day of Rest

Thus the heavens and the earth were finished, and all the host of them. And on the seventh day God finished His work which He had made; and He rested on the seventh day from all His work which He had made. And God blessed the seventh day, and made it holy; because on it He rested from all His work which God in creating had made. *(Genesis 1, 2)*

II.

EVIL ENTERS THE GOOD WORLD

The story of the garden of Eden tells how evil entered the good world. The serpent, according to our sages, persuaded Adam and Eve to become "independent of God," that is, to rebel against Him and disobey His command. God had given Adam and Eve the power to choose between right and wrong, otherwise they would not have been free creatures. When Adam disobeyed God's command and ate the fruit, the seed of evil was planted in the world, for by that act man showed that he denied God's rule in the world and that he set himself up "as God," that is, he wanted to exercise unlimited power like God. As a result of their rebellion against God's laws, on which their very lives depended, Adam and Eve began for the first time to feel guilt, shame and fear. Their happiness was changed into unhappiness. And their wrongdoing brought pain, suffering and death into the world.

THE Lord God planted a garden eastward, in Eden; and He put there the man, Adam, whom He had formed. From the ground the Lord God made grow all kinds of trees that were pleasant to the sight and good for food. The tree of life and the tree that gives knowledge of good and evil He placed in the middle of the garden. And there was a river flowing from Eden to water the garden.

The Lord God took the man and put him in the garden of Eden to till it and to guard it. And the Lord God commanded the man:

"You are free to eat from every tree in the garden; but you must not eat from the fruit of the tree that yields knowledge of good and evil, for on the day you eat from that tree you shall die" (that is, become subject to death).

From the ground God formed every beast of the field and every bird of the air, bringing them to the man to see what he would call them; whatever the man called any living creature, that was to be its name. The man named all the animals and the birds and every beast of the field, but no companion could be found to suit the man, Adam, himself.

Then the Lord God said:

"It is not good that the man should be alone; I will make a companion to suit him."

Then the Lord God caused a deep sleep to fall upon the man; and while he slept, He took one of the man's ribs, closing up the flesh in its place. The rib He had taken from the man, the Lord God shaped into a woman, and brought her to the man. Then the man said:

> "This is now bone of my bones,
> And flesh of my own flesh;
> She shall be called Woman,
> For out of Man was she taken."

This is why a man leaves his father and mother to marry a wife, and they become one.

Both the man and his wife were naked, but they felt no shame.

Now the serpent was more cunning than any other creature that the Lord God had made. And it said to the woman:

"Has God said that you are not to eat fruit from any tree in the garden?"

"We may eat fruit from the trees in the garden," said the woman, "but of the fruit of the tree in the center of the garden, God has said: 'You shall not eat from it, neither shall you touch it, lest you die.' "

Then the serpent said to the woman:

"No, you shall not die; God knows that the day you eat from it, your eyes will be opened and you will be as God, knowing what is good and what is evil."

When the woman learned that the fruit of the tree was good for food, and that it was a delight to the eyes, and that the fruit of the tree would make one wise, she took some of the fruit and ate it; she also gave some to her husband, and he ate. Then the eyes of them both were opened, and they realized that they were naked; and they sewed fig-leaves together, and made themselves clothes. In the cool of the day, when they heard the voice of the Lord God walking in the garden, the man and his wife hid themselves from the presence of the Lord God among the trees of the garden. But the Lord God called to the man and said:

"Where are you?"

"I heard Thy voice in the garden," he replied, "and I was afraid, because I was naked; so I hid myself."

"Who told you that you were naked?" He asked. "Have you eaten from the tree from which I forbade you to eat?"

The man said:

"The woman Thou hast given me as a companion, she gave me some fruit from the tree, and I ate it."

Then the Lord God said to the woman:

"What is this that you have done?"

The woman said:

"I ate it because the serpent misled me."

Then the Lord God said to the serpent:

> "Because you have done this,
> Most cursed shall you be of all beasts!
> On your belly shall you crawl,
> And eat dust all the days of your life.
> Always shall men and serpents be enemies.
> They shall bruise your head,
> And you shall bruise their heel."

To the woman He said:

"I will make your pain at childbirth very great; in pain shall you bear children. You shall strongly desire your husband, and he shall rule over you."

And to the man He said:

"Because you have hearkened to what your wife said and have eaten from the tree from which I forbade you to eat,

> "Cursed shall be the ground because of you;
> In toil shall you eat of it all the days of your life;
> Thorns and thistles shall it bring forth to you;
> In the sweat of your face shall you eat bread,
> Till you die and return to the ground;
> For out of it were you taken;
> For dust you are,
> And to dust shall you return."

The man named his wife Eve (*Havvah* — the one who gives life), because she was the mother of all human beings.

And the Lord God made garments of skins for Adam and his wife, and clothed them.

Then the Lord God said:

"Behold, the man has become like one of us; he knows good and evil. He might put out his hand now to take also of the tree of life, and by eating of it, live for ever!"

Therefore, the Lord God sent Adam forth from the garden of Eden, to till the ground from which he was taken. And He placed at the east of the garden of Eden the cherubim (angels), and the flaming sword which flashed in every direction, to guard the path to the tree of life. *(Genesis 2, 3)*

III.

THE CLEANSING FLOOD

Men multiplied and spread over the earth, and evil increased with them. So heartless did they become that, according to our sages, they put clothes on their marble statues to protect them against the winter's storms, but neglected the poor who died of the bitter cold. It was such wrongdoing that brought about the destruction of mankind by the flood. Only one family escaped — that of the righteous Noah. Many ancient peoples believed that a flood had once destroyed almost all mankind, but only the Bible explained it to be the result of man's evil deeds.

Cain and Abel

ADAM and Eve had two sons, Cain and Abel. Abel was a shepherd, Cain a farmer.

In the course of time, Cain brought some fruit of the earth as an offering to the Lord. And Abel brought some of the first-born of his flock and sacrificed them to the Lord. The Lord favored Abel and his offering; but He did not favor Cain and his offering.

Cain was very angry, and his face showed it. The Lord said to Cain:

"Why are you angry? and why are you downcast? If you do what is right, will not your offering be accepted? But if you do wrong, sin crouches at the door; and the desire to sin will master you; but you may master it."

Then Cain quarrelled with his brother Abel, and when they were out in the field, Cain rose up against Abel his brother, and slew him.

And the Lord said to Cain:

"Where is Abel your brother?"

Cain answered:

"I do not know. Am I my brother's keeper?"

The Lord said:

"What have you done? The voice of your brother's blood cries to Me from the ground! And now you shall be cursed by banishment from the very ground that has opened its mouth to swallow the brother's blood you shed. After this, when you till the ground, it shall not yield you its fruits; a fugitive and a wanderer shall you be on the earth."

And Cain said to the Lord:

"My punishment is greater than I can bear. Behold, Thou hast driven me out this day from this land; and from Thy face shall I be hidden; and I shall become a fugitive and a wanderer on the earth; and whoever finds me will slay me."

The Lord said to him:

"Whoever slays Cain shall be punished sevenfold."

And the Lord set a mark on Cain, to prevent anyone who found him from killing him. Then Cain left the presence of the Lord and lived in the land of Nod, on the east of Eden.

Cain and his wife had a son, Enoch; and Cain built a city and named it after his son, Enoch. To Enoch was born Irad; and Irad was the father of Mehujael; and Mehujael was the father of Methushael; and Methushael bore Lamech.

Beginnings of Arts and Crafts

Now Lamech married two wives; the name of one was Adah, and the name of the other Zillah. Adah bore Jabal, the ancestor of shepherds who dwell in tents. His brother's name was Jubal, the ancestor of all who play the harp and the pipe. And Zillah bore Tubal-cain, the smith, who forged instruments of copper and iron.

The boastful Violence of Lamech

Lamech said to his wives:

"Adah and Zillah, hear my voice;
    You wives of Lamech, hear what I say:
    I have slain a man for wounding me.
    If Cain shall be avenged sevenfold,
    Truly Lamech seventy and sevenfold."

The Ancestry of the Righteous

Adam and Eve bore another son and called him Seth, saying:
"God has given another child to us instead of Abel whom Cain killed."

Seth also had a son born to him called Enosh. Then men began to worship God by His name.

Evil grows and spreads

Now it came to pass when men began to multiply on the face of the earth, and daughters were born to them, that the angels saw the daughters of men that they were beautiful; and they married them, whomsoever they chose. In those days the Nephilim (giants) were on the earth, and also after that, when the angels and the daughters of men married, they had children; these were the mighty men that were of old, the men of renown.

When God saw that the wickedness of man was great on the earth and that his thoughts were bent on evil continually, He was sorry that He had made man on the earth; it caused grief to Him. Then the Lord said:

"I will blot out man whom I have created from the face of the earth, both man and beast and reptile and bird; for I am sorry that I have made them."

One righteous Man — Noah

In those days there lived Noah, a righteous and upright man. He was the father of three sons: Shem, Ham and Japheth. Noah lived close to God, and found favor with the Lord. When God saw that the earth was corrupt and was filled with violence and outrage, He said to Noah:

"I have decided to put an end to every human being. They have filled the earth with violence and outrage; I will destroy them and the earth together. Make yourself an ark of wood. Build rooms in the ark and cover it inside and outside with pitch. Make a roof for it and in it a window, and put the doorway of the ark in its side; also put three decks in it. For I am sending a flood of waters on the earth, to destroy every living creature under heaven; everything on earth shall perish."

And God continued to speak to Noah:

"But I will make a covenant with you; you shall enter the ark accompanied by your sons, Shem, Ham and Japheth, your wife, and your sons' wives. And you shall bring into the ark seven pairs of clean creatures of every kind, to keep them alive along with you; one of every pair is to be male and one female. And of the beasts that are not clean you shall take two pairs, the male and his mate, that they may be kept alive. Go now and gather every kind of edible food, and store it away to be food for you and for them."

Noah did all that God commanded him. Then the Lord said to him:

"Enter now, you and all your household into the ark, for I have judged you of all the men of today to be upright before Me. In seven days' time I will make it rain on the earth forty days and forty nights, and I will blot off the face of the earth every living creature that I have made."

Noah did all that the Lord had commanded.

At the end of the seven days, the waters of the flood covered the earth; and Noah went into the ark along with his sons and his wife and his sons' wives, driven by the waters of the flood. Then the Lord shut him in.

For forty days and forty nights rain fell upon the earth; the waters increased, and the ark was lifted and raised above the earth. The waters rose higher and higher, till the tallest mountains were all covered. Every creature that moved on the earth, men, beasts, reptiles, and birds perished; they were blotted out from the earth. Only Noah and they that were with him inside the ark were left.

Then God remembered Noah and all the living creatures and the animals that were with him in the ark. God made a wind to blow over the earth, till the waters went down; the rain from heaven ceased; and the waters withdrew more and more from the earth; and the ark rested on the mountains of Ararat.

Noah then opened the window that he had made in the ark, and sent out a raven which went flying to and fro, till the waters had diminished from off the earth. He waited seven days and sent a dove to see if the waters had drained off the face of the ground; but the dove found no resting-place for her feet, and returned to the ark. He put forth his hand and caught her and took her into the ark. After waiting seven days more, he again sent the dove out of the ark. In the evening the dove came back to him, and in her beak was a freshly plucked olive leaf. Noah then knew that the waters had gone from the earth. After waiting seven days more, he sent forth the dove, but she never came back to him. The waters had diminished from off the earth.

The Rainbow — God's Pledge

Noah then removed the covering of the ark and looked, and, behold, the face of the ground was dried!

And God said to Noah:

"Leave the ark, you and your wife and your sons and your sons' wives, and take out every living thing that is with you, every creature, bird and beast and reptile, that they may swarm on the earth, and be fruitful and multiply."

Noah did so. Then he built an altar to the Lord; and he offered up sacrifices on the altar. And the Lord said to Himself:

"I will not again curse the ground, though the bent of man's heart is evil from his youth; never again will I destroy every living creature as I have done. So long as earth remains, seedtime and harvest, cold and heat, summer and winter, day and night, shall not cease."

God blessed Noah and his sons, bidding them:

"Be fruitful and multiply and fill the earth. The fear of you and the dread of you shall be on every beast of the earth and on every bird of the air; for they are now in your power with every reptile of the land and every fish within the sea. Every moving thing that lives shall be food for you; I give you them all as once I gave you the green herbs. Only, you must never eat flesh with the life (that is, the blood) in it."

And God continued:

"As for Me, I establish My covenant with you and with your descendants after you and with every living creature that is with you, that never again shall all living creatures be destroyed by the waters of a flood."

Further God said:

"This is the symbol of the covenant which I make for all time between Me and you and every living creature that is with you: I have set My rainbow in the cloud, and it shall be a symbol of the covenant between Me and the earth. Whenever I bring clouds over the earth, the rainbow is seen in the cloud, I will see it, and I will remember My everlasting covenant with you and every living creature whatsoever; and the waters shall no more become a flood to destroy them."

Now the sons of Noah who came out of the ark were Shem, Ham and Japheth; and from these three, people spread all over the earth. *(Genesis 4–9)*

IV.

THE TOWER OF BABEL

Even after the flood men continued their wrongdoing until, in the pride of their power, they wanted to conquer the heavens. The building of the tower of Babel, according to our sages, was "rebellion against God" and His rule over the world. God had promised not to destroy the whole world again; and so, to prevent man's evil from spreading, God divided mankind into nations, speaking different languages. Each nation would restrain the other's wrongdoing; and thus the growth of evil in the world would be checked.

NOW all the people of the earth spoke one language; and as they travelled from the east, they found a broad valley in the land of Shinar (Babylonia); and they made their home there. Then they said to one another:

"Come, let us make bricks and burn them thoroughly."

Then, as they had bricks for stone and asphalt for mortar, they said:

"Come, let us make a name for ourselves by building a city and a tower with its top in heaven; it will keep us from being scattered abroad upon the face of the whole earth."

The Lord came down to see the city and the tower which human beings had built. The Lord said:

"They are one people, and they have one language; if this is what they do, almost at the very start, nothing that they ever undertake will prove too hard for them. Come, let us go down, and there make a babble of their language, so that they may not understand one another's speech."

So the Lord scattered them abroad from there upon the face of all the earth; and they gave up building the city. Therefore, they named it Babel, because it was there that the Lord made a babble of the language of the whole earth, and from there that the Lord scattered men abroad over all the earth. *(Genesis 11)*

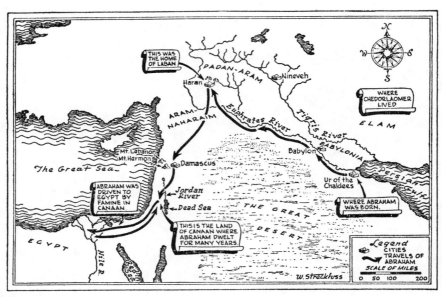

THIS WAS THE HOME OF LABAN

PADAN-ARAM

Haran

Nineveh

WHERE CHEDORLAOMER LIVED

ELAM

ARAM-NAHARAIM

Euphrates River

Tigris River

BABYLONIA

Babylon

Mt. Lebanon
Mt. Hermon

Damascus

The Great Sea

ABRAHAM WAS DRIVEN TO EGYPT BY FAMINE IN CANAAN.

Jordan River

Dead Sea

THIS IS THE LAND OF CANAAN WHERE ABRAHAM DWELT FOR MANY YEARS

THE GREAT DESERT

Ur of the Chaldees

WHERE ABRAHAM WAS BORN.

PERSIAN GULF

EGYPT

Nile River

W. Streckfuss

Legend
CITIES
TRAVELS OF ABRAHAM
SCALE OF MILES
0   50   100   200

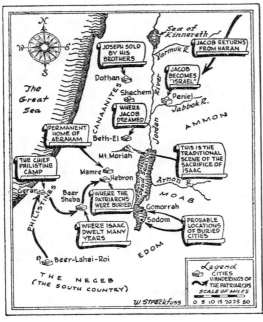

Sea of Kinnereth

JOSEPH SOLD BY HIS BROTHERS

JACOB RETURNS FROM HARAN

Yarmuk R.

Dothan

Shechem

JACOB BECOMES "ISRAEL"

Peniel

Jabbok R.

The Great Sea

WHERE JACOB DREAMED

AMMON

PERMANENT HOME OF ABRAHAM

Beth-El

Mt. Moriah

CANAANITES

THE CHIEF PHILISTINE CAMP

Mamre

Hebron

THIS IS THE TRADITIONAL SCENE OF THE SACRIFICE OF ISAAC

Gerar

Beer Sheba

WHERE THE PATRIARCHS WERE BURIED

Arnon R.

MOAB

Gomorrah

Sodom

PHILISTINES

WHERE ISAAC DWELT MANY YEARS

PROBABLE LOCATIONS OF BURIED CITIES

Beer-Lahai-Roi

EDOM

THE NEGEB
(THE SOUTH COUNTRY)

W. Streckfuss

Legend
CITIES
WANDERINGS OF THE PATRIARCHS
SCALE OF MILES
0 5 10 15 20 25 30

The World of the Patriarchs—Abraham, Isaac, Jacob-Israel and Joseph

V.

ABRAHAM — FOUNDER OF A PEOPLE

Thus far, the Bible has told what our ancestors thought about the beginnings of the world and civilization; and it has described the coming of evil into the world, and how it grew. Now the Bible records what our ancestors believed about the origins of the Jewish people, and tells at great length about its founders, "the Patriarchs," and describes its part in God's plan for all mankind. Mankind, even after the flood, was still bent on doing evil. They needed help to overcome their evil tendencies. It was God's plan to give them a Law, obedience to which would enable them to strengthen their desire to do good and overcome their desire to do evil. Therefore, God chose Abraham, Isaac and Jacob to found and develop a people who would gladly receive and obey that Law, and through the Law help mankind to bring forth the best within themselves, and to make a better world in which to live. This was the meaning of the covenant, or agreement, between Abraham and God, a covenant that would be a blessing to all mankind.

FROM Shem, Noah's eldest son, descended Terah. Terah was the father of Abram, Nahor, and Haran; Haran, the father of Lot, died. Terah took Abram, his son, and Lot his grandson, and Sarai his daughter-in-law, the wife of Abram, and led them from Ur of Chaldees↓ to go to the land of Canaan. But when they reached the city of Haran, they dwelt there. And in Haran, Terah died.

The Call of Abraham

Now the Lord had said to Abram:

"Leave your country, your kindred, and your father's home for the land that I will show you; I will make a great nation of you; I will bless you and make your name great, so that you shall be a blessing. And all the families of the earth shall find themselves blessed through you."

So Abram went, as the Lord had told him. And Abram took his wife Sarai and his nephew Lot, with all the property they had accumulated in Haran, and they started for the land of Canaan; and they came to the land of Canaan. Then the Lord appeared to Abram, and said:

↓For archaeological note see Item 1, p. 549 in the back of the book.

"I give this land to your descendants."

And Abram built an altar there to the Lord who appeared to him.

Lot, Nephew of Abraham

Abram was very rich in cattle, silver and gold. Lot also, who went with Abram, had flocks, and herds, and tents. And the land was not able to support them both. So strife arose between the herdsmen of Abram and the herdsmen of Lot. And Abram said to Lot:

"There must be no quarrel between you and me, nor between your herdsmen and mine; for we are kinsmen. Does not this whole land lie before you? Separate yourself, then, from me. If you will take the left hand, I will take the right; or if you take the right, I will take the left."

Lot looked round and saw all the plain of the Jordan, that it was well watered in every direction. He chose for himself all the valley of the Jordan plain; and he moved his tent as far as Sodom. The men of Sodom were wicked, and they sinned openly against the Lord. But Abram settled in the land of Canaan.

The Promise to Abraham

After Lot had separated from him, the Lord said to Abram:

"Look abroad now from where you are, north, south, east and west; for all the land which you see, I will give to you and your descendants for ever. I will make your descendants as numerous as the dust of the earth; so that if the dust of the earth can be counted, your descendants can be counted. Go and travel the length and the breadth of the land; for I will give it to you."

Then Abram moved his tent, and came and dwelt beside the oaks of Mamre at Hebron; and he built there an altar to the Lord.

Abraham the Warrior

At that time the king of Sodom and the king of Gomorrah, together with three others, waged war against Chedorlaomer and three neighboring kings. They met in battle in the valley of Siddim.

The valley of Siddim was full of slime pits, and when the kings of Sodom and Gomorrah fled, some of their followers fell in them, while the survivors made for the hills. The four kings captured all the goods and all the provisions of Sodom and Gomorrah and went away; they also carried off Lot, the son of Abram's brother, who lived in Sodom, and his goods.

Then one of the survivors came and told Abram the Hebrew, who was living beside the oaks of Mamre, that Lot had been captured. As soon as Abram heard that Lot had been taken prisoner, he led forth his faithful followers and went in pursuit. Dividing his forces by night, he routed the enemy and pursued them to the north near Damascus. He brought back the people and all the goods, and he also recovered his nephew Lot with his goods.

On returning from his defeat of the kings, Abram was met by the king of Sodom who said to Abram, "Keep the goods yourself, and let me have the persons."

Then Abram answered the king of Sodom:

"By this hand raised to the Lord, God Most High, Creator of heaven and earth, I swear I will not take a thread or a shoe-string of yours, lest you should say, 'I have made Abram rich.' Save only what the troops have eaten, let my comrades take their share of the spoil!"

Abraham yearns for a Son

After these events, the Lord came to Abram in a vision and said:

"Fear not, Abram; I am your shield; your reward shall be very great."

Abram said:

"O Lord God, what wilt Thou give me, seeing I go hence childless?"

Then God took Abram outside his tent, and said:

"Look now toward heaven, and count the stars, if you can. So numerous shall your descendants be."

And Abram believed in the Lord.

Hagar, the Egyptian Maid

Abram had been living ten years in the land of Canaan, and his wife Sarai had borne him no children. So she took her handmaid, Hagar the Egyptian, and gave her in marriage to Abram her husband.

Hagar bore a son to Abram, and Abram called his son, born of Hagar, by the name of Ishmael. He grew up a wild man.

When Abram was ninety-nine years old, the Lord appeared to him and said:

"I am God Almighty; conduct yourself before Me so as to be blameless; and then I will establish My covenant with you and multiply your descendants greatly."

Thereupon Abram bowed with reverence before the Lord.

And God continued: *The Change of Names*

"My covenant is with you: you shall be the father of a multitude of nations. Your name shall no longer be called Abram, but your name shall be Abraham; for the father of a multitude of nations have I made you. And as for you, you shall keep My covenant, and likewise your descendants after you. The sign of the covenant which you shall keep between Me and yourself and your descendants after you is this: every male among you shall be circumcised, when he is eight days old (*Brith Milah*). As for your wife Sarai, you shall not call her Sarai, but Sarah. I will bless her and, furthermore, I will give you a son by her; I will bless her, and she shall become a mother of nations; and kings of peoples shall come from her."

Abraham bowed deeply and laughed. He said to himself:

"Shall a man who is a hundred become a father? Sarah is ninety now, and shall she become a mother?"

Then Abraham said to God:

"O that Ishmael might be under Thy care!"

God answered:

"Sarah your wife shall indeed bear you a son; you must call him Isaac (the name meaning 'laughter'). As for Ishmael, I heard what you ask; I have a blessing for him also; I will make him fruitful and multiply him greatly, and I will make him a great nation. Nevertheless, I will fulfill My covenant with Isaac, whom Sarah shall bear to you when the time comes round next year."

Having finished speaking with him, God left Abraham.

Then Abraham was circumcised, and all the men of his house with him.   (*Genesis 12–27*)

VI.

TWIN CITIES OF SIN

The ancient cities of Sodom and Gomorrah were destroyed by earthquake and fire because of the cruelty and violence of their inhabitants. Our sages traced their wickedness to their greed for wealth. They told this tale: If the men of Sodom and Gomorrah saw that a man owned great riches, two of them would lure him to the vicinity of ruins, and while one kept him on the spot by pleasant conversation, the other would undermine the wall near which he stood, until it suddenly crashed down upon and killed him. Then the two plotters would divide up his wealth between them. Our sages further stated that God had acted mercifully towards these cities, for He had warned Sodom and Gomorrah for fifty-two years; but they would not heed His warning. Abraham's nobility of character, his keen sense of justice, and his deep human pity shone like lights in that dark age of violence.

Abraham's Hospitality

AS Abraham sat in the tent-door at noon one day, the Lord appeared to him beside the oaks of Mamre. Abraham raised his eyes, and three men stood before him. They were really angels, who had been sent by the Lord. When he saw them, he ran from the door of the tent to welcome them, and bowing said:

"Pray, sirs, if I have found favor with you, do not pass by your servant. Since you have come to your humble servant, have a little water to wash your feet; then lie down under the tree till I bring you some food to refresh yourselves; after that you can go on."

They said, "Do as you have spoken."

Then Abraham ran to the herd and took a tender, plump calf, which he handed to his servant, who hurried to prepare it. Taking curds and milk and the veal he had prepared, he placed them before the men, and stood beside them under the tree as they ate.

Then they asked him:

"Where is your wife Sarah?"

He said, "Inside the tent there."

"Well," the Lord said to Abraham, "I will come back to you next spring, when your wife Sarah shall have a son."

Then the men started to leave, and looked towards Sodom.

Sodom and Gomorrah

Abraham went part of the way with his departing guests, and the Lord thought, "Shall I hide from Abraham what I am going to do?"

Then the Lord said to the men in the presence of Abraham:

"Because the outcry against Sodom and Gomorrah is great, and their sin very grave, I must go down and see whether or not their conduct entirely answers to the outcry against them that has reached Me; I would know whether it is so."

The men turned towards Sodom, but Abraham remained standing before the Lord. Then Abraham went nearer and said:

"Wilt Thou really destroy the righteous and the wicked together? Suppose there are fifty righteous in the city; wilt Thou really destroy it and not forgive it for the sake of the fifty righteous in it? Far be it from Thee to act like that, to slay the righteous and the wicked together, letting the righteous fare as the wicked fare! Far be it from Thee! Shall not the Judge of all the earth Himself act justly?"

The Lord said:

"If I can find fifty righteous in Sodom, I will forgive all the city for their sake."

Then Abraham went on:

"Here am I venturing to speak to the Lord, I who am mere dust and ashes! Suppose five are wanting out of the fifty righteous, wilt Thou destroy all the city for the lack of five?"

He replied:

"I will not destroy it, if I can find forty-five in it."

Once more Abraham asked Him:

"Perhaps forty may be found in it."

He said, "I will spare it for the sake of the forty."

Then Abraham said:

"O let not the Lord be angry, let me say one word: Suppose thirty are found in it?"

ABRAHAM PLEADS FOR SODOM

"Shall not the Judge of all the earth Himself
act justly?"   (*Genesis 18.25*)

see page 24

JACOB'S STRUGGLE

"Your name shall be called no more Jacob,
but Israel . . . " *(Genesis 32.29)*

see page 45

He answered, "I will spare it, if I can find thirty there."
Abraham said:

"Here am I venturing to speak to the Lord: Suppose there are twenty found in it?"

God replied, "I will not destroy it for the sake of the twenty found in it."

Then Abraham said:

"O let not the Lord be angry, let me say one word more: Suppose ten are to be found in it?"

He replied, "I will not destroy it for the sake of the ten."

The Lord went away, and Abraham went home.

Lot and his Family escape

In the evening two of the angels reached Sodom. Lot was sitting in the gateway of Sodom, and when Lot saw them he rose to welcome them, saying:

"Step aside, sirs, I beg you, into the house of your servant to pass the night; you can rise early and go on your way."

"No," they said, "we will stay in the open square all night."

However, as he pressed them, they turned with him and entered his house, where he made a feast for them. Before they lay down to rest, all the inhabitants of Sodom, young and old from every quarter, beset the house and sought to injure them. The people of Sodom shouted to Lot:

"Where are the men who came to visit you tonight? Bring them out to us."

Lot went out to them and shut the door behind him. He said:

"Pray, friends, be not so wicked. Let these men alone — they have sought shelter under my roof!"

"Out of the way!" shouted the crowd.

"This fellow settled among us as a stranger, and he would lay down the law for us! Now we will treat you worse than them!"

So they crowded around Lot and were on the point of breaking into the house, when the men put out their hands, pulled Lot inside, and closed the door. Then they struck the people of the city, young and old, with blindness, till they tired themselves out with groping for the door.

The men said to Lot:

"If you have anyone else in the city, sons-in-law, daughters, anyone belonging to you, get them away for we intend to destroy this place. The outcry against it has come loud before the Lord, and the Lord has sent us to destroy it."

Lot then went out and told his sons-in-law, and he said:

"Up and away, for the Lord is going to destroy this city."

His sons-in-law, however, thought he was merely jesting.

When the dawn appeared, the angels urged Lot on:

"Be off with your wife and your daughters so that you are not destroyed when the city is punished."

He hesitated. But the men seized him and his wife and his two daughters by the hand; thanks to the Lord's pity for him, they got him away and left him outside the city. When they had got the party outside, one of the angels said to him:

"Now, flee for your life; don't look behind you, stay nowhere in all the valley, but flee to the hills, lest you be destroyed."

The sun had risen on the earth when Lot reached Zoar, and then the Lord rained sulphur and fire from heaven on Sodom and Gomorrah, destroying those cities and whatever grew upon the ground.

Lot's wife looked back, and she became a pillar of salt.

In the morning when Abraham arose and went to the place where he had stood before the Lord, he looked in the direction of Sodom and Gomorrah, and there was smoke rising from the land like smoke from a furnace.   (*Genesis 18–19*)

VII.

ABRAHAM'S SUPREME TEST

Abraham had to face many trials in his life, to prove that he was worthy of being the founder of the Jewish people. His faith in God was put to the supreme test when God commanded him to sacrifice Isaac, the son for whom he had so long hoped and prayed. From this experience of Abraham we learn also that God forbade child-sacrifice. Recent diggings in Palestine have brought to light jars containing the skeletons of little children, who had been sacrificed in ancient times to the gods. The new religion Abraham founded taught that God held human life sacred, and, therefore, those who worshipped Him must not take human life. Thus a great step forward was made in the way men thought about God, when Abraham taught men a new way to worship Him. From this story, we learn also about the obedience and faith of Isaac, who proved himself worthy of carrying on the great mission of Abraham.

THE Lord dealt with Sarah, as He had promised. Sarah bore a son. Abraham gave the name of Isaac to his son; and as God had commanded him, Abraham circumcised Isaac when he was eight days old. The child grew, and was weaned. And on the day that Isaac was weaned, Abraham held a great feast.

Hagar and Ishmael sent away

One day Sarah saw Ishmael, the son of Hagar, the Egyptian, whom the latter had borne to Abraham, playing along with her son Isaac; and she told Abraham:

"Cast out that slave-girl and her son; the son of that slave-girl shall not be heir along with my son, Isaac."

Abraham was greatly displeased, because the boy was his son by Hagar. But God said to Abraham:

"Do not be displeased on account of the lad and your slave-girl. Hearken to Sarah's bidding, for it is through Isaac that your name shall be carried on. I will also make a nation out of the son of your slave-girl, because he is your child."

Early next morning Abraham arose, and gave Hagar some food and a bottle of water. He put the child upon her shoulder and sent her away. She departed and wandered in the desert of Beer-sheba. When the water in the bottle was gone, she cast the child under a bush. She sat down a short distance from him, saying to herself, "Let me not see the child die."

While she sat there, she wept and the boy wept also, and God heard their cries. Then the angel of God called from heaven to Hagar:

"Hagar, what is the matter with you? Fear not; for God has heard the cry of the boy where he is lying. Arise, lift up the boy and hold him; for God will make him a great nation."

And God opened her eyes. And she saw a well of water. Then she went and filled the bottle with water and gave the boy a drink. God was with him, and he grew; and he dwelt in the desert and became an archer. He lived in the desert of Paran; and his mother took a wife for him out of the land of Egypt.

The Binding of Isaac

Some time later God put Abraham to the test.

"Abraham!" He said.

"Here am I," Abraham answered.

"Take now your son," He said, "your only son, whom you love, even Isaac, and go to the land of Moriah; and offer him there as a sacrifice↓ on one of the hills which I will tell you of."

Early next morning Abraham arose, and saddled his donkey, and took two of his young men with him and his son Isaac. He cut wood for burning the sacrifice and started for the place of which God had told him. On the third day Abraham looked up and saw the place at a distance. Then he said to his young men:

"You stay here with the donkey; the lad and I are going over there to worship. When we have worshipped, we will come back to you."

Abraham took the wood for burning the sacrifice and laid it on his son Isaac, while he himself carried the fire and the knife. And the two went off together.

"Father!" said Isaac to Abraham.

↓For archaeological note see Item 2, p. 549 in the back of the book.

"Yes, my son," he answered.

"Here are the fire and the wood," Isaac said, "but where is the lamb for the sacrifice?"

"God will provide Himself with a lamb for the sacrifice, my son," said Abraham.

So they went both of them together.

When they came to the place of which God had told him, Abraham built the altar there, and laid the wood in order, and bound his son Isaac, and laid him upon the wood on the altar. Then Abraham stretched forth his hand and lifted the knife to slay his son. But the angel of God called to him from heaven:

"Abraham, Abraham!"

"Here am I," he said.

"Do not lay your hand on the boy," the angel said, "do nothing to him; I now know that you revere God, seeing you have not withheld your son, your only son, from Him."

Then Abraham looked up, and glanced round, and behind him there was a ram caught in the thicket by its horns! Abraham freed Isaac. He then took the ram and offered it as a sacrifice instead of his son.

The angel of the Lord called to Abraham a second time and said:

"The Lord declares, 'Because you have done this, and have not withheld your son, your only son, I will indeed bless you. I will make your descendants as numerous as the stars of the heaven and as the sand on the seashore; and your descendants shall conquer their foes; and in your descendants shall all the nations of the earth be blessed; because you have obeyed My command!' "

Abraham then went back to where his young men awaited him and Isaac, and they started together for Beer-sheba.

(Genesis 21, 22)

VIII.

ISAAC AND REBEKAH

When Sarah, his wife, died, Abraham bought a field with a cave in it from the Hittites, one of the many peoples who dwelt in the land of Canaan. This act made Canaan his permanent home and showed his faith that Canaan would be the home of the people he founded for all generations. Fearful lest his descendants be absorbed, by intermarriage, into the pagan peoples about them, and thus disappear, Abraham forbade Isaac to marry a Canaanite woman. He sent Eliezer, his steward, to his old home in Aram to choose a wife for Isaac from among his own people. Thus, Abraham remained faithful to his mission of beginning a new people, dedicated to a new religion and a better way of life.

The Cave of Machpelah

SARAH lived a hundred and twenty-seven years; and she died at Hebron in the land of Canaan. And Abraham came to mourn for Sarah and to weep for her. And he rose up from before his dead, and said to the Hittites:

"I am a stranger, residing among you; let me have a burying-place among you, that I may bury my dead."

The Hittites answered Abraham:

"Hear us, my lord: you are a mighty prince among us; bury your dead in the choicest of our sepulchers; none of us shall withhold from you his burying-place for your dead."

Abraham rose up and bowed to the Hittites, the natives of the land. He spoke to them, saying:

"If it be your mind that I should bury my dead, hear me; speak for me to Ephron, that he may give me the cave of Machpelah that belongs to him, at the corner of his field; let him give it to me in your presence for its full value, that I may have it as a burying-place."

Ephron was sitting among the Hittites. And Ephron the Hittite answered Abraham in the presence of the Hittites, at the gate of his city, saying:

"No, my lord, hear me: I give you the field, I give you the cave in the field; in the presence of the sons of my people I give it to you; bury your dead."

Abraham bowed low before the people of the land, and said to Ephron:

"If only you will, I beg you, hear me! I will give the price of the field; take the money for it, and I will bury my dead there."

Ephron answered Abraham:

"My lord, hearken to me: a piece of land worth four hundred shekels of silver, what is a trifle like that between me and you? So bury your dead."

Abraham hearkened to what Ephron said, and he weighed out for Ephron the sum he had named in the presence of the Hittites. Thus the field of Ephron at Machpelah, east of Mamre, the cave in the field and all the trees in the field and on its borders were sold to Abraham in the presence of the Hittites, before all the inhabitants of Ephron's city.

Abraham then buried his wife Sarah in the cave of the field of Machpelah in Hebron, in the land of Canaan.

Eliezer's Mission

By this time Abraham was well advanced in years; and the Lord had blessed him in every way. And Abraham gave to Isaac all his possessions. Then Abraham said to Eliezer, his oldest servant and the man who took charge of all his affairs:

"Swear by the Lord, the God of heaven and earth, that you will not let my son marry a daughter of the Canaanites among whom I dwell. You shall go to my own country and kindred and there choose a wife for my son Isaac."

Then Eliezer said to him:

"Suppose the woman will not be willing to follow me to this land; am I to take your son back to the land from which you came?"

Abraham said to him:

"Beware that you do not take my son back there! The Lord, the God of heaven, who took me from my father's house and from the land of my birth, and who spoke to me, and who swore to me that He would give this land to my descendants, He will send His angel before you and you shall take a wife for my son from there. If the woman be not willing to follow you, then you shall be free from your oath. Only you shall not take my son back there."

Eliezer made the promise, and took the oath.

Then the old servant took ten of his master's camels and set out with precious gifts from his master. He arrived at the city where Nahor, the brother of Abraham, dwelt. It was towards evening, at the time when the women came out to draw water; he made the camels kneel by the well outside the city.

Eliezer's Test — Kindness

Then Eliezer prayed:

"O Lord, the God of my master Abraham, give me success, I pray Thee, today, and deal kindly with my master, Abraham. Here I stand beside the well of water. The daughters of the townsmen come out to draw water. Let it come to pass, that the maiden to whom I say, 'Pray lower your pitcher, that I may drink,' and she shall say, 'Drink, and I will give your camels drink also,'— may she be the maiden Thou hast chosen for Thy servant Isaac! Thereby shall I know that Thou hast dealt kindly with my master."

Before he finished speaking, Rebekah came out, who was a daughter of Bethuel and the granddaughter of Nahor, Abraham's brother. She carried a pitcher upon her shoulder. The maiden was young and very beautiful. She went down to the well, and filled her pitcher; and as she came up, the servant, Eliezer, ran to meet her, and said:

"Let me drink, I beg you, a little water from your pitcher."

"Drink, sir," she said; and she quickly lowered the pitcher from her shoulder and gave him drink. When she had finished giving him drink, she said:

"Let me draw water for your camels also, until they have enough."

She quickly emptied her pitcher into the trough and ran again to the well to draw some more water. She drew water for all his camels, while the man gazed upon her, eager to know whether the Lord had made his journey successful or not. When the camels finished drinking, Eliezer took a golden ring and two bracelets and gave them to her. Then he said:

"Whose daughter are you? Tell me I beg you. Is there room in your father's house for me to put up in?"

"I am the daughter of Bethuel and the granddaughter of Nahor," she replied. She said moreover to him, "We have plenty of straw and feed, and there is room to lodge in."

Eliezer bowed his head, and worshipped the Lord, saying:

"Blessed be the Lord, the God of my master Abraham! And as for me, the Lord has led me straight to the house of my master's brethren."

Eliezer negotiates for Rebekah

The maiden ran and told her mother's household what had happened. Now Rebekah had a brother named Laban. When he saw the ring and the bracelets on his sister's wrists, and heard his sister telling what the man said to her, Laban went out to greet the man. He found Eliezer, standing beside the camels at the well.

"Come in!" he said. "Why do you stand outside? I have the house all ready, and made room for the camels."

Laban brought Eliezer into the house, having taken the packs off the camels. He brought straw and feed for the camels and water for Eliezer and the men who were with him to wash themselves. Food was then set before him to eat; but Eliezer said:

"I will not eat until I have told my errand."

"Speak on," Laban said.

"I am Abraham's servant," he said. "My master made me promise: 'You must go to my father's house, and to my own kindred, and take a wife for my son.'

"Today, when I came to the well, I met Rebekah there, with her pitcher on her shoulder. When she had given me and my camels water to drink, I asked her whose daughter she was, and she told me that she was the daughter of Bethuel and the granddaughter of Nahor. Then I gave her the golden ring and the bracelets, and I blessed the Lord, the God of my master Abraham, who had led me to Rebekah, daughter of my master's brethren, to be a wife for Isaac.

"Now then, tell me whether or not you will deal kindly and truly with my master, so that I may know what to do next!"

Laban and Bethuel answered:

"This is the Lord's doing; we cannot interfere. Here is Rebekah; take her and go, and let her be the wife of your master's son, as the Lord has said."

When Eliezer heard their words, he bowed himself down to the earth before the Lord. He then brought out jewels of silver and of gold, and garments, and he gave them to Rebekah; he also presented costly gifts to her brother and her mother. He and his men then ate and drank, and stayed all night.

Next morning, when he arose, he said:

"Send me away to my master."

Her brother and mother said:

"Let the maiden remain with us a few days, at least ten; then she may go."

"Do not delay me," Eliezer said to them. "The Lord has made my errand a success. Send me away that I may go to my master."

"We will call the maiden," they said, "and ask her wishes."

They called Rebekah, and asked her:

"Will you go with this man?"

And she replied, "I will go."

They sent away Rebekah, and her maid, and Abraham's servant, and his men. And they blessed Rebekah, and said to her:

"Sister, may you be the ancestress of thousands and ten thousands!"

Thus Rebekah and her maidens, riding on camels, set out after Eliezer.

Love at first Sight

Isaac had gone out to meditate in the field at the eventide. As he looked up, he saw camels coming. And Rebekah looked up, and when she saw Isaac, she alighted from her camel and asked Eliezer:

"Who is the man that is walking in the field to meet us?"

"He is my master," said Eliezer.

Then she took her veil, and covered herself.

Eliezer told Isaac all that had happened. And Isaac brought Rebekah into his mother Sarah's tent, and Rebekah became his wife. Isaac loved Rebekah, and he was comforted for his mother.

Abraham's Death

Now Abraham lived a hundred and seventy-five years. He died in ripe old age, after a full and complete life. Isaac and Ishmael, his sons, buried him in the cave of Machpelah, beside his wife Sarah.

And after Abraham's death, God blessed his son Isaac.

(Genesis 23–25)

IX.

JACOB OBTAINS THE COVENANT

The birthright and covenant over which Jacob and Esau struggled involved the spiritual leadership of the tribe, for the head of the tribe acted as priest. Jacob put Esau to the test to see whether he valued this privilege and dignity as the first-born son. His refusal to give Esau the pottage could have no fatal result; meanwhile, he could find out what Esau really thought of his birthright. This struggle over the birthright revealed the different natures of the two men. Esau, the hunter, was a man of violence; he was impulsive, and readily yielded to his physical desires. Jacob, on the other hand, was self-controlled. Although he had faults and weaknesses, he respected the birthright and wanted to become the responsible leader of his people. Nevertheless, Jacob had to go through many trials and sufferings before he became fully worthy of having entrusted to him the covenant which God had made with Abraham and Isaac.

ISAAC was forty years old when he took Rebekah to be his wife. He prayed to the Lord on behalf of Rebekah, because she had no child. The Lord answered his prayers, and He said to Rebekah:

"Two nations are within you,
And two peoples shall be separated from you;
They shall be rivals, each to the other.
One people shall be stronger than the other;
But the elder shall serve the younger."

Rebekah later gave birth to twin sons. The first came forth ruddy and hairy all over like a hairy mantle; and they called his name Esau. And after that came forth his brother, and his hand grasped Esau's heel; and his name was called Jacob. The boys grew up. Esau was a skillful hunter, a man who lived in the fields; Jacob was a quiet man, who lived in a tent. Now, Isaac loved Esau, but Rebekah loved Jacob.

Esau sells his Birthright

One day Jacob was cooking some food, and Esau came in from the fields and he was faint. Esau said to Jacob:

"Let me swallow, I beg you, a mouthful of this red, red pottage; for I am faint." Hence Esau was also called Edom which means "Red."

Jacob said, "Sell me first your birthright."

And Esau answered:

"Here I am dying of hunger! What profit shall the birthright bring to me?"

Jacob said, "Swear to me first."

And Esau swore to him, and he sold his birthright to Jacob. And Jacob gave Esau bread and pottage of lentils. And Esau ate, and drank, and got up, and went his way. So Esau despised his birthright.

Rebekah's Scheme

When Isaac was an old man, his sight was so dim that he could not see. He called Esau his elder son, and said to him:

"My son!"

"Here am I," Esau replied.

"I am an old man now," Isaac went on, "I do not know how soon I may die. Take your hunting weapons, I beg you, your quiver and your bow, and go out to the field, and get me some venison; make me savory food, such as I love, and bring it to me to eat, so that I may give you my blessing before I die."

Rebekah overheard what Isaac said to Esau. When Esau had gone off to the fields to hunt for venison to give his father, Rebekah said to her son Jacob:

"I heard your father speak to your brother Esau, that he should bring him venison, and make him savory food, so that he might eat and bless him in the presence of the Lord before he died. Now, my son, do exactly as I tell you. Go to the flock and bring me two tender kids. I will make them savory food such as your father loves; and you shall bring it to your father to eat, so that he may bless you before he dies."

Then Jacob said to Rebekah his mother:

"My brother Esau is a hairy man, while my skin is smooth.

Suppose my father should feel me? I would appear to him as a deceiver, and I shall bring a curse upon myself, and not a blessing."

"Upon me be your curse, my son!" his mother replied. "Only obey me, and go and get the kids for me."

He went and got them and brought them to his mother; and his mother made savory food, such as his father loved. Then Rebekah took the best clothes of Esau her elder son, which she had in the house, and dressed Jacob her younger son in them. She spread the skins of the kids upon his hands and upon the smooth part of his neck. And she put the savory food and the bread, which she had prepared, into the hands of her son Jacob. He came to his father, and said:

"My father!"

"Here am I," Isaac said, "who are you, my son?"

Jacob answered his father:

"I am Esau, your first-born; I have done as you told me. Arise, I beg you, sit and eat of my venison, that you may give your blessing to me."

Isaac said to his son:

"How did you find it so quickly, my son?"

"Because," he said, "the Lord your God sent me good speed."

Isaac then said to Jacob:

"Come near to me, I beg you, that I may feel you, my son, whether you are my very son Esau or not."

Jacob went near to his father Isaac; and he felt him, and said:

"The voice is the voice of Jacob, but the hands are the hands of Esau."

Blessing but not Covenant

Isaac did not recognize him, for his hands were hairy, like his brother Esau's. And Isaac said:

"Bring me my son's venison, I will eat it, and then give you my blessing."

Jacob brought it near him, and he ate; he brought him wine, and he drank. Then his father Isaac said:

"Come here now, and kiss me, my son."

He came near, and kissed him. And Isaac smelled the smell of his clothes, and he blessed him, and said:

"See, the scent of my son
　Is like the scent of a field which the
　　Lord has blessed.
So may God give you of the dew of heaven,
And of the fat places of the earth,
And plenty of corn and wine.
May peoples be your servants,
And nations bow down to you!
Be master over your brethren,
And may your mother's sons bow down to you!"

Esau threatens Jacob

No sooner had Isaac finished blessing Jacob — indeed, Jacob had just left his father Isaac — when his brother Esau came in from the hunt. He, also, made savory food and brought it to his father.

"Let my father arise," he said to Isaac, "and eat his son's venison, that you may give me your blessing."

"Who are you?" said Isaac his father.

"Your son," he answered, "your first-born, Esau!"

This made Isaac tremble violently, and he said:

"Who then is he who brought venison to me? I ate it all before you came, and I have blessed him! Indeed, he shall remain blessed!"

When Esau heard what his father said, he cried loud and bitterly, and said to his father:

"Bless me also, my father!"

Isaac said:

"Your brother came with guile, and has taken away your blessing."

"Is he not rightly named Jacob?" Esau said, "for he has supplanted me these two times. He took away my birthright; and now he has taken away my blessing!"

And he said:

"Have you not reserved a blessing for me?"

Isaac answered Esau:

"I have made him your master; I have appointed all his brethren to be his servants; I have given him corn and wine to sustain him. What then shall I do for you, my son?"

Esau said to his father:

"Have you but one blessing, my father? Bless me, also, O my father."

And Esau wept aloud. Then his father Isaac answered him:

"Behold, in the fat places of the earth shall be
 your dwelling,
And of the dew of heaven from above shall your land
 be watered;
And by your sword shall you live,
And you shall serve your brother."

Esau hated Jacob because of the blessing with which his father had blessed him; and Esau muttered:

"My father will soon die; then I will kill my brother Jacob."

Jacob receives the Covenant

When the words of her son Esau were told to Rebekah, she sent and called for her younger son Jacob, and said to him:

"Your brother Esau intends to kill you. Now, my son, do what I tell you: run away to my brother Laban in Haran, and stay with him a while, until your brother is no longer angry and he forgets what you have done to him. Then I will send and bring you back. Why should I be bereaved of you both in one day?"

Then Rebekah said to Isaac:

"If Jacob marries a Hittite woman, one of the daughters of the land, what good shall my life do me?"

So Isaac called Jacob, and said to him:

"You shall not take a wife of the daughters of Canaan. Go to the house of Bethuel, your mother's father, and take a wife there among the daughters of Laban, your mother's brother. God Almighty will bless you, and make you fruitful, and multiply you, that you may become a company of peoples! May He give the blessing of Abraham to you and to your descendants after you, that you may inherit the land where you now merely reside, the land which God gave to Abraham."

Jacob's Dream

Isaac then sent Jacob away; and Jacob started to go to Haran in Padan-Aram, where Laban lived.

Setting out from Beer-sheba, Jacob travelled all the day towards his destination. At a certain place on the road, Jacob spent the night, for the sun had set. He took one of the stones of the place, and put it under his head, and lay down to sleep. He dreamed. He saw a ladder set up on the earth, and the top of it reached to heaven. And the angels of God were ascending and descending on it.

The Lord stood beside him, and said:

"I am the Lord, the God of Abraham your ancestor, and the God of Isaac. The land on which you are lying, I will give to you and to your descendants. Your descendants shall be as numerous as the dust of the earth; you shall spread abroad to the west, and east, and to the north, and to the south. And in you and in your descendants shall all the families of the earth be blessed. I am with you, and will guard you wherever you go, and I will bring you back into this land; for I will not leave you until I have done what I have promised you."

Jacob awoke from his sleep, and he said:

"Surely the Lord is in this place; and I did not know it."

He was filled with awe, and said:

"Truly this place must be a house of God, a gate of heaven."

When Jacob rose up in the morning, he took the stone that he had put under his head, and set it up as a sacred altar, and poured oil upon it. He named that place Beth-el, which means the house of God. *(Genesis 25, 27, 28)*

X.

THE NEW NAME — "ISRAEL"

On Jacob's return from Padan-Aram, he had a strange experience, that brought about the change of his name to "Israel." The ancients believed that the name described a person's character; hence a change of name indicated a change of character. Undoubtedly, Jacob's many trials and sufferings had developed his better nature and so ennobled him that he became truly worthy of being the "Champion of God," which is the meaning of "Israel." In this story we learn how the people Abraham had fathered came to bear the name "Israel."

JACOB went on his journey and came to the land of the people of the East. As he looked, he saw a well in the open country, besides which three flocks of sheep were resting. From this well men watered their flocks. A heavy stone lay on the mouth of the well. When the flocks gathered there, the men rolled the stone from the mouth of the well, and watered the sheep; after which they replaced the stone on the mouth of the well. And Jacob said to the men:

"My brethren, where do you come from?"

"From Haran," they replied.

He said to them:

"Do you know Laban, the descendant of Nahor?"

"We know him," they answered.

"Is he well?" asked Jacob.

"Yes," they answered, "and here is his daughter Rachel coming with the sheep!"

"Why," said Jacob, "the sun is still high; it is not time yet for you to collect your flocks; water the sheep yourselves, go and attend to them."

"We cannot," they answered, "until all the flocks have been gathered together, and the stone is rolled from the mouth of the well; then we water the sheep."

Jacob's strange Courtship

While Jacob was still speaking with them, Rachel came with her father's sheep, for she was a shepherdess. When Jacob saw

Rachel, the daugher of Laban, his mother's brother, he went forward and, rolling the stone from the mouth of the well, watered the flock of Laban. And happy at meeting one of his kinsfolk, he kissed her.

Jacob told Rachel that he was Rebekah's son and her father's nephew; and she ran to tell her father. As soon as Laban heard that Jacob was his sister's son, he went to meet him, embraced and kissed him many times, and took him to his house.

Jacob told Laban all about himself, and Laban said to him:

"Surely, you are my bone and my flesh!"

Jacob stayed with him a whole month. Then Laban said to him:

"Because you are my kinsman are you to serve me for nothing? Tell me, what shall your wages be?"

Now Laban had two daughters, the elder called Leah and the younger called Rachel. Leah's eyes were weak; but Rachel was beautiful in form and fair to look upon. Jacob loved Rachel; and he said to Laban:

"I will serve you seven years for Rachel, your younger daughter."

And Laban said, "It is better that I give her to you, than that I should give her to another man; stay on with me."

Jacob served seven years for Rachel; and they seemed to him but a few days, such was his love for her. Then Jacob said to Laban:

"Give me my wife, for I have fulfilled my days of service."

Laban gathered together all the men of the place, and made a feast. During the evening he took his daughter Leah, and brought her secretly to Jacob in his tent. Laban gave Zilpah to Leah as her maid. In the morning Jacob found that he had married Leah; and he said to Laban:

"What is this you have done to me? Did I not serve you for Rachel? Why then have you cheated me?"

Laban answered:

"It is not so done in our country, to marry the younger daughter before the elder. Fulfill the week of this one, and we will give you the other also for seven more years' service."

Jacob did so and fulfilled her week; and then Laban gave him his daughter Rachel in marriage. Laban gave Bilhah to Rachel as a maid. And Jacob loved Rachel more than Leah, and he served with Laban for seven more years.

Jacob sets out for Canaan

Jacob's family increased in number; and he became very rich and had large flocks and male and female slaves and camels and asses.

But he heard Laban's sons saying:

"Jacob has taken away all our father's property; he has acquired all this wealth from what our father had."

Jacob also saw that Laban's looks were not as friendly as they were before.

And the Lord said to Jacob:

"Return to the land of your fathers and to your kinsfolk; and I will be with you."

Then Jacob arose, and mounted his children and his wives on camels; and he drove off all the livestock which he had accumulated in Padan-Aram, to go to his father Isaac in the land of Canaan. The caravan started out on the long journey home. And Rachel stole the images that belonged to her father, Laban.↓

Jacob fears meeting Esau

Jacob sent messengers ahead to his brother Esau, who lived in the land of Seir, the country of Edom, with these instructions:

"You shall say to my lord Esau: 'Your servant Jacob says: I have sojourned with Laban until now. I have oxen, asses, flocks and servants, male and female; and I have sent to tell my lord, that I may find favor with you.' "

The messengers returned to Jacob, and reported that they had gone to his brother Esau, who was already on his way to meet him, and four hundred men were with him.

Jacob was greatly afraid and was distressed. He divided his party, and the flocks and the herds and the camels, into two camps, thinking that, if Esau attacked and overpowered one camp, the other camp might escape.

Then Jacob prayed this prayer:

↓For archaeological note see Item 3, p. 549 in the back of the book.

"O Lord, God of my father Abraham and God of my father Isaac, O Lord, who saidst to me, 'Return to your country and your kinsfolk,' I am not worthy of all the kindness and of all the truth which Thou hast shown unto Thy servant; for with nothing but my staff I passed over the river Jordan, and now I have become two camps. Save me, I pray Thee, from the power of my brother Esau! I fear that he will come and attack me and kill the mother with the children. Thou didst promise, 'I will deal kindly with you and make your descendants like the sands of the sea which cannot be numbered for multitude.'"

And Jacob remained there for the night.

From what he had at hand he selected a present for his brother Esau: two hundred she-goats and twenty he-goats, two hundred ewes and twenty rams, thirty milch camels and their colts, forty cows and ten bulls, twenty female donkeys and ten foals. He put them in charge of his servants, each herd by itself; and he said to his servants:

"Go on before me, and leave a space between herd and herd."

And to the leader he gave this order:

"When Esau my brother meets you and asks you, 'To whom do you belong and these animals that you are driving?' say, 'To your servant Jacob; and these animals are a present sent to my lord Esau; and he himself is just behind us.'"

Jacob gave the same order to the second leader, and the third, and to all the others who were driving the herds, saying:

"Give this message to Esau, when you meet him. Also be sure to say, 'Your servant Jacob is just behind us.'"

"For," thought Jacob, "I will please him with the present that goes before me, so that when he sees me, he may perhaps receive me kindly."

Jacob thus sent the men with the present before him; and he himself spent that night in the camp.

Jacob becomes "Israel"

Later that night Jacob rose up and took his two wives, his two maid servants, and his children, and sent them over the river Jabbok.

Jacob was left alone; and a man wrestled with him until the

break of day. When the man found he could not master him, he struck the hollow of his thigh, so that Jacob's thigh was strained, as he wrestled with him. Then the man said:

"Let me go, for the day is breaking."

Jacob replied:

"I will not let you go, unless you bless me."

The man said to him, "What is your name?"

He answered, "Jacob."

And the man said:

"Your name shall be called no more Jacob, but Israel, Champion of God; for you have struggled with God and with men and have prevailed."

And Jacob asked him, "Tell me, I beg you, what is your name."

"Why ask for my name?" he answered. "It is a mystery."

And He blessed him there.

Jacob called the name of that place Peniel (the face of God). "For," he said, "I have seen God face to face, and yet I am alive!"

Jacob meets Esau

On the morrow, Jacob looked up, and he saw Esau coming and with him four hundred men. He divided the children among Leah, Rachel and the two maids, Bilhah and Zilpah, and put the maids and their children in front, then Leah and her children next, and finally Rachel and her son, Joseph, in the rear. Jacob himself went on before them, bowing seven times to the earth until he reached his brother. Esau ran to meet him and embraced him, and threw his arms around his neck and kissed him; and they wept.

When Esau looked up and saw the women and the children, he said:

"Who are these with you?"

Jacob replied, "The children whom God has so kindly given me."

Then the maidservants and their children came near and bowed to the ground. Leah and her children also came near and bowed down; and after them, Joseph and Rachel came and bowed down before Esau.

Esau asked, "What do you mean by all this camp which I met?"

"To find favor in your sight, my lord," Jacob replied.

"I have enough, my brother," said Esau. "Keep what you have."

Jacob said, "No, if I have found favor in your sight, receive my present from me, to show that you are pleased with me. Take, I beg you, my gift that I bring to you, for God has been generous to me and I have enough." And Jacob urged Esau, and he took it.

Then Esau started back that day to Seir, his home.

The Death of Isaac

Jacob travelled on and came to Isaac, his father, at Hebron. Isaac was very old. Soon he died and was gathered to his fathers, after a full life. And Esau and Jacob, his sons, buried him.

And Esau took his wives, and his sons, and his daughters, and all the people of his household, and his flocks and herds, and went into a land away from his brother Jacob. He made his home in the highlands of Seir.

Jacob, however, made his home in the land where his father had sojourned, in the land of Canaan.↓

These are the descendants of Jacob. Jacob had twelve sons and a daughter, Dinah. Leah's sons were Reuben, Simeon, Levi, Judah, Issachar and Zebulun. Rachel's sons were Joseph and Benjamin. The sons of Bilhah, Rachel's maid, were Dan and Naphtali; and the sons of Zilpah, Leah's maid, were Gad and Asher. *(Genesis 29–33, 35–37)*

↓For archaeological note see Item 4, p. 550 in the back of the book.

XI.

JOSEPH IN EGYPT

Jacob (Israel) dwelt in Canaan with his twelve sons, each one the head and leader of his own tribal family. This marked the beginning of the twelve tribes of Israel. Jacob loved Joseph more than his other sons, for he saw in him qualities which his other sons did not have. The brothers became jealous of Joseph and grew to hate him. They hoped to get rid of him by selling him as a slave to some passing tribesmen. Joseph escaped this fate, however, and made his own way to fame and fortune. So loyally did Joseph serve his adopted country Egypt that, when he died, according to our sages, "The whole of Egypt was in great grief, for he had been a compassionate friend to the Egyptians." From the story of Joseph we learn how his younger son Ephraim inherited the blessing of Abraham, and how the children of Israel, as the people of Abraham were now called, came to live in Egypt.

JOSEPH, at seventeen years, was a shepherd-lad, and tended the flocks along with his brothers. He brought evil report of them to his father. Now, Israel loved Joseph more than all his other sons, because he was born to him in his old age. He had a coat of many colors made for him. When his brothers saw that their father loved him more than all his brothers, they hated him and could not speak peaceably to him.

The Man of Dreams

Joseph one night dreamed a dream and he told it to his brothers; and they hated him more than ever. He said to them:

"Hear, I beg you, this dream which I have dreamed. We were binding sheaves of wheat in the field, and my sheaf stood upright, while your sheaves came round about and bowed down to my sheaf!"

His brothers said to him:

"Shall you indeed reign over us? Shall you have dominion over us?"

They hated him more than ever for his dreams, and for his words. Then he had another dream which he told to his brothers.

"I have dreamed yet another dream!" he said. "The sun and the moon and eleven stars bowed down to me!"

He told it to his father and his brothers; and his father rebuked him, and said:

"What is this dream that you have dreamed? Shall I and your mother and your brothers actually bow before you to the earth?"

His brothers became jealous of him; but his father kept in mind what he had said.

Joseph in the Pit

One day, when Joseph's brothers had gone off to pasture their father's flock at Shechem, Israel said to Joseph:

"Go now, and see how your brothers are, and the flock; and bring me back word."

Israel sent him from the valley of Hebron; and Joseph came to Shechem. A man found him wandering about in the fields, and asked him: "What are you seeking?"

"I seek my brothers," he answered. "Tell me, I beg you, where are they pasturing the flock?"

The man said, "They have gone from here; I heard them say, 'Let us go to Dothan.'"

Joseph went after his brothers, and he found them in Dothan. When they saw him in the distance, before he reached them, they plotted to kill him.

"Here comes this dreamer!" they said to each other. "Come now, let us slay him and cast him into one of the pits. We can say: A wild beast devoured him. Then we shall see what becomes of his dreams!"

Reuben heard this, and he saved Joseph from their hands, and said:

"Let us not take his life. Let us cast him into this pit in the wilderness, but do him no violence!" His idea was to rescue him, to restore him to his father.

When Joseph came to his brothers, they seized him, stripped him of his coat of many colors, and cast him into the pit. The pit was empty; there was no water in it.

Sold as a Slave

The brothers then sat down to eat. They looked up and saw a caravan of Ishmaelites coming from Gilead, and their camels were loaded with spices and balm which they were carrying down to Egypt. Then Judah said to his brothers:

"What profit is it if we slay our brother and conceal his murder? Come, let us sell him to the Ishmaelites instead, and let not our hands do him violence! After all, he is our brother!"

His brothers agreed with him, and drawing Joseph out of the pit, they sold him for twenty shekels of silver to the Ishmaelites. And they brought Joseph down to Egypt.

His brothers took Joseph's coat of many colors and dipped it in the blood of a goat they had killed; and they sent the coat of many colors to their father; and they said:

"We found this coat; know now whether it is your son's or not."

Jacob knew it, and cried:

"It is my son's coat; some wild beast has devoured him; Joseph is without doubt torn to pieces."

In his grief Jacob rent his clothes, and put sackcloth upon himself and mourned for his son many days. His sons and his daughters all tried to comfort him, but he refused to be comforted.

"No," he said, "I will go down to the grave mourning for my son."

And Israel grieved for Joseph.

In Potiphar's Service

Now Joseph was brought down to Egypt,↓ and Potiphar, an officer of Pharaoh's, the captain of the guard, bought him from the Ishmaelites. He lived in the house of his master, an Egyptian, who saw that the Lord gave Joseph success in everything he did. Joseph found favor in his sight, and he served him. And he appointed him overseer over his house, and he entrusted everything he had to him. From the time that Potiphar appointed Joseph his overseer, the Lord blessed the house of the Egyptian for Joseph's sake. Potiphar left everything in the hand of Joseph; not a thing did he trouble himself about, except his food.

↓For archaeological note see Item 5, p. 550 in the back of the book.

Joseph was of beautiful form and fair to look upon. By and by his master's wife cast her eyes on him and tempted Joseph to make love to her. But he refused, and said to his master's wife:

"My master does not trouble himself about anything in the house, and he has left everything in my hand; he is not greater in this house than I; he has kept nothing back from me except yourself, for you are his wife. How then can I do this great wickedness and sin against God?"

Day after day she spoke to Joseph, but he would not hearken to her appeal. One day, when he went into the house to do his work, and there was no man of the household within, she caught him by his garment. But he ran off, and left his garment in her hand, and got away. When she saw that he had run away, and left his garment in her hand, she called to her household:

"See, he has brought in a Hebrew into the house to insult me! I screamed, and when he heard me screaming aloud, he left his garment with me and ran off!"

She kept the garment beside her until his master came home. Then she told him this story:

"The Hebrew servant, whom you brought to us, came in to insult me. But when I screamed aloud, he left his garment with me and ran out!"

Joseph in Prison

When Joseph's master heard what his wife said, about how his servant had treated her, he was very angry. He took Joseph, and put him in prison, where the king's prisoners were held. But the Lord was with Joseph and was kind to him and helped him to win the friendship of the keeper, so that he put Joseph in charge of all the other prisoners, and held him responsible for anything they did. The keeper of the prison did not attend to anything Joseph undertook, for the Lord was with him; and whatever he did, the Lord made it prosper.

After this, it happened that the butler and the baker of the Pharaoh of Egypt offended their lord and king. And Pharaoh was angry at these two officers, the chief of the butlers and the chief of the bakers, and he put them in custody in the house of the captain of the guard, the very prison in which Joseph was held. The captain of the guard appointed Joseph to attend upon them. For some time they remained in his custody.

Then one night they both dreamed dreams, each man dreaming something with a meaning for himself. When Joseph went to attend them next morning, he noticed that they were sad. He asked them:

"Why are you looking so sad today?"

"We have dreamed a dream," they said, "and there is none that can interpret it."

Joseph said to them:

"Do not interpretations belong to God? Tell it me, I beg you."

The chief butler told his dream to Joseph.

"In my dream," he said, "there was a vine before me; and on the vine there were three branches. It seemed to bud; its blossoms shot forth; and the clusters brought forth ripe grapes. Pharaoh's cup was in my hand, and I plucked the grapes and squeezed them into Pharaoh's cup and handed the cup to Pharaoh."

Joseph then said:

"This is the interpretation: The three branches are three days. Within yet three days Pharaoh will release you, and restore you to your office; and you shall hand Pharaoh his cup, as you used to do when you were his butler. But have me in your remembrance when all goes well with you. Do me the kindness of mentioning my name to Pharaoh, and bring me out of here; for I was really stolen away out of the land of the Hebrews; and I have done nothing in this country for which they should put me into the dungeon."

When the chief baker saw that the interpretation was good, he said to Joseph:

"In my dream I, too, saw something; three baskets of white bread were on my head; in the uppermost basket there were all sorts of cake for Pharaoh; and the birds kept eating them out of the basket on my head."

Then Joseph said, "This is the interpretation: The three baskets are three days. Within yet three days Pharaoh will release you, and shall hang you on a tree; and the birds shall eat the flesh off you."

On the third day, which was Pharaoh's birthday, he made a feast for all his courtiers, and he released the chief butler and the chief baker. The chief butler he restored to his office, and he handed the cup to Pharaoh; but the chief baker he caused to be hanged.

Thus, it happened as Joseph had interpreted to them. The chief butler did not remember Joseph, but forgot him.

The Dreams of Pharaoh

Two years passed, and Pharaoh dreamed: and, behold, he was standing beside the Nile. Up came seven cows from the Nile, well-fed and fat; and they fed in the river grass. After them, seven other cows came up from the Nile, poorly fed and lean, and stood beside the other cows on the bank of the Nile. And the poorly fed, lean cows ate up the well-fed, fat cows. Then Pharaoh woke up.

When he again fell asleep, he had a second dream: and, behold, seven ears of corn came up on a single stalk, full and good. And seven ears, thin and blasted with the east wind, sprang up after them. And the thin ears swallowed up the seven ears that were full and good. Then Pharaoh awoke, and he found that it was a dream.

Next morning Pharaoh was worried; and he sent for all the magicians and wise men of Egypt. He told them his dreams; but none could tell him what they meant. Then the chief butler said to Pharaoh:

"I must recall my faults this day: Pharaoh was angry with his servants and put myself and the head baker in custody within the house of the captain of the guard. On the same night we dreamed dreams, he and I; each dreamed a dream with a meaning for himself. But there was a young man with us, a Hebrew, a servant belonging to the captain of the guard. When we told him our dreams, he interpreted them, telling each of us the meaning of his own dream. And as he interpreted them, so it was. I was restored to my office, and the other man was hanged."

Then Pharaoh sent for Joseph, and they brought him hurriedly from the dungeon. After he had shaved and changed his clothes, he came into Pharaoh's presence. Pharaoh said to Joseph:

"I have dreamed a dream, but there is none that can interpret it. I have heard it said of you that you know how to interpret dreams."

"Not I," said Joseph, "God alone can give Pharaoh a true answer."

Pharaoh then told Joseph his two dreams. "I told this to the magicians," he said, "but none of them could tell me the meaning."

Joseph said to Pharaoh:

"The dream of Pharaoh is one; what God is about to do He has revealed to Pharaoh. The seven good cows represent seven years; and the seven good ears represent seven years: it is one and the same dream. The seven lean and poorly fed cows that came up after them represent seven years, and also the seven empty ears, blasted with the east wind. There shall be seven years of famine. That is what I meant when I said to Pharaoh that God has shown Pharaoh what He is about to do. Seven years of great plenty are coming throughout all the land of Egypt; but there shall come seven years of famine after them; and all the plenty shall be forgotten in the land of Egypt. Famine will consume the land, so sore a famine that all the plenty will be forgotten in the land of Egypt.

"The dream was sent twice to Pharaoh, because the thing is established by God, and God will soon bring it to pass. Now, therefore, let Pharaoh find a wise and intelligent man and put him in control of the land of Egypt. Let Pharaoh act quickly, and appoint overseers throughout the land to collect a fifth of the produce of Egypt during the seven years of plenty. Let them gather all the food of the good years that are coming, and, by the authority of Pharaoh, store up the corn and hold it for food in the cities. The food shall be a reserve against the seven years of famine that are to be in the land of Egypt, that the country may not perish of the famine."

The plan pleased Pharaoh and all his courtiers.

Pharaoh then said to his courtiers:

"Can we find such a man as this, a man in whom is the spirit of God?"

Then he turned to Joseph and said:

"Since God has shown you all this, there is none so wise and intelligent as yourself. You shall be appointed over my house, and all my people shall obey your commands. Only in the throne shall I be greater than you." Then Pharaoh added:

"See, I have appointed you over all the land of Egypt!"

And Pharaoh took off his signet ring from his hand and put it upon Joseph's hand, and had him dressed in garments of fine linen, and put a gold chain about his neck. And Pharaoh made him ride in the second chariot which he had; and they cried before him, "Abrech!" (Bow the knee!).

Joseph was thirty years old when he became prime minister to Pharaoh, king of Egypt.

And Joseph went out from the presence of Pharaoh, and went throughout all the land of Egypt. During the seven years of plenty, the earth bore ample crops; and he gathered all the produce of the rich years over Egypt, and he stored up the food within the cities; in every city he stored the produce of the surrounding fields. Joseph stored up corn in huge quantities, like the sand of the sea.

The seven years of plenty in the land of Egypt came to an end, and then, as Joseph had foretold, the seven years of famine began. There was famine in every country other than Egypt; but in all the land of Egypt there was bread.

Then Joseph opened all the storehouses and sold the produce to the Egyptians. As the famine was all over the world, people from every country also came to Joseph in Egypt to buy grain — so severe was the famine everywhere on earth.

Joseph recognizes his Brothers

Now Jacob learned that there was corn for sale in Egypt; and he said to his sons:

"I have heard that there is corn for sale in Egypt. Go down there and buy some for us, that we may live and not die."

Joseph's ten brothers went to buy corn from the Egyptians; but Jacob did not send Benjamin, Joseph's brother, with the rest, for he was afraid lest harm should befall him.

As Joseph was prime minister of the country, he controlled the sale of corn to all the Egyptians. When the brothers of Joseph came to Egypt, they were brought before him. Joseph saw his brothers, and he recognized them, but he acted toward them as would a stranger. He spoke roughly to them, and said:

"Where do you come from?"

"From the land of Canaan," they replied, "to buy food."

And Joseph knew his brothers, but they knew him not.

Then Joseph remembered what he dreamed about them, and he said to them:

"You are spies; you have come to see how defenseless the land is."

"No, my lord," they said, "your servants have come to buy food. We are all the sons of one man; we are upright men, your servants are no spies."

Joseph answered:

"No, you have come to see how defenseless the land is."

"Your servants," they said, "are twelve brothers, the sons of one man in the land of Canaan; the youngest is at present with our father, and one is missing."

Joseph replied, "It is as I said: You are spies. But you shall be tested by this: As sure as Pharaoh lives, you shall not leave, unless your youngest brother comes here. Send one of your number, and let him bring your brother, while you remain here, that your words may be proved and show whether you are honest. Otherwise, as sure as Pharaoh lives, you are spies."

He then put them all together into prison for three days. On the third day Joseph said to them:

"Do this, and save your lives; for I fear God. If you are upright men, let one of you be held in prison, while the rest carry corn for your starving households; and bring your youngest brother to me. So shall your words be verified, and you shall not die."

They said one to another, "This distress has come upon us, because we are truly guilty concerning our brother; for we saw his distress but we would not hearken when he entreated us."

And Reuben answered them, "Did I not tell you not to sin against the child? But you would not hearken to me. Therefore, you see, there is a reckoning for his death."

They did not know that Joseph understood them; for there was an interpreter between them. But Joseph withdrew, and wept.

When he returned to them, he selected Simeon from among them and had him bound before their eyes. Then he gave orders to fill their bags with corn and to restore each man's money in his sack and to give them provisions for the journey. This was done. They loaded their donkeys with corn and went away.

At the place where they lodged for the night, one of them opened his sack to give fodder to his animal, when he saw his money at the mouth of his sack. He said to his brothers:

"My money has been restored! Here it is, inside my sack!"

At this their hearts sank, and they turned trembling one to another, saying, "What is this that God has done to us?"

When they reached Jacob their father in the land of Canaan, they told him all that had befallen them. Jacob their father said:

"You have bereaved me of my children: Joseph is no more, and Simeon is missing, and now you would take Benjamin away. See, what I have to bear!" And Jacob continued:

"My son shall not go with you; for his brother is dead and he only is left. If he came to any harm on the road, you would bring down my gray hairs with sorrow to the grave."

*Joseph tests his Brothers to find
out their Loyalty to Benjamin*

The famine raged in the land of Canaan. When they had eaten up the corn which they had brought from Egypt, Jacob said to his sons:

"Go again, buy us a little food."

"But," said Judah, "the man earnestly warned us, 'You shall not see me, unless your brother is with you.' We will go and buy food, if you send our brother with us; but if you refuse, we will not go."

"Well," said Jacob, "if it is to be, then do this: Take some of the choice fruits of the land in your vessels and carry them as a present to the man, a little balsam, a little honey, spices, fragrant gum, nuts and almonds; take double money with you; and carry back the money that was returned in your sacks, perhaps it was an oversight; take also your brother, and go again to the man. May God Almighty give you mercy before the man, that he may release to you your other brother and Benjamin. If I am to be bereaved of my children, I am bereaved!"

The men took the present, the double money, and Benjamin; they started south for Egypt, and made their way into the presence of Joseph.

When Joseph saw Benjamin with them, he said to the steward of his house:

"Take the men into the house, and slaughter the animals, and make all preparations; for the men shall dine with me at noon."

He did as Joseph told him. He took the men into Joseph's house. They were afraid, because they were brought into Joseph's house, thinking, "On account of the money that was replaced in our sacks at our first visit, he has us brought here; he wants to accuse us and attack us, and make us slaves, and seize our animals."

They told Joseph's steward about the money in their sacks, and said:

"We have brought it back, and we have brought other money to buy food. We do not know who put our money in our sacks."

"Peace be to you," he said, "you need not be afraid."

Then he brought Simeon out to them.

When Joseph came home, they brought the present to him in the house and bowed to the ground before him. He asked how they were. And he said:

"Is your father well, the old man of whom you spoke? Is he yet alive?"

They answered, "Your servant our father is well; he is yet alive."

They bowed in silence, and did homage to him.

Looking up, he saw Benjamin his brother, his mother's son, and asked:

"Is this your youngest brother of whom you spoke to me?" Then Joseph said, "God be gracious to you, my son!"

His heart yearned for his brother; and he sought a place to weep; and he entered into his chamber, and wept there. After washing his face, he came out; and controlling himself, he ordered dinner to be served.

So they feasted and drank with him. Meanwhile, Joseph ordered the steward of his house:

"Fill the men's sacks with food, as much as they can carry, put every man's money in the mouth of his sack; and in the mouth of the youngest man's sack, with his corn money, put my goblet, the silver goblet."

He did as Joseph told him.

As soon as the day dawned, the men set off with their animals. When they had left the city, but were not far away, Joseph said to his steward:

"Up, follow after the men! When you overtake them, ask them: 'Why have you returned evil for good? Why have you stolen the silver goblet, the very goblet out of which my lord drinks and with which he divines?* It is a wicked thing that you have done.'"

When the steward overtook them, he asked them this. And they said to him:

"Why should my lord speak like this? Your servants would never think of doing such a thing! Why, we even brought you back from Canaan the money that we found in our sacks! How then should we steal silver or gold out of your lord's house? If the goblet is found in the possession of any of your servants, let him die, and the rest of us will be slaves to my lord."

"As you say," replied the steward. "However, only the one in whose possession it is found shall become my slave; the rest of you shall be held blameless."

They hastened, and lowered their sacks to the ground. Every man opened his sack and the steward searched them, beginning at the eldest, and leaving off at the youngest. And the goblet was found in Benjamin's sack. Tearing their clothes in dismay, each reloaded his donkey, and they went back to the city.

*To find out where things are, or to foretell events by the use of magic.

When Judah and his brothers reached Joseph's house, he was yet there; they flung themselves on the ground before him.

"What is this you have done?" said Joseph. "Don't you know that a man in my position is able to divine?"

Judah answered, "What shall we say, my lord? What shall we speak? How shall we clear ourselves? God has found out the iniquity of your servants; now we are slaves to my lord, we and the man in whose possession the goblet was found."

"Far be it from me that I should do this," said Joseph. "The man in whose possession the goblet was found, he shall be my slave; but as for the rest of you, you may go in peace to your father."

Then Judah came near to him, and said:

"Oh, my lord, let your servant, I beg you, say one word to my lord, and be not angry at your servant; for you are like Pharaoh himself. My lord asked his servants, 'Have you a father, or a brother?' And we said to my lord, 'We have a father, an old man, and a child of his old age, a little one; and his brother is dead. He is the only child left of his mother, and his father loves him.' You said to your servants, 'Bring him down to me, that I may look at him.' And we said to my lord, 'The boy cannot leave his father; for if he should leave his father, his father would die.' You said to your servants, 'Unless your youngest brother comes along with you, you shall not see me again.' Well, when we went to your servant our father, we told him what my lord said. And when our father bade us return, and buy a little food, we said, 'We cannot go down. If our youngest brother goes with us, then we will go down; for we cannot see the man, unless our youngest brother is with us.' Your servant our father said to us, 'You know that my wife bore me two sons; one left me, and surely he must have been torn to pieces, for I have never seen him again. If you take this one also from me, and if harm befalls him, you will bring down my gray hairs with sorrow to the grave.'

"Now, if I return to your servant my father, and the boy is not with us, he will die, for his very soul is bound up with the boy's soul; and your servants will bring down the gray hairs of your servant our father with sorrow to the grave. Now then, I beg you, let your servant remain in the boy's place as my lord's slave, but let the boy go back with his brothers."

Joseph reveals Himself

Joseph could no longer control himself before all his attendants. He called out:

"Cause every man to go out from me."

No one was present, while Joseph made himself known to his brothers. And he wept aloud; and the Egyptians of Pharaoh's household heard him weeping. Then Joseph said to his brothers:

"I am Joseph. Does my father yet live?"

His brothers were so astounded that they could not answer him. Then Joseph said:

"Come near to me, I beg you."

They came near. He said:

"I am Joseph your brother, whom you sold into Egypt. Do not be ashamed or angry with yourselves, that you sold me here; for God sent me before you to preserve life. The famine has already been two years in the land; and there are yet five years, in which there shall be neither plowing nor harvest. God sent me before you to give you a remnant on earth and to save you alive for a great deliverance. It was not you but God who sent me here; and He has made me Pharaoh's prime minister, head of all his palace, and ruler over all the land of Egypt.

"Hasten back to my father, and give him this message from his son Joseph: God has made me lord of all Egypt; come down to me, do not tarry. You shall dwell in the land of Goshen, and you shall be near me, you, and your sons, and your grandsons, and your flocks and herds, and all you possess. I will provide for you here, lest you come to poverty, for there are yet five years of famine."

Then Joseph embraced his brother Benjamin and wept, and Benjamin wept with him. He kissed all his brothers; and after that his brothers talked with him.

Israel goes to Egypt

The report that Joseph's brothers had come spread throughout Pharaoh's palace; and it pleased Pharaoh well, and his courtiers. And Pharaoh said to Joseph:

"Say to your brothers: This is what you are to do: Load your animals, and go back to the land of Canaan; and take your father and your households, and come to me; and I will give you the best that the land of Egypt holds."

So Joseph sent his brothers away, and they returned to Jacob their father.

And they told Jacob:

"Joseph is still living, and he is prime minister over all the land of Egypt."

Jacob fainted when he heard the news; for he did not believe them. But when he saw the wagons that Joseph had sent for their use, his spirit revived. And Jacob believed them.

"Enough!" said Jacob. "Joseph my son is yet alive; I will go and see him before I die."

And Jacob took his journey with all that he had, and came to Beer-sheba, and offered sacrifices to the God of his father Isaac. In the visions of the night, God spoke to Jacob, and said:

"Jacob! Jacob!"

"Here am I," he answered.

And He said:

"I am God, the God of your father; fear not to go down to Egypt; for I will there make of you a great nation. I will go down to Egypt with you; and I will also surely bring you back again to Canaan."

Next morning Jacob set out from Beer-sheba. His sons took Jacob their father, their wives, and their little ones, in the wagons which Pharaoh had sent to carry them. With their livestock and all their possessions, Jacob and his family came into Egypt.

Jacob sent Judah before him to Joseph, to show the way to Goshen; and they came into the land of Goshen. And Joseph made ready his chariot and went to meet his father in Goshen.

He presented himself to him and embraced Jacob, and wept from joy as Jacob embraced him. Then Jacob said:

"Now that I have seen that you are yet alive, let me die!"

And Joseph settled his father and brothers in the best of the fertile land in Goshen, as Pharaoh had commanded.

Ephraim and the Covenant

Jacob lived in the land of Egypt for seventeen years. When he felt that his time to die had come, he summoned his son Joseph, and said to him:

"God Almighty appeared to me in the land of Canaan, and blessed me. He said to me, 'I will make you fruitful and multiply you, and I will make of you a company of peoples; and I will give you and your descendants this land for an everlasting possession.' Your two sons, who were born to you in the land of Egypt, before I came to you in Egypt, are mine; Ephraim and Manasseh are to be as much mine as Reuben and Simeon.

"Now bring them to me, I beg you, and I will bless them."

Joseph brought them to him. But Jacob's eyes were so dim with age that he could not see.

Israel (Jacob) blessed them, saying:

"The God before whom my fathers Abraham and Isaac walked, the God who has been my shepherd all my life to this day, the angel who has delivered me from all evil, bless the boys; and may they carry on my name, and the name of my fathers Abraham and Isaac; and let them grow into a multitude in the midst of the earth."

When Joseph saw that his father was laying his right hand on the head of Ephraim, it displeased him and he seized his father's hand to remove it from Ephraim's head to Manasseh's head. And Joseph said to his father:

"No, my father, here is the first-born; put your right hand on his head."

But his father refused.

"I know, my son," he said, "I know it; he also shall become a people, and he also shall be great; but his younger brother shall be greater than he, and his descendants shall become a multitude of peoples."

And he blessed them that day, saying:

"By you shall Israel bless, saying: God make you as Ephraim and Manasseh."

And he set Ephraim before Manasseh.

The Death of Jacob

Then Israel said to Joseph:

"I am about to die; but God will be with you, and will bring you back into the land of your fathers."

Israel then caused all his sons to be summoned and blessed them; and he gave to each the blessing suited to him.

Having blessed Reuben, Simeon and Levi, Israel said to Judah:

"Judah, your brothers shall praise you;
Your hand shall be on the neck of your enemies;
Your father's sons shall bow down before you.
Judah is a lion's whelp!
The scepter shall not depart from Judah,
Nor the ruler's staff from between his feet."

Then Israel continued to speak to Zebulun, Issachar, Dan, Gad, Asher and Naphtali. Before he closed his blessing with Benjamin, he spoke these words to Joseph:

"Joseph is a fruitful vine,
A fruitful vine by a fountain;
Its branches run over the wall.
Archers have dealt bitterly with him,
And shot at him, and hated him;
But his bow remained steady,
And his arms were made supple,
By the Mighty One of Jacob.
May the Almighty, the God of your father,
Bless you with blessings of heaven above.
Such blessings shall rest on Joseph,
The prince among his brothers."

When he was through with speaking to his sons, he gathered up his feet into the bed, and expired, and was gathered unto his people.

Israel's sons did with him as he had commanded them. His sons carried him to the land of Canaan and buried him in the cave of Machpelah which Abraham had bought from the Hittites.

After burying his father, Joseph and his brothers and all who had accompanied him returned to Egypt. Now that their father was dead, Joseph's brothers thought:

"Perhaps Joseph will hate us and will fully requite us all the evil we did to him!"

So they sent this message to Joseph: "Before he died, your father bade us to say to Joseph, 'Forgive, I beg you, the transgression and the sin of your brothers and the evil they did you!' Please forgive now the transgressions of the servants of the God of your fathers!"

When Joseph was told this, he broke down. Then his brothers came and fell down before him; and they said:

"See, we are your humble servants!"

Joseph said to them:

"Fear not; for am I in the place of God? You meant to do me evil; but God meant it for good, to bring to pass, as it is this day, to save the lives of many people. Do not be afraid; I myself will sustain you and your dependents."

Thus he comforted them, and spoke kindly to them.

Joseph's last Request

Joseph continued to live in Egypt, as did his father's family. Then the time came when Joseph said to his brothers:

"I am about to die; but God will surely remember you and bring you up out of this land to the land which He promised to give to Abraham, to Isaac and to Jacob."

Joseph then made the children of Israel swear an oath that they would take up his bones with them from Egypt.

And Joseph died, when he was a hundred and ten years old.

(Genesis 37, 39–50)

JOSEPH FORGIVES HIS BROTHERS

"You meant to do me evil; but God meant
it for good."   (*Genesis 50.20*)

see page 64

THE SONG OF FREEDOM

"I will sing to the Lord, for He has gloriously triumphed . . ."   (*Exodus 15.1*)

see page 80

שְׁמוֹת

EXODUS

THE children of Israel increased in numbers. After the death of Joseph, however, they became enslaved to the Egyptians.↓ They won their freedom from Egypt under the leadership of Moses. For forty years the Israelites were governed by Moses, the great Prophet and Liberator, and under his guidance they became a nation of free men. After their escape from Egypt, they survived the hardships of the wilderness and were led by Moses to the borders of the Promised Land.

How did the Israelites become slaves in Egypt? How did they win their freedom? What kind of a man was Moses? What united these freed slaves, so that they became one people?

These questions the Book of Exodus answers. From it, we learn how Israel became a religious people at Mount Sinai where they received the written Covenant, or Law, which ever afterwards shaped their ideas of right and wrong and made the Jewish religion their way of life. It also tells about the origin of the Passover Festival; how the Jewish people began to worship God in a special place called a Sanctuary; how many obstacles Moses had to overcome to mold the Israelites into a united people; and how difficult it was for them to free themselves from Egyptian idol-worship.

But, above all, Exodus describes how the God of Israel upheld the cause of slaves against rich and powerful tyrants, and so reveals that God seeks justice, mercy and kindness in human life; that He holds men sacred; and that He wants all men to have and enjoy freedom.

Exodus, the second Book of Moses, receives its name from the departure, or exodus, of the Israelites from Egypt. Its Hebrew name is *Shemot* (Names), because it begins with a list of the names of Israel's sons in Egypt.

↓For archaeological note see Item 6, p. 550 in the back of the book.

I.

MOSES — THE LIBERATOR

Moses was the hero of Israel's struggle for freedom. Our sages wove many legends about his life. Among others, they told this story: Moses was a prince in Pharaoh's palace. When he saw the cruel burdens placed on the Israelites, he was saddened, and he said, "Woe is me for you. Would that I could die for you!" Then he went out among the people and shared their heavy labor. God saw this, and appeared to Moses and said, "You have put aside your work and have gone to share the sorrows of Israel, behaving to them like a brother. I will leave My place on high and speak only with you." Perhaps, because the mother of Moses — a member of the Levites who were teachers in Israel — nursed and raised him, Moses learned from her about his ancestors and the God of Israel who wanted kindness, justice and freedom, and about His covenant with Abraham, Isaac and Jacob.

JOSEPH died and all his brothers and all that generation. But the children of Israel had been fruitful; and they increased in numbers till the land was filled with them. Meanwhile, a new king rose and ruled over Egypt, who did not know Joseph.

The cruel Pharaoh

Then Pharaoh said to his people:

"Behold, the Israelites are too many and too mighty for us! We must deal wisely with them, lest they multiply still more and then, if we happen to be at war, join our enemies and fight against us so as to escape from the country."

Thereupon, the Egyptians put the Israelites under taskmasters, who were the captains of labor gangs, to crush them with heavy burdens; and they built for Pharaoh the store-cities of Pithom and Raamses. The Israelites were forced to slave for the Egyptians; their life was made bitter with hard and cruel service; they were forced to build with mortar and brick and to do all manner of hard labor and field-work.

But the more the Israelites were afflicted, the more they multiplied and increased, till the Egyptians dreaded the Israelites. Then Pharaoh ordered all his people to throw every son born to the Israelites into the Nile, but to save every girl alive.

How Moses was saved

Now a man named Amram, belonging to the tribe of Levi, married Jochebed, a woman of the same tribe; and she gave birth to a son. When Jochebed saw that he was a handsome boy, she hid him three months. When she could hide him no longer, she placed the child in a basket made of papyrus reeds, daubed with mortar and pitch, and laid the basket among the bulrushes by the bank of the river Nile. His sister, Miriam, stayed near by to see what would happen to him.

Presently Pharaoh's daughter came down to bathe in the river. She and her maidens were walking along the river-bank, when she saw the basket among the bulrushes. She sent her slave-girl to get it. On opening it, she saw that the child in it was a boy crying. She pitied him, and said:

"This is one of the Israelite children."

Then Miriam said to Pharaoh's daughter:

"Shall I go and get you an Israelite nurse, to nurse the child for you?"

"Go," said Pharaoh's daughter.

Miriam went, and brought the child's mother, and Pharaoh's daughter said to her:

"Take this child away and nurse it for me, and I will pay you your wages."

Jochebed took the child and nursed him, and when he grew up she brought him to Pharaoh's daughter, who then adopted him as her son. She called him Moses (the one drawn out). "For," she said, "I drew him out of the water."

Moses protects the Weak

One day, after Moses was grown up, he went out to observe what his own people were doing; and as he was watching them at their hard labor, he saw an Egyptian beating an Israelite. He looked around and did not see any other person. He struck down the Egyptian and hid his body in the sand. Next day, when he went out, he saw two Israelites quarreling. Moses said to the man who was in the wrong:

"Why do you strike your fellow?"

The man replied:

"Who made you a ruler and judge over us? Do you intend to kill me as you killed the Egyptian?"

This answer made Moses afraid; he thought that what he had done must be known.

When Pharaoh heard of the Egyptian's death, he sought to have Moses put to death, but Moses escaped from Pharaoh to the land of Midian.

Moses again protects the Weak

As Moses was sitting beside a well, the seven daughters of Jethro, the priest of Midian, came and drew water to fill the troughs for their father's flock. But some shepherds came and sought to drive them from the well. Moses went to their rescue, and also helped them to water their flock. When they came home to their father, Jethro asked them:

"How is it that you have come back so early today?"

"An Egyptian," they answered, "protected us from the shepherds. He even drew water for us and watered the flock."

"Where is he?" the man asked his daughters. "Why have you left him behind? Ask him to have a meal with us."

Moses came and agreed to make his home with Jethro. Later Jethro gave Moses his daughter, Zipporah, to be his wife.

The burning Bush

During this long time the Pharaoh of Egypt died. The Israelites still were groaning under their bondage, and the wail of their cries for help came up to God. God heard their moaning, and He remembered His covenant with Abraham, Isaac and Jacob; and He determined to end their plight.

One day, as Moses was tending the flock of his father-in-law, he led the flock to the western side of the desert and came to the sacred mount of Horeb (Sinai). Suddenly he looked, and there was a bush ablaze with fire, yet the bush was not consumed.

"I will turn aside," said Moses, "and see this marvel, why the bush is not burned up."

When the Lord saw that he had turned aside to look at it, He called to him out of the bush:

"Moses, Moses!"

"Here am I," Moses answered.

"Do not come close," He said. "Remove your sandals from your feet, for the place where you are standing is sacred ground. I am the God of your forefathers, the God of Abraham, of Isaac, and of Jacob."

Moses covered his face; he was afraid to look.

"I have indeed seen the affliction of My people in Egypt," the Lord said, "and I have heard them wailing under their slave-drivers; and I have come down to rescue them from the Egyptians and bring them out of that land to a good, large land, flowing with milk and honey, the country of the Canaanites. Come, I will send you to the new Pharaoh that you may bring My people the Israelites out of Egypt."

The Modesty of Moses

Then Moses said to God:

"Who am I, to go to Pharaoh and bring the Israelites out of Egypt?"

"I will be with you," God answered; "and this shall be the sign for you that I have sent you. When you bring the people out of Egypt, you shall worship God at this very mountain."

"But," said Moses to God, "when I go to the Israelites and tell them that the God of their fathers has sent me to them, and when they ask me, "What is His name?" what am I to say to them?"

The Lord answered:

"You must tell the Israelites that the Lord, the God of their fathers, the God of Abraham, of Isaac and of Jacob has sent you to them; tell them: This is My name for all time, this is My title for all ages.

"They will listen to what you say. Then you, together with the elders of Israel, must go to Pharaoh and tell him: 'The Lord, the God of the Israelites, has met us. Pray, let us make a three days' journey into the desert, that we may sacrifice to the Lord our God.'

"Well do I know that the king of Egypt will not let you go without the use of force. So I will stretch out My hand and strike Egypt with all the marvels that I shall perform there; after that he will let you go."

Then Moses said, "But, O Lord, I am no speaker, for I am tongue-tied, and I have no command of words."

The Lord said to him:

"Who gives man his mouth? Who makes one man dumb or deaf, who gives him sight or makes him blind? Is it not I, the Lord? Go, then, I will help you speak and will instruct you what to say. Your brother Aaron shall be your spokesman to the people; he shall serve as a mouthpiece for you, and you shall inspire him what to say."

Moses returns to Egypt

Moses went back to Jethro, his father-in-law, and said to him:

"Pray, let me return to my people in Egypt, to see if they are still alive!"

"Go with my blessing," said Jethro.

Whereupon, Moses took his wife and the sons who had been born to them, and returned to the land of Egypt.

Meanwhile, the Lord said to Aaron, the brother of Moses:

"Go into the desert to meet Moses."

Aaron went, and he met Moses at the sacred mount. Then Moses told Aaron all that the Lord had commanded him. Moses and Aaron then gathered all the elders of Israel, and Aaron told them what the Lord had said to Moses.

And the people believed. When they heard that the Lord remembered the Israelites and that He had seen their affliction, they bowed their heads and worshipped. *(Exodus 1–4)*

II.

PHARAOH VERSUS GOD

The Egyptians believed that Pharaoh was not only a king but a god, and they worshipped him in addition to their other gods. As befitted a god, Pharaoh built great temples for his worship and pyramids which were really tombs. He required vast amounts of human labor for his many buildings, and he forced his people to work for him. To Pharaoh human life was very cheap. Indeed, Egyptian civilization was founded on human slavery. It was outwardly a magnificent civilization, but cruel and unjust. In the name of the God of Israel, Moses and the Israelites revolted against Pharaoh and the slavery, cruelty and inhumanity which he represented. For the God of Israel held human beings to be sacred, and He wanted them to be free.

AFTER speaking with the elders, Moses and Aaron went to Pharaoh and told him that the Lord, the God of Israel, said, "Let My people go, that they may hold a festival in My honor in the desert."

"Who is the Lord," asked Pharaoh, "that I should listen to His orders to let Israel go? I know nothing about the Lord; besides, I will not let Israel go."

Moses and Aaron replied:

"Pray, let us make a three days' journey into the desert that we may sacrifice to the Lord, our God, lest He fall upon us with pestilence or with the sword."

Pharaoh then said, "Moses and Aaron, why would you draw the people from their labors? Mind your own business. The work-people are lazy as it is, and yet you would relieve them of their tasks!"

Bricks without Straw

That same day Pharaoh ordered the slave-drivers and the foremen:

"You must no longer give the Israelites straw for making bricks; after this, let them go and gather the straw for themselves. But you must demand from them the same number of bricks as they have had to make till now; you must not reduce their quantity. They are lazy; that is why they are crying, 'Let us go and sacrifice to our God!' Make the men do heavier work, that they may attend to that instead of attending to lying words."

The slave-drivers and the foreman told the Israelites what Pharaoh had ordered.

The people scattered all over Egypt in search of stubble for straw, while the slave-drivers continued to urge them on to complete their daily amount of bricks, as when straw had been provided.

The foremen of the Israelites went and appealed to Pharaoh, "Why do you treat your servants so? Your servants have no straw supplied to them and yet we are told to make bricks; and your servants get beaten, whereas the fault lies with you."

Pharaoh answered angrily:

"You are lazy, lazy; that is why you say, 'Let us go and sacrifice to the Lord.' Be off now to your work; you shall get no straw, but you must deliver your quantity of bricks."

After they had left Pharaoh, the foremen met Moses and Aaron, who were waiting for them, and cried out:

"May the Lord punish you! You have given us a bad reputation with Pharaoh and his officers, putting a weapon into their hands to kill us!"

God promises Freedom

Moses appealed to the Lord and said:

"O Lord, why hast Thou ill-treated this people? Why didst Thou send me here? Ever since I came to speak to Pharaoh in Thy name, he has treated this people even worse; and Thou hast done nothing to rescue Thy people!"

The Lord answered:

"I have heard the groaning of the Israelites whom the Egyptians have enslaved, and I remember My covenant. Tell the Israelites that I am the Lord. I will free them from the burden of the Egyptians and rid them of their bondage. I will deliver them by

an outstretched arm and by mighty acts of judgment; I will take
them to Me for a people and I will be to them a God. I will bring
them into the land that I solemnly swore to give to Abraham,
Isaac, and Jacob, and I will give it to them as an inheritance. I
am the Lord."

And He continued:

"Now you shall see what I will do to Pharaoh; he will be
compelled to let them go; he will be forced to drive them out of
his country. And the Egyptians shall know that I am the Lord,
when I stretch out My hand against Egypt and bring the Israelites
from their midst."   (*Exodus 4–6*)

III.

PASSOVER — THE FESTIVAL OF FREEDOM

Pharaoh was not easily persuaded to let the Israelites leave Egypt. Time and again he promised to let them go, but each time he withdrew his promise. Nine plagues then came to torment the land — blood, frogs, flies, gnats, cattle diseases, sores, hail, locusts and darkness. Only the tenth plague — the destruction of the first-born of the Egyptians — was so terrible that Pharaoh had to yield. Our sages commented on the human misery caused by the stubbornness of Pharaoh and pointed out how the plagues revealed the long-suffering patience of God, for He had given Pharaoh many opportunities to free his slaves. Before the last plague came, the Israelites were told to celebrate the sacred gift of freedom for all time to come. This celebration later came to be known as the Festival of Passover.

THE Lord said to Moses:

"One more plague will I bring on Pharaoh and on Egypt, and then he will let you go; indeed, when he shall let you go, he shall surely drive you out of the country."

Moses' final Warning

Moses came again before Pharaoh and said:

"The Lord declares that He will pass through Egypt about midnight, when all the first-born in Egypt shall die, from the eldest son of Pharaoh on the throne to the eldest son of the slave-girl at the mill, and the first-born of all the cattle. Then shall a loud wail ring through all the land of Egypt, such as there never has been and never will be heard again. And not even a dog shall bark against any of the Israelites nor their animals — to teach you that the Lord does make a difference between the Egyptians and Israel. And all your officers shall come to me and bow down, begging, 'Go away, together with all the people that follow you.' After that I will leave the country."

Moses then left the presence of Pharaoh.

Passover — Festival of Freedom

The Lord then said to Moses and Aaron:

"Tell the whole community of Israel: 'This month shall be to you the first month of the year.'

"On the tenth day of this month they shall provide for themselves one lamb each for their families, a lamb for each household. They shall keep it until the fourteenth day of the month, when every member of the community of Israel shall kill it between sunset and dark. Then they shall take some of the blood and smear it on the two doorposts and the lintel of the houses where the lamb is eaten.

"And this is how you are to eat it: Your belt tight round your waist, your sandals on your feet, and your staff in your hand; you shall eat it in haste. For it is the Lord's passover. This very night I will pass through the land of Egypt, striking down all the first-born in Egypt, man and beast alike, and dooming all the gods of Egypt. I am the Lord. The blood shall mark the houses where you live, and when I see the blood I will pass over you, sparing you the deadly plague, as I strike down the land of Egypt."

And the Lord continued:

"This day shall be a memorial day for you to be kept as a festival for the Lord; age after age you shall keep this as a permanent festival. For seven days you shall eat unleavened bread (*Matzah*); on the first day you shall clean your houses of all leaven (*Hometz*). On the first day also you shall hold a religious gathering, and on the seventh day also a religious gathering. You shall do no business on these days, no work except in preparing the food that everyone needs."

And the Lord added:

"When you enter the land which the Lord shall give you, as He promised, you shall keep up this service. When your children say to you, 'What do you mean by this service?' you shall answer, 'It is the Passover-sacrifice to the Lord, for He passed over the houses of the Israelites in Egypt when He struck down the Egyptians; but He kept our houses safe.' "

Moses and Aaron spoke these words to the Israelites, and after they heard them, the people bowed their heads, and worshipped. Then they went and did as the Lord had commanded Moses and Aaron.

The Plague of the First-born.
Pharaoh expels the Israelites.

And it came to pass at midnight that the Lord struck down all the first-born in the land of Egypt, from the eldest son of Pharaoh on the throne to the eldest son of the prisoner in the dungeon, as well as the first-born of all the cattle, but He did no harm to His people, the Israelites.

There was a loud wail of sorrow in Egypt, for there was not a house where someone was not dead. Pharaoh arose in the night, together with all his officers and all the Egyptians.

And Pharaoh summoned Moses and Aaron, and said to them:

"Go away from among my people, both you and the Israelites; go and worship the Lord, as you have asked. Take with you your flocks and herds, as you demand, and go; and ask a blessing for me also."

The Egyptians pressed the Israelites to hurry out of the land, crying, "We shall all perish!"

The Israelites hastily snatched up their unbaked dough, unleavened as it was, and wrapped their kneading-bowls inside their cloaks and carried them on their shoulders.

The Israelites did exactly as the Lord had ordered Moses and Aaron. And on that very day the Lord brought the Israelites out of the land of Egypt. (*Exodus 11, 12*)

IV.

GOD TRIUMPHS OVER PHARAOH

After the Israelites had left Egypt and crossed the Red Sea, Moses sang his thrilling Song of Triumph. Our sages tell us that the angels also wanted to sing God's praises that day before Him, but He silenced them out of His great grief and compassion for the dying Egyptians. "They are My children," He cried, "the work of My hands; would you sing Me a song while they drown in the sea?"

WHEN Pharaoh had let the Israelites go, God did not take them by the road leading directly to the land of Canaan, although that was near; for God thought that perhaps the Israelites might have regrets, if they had to fight, and desire to return to Egypt. But God led the people by a roundabout road in the direction of the desert, towards the Red Sea.

The Israelites went up armed out of Egypt. Moses himself took the bones of Joseph; for Joseph had made the Israelites promise that they would do this. The Lord went in front of them, in a pillar of cloud, to lead them by day, and in a pillar of fire, to light them through the night, so that they might march both by day and by night.

Pharaoh pursues Israel

When Pharaoh was told that the Israelites had left, he and his officers changed their minds about permitting them to leave Egypt.

"What have we done," they cried, "to let the Israelites leave our service?"

Pharaoh got his chariots ready and took his men with him, six hundred picked chariots and all the rest of the chariots of Egypt, manned by their captains. The Lord let the heart of Pharaoh remain stubborn, and he followed the Israelites to the shores of the Red Sea.

When Pharaoh and his army drew near, the Israelites looked back, and saw that the Egyptians were coming after them. They became terribly afraid. They cried to the Lord. And they said to Moses:

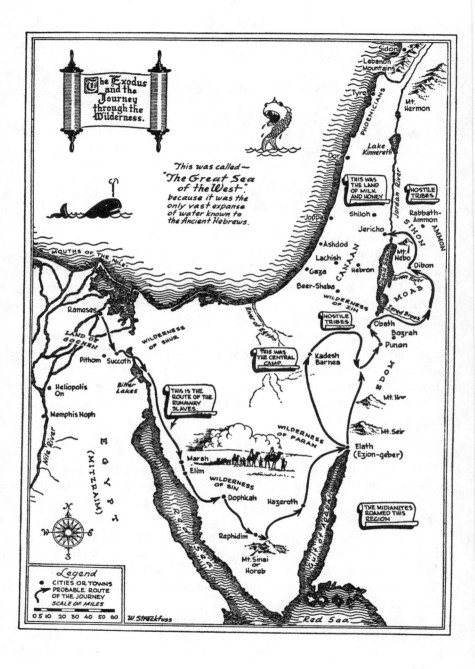

The Exodus and the Journey through the Wilderness.

This was called —
"The Great Sea
of the West":
because it was the
only vast expanse
of water known to
the Ancient Hebrews.

MOUTHS OF THE NILE

Sidon
Lebanon Mountains
Tyre
Mt. Hermon
PHOENICIANS
Lake Kinnereth
Dor
THIS WAS THE LAND OF MILK AND HONEY
HOSTILE TRIBES
Joppa
Shiloh
Rabbath-Ammon
Jericho
Jordan River
SIHON
AMMON
Ashdod
Mt. Nebo
Lachish
Dead Sea
Dibon
Gaza
Hebron
CANAAN
Beer-Sheba
Arnon River
MOAB
WILDERNESS OF ZIN
Jered Brook
River of Egypt
HOSTILE TRIBES
Obath
THIS WAS THE CENTRAL CAMP
Kadesh Barnea
Bozrah
Punon
EDOM

Rameses
LAND OF GOSHEN
WILDERNESS OF SHUR
Pithom Succoth
Heliopolis On
Bitter Lakes
Memphis Noph
Nile River
EGYPT (MITZRAIM)
THIS IS THE ROUTE OF THE RUNAWAY SLAVES
WILDERNESS OF PARAN
Mt. Hor
Mt. Seir
Elath (Ezion-geber)
Marah
Elim
WILDERNESS OF SIN
Dophkah
Hazeroth
THE MIDIANITES ROAMED THIS REGION
Raphidim
Red Sea
Mt. Sinai or Horeb
Gulf of Akaba

N W E S

Legend
• CITIES OR TOWNS
PROBABLE ROUTE OF THE JOURNEY
SCALE OF MILES
0 5 10 20 30 40 50 60

W. Streckfuss

Red Sea

"Was it because there were no graves in Egypt that you have brought us to die in the desert? Why have you misguided us by bringing us out of Egypt? Did we not tell you in Egypt to let us alone that we might serve the Egyptians? Better for us to serve the Egyptians than die in the desert!"

Moses answered:

"Have no fear, stand still, and watch the Lord deliver you today; for though you see the Egyptians today, you shall never see them again. The Lord will fight for you, and you have only to keep still."

Crossing the Red Sea

The Lord then said to Moses:

"Why do you cry to Me? Tell the Israelites to march forward. And as for you, raise your staff and stretch out your hand over the sea, and divide it; and the Israelites shall march on dry ground through the sea."

Then the pillar of cloud which had been before the Israelites moved to behind them and remained between the army of Egypt and the army of Israel. When darkness came, the cloud lit up the night where the Israelites were but not where the Egyptians marched, so that the one army did not overtake the other that night. Then the Israelites came to the Red Sea.

Moses stretched his hand out over the sea; and the Lord swept the sea along by a strong east wind, all night, till the bed of the sea was dry. The Israelites marched through the sea on dry ground, the waters forming a wall to right and a wall to left. The Egyptians pursued them right into the sea. In the morning, before dawn, the Lord threw them into a panic. He struck off their chariot-wheels and caused them to advance with difficulty. The Egyptians cried:

"Let us flee from the Israelites! The Lord fights for them against us!"

Then the Lord said to Moses:

"Stretch your hand out over the sea to make the waters flow back upon the chariots and cavalry of the Egyptians."

Moses stretched his hand out over the sea; and, as morning broke, the sea returned to its level, and while the Egyptians were fleeing before the returning water, the Lord overwhelmed them in the midst of the sea.

Thus the Lord saved Israel that day from the Egyptians; and Israel saw the Egyptians lying dead upon the seashore. And when Israel saw the mighty act of the Lord against the Egyptians, they stood in awe of the Lord; and they believed in the Lord and in His servant, Moses.

The Song of God's Triumph

Then Moses and the Israelites sang this song to the Lord:

"I will sing to the Lord, for He has gloriously
      triumphed;
   The horse and his rider has He thrown into the sea.
   The Lord is my strength and song,
   And He has saved me.
   He is my God, and I will glorify Him;
   My father's God, and I will exalt Him.
   The Lord is a man of war,
   The Lord is His name.
   Pharaoh's chariots and his host has He cast into
      the sea;
   And his chosen captains are sunk in the Red Sea.
   The deeps cover them;
   They sank into the depths like a stone.

   Thy right hand, O Lord, glorious in power,
   Thy right hand, O Lord, dasheth in pieces the foe.
   At Thy blast the waters were piled up;
   The floods stood upright as a heap;
   The deeps turned hard in the heart of the sea.
   The foe said, 'I will pursue them, I will overtake
      them,
   I will divide their spoil;
   My lust shall be satisfied upon them;
   I will draw my sword, and destroy them!'
   But Thou didst blow Thy blast and the sea covered
      them;
   Like lead they sank into the mighty waters!

Who is like unto Thee, O Lord, among the mighty?
Who is like unto Thee, glorious in holiness,
Fearful in praises, doing wonders?
The Lord shall reign for ever and ever!"

Miriam and the Women

And Miriam, the prophetess, the sister of Aaron and Moses, took a tambourine in her hand. She was followed by all the women dancing with their tambourines. And Miriam sang to them:

"Sing to the Lord, for He has gloriously triumphed;
The horse and his rider has He thrown into the
   sea." (*Exodus 13–15*)

V.

STARTING THE LONG JOURNEY

The journey to Canaan was a long, hard trek for a people who were not accustomed to desert life and travel. Their forty years in the wilderness proved a time of trial and testing. Moses had to train the Israelites and get them ready for receiving the Law and for the invasion of the Promised Land. He had to rid their minds of their slavish spirit and toughen them to bear hardships like true pioneers. Moreover, he wanted to strengthen their character and weld them into a united nation. But Moses possessed genius and untiring patience that in time overcame the murmurings, complaints, difficulties and even rebelliousness of this horde of slaves, and changed them into a holy people.

FROM the Red Sea Moses led the Israelites forward into the Wilderness of Shur; and they marched for three days into the desert, and they found no water.

Complaints for Water

When they reached the oasis of Marah, they could not drink the water there, it was so bitter; therefore its name was Marah which means "Bitterness." And the people grumbled against Moses and cried:

"What shall we drink?"

Moses appealed to the Lord; and the Lord showed him a tree. Moses took a branch of it and threw it into the waters, and the waters became sweet.

Then they marched on and came to Elim, where there were twelve springs of water and seventy palm trees; there they camped beside the springs.

Marching from Elim, the Israelites came to the Wilderness of Sin, between Elim and Sinai.

Murmurings for Food

Again the Israelites grumbled against Moses and Aaron in the desert crying:

"Would that we had died by the hand of the Lord in Egypt, where we could sit beside the flesh-pots and where we had plenty to eat! Here you have brought us into the desert to starve this whole people to death!"

The Lord said to Moses:

"I have heard the Israelites grumbling; tell them that at dusk they shall eat flesh, and in the morning they shall be filled with bread — to teach them that I am the Lord their God."

Moses and Aaron told all the Israelites:

"In the evening you shall find that it was the Lord who brought you out of the land of Egypt, and in the morning you shall see the Lord manifested in might, since He has heard you grumbling."

In the evening quails flew up and dropped all over the camp, and in the morning there was a fall of dew round the camp. When the dew evaporated, there, on the ground, lay thin flakes, like frost. When the Israelites saw it, they said to one another:

"What is it?" — for they did not know what it was.

"That," said Moses, "is the food the Lord gives to you. Gather it for six days, but on the seventh day, on the Sabbath, there shall be none. However, on the sixth day there will be food enough for two days."

The children of Israel called this food *manna*. It was white as coriander seed and tasted like wafers made with honey. And for forty years the Israelites ate manna.

From the Wilderness of Sin the Israelites travelled by stages, as the Lord commanded them, and they camped at Rephidim.

Amalek — *The eternal Enemy*

It was at Rephidim that Amalek, a fierce and warlike tribe of nomads, came and fought against Israel. Moses said to Joshua, captain of the hosts of Israel:

"Pick out some men to go and fight against Amalek; tomorrow I will stand on the top of the hill, holding the rod of God in my hand."

Joshua did as Moses told him. He fought against Amalek, while Moses, Aaron and Hur went up to the top of the hill. Whenever Moses raised his hand, then Israel won; whenever he lowered his hand, then Amalek won. But the hands of Moses grew tired; so they put a stone below him, on which he sat. And Aaron and

Hur held up his hands, one on one side and the other on the other side, so that his hands remained steady till sunset. Joshua finally defeated Amalek, and put the enemy to the sword.

The Lord said to Moses:

"Write this down in a book in commemoration of the day, and read it aloud to Joshua. For I mean to blot out the memory of Amalek from under the heavens."

And Moses built an altar and he called it *Adonai-nissi* (The Lord is my banner). And he declared:

"We pledge loyalty to the Lord in His war against Amalek from age to age!"

Organizing the People

Now Jethro heard of all that God had done for Moses and for His people Israel. Jethro came into the desert where Moses was encamped, at the hill of God. Moses was told: "Here is your father-in-law, Jethro, coming to you."

Moses went to meet his father-in-law. They asked about each other's health and went inside the tent, where Moses told Jethro all that the Lord had done to Pharaoh and the Egyptians for Israel's sake, all the distress they had suffered on their journey, and how the Lord had preserved them.

Jethro rejoiced over the goodness of the Lord to the Israelites, in rescuing them from the Egyptians.

Next day, as Moses was holding a people's court, with the people surrounding him from morning to night, Jethro noticed all his labor for the people, and said to him:

"What is this you are doing? Why sit alone as a judge, with the people all around you from morning to night?"

Moses answered his father-in-law:

"Because the people come to me to inquire of God. Whenever they have any disputes, they come to me; and I decide between a man and his neighbor, and I make them know the rules and instructions of God."

Jethro said to him:

"You are not doing right. You will wear yourself out, you and your people. This work is too burdensome for you, and you cannot manage it alone. Now listen to me, let me advise you, that God may be with you. You yourself may represent the people before God, laying their cases before Him, and instructing them in His rules and commands, letting them see how they are to live and what they are to do. But, select some capable men from among the people, religious and honest men, who scorn unjust gain, and appoint them to supervise groups of thousands, hundreds, fifties, and tens. Let them act as judges in ordinary cases. They can refer any special case to you and judge lesser matters themselves. That will make things easier for you, as they share the work with you."

Moses listened to what his father-in-law said, and did exactly as he had been told. Then Moses let Jethro depart. And Jethro returned to his own country.

Leaving Rephidim, the Israelites travelled until they reached the Wilderness of Sinai.   (*Exodus 15–19*)

VI.

THE COVENANT AT MOUNT SINAI

The Covenant or agreement between God and Israel stated that God would guide and help His people *if* they would be true and faithful to Him. But, how would the people know what being faithful to God meant? For such purpose, the people needed rules or laws to tell them what they should do and how they should conduct themselves to be loyal to God and to fulfill their agreement with Him. Hitherto, the Covenant had been verbal and had been made between God and the great patriarchs — Abraham, Isaac and Jacob. Now, at Mount Sinai, the Covenant was written and was made between God and the entire people of Israel. Moses received the Ten Great Words ("Ten Commandments," or "Decalogue") for Israel. And as their national life developed, additional rules or laws carried forward the spirit of the Ten Great Words.

THE third month after leaving the land of Egypt, the Israelites entered the Wilderness of Sinai. They pitched camp in front of the mountain, and Moses went up to God.

Moses prepares Israel

The Lord called to Moses from the mountain, saying:

"Tell this to the house of Jacob, tell the Israelites: 'You have seen for yourselves what I did to the Egyptians and how I bore you safe on eagle's wings and brought you hither to Myself. Now then, if you will listen to what I say and keep My solemn Covenant, you shall be My own treasure among all nations, for all the world is Mine. You shall be a nation of priests for Me, a holy nation.' "

The Lord then added:

"I am coming to you in a thick cloud, so that the people may hear Me speaking to you and always believe you also.

"Go to the people and consecrate them today and tomorrow; let them wash their clothes and be ready for the third day, for on the third day I will descend upon Mount Sinai in the sight of all the people."

The Ten Commandments

Our sages tell us that God had offered the Law to several nations but that one after the other they had refused it, because they would have had to change their unethical ways of living. Only after their refusal did God give the Law to Israel, who promised to obey it. They also tell us that, when God spoke the great words on Mount Sinai, the divine voice divided itself into seventy languages so that all mankind might hear and understand them.

On the morning of the third day, there was thunder and lightning, and a dense cloud shrouded the mountain, and a loud trumpet-blast was heard, till all the people in the camp trembled. Moses brought the people out of the camp to meet God; they took their stand at the foot of the mountain.

Mount Sinai was completely wrapped in smoke, as the Lord descended in fire upon it; the smoke ascended like smoke from a furnace; and when the mountain shook violently, the people trembled. As the blast of the trumpet grew louder and louder, Moses spoke and God answered him.

Then God spoke all these words:

"I am the Lord thy God, who brought thee out of the land of Egypt, out of the house of bondage.

"Thou shalt have no other gods before Me. Thou shalt not make unto thee a graven image, nor any manner of likeness of anything that is in heaven above, or that is in the earth beneath, or that is in the water under the earth; thou shalt not bow down unto them, nor serve them; for I the Lord thy God am a jealous God, visiting the iniquity of the fathers upon the children unto the third and fourth generation of them that hate Me; and showing mercy unto the thousandth generation of them that love Me and keep My commandments.

"Thou shalt not take the name of the Lord thy God in vain; for the Lord will not hold him guiltless that taketh His name in vain.

"Remember the Sabbath day to keep it holy. Six days shalt thou labor, and do all thy work; but the seventh day is a Sabbath unto the Lord, thy God; in it thou shalt not do any manner of work, thou, nor thy son, nor thy daughter, nor thy man-servant, nor thy maid-servant, nor thy cattle, nor thy stranger that is within thy gates; for in six days the Lord made heaven and earth, the sea, and all that in them is, and He rested on the seventh day; wherefore the Lord blessed the Sabbath day, and hallowed it.

"Honor thy father and thy mother, that thy days may be long upon the land which the Lord thy God giveth thee.

"Thou shalt not murder.

"Thou shalt not commit adultery.

"Thou shalt not steal.

"Thou shalt not bear false witness against thy neighbor.

"Thou shalt not covet thy neighbor's house; thou shalt not covet thy neighbor's wife, nor his man-servant, nor his maid-servant, nor his ox, nor his ass, nor anything that is thy neighbor's."

The Lord said to Moses:

"Write down these words, for in accord with these words, I have made a solemn Covenant with you and with Israel."

Then Moses called together the elders of the people and set before them all these words which the Lord had commanded him. And all the people answered together:

"Whatever the Lord commands, we will do and we will obey."

Influence of Egypt — The golden Calf

Then the Lord said to Moses:

"Come up beside Me on the mountain, and I will give you the stone tables with the directions and orders I have inscribed for the guidance of the people."

Moses rose and went up the mountain of God with his attendant Joshua, telling the elders of Israel to wait below for them till they returned.

"You have Aaron and Hur," he said. "Anyone with a dispute can take it to them."

The radiance of the Lord rested on the mountain of Sinai; it looked to the Israelites like blazing fire on the top of the mountain; for six days the cloud covered it, and on the seventh day He called from the cloud to Moses. Moses entered the cloud and went up the mountain, and he remained on the mountain forty days and forty nights.

When the people saw that Moses delayed in returning to them, they gathered around Aaron, saying:

"Come, and make us some god to go in front of us; as for this Moses, the man who brought us out of the land of Egypt, we do not know what has become of him!"

Aaron said to them:

"Break off the golden earrings from the ears of your wives and sons and daughters, and bring them to me."

The people all broke off their earrings and handed them to Aaron, who melted them into one piece, and carved it with a tool into a metal calf. And the people exclaimed:

"Here is your God, O Israel, who brought you out of the land of Egypt!"

Thereupon, Aaron erected an altar in front of the calf and proclaimed a festival on the next day for the Lord. The next morning the people rose, and offered sacrifices. Then the people sat down to the sacrificial-feast, after which they rose to amuse themselves.

Now the Lord said to Moses:

"Go down, for your people whom you brought out of the land of Egypt have dealt wickedly. They have turned aside quickly out of the way which I commanded them; and they have made themselves a metal calf, worshipping it, sacrificing to it, crying, 'Here is your God, O Israel, who brought you out of the land of Egypt!'"

The Lord continued:

"I have watched this people, and it is a stiff-necked, obstinate people. Now let Me alone, that My wrath may blaze against them and burn them up! I will make a great nation of you."

Moses pleaded with the Lord, his God.

"O Lord," he cried, "why doth Thy wrath blaze against Thine own people whom Thou didst bring out of the land of Egypt with great power and a mighty hand? Why should the Egyptians sneer, 'He led them away to harm them, to slay them among the hills and to consume them from the face of the earth?' Cease Thy fierce anger and change Thy mind about punishing Thy people thus. Remember Abraham and Isaac and Jacob, Thy servants, to whom Thou didst swear that Thou wouldst make their descendants as numerous as the stars in heaven and give all this land, of which Thou didst speak, to their descendants as a possession for all time."

So the Lord changed His mind about the punishment He had threatened to His people. Moses turned away to go down the mountain, with the two Tables of the Law in his hands, tables written on both sides that were the work of God.

The first Tables broken

When Joshua heard the noise of the people as they shouted, he said to Moses:

"That is the noise of war in the camp."

"No," said Moses, "it is not the voices of men conquering nor the voices of men being conquered; what I hear is the noise of people singing."

As soon as Moses came near the camp, he saw the calf and the people dancing round it. He blazed with anger. He flung down the Tables of the Law and broke them at the foot of the mount; he took the calf they had made and burned it with fire, and ground it to powder, which he threw into water and made the Israelites drink it. And the Lord punished the people for the calf which Aaron made.

Then Moses asked Aaron:

"What did this people do to you, that you have let them incur this great guilt?"

Aaron answered:

"Let not my lord's anger blaze; you know how determined the people are to do wrong. They told me to make gods for them, to go in front of them, crying, 'As for this man Moses, the man who brought us out of the land of Egypt, we do not know what has become of him!' I told them to bring any gold they possessed; and they brought the gold to me. I cast it into the fire, and there came out this calf!"

Next day Moses said to the people:

"You have committed a great sin. I will go up to the Lord; perhaps I may make atonement for your sin."

Then Moses went back to the Lord and said:

THE LAW AT MOUNT SINAI

"Moses turned away to go down the mountain,
with the two Tables of the Law in his hands . . ."

(*Exodus 34.29*)

see page 90

BEZALEL, THE ARTIST

"And let them make Me a sanctuary, that I may
dwell among them."   (*Exodus 25.8*)

see page 92

"Alas, this people has committed a great sin, making a golden god for themselves! Yet, wilt Thou not forgive their sin? If Thou wilt not, blot me, I pray Thee, out of the book which Thou hast written!"

The Lord answered Moses:

"I blot sinners out of My book. And now go, and lead the people where I told you; see, My angel shall go ahead of you. Nevertheless, on the day when I do punish, I will punish them for their sin."

The second Set of Tables

Then the Lord said to Moses:

"Cut two tables of stone like the former ones, and I will write on them what was written on the former tables which you broke."

Moses cut two tables of stone like the former ones; and early in the morning Moses went up Mount Sinai, carrying the two tables of stone in his hand.

The Lord passed by before him, and proclaimed:

"The Lord, the Lord, God, merciful and gracious, long-suffering, and abundant in goodness and truth; keeping mercy to the thousandth generation, forgiving iniquity and transgression and sin; and that by no means will clear the guilty; visiting the iniquity of the fathers upon the children, and upon the children's children unto the third and the fourth generation."

Moses hastened to bow his head to the ground.

Then the Lord said to Moses:

"Write these words down, for these are the terms of the Covenant I have made with you and Israel."

Moses wrote on the tables the words of the Covenant, the Ten Commandments.

When Moses came down from Mount Sinai with the two Tables of the Law in his hand, he did not know that his face glowed after speaking to God. But when Aaron and the Israelites saw Moses, his face was in a glow. They were afraid to come near him, till Moses called to them. Then Aaron and all the elders came to him, and Moses talked with them. After that, all the Israelites came near, and he set before them all the words of the Lord. (*Exodus 19–20, 24, 32–34*)

VII.

THE TABERNACLE — GOD'S PALACE

The children of Israel had met God on Mount Sinai. They were now to travel to the Promised Land. Would God leave Mount Sinai to go with them to Canaan? If so, how would they know that He was with them? To satisfy the people's need for a symbol of God's presence, Moses set aside a large tent which he called the Tabernacle, or God's Dwelling Place. Since Moses and the people could meet with God there, he called it also the Tent of Meeting. Moses made an oblong box with poles on its sides with which the box — later known as the Ark of the Covenant — could be carried. He put the Tables of the Law into this box. The Ark was placed inside the Tabernacle, so that the Lord, the God of Israel, now had His Palace — the Tabernacle. And the priests and Levites were like royal courtiers who served the King. Bezalel was the first Jewish artist. He built the Tabernacle and made all its utensils.

THE Lord said to Moses:

"Speak to the Israelites, that they gather contributions from everyone whose heart is willing. And let them make Me a Sanctuary, that I may dwell among them."

He further said:

"The Tabernacle itself you shall make out of ten curtains, making them of fine twisted linen, violet, purple and scarlet material, the work of artists.

"They shall make an Ark of acacia-wood, and a Table of acacia-wood overlaid with pure gold.

"You shall make a Candlestick of gold. And you shall make the Altar of acacia-wood, with horns on its four corners, the horns to be one piece with it; you shall overlay it with bronze.

"You shall make a bronze Basin with a bronze base for washing, and place it between the Tent of Meeting and the Altar, putting water in it, so that Aaron and his sons may wash themselves from it, whenever they enter the Tent of Meeting or approach the Altar to minister.

"And you shall order the Israelites to bring you pure oil from crushed olives for the light, to cause a Lamp to burn continually." (*Ner Tamid*)

Voluntary Contributions

Moses then said to the assembly of Israel:

"This is what the Lord commands: You shall gather a special offering for the Lord, to be made by everyone who has a willing heart. Let every skilled workman among you come and help make the Tabernacle, its curtains and its vessels, the priestly robes for service in the sacred place, and the sacred garments to be worn by Aaron the priest and by his sons in their priestly service."

The assembly of Israel then broke up. Everyone who felt moved, everyone whose heart was willing, came with his special offering for the Lord, to work at the Tabernacle, its curtains and its vessels, and the sacred garments of the priests.

Bezalel, the Jewish Artist

Then Moses said to the Israelites:

"The Lord has especially chosen Bezalel, inspiring him with the spirit of God, in skill and knowledge and ability in every craft, to create artistic works; and He has given Bezalel ability to instruct others. Both to him and Oholiab the Lord has given skill to do all kinds of artistic work — that of the engraver, the artisan, the worker in materials, and the creator of beautiful things."

Under the supervision of Moses, the artists received all the contributions which the Israelites brought, until they said to Moses:

"The people are bringing far more than is needed for the work the Lord has ordered."

Moses then issued an order:

"No more contributions are necessary for the Tabernacle."

Moses dedicates the Tabernacle

In time, all the work on the Tabernacle was finished, and the Israelites did as the Lord had commanded Moses. They brought the Tabernacle and all its parts to Moses; and when Moses saw that they had carried out all the work just as the Lord had commanded, Moses blessed them and caused the Tent of Meeting to be set up.

Then the cloud covered the Tent of Meeting, and the glory of the Lord filled the Tabernacle. The Israelites prepared themselves to march. Whenever the cloud was raised above the Tabernacle, the Israelites would march ahead, throughout all their journeys; but whenever the cloud was not raised, they would not move till the day it did lift.

The cloud of the Lord was above the Tabernacle by day, and there was fire in it by night, in sight of all the house of Israel throughout all their journeys.　(*Exodus 25–27, 30–31, 35–40*)

וַיִּקְרָא

LEVITICUS

WHAT shall we do to live as Jews? What must Jews do and be in order to become a holy people? What way of life does the Jewish religion hold to be most worth while?

We often ask questions like these today. Our ancestors asked similar questions of Moses centuries ago. They received their answers in the written Covenant of Mount Sinai and in the teachings of Moses, for Moses was not only the Liberator of the Jewish people, he was also their great Lawgiver.↓

The readings given in the following chapters have been selected from Leviticus, Numbers and Deuteronomy, and have been arranged into groups according to subject. They answer such questions as: What should be the attitude of a Jew towards his parents? towards the aged? What are the duties of a Jew towards charity, the poor, the widow, the orphan, the stranger, the laborer? Who were the religious leaders of Israel before there were rabbis? What are some important Jewish festivals and fasts? What are the dietary laws?

Among Jewish national problems were: What was the attitude of the Jewish people towards their king? What of the judges and the courts? Did women have legal rights? What about the ownership of land? How were the Jewish people to wage war, if that became necessary?

All these were very important matters. For the Jewish people were to be a holy people. This meant that they were to separate themselves from all that displeased God, and were to lead pure and upright lives. Time and again holiness was the reason given for the laws and commandments: "You shall be holy: for I the Lord your God am holy."

Leviticus is the third Book of Moses. It deals mostly with the duties of the priests and Levites. Originally this book was called *Torat Kohanim*, "The Law of the Priests." Its present Hebrew name is *Va-Yikra*, the word with which it begins, and it means "And He called (to Moses)."

↓For archaeological note see Item 7, p. 551 in the back of the book.

I.

PRIEST AND LEVITE

In ancient times the Israelites worshipped God by bringing animal sacrifices to the altar. There they said prayers and performed various ceremonies. The priests and Levites conducted the worship. Moses, at the command of God, appointed Aaron as High Priest, and the tribe of Levi as the caretakers and servants of God's Tabernacle. The Levites also had charge of the education of the people. Today, of course, the Jewish people do not use this ancient method of worship. In the course of time, Judaism substituted prayers for sacrifices.

The Priesthood

THE Lord said to Moses:

"Take Aaron and his sons, the garments of their sacred office and the anointing oil, and the sacrifices, and gather all the community at the entrance to the Tent of Meeting."

Moses did as the Lord commanded him. And when the entire community had assembled, Moses said:

"This is what the Lord has ordered to be done."

Moses took some of the anointing oil and poured it over the head of Aaron to consecrate him.

Moses next brought forward Aaron's sons, clothed them with tunics, girdled them with sashes, and fastened caps on them, as the Lord had commanded. He then brought forward the sacrifice and slaughtered it.

And Aaron and his sons carried out all the commands which the Lord gave through Moses. (*Leviticus 8–9*)

The Levites: Servants and Teachers

The Lord said to Moses:

"Bring the tribe of Levi forward and present them before Aaron the priest, to be at his service. They shall do duty for him and for the whole community before the Tent of Meeting, to look after the Tabernacle, taking charge of all the equipment of the Tent of Meeting. Assign the Levites to Aaron and his sons; they belong to him, out of the Israelites." *(Numbers 3.5)*

And Moses wrote this Law, and delivered it to the priests, the sons of Levi, who carried the Ark of the Covenant of the Lord, and to all the elders of Israel. And Moses commanded them as follows:

"At the end of every seven years, at the Feast of Booths, when all Israel comes to appear before the Lord your God at the Sanctuary He chooses, you shall read this Law aloud in the hearing of all Israel. Assemble the people, men, women and children, and any strangers in your employ that are in your community, that they may hear and learn it, and revere the Lord your God, and be careful to observe all the words of this Law; and that their children, who do not know it, may hear and learn to revere the Lord your God, as long as you live in the land into which you are going." *(Deuteronomy 31.9)*

The priestly Benediction is used to this Day

And the Lord gave Moses this command for Aaron and his sons:

"You shall bless Israel in these words:

'The Lord bless thee, and keep thee;

'The Lord make His face to shine upon thee, and be gracious unto thee;

'The Lord lift up His countenance upon thee, and give thee peace!'

"So shall they put My name upon the children of Israel, and I will bless them." *(Numbers 6.22)*

II.

FEAST AND FAST

Besides the Sabbath, the three leading festivals of the Jewish year are: Passover (*Pesah*) in the early spring, the Feast of Weeks (*Shabuot*) in the early summer, and the Feast of Booths (*Succot*) in the early autumn. In ancient times, pilgrimages were made to the Temple in Jerusalem on these festivals and they became known as the "Pilgrim Festivals." The Hebrew month Nisan, in which Passover falls, was considered the first month of the Jewish year. The first day of the seventh month, however, named Tishri, marked the beginning of the New Year (*Rosh Hashanah*) in the Jewish calendar. Ten days later came the solemn Day of Atonement (*Yom Kippur*), the day of the Great Fast.

THE Lord directed Moses to give these commands to the Israelites:

"These are the fixed festivals of the Lord which you shall proclaim as religious assemblies, each in its proper season."

The Sabbath Day

"And the children of Israel shall keep the Sabbath, to observe the Sabbath throughout their generations, for a perpetual covenant. It is a sign between Me and the children of Israel for ever; for in six days the Lord made heaven and earth, and on the seventh day He ceased from work and rested." (*Exodus 31.16, 17*)

"During six days work may be done; but on the seventh day there is to be a Sabbath of complete rest, a religious assembly, when you shall do no work; it is to be kept as a Sabbath for the Lord in all your dwellings."

Pesah — The Passover

"On the fourteenth day of the first month (Nisan), towards evening, the Passover of the Lord begins. On the fifteenth of the same month the Feast of Unleavened Bread begins; for seven days you shall eat unleavened bread. On the first day of the festival you shall hold a religious assembly; you shall do no hard work. For seven days you shall offer sacrifices to the Lord; on the seventh day you shall hold another religious assembly, doing no hard work.

Shabuot — The Feast of Weeks

"From the second day of Passover, the day you bring the sheaf of the wave-offering, you shall count seven full weeks, counting fifty days to the day following the seventh week, and then you shall offer a cereal-offering of new grain to the Lord. On that day you shall proclaim and hold a religious assembly, when you shall do no hard work. It is to be an everlasting law in all your dwellings throughout your generations.

Rosh Hashanah — The New Year

"The first day of the seventh month (Tishri) you shall hold as a day of complete rest, a day of remembrance, celebrated by the blowing of trumpets, a religious assembly; you shall do no hard work, and you shall offer a sacrifice to the Lord.

Yom Kippur — The Day of Atonement

"On the tenth day of the seventh month (Tishri) which is the Day of Atonement, you shall hold a religious assembly; you shall afflict your souls (observe a fast), and offer a sacrifice to the Lord. You shall not do any kind of work on that day, for it is a day of atonement, on which atonement is made for you before the Lord your God. It is to be an everlasting law throughout your generations in all your dwellings. You shall observe it as a Sabbath of complete rest, and you shall abstain and fast; from sunset on the ninth day to sunset on the tenth day you shall keep your Sabbath.

Succot — The Festival of Booths

"On the fifteenth day of this seventh month (Tishri) the seven-day Feast of Booths in honor of the Lord begins. On the first day there shall be a religious assembly when you shall do no hard work. For seven days you shall offer sacrifices to the Lord; on the eighth day (*Shemini Azeret*) you shall hold a religious assembly, and offer sacrifice to the Lord; it is a sacred assembly, and you shall do no hard work. On the first day you shall take the fruit of the beautiful trees (*Etrog*), the branches of palm trees, the boughs of leafy trees (myrtle), and water-willows (these last three together make the *Lulab*), and rejoice before the Lord your God for seven days. These seven days you shall live in booths (*Succot*); all the native-born Israelites shall live in booths, that your descendants may know that I made the Israelites live in booths when I brought them out of the land of Egypt; I am the Lord your God."

Thus did Moses announce to the Israelites the fixed festivals of the Lord, and the day of the Great Fast.   (*Leviticus 23*)

III.

LAWS OF PURITY

The most important word in religion, next to the name of God, is "holiness." The simplest meaning of the word holiness is purity; that is, purity of life, thought and action. The Jewish religion maintained that a pure spirit could be found only in a clean and healthy body. Thus the laws of holiness were concerned not only with justice and love toward one's fellowmen, but also with the healing of diseases, proper relations between men and women, and the daily diet (Dietary Laws). Since the daily diet affected a man's whole being, the kinds of food a Jew was permitted to eat held an important place in the laws of holiness. Furthermore, the manner of preparing animals for food was also regarded as highly important.

The Dietary Laws (Kashrut)

THE Lord said to Moses:
"Say to the Israelites: 'I am the Lord your God, who have separated you from other peoples. You shall, therefore, make a distinction between clean animals and unclean, clean birds and unclean. You shall not make your souls impure with beast or bird or reptile, which I have separated as unclean for you. You shall be holy unto Me; for I, the Lord, am holy, and I have separated you from other peoples, to make you Mine.' "

(Leviticus 20.24–25)

Fit and unfit Animals

The Lord spoke to Moses and Aaron and gave them these commands for the Israelites:
"These are the living things that you may eat of all animals on earth. Any of the animals with a parted hoof, that has its hoof divided through, and that chews the cud, you may eat. But, of those that chew the cud or have a parted hoof, you shall not eat the following: the camel, because though it chews the cud, it has not a parted hoof; it is therefore unclean for you; and the pig, because, although it has a parted hoof, it does not chew the cud; it is therefore unclean for you." (Leviticus 11.1–8)

Shell-fish forbidden

"You may eat anything with fins and scales that lives in the water, in sea or in stream. But things in sea or stream that have no fins and scales, you shall not eat of their flesh." *(Leviticus 11.9–12)*

Of Birds and Insects

"Of birds you shall detest the birds of prey; they are not to be eaten, since they are detestable."

"Every swarming insect on earth is detestable for you; not one shall be eaten. Whatever crawls on its belly, whatever goes on four legs, any swarming insect whatever on earth, you shall never eat; such are detestable." *(Leviticus 11.13–23)*

> Our sages developed a set of regulations how animals should be prepared for food so that they suffer as little as possible when slaughtered, and so that their blood be quickly drained off. These regulations are called, in Hebrew, the laws of *Shehitah.*

The Lord gave Moses these commands for Aaron, his sons and all the Israelites:

"Any Israelite who in hunting catches an animal or a bird that may be eaten, shall pour out its blood and cover it with dust. For the life of every creature is bound up with its blood. Hence I command the Israelites: You shall never taste the blood of any creature, for the life of every creature lies in its blood." *(Leviticus 17.13–14)*

IV.

A MAN AND HIS NEIGHBOR

How should a Jew act in his daily relations with his fellow-men? In all his dealings with others, what should be the main principle of his conduct? The great rule of the Jewish religion is that *every* human being must be held sacred, for no matter what place he occupies in life, each person has in him some of the divine spirit, and is a child of God. When we have this attitude towards our fellowmen, then the spirit of holiness is present in our every act.

The Foundation Stones

"I AM the Lord your God; you shall be holy, for I, the Lord your God, am holy." *(Leviticus 19.1)*

"You shall love your neighbor as you love yourself; I am the Lord." *(Leviticus 19.18)*

Toward Parents

"You shall revere your mother and your father, every one of you, for I, the Lord your God, am holy." *(Leviticus 19.3)*

Towards Old Age

"You shall rise up before a man with white hair, and honor the person of an old man, standing in awe of your God: I am the Lord." *(Leviticus 19.32)*

Towards Honesty

"You shall not steal; you shall not cheat; you shall not tell a lie to one another. You shall not take a false oath in My name. You shall not deceive your neighbor, nor rob him; you shall not withhold the wages of a hired laborer over night until the next morning." *(Leviticus 19.11–13)*

"You shall not keep weights of different sizes in your bag, a large one and small one; you shall keep a full, just weight, that you may have a long life in the land which the Lord your God is giving you. For everyone who acts dishonestly, everyone who practices injustice, is hateful to the Lord your God." *(Deuteronomy 25.13–16)*

Kindness towards Animals

"You shall not withhold your help from any ox or sheep of a neighbor which you see going astray; you shall surely bring them back to your neighbor. You shall not withhold your help from your neighbor's donkey or ox fallen by the wayside; you shall surely help him to raise them up.

"If you happen to come upon a bird's nest on a tree or on the ground with young ones or eggs, you shall not take away the mother-bird with her young. You shall rather let the mother-bird go, and take only the young for yourself, that you may prosper, and have a long life." *(Deuteronomy 22.1–7)*

Towards Enemies

"You shall not hate your brother in your heart. You shall warn him of his fault, lest you bring guilt upon yourself. You shall not take vengeance, nor bear any grudge against him, but you shall love your neighbor as yourself." *(Leviticus 19.17–18)*

"If you see the animal of a man who hates you lying helpless under its load, you shall not desert him in his trouble; you shall help him to release the animal." *(Exodus 23.5)*

Strangers and Aliens

"You shall not injure or mistreat an alien or stranger among you; for you were once strangers yourselves in the land of Egypt." *(Exodus 22.20)*

"And if a stranger is living with you in your land, you shall not harm him; you shall treat him like the native born among you and love him as one of your own, since I, the Lord, am your God; for you were once strangers in the land of Egypt." *(Leviticus 19.33, 34)*

The Poor and their Needs

"If you have a poor man among you, any of your neighbors in any of your communities in the land which the Lord your God is giving you, you shall not harden your heart nor shut your hand against your needy brother; you shall open wide your hand to him and freely lend him enough for his needs. You shall give to him and give cheerfully, for that will make the Lord your God bless you in all your work and in whatever you undertake.

"The poor will never cease to be in the land; that is why I command you to open your hand to the destitute and the needy in your land." (*Deuteronomy 15.7–11*)

"When you reap your harvest, you shall not reap your field to the very corners, nor gather the stray ears of your harvest; you shall not glean your vineyards bare, nor pick up the fallen grapes; leave them for the poor and the strangers who live with you: I am the Lord your God." (*Leviticus 19.9, 10*)

"You shall never tamper with a poor man's rights in court."
(*Exodus 23.6*)

Crime and Punishment

"If anyone takes another person's life, he shall be put to death. Whoever takes an animal's life shall make it good — a life for a life. If a man disfigures his neighbor, then, as he has done, so it shall be done to him, limb for limb, eye for eye, tooth for tooth; as he has disfigured his neighbor, so shall he be disfigured.* You shall have one and the same law for alien and native-born alike; for I am the Lord your God." (*Leviticus 24.17–22*)

"In every case of murder, the murderer shall be put to death on the evidence of witnesses; the evidence of a single witness is insufficient to condemn anyone to death. You shall not accept a money payment on behalf of a murderer who has been guilty of wilful murder; he shall be put to death without fail."
(*Numbers 35.30, 31*)

---

*This was the ancient law of the desert and showed an attempt to reach even-handed justice. But, according to Jewish tradition, it was not to be taken literally; it was to be interpreted to mean that the injured person should be compensated according to his injury.

"When you cross the Jordan into the land of Canaan, you shall select suitable cities to serve as cities of refuge for you, so that any seeming murderer who kills a person accidentally may flee there. These cities shall provide you with a refuge from the avenger, so that the seeming murderer may not die before he has appeared before the community to be tried." *(Numbers 35.10–12)*

Fringes for Remembrance

"Speak to the Israelites and tell them that throughout their generations they shall make fringes (*Tsitsit*) for themselves on the corners of their garments, fastening the fringe to each corner with a blue thread.

"The fringe will serve to catch your eye and remind you to obey all the commands of the Lord, not to follow your own wandering desires and fancies, but to remember all My commands, and be loyal to your God.

"I am the Lord your God, who brought you out of the land of Egypt in order to be your God; I am the Lord, your God." *(Numbers 15.38–41)*

V.

NATIONAL PROBLEMS

Among the great problems that faced Israel, as they face every nation, were the problems of government and justice, the legal rights of women, and the use of slaves and slave labor. The ownership of land and the waging of war against enemies were also important national problems. Moses, at the command of God, sought to deal with these matters so that Israel might establish justice and peace in their national life, and thus protect the weak and the poor from the rich and the strong.

Government

The Israelites had to wait a long time before they entered Canaan and set up a government there. But the Torah discussed the duties of the king who would some day rule them. The king was instructed that he was subject to the people's will, and he was to submit to the laws of the Covenant.

"WHEN you enter the country which the Lord your God gives you and take possession of it and settle down in it, if you say to yourself, 'I must have a king over me like all nations around me,' then you may appoint a king whom the Lord your God chooses.

"You shall make one of your own brothers king over you; you shall not put a foreigner over you, one who is not your brother.

"He shall not multiply his war-horses, nor cause the people to return to Egypt again in order that he should multiply war-horses; for the Lord has forbidden you ever again to return to Egypt.

"Neither shall he multiply many wives for himself, lest his heart be led astray from his duties; nor shall he multiply silver and gold for himself in great quantities.

"When he is seated on his royal throne, he shall have a copy of this Covenant written for himself, taken from the copy in charge of the Levitical priests. He shall keep the book beside him, and he shall study it all the days of his life, that he may learn to revere the Lord his God and obediently keep all the commands and laws of this Covenant, so that his heart may not be lifted proudly over his fellow-countrymen, and that he may not turn to the right or to the left from what he is commanded, but that he and his children may continue long on the throne in Israel."

(Deuteronomy 17.14–20)

Legal Justice

> Courts of law were to be set up whose sole purpose was to mete out justice. The priests were the early judges, and they were expected to deal impartially with all who came before them.

"You shall appoint judges and officials throughout your tribes to rule the people with right justice, in all the communities granted you by the Lord your God.

"You shall not interfere with justice; you shall not be partial to anyone; and you shall not accept a bribe — for a bribe blinds even men whose eyes are open, and it destroys the case of a good man.

"Justice, justice shall you follow, that you may live and inherit the land which the Lord your God gives you." (Deuteronomy 16.18–20)

"If a question should arise in your local community which is too hard for you to decide, a question of bloodshed, of property, of compensation for injury, you shall set out and go up to the Sanctuary chosen by the Lord your God, and consult the Levitical priests and the judge who is in office at that time; ask them, and after inquiry they will let you know the right answer. You shall be guided by the decision they announce to you, and you shall be careful to do just as they direct you."

(Deuteronomy 17.8–11)

Legal Rights of Women

> In Israel women were always held in high esteem. The Matriarchs, the wives of the founders of Israel, played an important part in the destiny of the Jewish people. In the Ten Commandments, mothers received equal consideration with fathers. But, if a woman's father died, leaving no male heir, could she inherit his property? The famous incident of the daughters of Zelophehad settled this matter for all time.

The daughters of Zelophehad came forward and took their stand before Moses and Eleazar, the priest, the princes and all the community at the entrance of the Tent of Meeting, and said:

"Our father died in the desert, leaving no sons. Why should our father's name be lost, just because he had no son? Let us hold property along with our father's kinsmen."

Moses laid their plea before the Lord, and the Lord said to Moses:

"The daughters of Zelophehad are right; you shall certainly let them hold property along with their father's kinsmen; let their father's share pass to them. And direct the Israelites to let a man's property always pass to his daughters, if he dies without leaving a son.

"This is to be a fixed law for the Israelites, as the Lord has commanded them through Moses." (*Numbers 27.1–11*)

Slaves and Slave Labor

The laws that dealt with slavery are filled with a spirit of social justice. Of course, a distinction was drawn between Israelite slaves and those of other peoples. But in view of the cruelties of the institution of slavery, even far into modern times, the ancient laws of the Israelites were most humane. At all times just and humane treatment of the slave was demanded in the Torah, for the slave, too, was considered a child of God.

"If a fellow-countryman becomes poor so that he cannot pay his debts, then you shall relieve him and enable him to live with you. Take no interest from him in money or in kind; let your fellow-countryman live with you, and never ask interest on your money loans to him nor on the food which you furnish him.

"If a fellow-countryman becomes poor and sells himself to you, then you shall not make him serve as a slave; you shall let him live with you as a hired servant. You shall not lord it over him harshly, but stand in awe of your God." (*Leviticus 25. 35–43*)

"If a Hebrew man or woman is sold to you, he shall serve you for six years, but in the seventh year you shall set him free. And in setting him free you shall not let him go empty-handed; you shall furnish him liberally out of your flock and threshing-floor and wine-press, giving him a present as the Lord your God has prospered you.

"Remember you were once a slave in the land of Egypt, and that the Lord your God rescued you; that is why I command you to do this today.

"If, however, he says to you, 'I will not leave you,' because he is fond of you and your household, since he has fared well with you, then you shall take an awl and thrust it through his ear into the door; then he shall be your slave for all time. And the same applies to your female slave.*

"You shall not think it hard to let him go free from your service; for six years he has served you at half the cost of a hired servant. Then shall the Lord your God prosper you in all you undertake." (*Deuteronomy 15.12–18*)

The Ownership of Land

The Israelites were an agricultural people in Canaan. The ownership of land, therefore, was a most important matter. Then, as today, a small number of persons acquired most of the land and thus forced many to become landless serfs. Moses commanded the observance of two notable laws. One was called the law of *Shemitah*, or the Sabbatical Year, a year of rest for the land to prevent its becoming exhausted. This came every seventh year, and whatever the soil yielded of itself during that year was free to all. The other was the law of *Yobel*, or the Jubilee Year. It came at the end of seven Sabbatical cycles, or every fiftieth year. In that year every Israelite slave was set free, and all land which had been sold, or which had otherwise passed out of the hands of the original owner, was to be restored to him or to his heirs.

The Lord spoke to Moses on Mount Sinai and gave him these further commands for the Israelites:

"When you enter the land I give you, the land shall enjoy a sabbath rest for the Lord. For six years you may sow your field, and for six years you may prune your vineyard and gather in its produce; but the seventh year shall be a sabbath of complete

---

*The piercing of the ear was a sign of shame. Our sages explained that the ear was selected for this sign because it had heard the announcement of human freedom at Mount Sinai, and now should bear the mark of shame at a man's willingness to reject this freedom.

rest for the land, a sabbath in honor of the Lord; you shall not sow your field nor prune your vineyard. You shall not even gather in the aftergrowth of your harvest, nor the grapes from your undressed vines; it shall be a year of complete rest for the land.

"You shall count seven cycles of years, seven times seven years; so that the seven cycles of years amount to forty-nine years. Then, on the tenth day of the seventh month, you shall sound a loud trumpet-blast throughout the land; the trumpet-blast shall sound aloud on the Day of Atonement.

"You shall hallow the fiftieth year, and proclaim liberty throughout the land to all the inhabitants thereof; it shall be a jubilee year for you, when each of you shall return to his own property and family.

"And the land shall not be sold for ever; for the land is Mine; and you are only strangers and settlers with Me. You shall allow the land to be bought back anywhere in the country you shall possess." (*Leviticus 25.1–24*)

Attempts to civilize War

The great ideal of Judaism is peace. Time and again, the Bible emphasized the importance of peace. The blessing of the officiating priests ended with the hope of peace. But the Israelites lived in a cruel and warlike world, where they had to fight to keep their right to live as a people. Though they had to learn the arts of war, Moses sought to make the conduct of war less cruel and brutal than it was usually waged in those days. He sought to "civilize" war, with the hope that in time men would settle their disputes not by violence, force and death, but by reason, law and justice.

And Moses said to the Israelites:

"When you go out to battle against your enemies, you shall not fear. On the eve of battle the priest shall come up and address the army thus:

'Hearken, Israel, you are opening a campaign today against your enemies; do not lose heart, fear not, tremble not, be not afraid of them, for the Lord your God goes with you, to fight for you against your enemies and to give you the victory.'

"Then the officers shall tell the army:

'Whoever has built a new house, but has not used it, may leave and return home, lest he die in battle and another man use it.

'Whoever has planted a vineyard, but has not enjoyed the fruit of it, may leave and return home, lest he die in battle and another man enjoy the fruit of it.

'Whoever has betrothed a wife, but has not married her, may leave and return home, lest he die in battle and another man marry her.' " (*Deuteronomy 20.1–7*)

"When a man is newly married, he is not to go out with the army, nor be counted with it for any duty; he is to be free at home for one year, to rejoice with his wife whom he has married." (*Deuteronomy 24.5*)

"The officers shall tell the army further:

'Whoever is afraid and faint-hearted shall leave and return home, lest his fellows lose heart like him.

'When you besiege a city, you shall first offer it terms of peace.

'When you have to besiege a city a long time in order to capture it, you shall not destroy its trees by taking an axe to them; you may eat their fruit but you shall not cut them down. Is a tree a human being that you should lay siege to it? Only trees which you know are not fruit trees may be destroyed and cut down that you may build siege-works to reduce the city that makes war against you.' " (*Deuteronomy 20.8–20*)

VI.

IDOLATRY — THE GRAVEST OF ALL SINS

Time and again Moses warned the Israelites against idolatry.
This form of worship threatened the very idea of a holy people,
for idolatry was associated with impure and cruel practices,
including even human sacrifices such as burning children in
fire to the fire-god, Moloch. Idols were easy to worship for
they did not demand of the worshipper righteousness and
justice, kindness and mercy. Moreover, idols were fixed images
of stone or metal or wood, whereas God is a spirit. Idols were
attached to one place, while God is everywhere. Idolatry
denied all that the God of Israel stood for. Hence, it was the
gravest of all sins and the root of all other sins. Moses feared
lest the Israelites might be influenced by the idol-worship of their
pagan neighbors, and so he commanded the destruction of such
idol-worshipping nations. He also prohibited intermarriage
with idol-worshippers.

"YOU shall make no idols for yourselves, nor erect any carved
or sacred pillar (obelisk), you shall not put up any figured
stone for worship in your land; for I am the Lord your God."

(*Leviticus 26.1*)

"Do not turn to the idols, nor make yourselves metal gods:
I am the Lord your God." (*Leviticus 19.4*)

"When the Lord your God puts an end to the nations before
you as you advance to dispossess them, take care not to be tricked
into copying them, after they have been destroyed before you;
beware of appealing to their gods, asking, 'How did these nations
worship their gods?— that I may do the same thing.'

"You shall not worship the Lord your God thus; for they
offered their gods all that is hateful to the Lord, burning in fire
even their sons and daughters to their gods." (*Deuteronomy 12.29–31*)

The Lord gave Moses these commands for the Israelites:

"Anyone belonging to Israel or any alien settled in Israel who
gives any of his children to Moloch shall be put to death; the

people of the land shall stone him, because he gave his children to Moloch, making impure My Sanctuary and unclean My holy name. If the people of the land ever ignore his sin of giving children to Moloch and fail to put him to death, then I will set My face against that man and his family. I will cut off from their kinsfolk both him and all who follow him in deserting Me for Moloch." (*Leviticus 20.1–5*)

VII.

REWARDS AND PUNISHMENTS

The Covenant sets forth the rewards that result from obeying the laws of God, as well as the punishments for disobeying these laws. As the physical laws of Nature command obedience, so do the spiritual laws of Life. When men obey the physical laws of Nature, they prosper, for the Creator of the world intended them for men's good; but if men break those laws, they suffer harm and even death. So, too, with the spiritual laws of human relations. When men practice truth, justice and peace, they enjoy security and happiness. But when men practice falsehood, injustice and violence, they lose confidence in each other. They begin to fear, then hate their fellowmen, and they cause strife which brings destruction and death into the world. Moses appealed to Israel to obey God's Covenant with them, so that it would bring them His blessings and they would enjoy a worth-while life.

"IF YOU live by My laws and follow My commands obediently, I will give you the rains in due season, the land will bear its crops, and the trees shall bear their fruit; your threshing shall last till the time for vintage, and your vintage shall last till the time for sowing.

"You shall have plenty to eat, and you shall live securely in your land. I will grant you peace in your land, so that you shall rest with none to frighten you.

"I will set My dwelling in your midst, and will move about among you and be your God, while you shall be My people. I am the Lord your God, who brought you from the land of Egypt to save you from bondage to the Egyptians; I have broken the bars of your yoke and made you walk upright.

"But if you will not listen to Me, if you will not do all I command you, if you reject My commands and break My laws, I will set My face against you till you are beaten by your enemies, till those who hate you shall rule over you and you shall flee when no one pursues you.

"I will break the power of which you are so proud. I will make the skies hard as iron for you and the earth as hard as bronze, till you spend your strength in vain; for your land shall bear no crops, and your trees shall bear no fruit.

"I will scatter you among the nations, unsheathing the sword of war upon you, till your land lies waste, and your cities lie desolate.

"Yet, even when they are in the land of their enemies, I will not reject them so as to destroy them entirely and so break My Covenant with them; for I am the Lord their God.

"But I will remember for their sakes the Covenant with their ancestors whom I brought out of the land of Egypt in the sight of the nations to be their God.

"I am the Lord!"   (*Leviticus 26*)

בְּמִדְבַּר

NUMBERS

THE Israelites remained at Mount Sinai about a year. At Mount Sinai they had received the written Covenant of the Law which became their Constitution and which made them into a religious people. After that great event, the Israelites travelled, under the leadership of Moses, to the Promised Land, where they hoped to develop their religious way of life.

What took place during their years of wandering in the wilderness? Were the Israelites equal to the tasks of their new freedom? Did they loyally undertake to follow Moses' leadership? Could they quickly change from a people of slaves to courageous freemen who were willing and able to undergo hardships and suffering? Or, did that generation have to pass away and a new generation be born that could better endure the trials of true pioneers?

The Book of Numbers records what happened to the Israelites from the time they left Mount Sinai until they reached the borders of Canaan. It describes how the old Israel became the new Israel, so that even a heathen prophet, who came to mock and curse them, praised and blessed them instead. Moses, with patience and wisdom, molded the Israelites into a powerful, united people, prepared to undertake the conquest of the land. During those forty years of wandering, marching and preparation, God's loving care protected them in times of trouble, want and distress.

Numbers, the fourth Book of Moses, is called, in Hebrew, *Be-Midbar*, from its first important word meaning, "In the Wilderness." In English, however, it is named "Numbers," because it begins with the numbering, or census, of the Israelites as they began their journey towards Palestine.

I.

JOURNEY'S BEGINNING

After Moses had given the Law of the Covenant to Israel, God commanded him to take a census of those who could bear arms and to organize the tribes in their marching order. This Moses did. The Ark of the Covenant was carried at the head of the marching hosts. It was the symbol of God's presence and protection. When the Levites started to carry it forward, and when they brought it to rest, Moses said a prayer. To this day the prayers of Moses are chanted at the opening and closing of the Ark, whenever the Torah is read.

Taking the Census

IN THE second year after the Israelites had left the land of Egypt, the Lord spoke to Moses in the Tent of Meeting, in the Wilderness of Sinai, and said:

"Count the number of all the members of the community of Israel, tribe by tribe and family by family; and also count the male individuals from twenty years old and upward, who are able to go out to war. One man from each tribe is to help you in this census."

Moses and Aaron then took the men selected from the community, the heads of their tribes, and having assembled all Israel, family by family, they counted the individuals from twenty years old and upward.

The number of Israelites, family by family, over twenty years old who were able to go to war, amounted to six hundred and three thousand five hundred and fifty.

The Order of the March

The Lord told Moses and Aaron:

"The Israelites shall pitch their tents according to their respective companies, each by the flag of its tribe, facing the Tent of Meeting on every side."

The Israelites carried out this order. Exactly as the Lord had commanded, they encamped by their respective companies, and marched tribe by tribe and family by family.

The protecting Presence

On the day when the Tabernacle was set up, a cloud covered
the Tabernacle — the Tent of the Testimony — and in the night
something like the appearance of fire hung over the Tabernacle
until the morning.

Whenever the cloud rose above the Tabernacle, the Israelites
marched forward; when the cloud stopped, the Israelites encamped.
At the bidding of the Lord the Israelites advanced; and at His
signal they encamped. On the day or days that the cloud remained over the Tabernacle, they remained in camp. No matter
how long the cloud remained over the Tabernacle, the Israelites
obeyed the command of the Lord and did not advance.

Sometimes the cloud remained over the Tabernacle only for
a few days; then, as the Lord ordered, they remained in camp;
and sometimes the cloud was there from evening to morning and
rose in the morning, so that they moved forward; sometimes the
cloud would remain for a day and a night, sometimes for two
days or for a month or longer. But the Israelites always encamped
at the bidding of the Lord; and they obeyed the command of the
Lord, as He gave it through Moses.

Prayers before the Ark

The long journey now began.

The Israelites set forward from the Mount of the Lord three
days' journey, and the Ark of the Lord's Covenant went before
them to seek out where they were to encamp. And the cloud of
the Lord was over them by day, when they set forward from the
camp.

When the Ark set forward, Moses would say:

"Rise up, O Lord, and let Thine enemies be scattered;
    And let them that hate Thee flee before Thee."

And when the Ark rested, he would say:

"Return, O Lord, unto the ten thousands of the families
    of Israel."   (*Numbers 1, 2, 9, 10*)

II.

BURDENS OF THE LEADER

Hardly had the march begun when the slavish Israelites murmured and complained. The troubles of Moses increased, until his despair and discouragement almost overwhelmed him. He then began to realize that that generation could not face the responsibilities of a free people.

The People want Food

THE Israelites complained bitterly to Moses:
"Would that we were given flesh to eat! We remember the fish that we used to eat in Egypt for nothing; the cucumbers, and the melons, and the leeks, and the onions, and the garlic. But now we are hungry, and there is nothing but this manna!"

Moses heard the people weeping. Then he said to the Lord:

"Why hast Thou dealt ill with Thy servant? Why have I not found favor in Thy sight? Thou layest the burden of all this people upon me! Was it I who gave birth to this people that Thou shouldst order me to carry them in my arms, as a nurse carries a suckling infant, to the land which Thou hast sworn to their fathers to give them? I am not able to carry all this people by myself."

The seventy Elders

The Lord answered Moses:

"Gather to Me seventy of the elders of Israel, and bring them to the Tent of Meeting, to stand beside you. I will come and speak to you there, and I will inspire them with part of your spirit, that they may share the burden of the people with you, and you shall not bear it by yourself."

Moses gathered seventy of the elders of the people and placed them round the Tent. The Lord came down in the cloud and talked to him, and inspired the elders with his spirit; and when the spirit rested on them, they prophesied — then stopped.

Eldad and Medad

Two men, however, had remained in the camp. One was named Eldad and the other Medad. The spirit rested on them also, and they also prophesied inside the camp — for although they were included among the seventy, they had not gone to the Tent. Whereupon a young man ran to tell Moses:

"Eldad and Medad are prophesying inside the camp!"

Joshua, the son of Nun, who had served Moses ever since he was a youth, answered and said:

"My lord, Moses, stop them!"

But Moses said to him:

"Are you jealous for my sake? Would that the Lord's people were all prophets, that the Lord would inspire them all with His spirit!"

Then Moses and the elders returned to the camp.

Moses grows weary

Moses then asked the Lord:

"Where can I get flesh to give to all this people? For they weep and cry, 'Give us flesh to eat.' If this is to be Thy treatment of me, pray kill me at once, if I find any favor with Thee, and let me see no more of my trouble."

The Lord bade Moses tell the people:

"Sanctify yourselves in readiness for tomorrow, that you may eat flesh. You have let the Lord hear you weeping and complaining, 'O that we had flesh to eat! For it was well with us in Egypt!'

"Therefore, the Lord will give you flesh to eat; you shall eat flesh not one day, nor two days, nor five days, nor ten days, nor twenty days, but a whole month, till you cannot bear the smell of it, till you loathe it — because you have spurned the Lord who is in your midst, and have wept before Him, regretting that you ever left Egypt!"

Then Moses said:

"The people with me number six hundred thousand as they stand, and yet Thou sayest, 'I will give them flesh to eat for a whole month!' Can flocks and herds enough be slaughtered for them? Can all the fish of the sea be gathered to satisfy them?"

The Lord answered:

"Is the Lord's power so limited? You shall see now whether My promise comes true or not."

The Coming of Quail

Moses then told the people what the Lord had said.

And a wind blowing from the Lord brought up quails from the sea, and let them fall near the camp, about a day's journey on each side of it all round the camp, and about three feet thick above the face of the earth.

All that day and night and all the next day, the people gathered quails.

As the people were devouring this food, before the supply gave out, the anger of the Lord blazed in fury against them, and He struck them with a terrible plague.

That place was called Kibrot-hattaavah (Graves of Greed), because they buried there the people who had been greedy for flesh.   (*Numbers 11*)

III.

CRISIS AND DECISION

The Israelites reached the large oasis of Kadesh-Barnea, where Moses sent out twelve spies to bring back information about the land of Canaan and its inhabitants. The unfavorable report of the ten spies disheartened the people to the point of rebellion. Then came God's great decision: That generation was slave-spirited; a new generation, bred to the hardships of freedom, had to come into existence before the Promised Land could be invaded.

Moses sends out the Spies

THE Israelites encamped at Kadesh-Barnea, in the Wilderness of Paran.

There the Lord told Moses to send some men to spy out the land of Canaan, which He intended to give to the Israelites. He was to send a man from every tribe, all of them leading men. So Moses ordered:

"Go and see what the land is like, and whether the people who are living in it are strong or weak, whether they are few or many; what the land is like, whether it is good or bad; and what the cities are like in which they are living, whether they are open, or fortified; and whether the land is rich or poor, whether it is wooded or not. Also do your best to bring back some of the fruit of the land."

Moses then despatched the spies from the Wilderness of Paran. The season was that of the first ripe grapes.

They went to Canaan, and spied out the land. They reached the Valley of Eshcol, they cut a branch from there with a single cluster of grapes, and it was so large that it took two of them to carry it on a pole; they took also some pomegranates and some figs.

Conflicting Reports

At the end of forty days they returned. They came to Moses and Aaron and all the Israelites encamped at Kadesh-Barnea, and gave their report:

"We came into the land to which you sent us, and surely it flows with milk and honey; and here is some of its fruits. The people there, however, are fierce and the cities are fortified and very great; and besides we saw the Anakim (giants) there."

Thus they gave the Israelites a discouraging report of the land they had spied out, and they continued:

"The land through which we passed as spies is a land that consumes its inhabitants, and all the people we saw in it are giants. To ourselves we looked like grasshoppers, and we must have looked the same to them."

Upon hearing this, all the Israelites wailed, and they murmured against Moses and Aaron.

"Would that we had died in Egypt!" they cried. "Would that we had died here in the desert! Why does the Lord bring us into this land only to fall by the sword? Our wives and our children will be a prey. Shall we not rather return to Egypt? Let us appoint a captain, and let us return to Egypt!"

Caleb, who represented the tribe of Judah, silenced this clamor of the people, and said:

"We ought to go up and seize the land; for we are well able to master it."

But the other spies said:

"We are not able to march against the people there; they are too strong for us."

Moses and Aaron then fell on their faces before the assembled Israelites, while Joshua, the son of Nun, and Caleb, the son of Jephunneh, two of the spies, argued with the whole community:

"The land over which we have gone as spies is a good, fertile country. If the Lord is pleased with us, He will bring us into this land, and give it to us — a land flowing with milk and honey. Only do not rebel against the Lord! Do not be afraid of the people there! Their protection has failed them, and the Lord is with us; fear them not!"

The People grow rebellious

The whole community was on the point of stoning Joshua and Caleb, when the glory of the Lord appeared to all the Israelites at the Tent of Meeting. And the Lord said to Moses:

"How long will this people complain against Me? How long are they to distrust Me, in spite of all the proofs that I have shown them? I will smite them and destroy them, and I will make a nation out of you greater and mightier than they."

But Moses said to the Lord:

"When the Egyptians hear this, they will say, 'The Lord has killed them in the wilderness because He was not able to bring this people into the land which He had sworn to give them.' Forgive, I pray Thee, the guilt of this people, as Thou hast forgiven this people ever since they left Egypt, because Thy love is rich."

Whereupon the Lord answered:

"I have pardoned them as you have asked. But, as surely as I live and as surely as one day the whole earth will be full of the glory of the Lord, not one of the men who have seen My glory and the proofs I wrought in Egypt and the desert, and who yet have put Me to the proof over again, refusing to listen to Me, not one of them shall live to see the land which I swore to their fathers to give them . . .

A new Generation needed

"Your children, however, who you said would become a prey, I will bring in, to let them possess the land you despise. As for the rest of you, your dead bodies shall fall in this wilderness, and your children shall be wandering shepherds there forty years, paying the penalty of your unfaithfulness, until all your bodies have perished in the desert."

The men sent by Moses to spy out the land, who, when they returned, made all the Israelites murmur against him by giving a bad report of the land, these men later died by a plague before the Lord.

But Joshua, the son of Nun, and Caleb, the son of Jephunneh, remained alive. (*Numbers 13–14*)

IV.

KORAH'S REBELLION

Immediately after the incident of the spies, Korah, together with Dathan and Abiram, openly revolted against Moses' leadership. Korah used the language of idealism to hide his jealousy of Moses and his desire for personal power. Unfortunately, many of the leaders and the people joined Korah. Our sages used Korah's rebellion as an example of a controversy waged for selfish purposes. They called his quarrel "a controversy not waged in the name of Heaven."

Rebellion breaks out

NOW, Korah, with Dathan and Abiram, and two hundred and fifty other Israelites, who were leaders of the community and men of renown, combined to oppose Moses and Aaron. They said to them:

"You take too much upon yourselves! The whole community is holy, every man of them, and the Lord is among them. Why do you raise yourselves above the Lord's assembly?"

When Moses heard this, he said to Korah and those associated with him:

"In the morning the Lord will show who belongs to Him; He will allow those who are really holy to approach Him."

"Listen to me, you Levites," continued Moses to Korah. "Is it not enough for you that the God of Israel has singled you out from the whole community and allowed you near His presence to do the work of the Tabernacle, and to be servants of the community, permitting you and all your fellow Levites to approach Him? You want to be priests as well? It is accordingly against the Lord that you and your company are gathered. For what has Aaron done that you should murmur against him?"

Moses then sent for Dathan and Abiram, but they refused to obey, saying:

"No, we will not come up. Is it not enough that you have taken us away from a land flowing with milk and honey, to kill us in the wilderness, that you would make yourself a prince over us?

Moreover, you have not brought us into a land flowing with milk and honey, nor have you given us an inheritance of fields and vineyards. Will you throw dust in the eyes of these men? No, we will not come up before you!"

The destroying Earthquake

Moses then said to Korah:

"Tomorrow, you and all your followers appear before the Lord, together with Aaron. Let each of you take his fire-pan, and put incense in it, and all bring them up to the Lord."

Each of them took his fire-pan, put burning coals in it and incense on the top. Then each took his place at the entrance of the Tent of Meeting, along with Moses and Aaron.

Korah had caused all his followers to assemble at the entrance of the Tent of Meeting, and the glory of the Lord appeared to the whole assembly.

Then Moses said:

"Hereby you shall know that the Lord has sent me to do this thing, and that I am not doing it of my own mind. If these men die the common death of all men and suffer as all men suffer, then the Lord has not sent me. But if the Lord does something new, if the ground opens its mouth and swallows them up, then you shall understand that these men have despised the Lord."

As Moses finished speaking, the ground split under Korah's followers. The earth opened its mouth and swallowed them up with all their households. They and theirs went down alive into the pit; and the earth closed over them, and they vanished from the community.

All the Israelites around fled at their shrieks, fearing lest the earth might swallow them also.

The blossoming Rod

Next day the community of Israel still murmured against Moses and Aaron, saying:

"It is you who have slain the Lord's people."

When the community gathered against Moses and Aaron, they turned to face the Tent of Meeting, and there was the cloud covering it! — the Lord's glory appeared.

The Lord spoke to Moses:

"Tell the Israelites to take a rod from each leader of each tribe, and write the name of each one on his rod, and Aaron's name upon the rod of Levi. Lay them in front of the Ark inside the Tent of Meeting, where I meet with you; and the man whom I choose, his rod shall blossom. Thus will I stop and silence any murmuring on the part of the Israelites against you."

Moses did as he was ordered.

When Moses entered the Tent next day, he found that the rod of Aaron, representing the tribe of Levi, had blossomed; it had produced blossoms and borne ripe almonds.

Moses brought all the rods out from the Tent, before all the Israelites. They looked at them, and each man took his rod.

The Lord then said to Moses:

"Put Aaron's rod back in front of the Ark to be kept as a sign for rebellious men; and that there may be an end of their murmurings against Me, else they will die."

And Moses did as the Lord commanded him.   (*Numbers 16, 17*)

V.

THE SIN OF MOSES

Unlike the fickle Israelites, Moses was steadfast and faithful through all these years of trial. Only once did his patience give way to anger; and his anger caused him to doubt for a moment God's power to fulfill His promise. For this, Moses merited punishment. He lost his right to enter the Promised Land.

The Death of Miriam

WHILE the Israelites were staying at Kadesh-Barnea, Miriam, the sister of Moses and Aaron, died and was buried there.

The Israelites now came into the Wilderness of Zin; there was no water for the people.

Once more the people quarrelled with Moses, complaining:

"Why have you brought the people of the Lord into this desert only to let us die, both us and our cattle? Why did you make us leave Egypt for this evil place? It is no place of grain, of figs, or of vines, or of pomegranates; neither is there any water to drink!"

The Sin of Moses

The Lord said to Moses:

Take your rod, and assemble the people, you and Aaron your brother, and bring water from the rock for them, to let them and their cattle drink. When you have gathered the community, in their presence *speak* to the rock that it give forth its waters."

Moses took his rod and he and Aaron gathered the assembly in front of the rock.

Moses then said to the people:

"Listen, you rebels: must we bring you water out of this rock?"

Then, lifting his hand, Moses *struck* the rock with his rod twice; and the waters came forth abundantly, and the people drank, and so did their cattle.

The Lord then said to Moses and Aaron:

"Because you believed not in Me, to sanctify Me before the Israelites, you shall not lead this people into the land which I have given them."

The Waters of Meribah

These springs were called the waters of Meribah (Strife), because there the Israelites strove against the Lord, and there He sanctified Himself before them.   (*Numbers 20*)

VI.

ISRAEL MEETS HOSTILE NATIONS

Forty years had passed since the Israelites had left Egypt. The old generation of slaves who had been freed had died out. Moses now led a new generation born in freedom. The time for battles had come. The Israelites respected the territory of Edom, for Edom was descended from Esau; they also respected the lands of Moab and Ammon, descended from Lot, the nephew of Abraham. Therefore, Moses went northward to lead the Israelites against the Amorites.

Edom refuses Passage

FROM Kadesh-Barnea Moses sent messengers to the king of Edom, from his "brother Israel," saying:

"You know all the hardship that has befallen us; how our fathers went down to Egypt, how we dwelt in Egypt a long time; and we were badly treated, we and our fathers, by the Egyptians; and when we cried to the Lord, He heard our voice, and brought us out of Egypt. Now here we are at Kadesh-Barnea, a city on the border of your territory. Pray, let us pass through your land.

"We will not pass through any field or vineyard, nor will we drink the water of your wells; but we will go along the royal highway, turning neither to right nor to left, until we pass beyond your border."

Edom answered Israel:

"No, you shall not pass through; if you do, I will attack you."

The Israelites said to him:

"We will keep to the highway, and we will pay you for any water that we or our cattle drink; pray let us pass through quietly; there is no harm in that!"

"No," said Edom, "you shall not pass through," and he came out with a large army to stop them.

Thus Edom refused to let Israel pass through his territory.

Israel had to turn aside.

Death of Aaron: Eleazar his Son becomes High Priest

The Israelites journeyed from Kadesh-Barnea and came to Mount Hor. At Mount Hor on the borders of Edom, the Lord said to Moses and Aaron:

"Aaron shall now be gathered to his people, for he shall not enter the land I have given to the Israelites, because you and he were faithless to My word at the waters of Meribah. Take Aaron and his son Eleazar up Mount Hor. Strip Aaron of his robes and put them on Eleazar; and Aaron shall die there."

Moses did as the Lord told him. Aaron and he went up Mount Hor before the eyes of all the community. And Moses stripped Aaron of his robes and put them on Eleazar his son; and Aaron died on the mountain-top. Then Moses and Eleazar came down the mountain. When all the assembly saw that Aaron was dead, they mourned for Aaron thirty days.

King Sihon and King Og

Moses now sent messengers to Sihon, king of the Amorites, saying:

"Let us pass through your land; we will not turn aside into any field or vineyard; we will not drink any water from your wells; we will march along the royal highway until we have passed beyond your border."

But Sihon gathered all his forces and marched against Israel in the desert. He reached Jahaz and there attacked Israel. But Israel routed him, giving no quarter. They seized his country from the river Arnon to the Jabbok.

Israel then settled in the land of the Amorites.

Moses now turned to march in the direction of Bashan to the north. Og, king of Bashan, with all his forces, marched against the Israelites to give battle at Edrei. The Lord said to Moses:

"Fear him not, I put him into your hands, with all his forces and his land; you shall deal with him as you dealt with Sihon, king of the Amorites."

Whereupon the Israelites routed Og and his army, till not one of his men survived. Then the victors seized his land.

The Israelites then set out and encamped opposite Jericho, on the plains of Moab, east of the river Jordan. (*Numbers 20, 21, 22*)

VII.

BALAAM BLESSES THE NEW ISRAEL

The neighboring peoples and their kings, especially Balak, king of Moab, began to fear the Israelites. Balak thought that he could overcome them with magic more successfully than with weapons, so he enlisted the aid of the magician-prophet, Balaam, to curse the Israelites. The ancients believed in the power of curses, as they believed in the power of blessings. But, try as he would, Balaam could not curse Israel; instead he felt compelled to express his wonder and admiration for Israel and blessed them. Thus, Balaam the heathen prophet, stood witness to the miraculous change in Israel that had transformed them from a despised, slave people into a brave, free nation. The exodus began with Pharaoh, king of Egypt, despising the old Israel as slaves; now, at its end, through Balaam his prophet, Balak, the king of Moab, was compelled to praise the new Israel. Moses, through divine power, had accomplished his great undertaking.

NOW Balak, king of Moab, had observed all that Israel had done to the Amorites; and he was in dread of the Israelites, for they were very numerous.

Moab was overcome with dread of the Israelites, and he said to the elders of neighboring Midian:

"This multitude will lick up all the pasture that is round us as the ox licks up the grass in the field."

Balak also sent messengers to Balaam, the son of Beor, in the land of the Ammonites, with his summons:

"Behold, there is a people that has come from Egypt! They cover the face of the earth, and they have now settled opposite me! Come now, therefore, I beg you, and curse this people for me; for they are stronger than I am; perhaps, I may be able to defeat them and drive them out of the land. For I know that he whom you bless is blessed, and he whom you curse is cursed."

Balaam consents to go

After a time Balaam came to Moab, and he said to King Balak:

"Well, I have come to you! But have I any power at all to say a single word? The word that God puts into my mouth, that word must I speak."

On the Heights of Baal

It came to pass next morning that Balak took Balaam to the Heights of Baal where he could catch sight of the outermost part of Israel.

Then the Lord put words into Balaam's mouth, and he said:

> "From Aram has Balak brought me,
> The king of Moab from the mountains of the East:
> 'Come, curse Jacob for me,
> Come, curse Israel!'
> How shall I curse, whom God has not cursed?
> From the top of these rocks I see them,
> From these heights I behold them:
> Lo, it is a people that is a nation apart,
> And shall not be reckoned among the nations.
> Who can count the multitudes of Jacob,
> Or number the myriads of Israel?"

On the Heights of Pisgah

"What have you done to me?" cried Balak in anger. "I brought you to curse my enemies, and now you have blessed them instead."

Balaam answered:

"Must I not be careful to speak whatever the Lord tells me to say?"

Balak then said:

"Pray, come with me to another place to see them, and curse them for me there!"

He took Balaam into the field of Zophim, to the top of Pisgah. Balaam said to Balak:

"Remain here, while I go to meet God yonder."

The Lord met Balaam and put words in his mouth, and bade him return to Balak, and told him what to say.

"What has the Lord said?" Balak asked.

Whereupon Balaam spoke these words:

> "Arise, Balak, and hear;
> Give ear to me, son of Zippor!
> God is not a man, that He should lie;
> Nor a human being that He should repent.
> When He has said something, will He not do it?
> Or when He has spoken, will He not make it good?
> See, I am bidden to bless;
> When He has given a blessing, I cannot call it back.
> No one has beheld iniquity in Jacob,
> Neither has one seen wrong in Israel;
> The Lord their God is with them,
> The King dwells among them."

On the Heights of Peor

Balak, enraged, cried to Balaam:

"Neither curse them at all, nor bless them at all!"

Balaam replied:

"Did I not tell you that I must do all that God told me to do?"

Then Balak said to Balaam:

"Come now, I will take you to another place; perhaps God will be pleased that you curse them for me there."

Balak took Balaam to the top of Peor, which looks down upon the desert.

When Balaam saw that the Lord was pleased to bless Israel, he did not use enchantments as usual, but he gazed out toward the desert. As he looked, he saw Israel lying encamped, tribe by tribe; and the spirit of God came over him, and he spoke these words:

> "How goodly are thy tents, O Jacob,
> Thy dwelling-places, O Israel!
> As far-stretching valleys,
> As gardens by the river-side,
> As oaks planted by the Lord,
> As cedars beside the waters.
> Blessed be everyone that blesseth thee,
> And cursed be everyone that curseth thee!"

Balaam is sent away

Balak's anger blazed against Balaam, and he struck his hands together.

"I called you to curse my enemies," cried Balak to Balaam, "and here you have actually blessed them these three times. Therefore, now flee to your home! I intended to give you great honor, but the Lord has prevented you from receiving your reward!"

Balaam answered:

"Did I not indeed say to the messengers whom you sent to me, that even if Balak were to give me his very house full of silver and gold, I could not go beyond the word of the Lord to do anything good or bad of my own accord? Whatever the Lord says, that I say. I go back, indeed, to my own people; but let me tell you what this people will do to your people in days to come."

Israel of the Future

Then Balaam spoke this prophecy:

"I see them, but not as they are now;
I behold them, but not as they are at present.
A star (a king) shall come forth out of Jacob,
And a scepter shall rise out of Israel,
And shall smite through the corners of Moab,
And break down all the sons of Seth.
And Edom shall be a possession;
Seir, also, shall become a possession,
They who were their enemies!
Israel shall win valiantly,
And Jacob shall conquer his foes!"

Then Balaam arose. He departed, and returned home. And Balak also went his way. (*Numbers 22–24*)

VIII.

JOSHUA — SECOND IN COMMAND

Moses' great labors had drawn to a close. He was old; and he was now concerned about who should lead Israel in the future. The Israelites, bred in the manly virtues of the desert, steadfast in their loyalty to the Covenant, zealous for their freedom, and eager to take possession of the Promised Land, needed young but experienced leadership. Such a leader was Joshua, son of Nun, and Moses appointed him to be his successor.

MOSES and Eleazar, the High Priest, took the census of the Israelites while they were encamped on the plains of Moab beside the river Jordan opposite Jericho. There was not a man among them who had been in the earlier census taken by Moses and Aaron, the priest, in the Wilderness of Sinai, except Caleb and Joshua; for, as the Lord had declared, all the others had perished in the desert.

The Appointment of Joshua

The Lord said to Moses:

"Ascend this mountain of Abarim and view the land which I have given to the Israelites. When you have seen it, you also shall be gathered to your people, as your brother Aaron was; because you and he were faithless to my instructions when the people complained in the Wilderness of Zin, where I commanded you to sanctify Me at the waters before their eyes."

Moses said:

"Let the Lord, the God of all human beings, appoint a leader over the people to guide all Israel's affairs and plans so that the people of the Lord may not be like sheep that have no shepherd."

And the Lord answered:

"Take Joshua, the son of Nun, a man in whom is spirit, and lay your hands upon him; place him before Eleazar, the priest, to receive directions from the Lord by means of the Urim (the sacred lots). At Eleazar's bidding, Joshua and all the people of Israel shall act and move."

Moses did as the Lord commanded him.

He placed Joshua before Eleazar, the priest, and before all the people. And he laid his hands on Joshua, and gave him his commission.   (*Numbers 26–27*)

דְּבָרִים

DEUTERONOMY

THE new Israel had been born and had grown up in the desert. They had not been eye-witnesses to the stirring events of the exodus from Egypt and the giving of the Covenant at Mount Sinai. Indeed, they had not actually accepted the Covenant of Mount Sinai, nor had they yet sworn allegiance to it. Moses, aware that the end of his life was close at hand, appealed to this new Israel to accept the Covenant between their forefathers and God, and to be ever loyal and faithful to it.

The Book of Deuteronomy reviews the history and the laws contained in the Books of Exodus, Leviticus and Numbers. Unlike the other books of the Pentateuch, Deuteronomy is cast in the form of orations, which retell the events that took place during the journey from Egypt to the threshold of Palestine. They give utterance to the spirit of Judaism in its sublime declaration of faith in One God: "Hear, O Israel: the Lord our God, the Lord is One." And they appeal to Israel's devotion and loyalty to the Covenant of God. The book closes with the magnificent song and blessing of Moses, just before the great Liberator, Teacher, Lawgiver and Leader died.

These noble orations have rightly been called the "Farewell Addresses" of Moses, the servant of God.

Our sages tell us that the last few verses, which describe the death of Moses — simple, solemn and touching — were not written by Moses, but by Joshua, his lieutenant.

The Book of Deuteronomy, fifth and last of the Books of Moses, was originally called *Mishneh Torah*, "The Law Repeated." Its present Hebrew name, *Debarim*, or "Words," comes from its first verse which reads, "And these are the *words* which Moses spoke."

I.

FIRST ORATION:
OBEDIENCE TO THE COVENANT

In the first half of this oration Moses reviewed the events
that had taken place from the time the Israelites left Egypt
to the moment they stood on the frontiers of Canaan. Throughout it, Moses emphasized God's care of Israel in all their
difficulties, and then urged upon the people to obey and carry
out the Covenant between them and God.

THESE are the words which Moses spoke to all Israel east of
the river Jordan.

The Source of Wisdom

"Now, O Israel, hearken to the rules and regulations which
I teach you, and obey them, so that you may live and go in and
possess the land which the Lord, the God of your fathers, is
giving you. Observe, therefore, and do them; for they will prove
your wisdom and your understanding in the eyes of the peoples; and
when they hear all these laws, they will say, 'This great nation is
indeed a wise and understanding people!' . . .

Sinai never to be forgotten

"What great nation has God so near to it as the Lord our God is,
whenever we call upon Him? What great nation has rules and
regulations so righteous as all this Covenant, which I set before
you this day? Only take heed to watch yourselves well, lest you
forget what you yourselves have seen, and let them depart from
your minds all the days of your life. Teach them to your children
and your children's children, the story of the day when you stood
before the Lord your God at Mount Sinai, when the Lord said
to me, 'Assemble the people round Me, and I will let them hear My
words, that they may learn to reverence Me all the days of their
life on earth, and that they may instruct their children in reverence;' the story of how you came near and stood at the foot of
the mountain; and the mountain flamed up to the very heart of
heaven, shrouded in darkness, clouds and gloom; and how the

Lord spoke to you out of the flames, but you saw no form; you heard only a voice. . . .

"He made His Covenant known to you, the Decalogue, which He ordered you to obey; and He wrote it on two Tables of stone. The Lord then ordered me at that time to teach you to observe the rules and regulations, that you might do them in the land which you are entering to possess . . .

"When you shall have children and children's children, and you shall have been long in the land, and shall deal corruptly, and make a graven image, even the form of anything, and shall do what is evil in the sight of the Lord your God, I call heaven and earth to witness against you this day, that you shall soon utterly perish from off the land which you go over the Jordan to possess. You shall not live long upon it, but shall utterly be destroyed. And the Lord shall scatter you among the peoples, and you shall be left few in number among the nations, whither the Lord shall lead you away. . . .

Israel's unfailing Protector

"Yet, even in exile, if you seek the Lord your God, you shall find Him, provided that you seek Him with all your heart and all your soul. When you are in distress, and many troubles come upon you, in the end you shall come back to the Lord your God and hearken to His voice.

"The Lord your God is a merciful God. He will not fail you, He will not destroy you, He will not forget the Covenant He swore to your fathers . . .

"He loved your fathers, and chose their descendants after them, and He brought you out of Egypt, and drove out nations greater and stronger than yourselves, that He might give you their land for an inheritance. . . .

Obedience brings Life

"Therefore, know this day, and lay it to your hearts that the Lord, He is God in heaven above and on the earth beneath; there is none else. You must obey His rules and regulations, which I command you this day, that you may prosper and your children after you, and that you may live long upon the land, which the Lord your God gives you for ever." (*Deuteronomy 4*)

II.

SECOND ORATION:
LOVE — THE SPIRIT OF THE COVENANT

In this, the longest of the orations, Moses summarized the laws of the Covenant. But, what is most striking about this oration was Moses' emphasis on the inner spirit of the laws. That spirit was God's love for Israel and the need of Israel's love for God. Love is truly the spirit of the Covenant. These commandments and statutes were more than dry laws that were to be accepted outwardly; they must be written inwardly upon the heart. They expressed the inner spirit of the Jewish religion; and, our sages said, they must be observed with *Simhah shel Mitzvah*, that is, with true joyousness of spirit, and with complete *Kavvanah*, sincerity of heart.

The Unity of God

"HEAR, O Israel: the Lord our God, the Lord is One.
"And thou shalt love the Lord thy God with all thy heart, and with all thy soul, and with all thy might. And these words, which I command thee this day, shall be upon thy heart; and thou shalt teach them diligently unto thy children, and thou shalt talk of them when thou sittest in thy house, and when thou walkest by the way, when thou liest down, and when thou risest up. And thou shalt bind them for a sign upon thy hand, and they shall be for frontlets between thine eyes (*Tefillin*). And thou shalt write them upon the doorposts of thy house, and upon thy gates, (*Mezuzah*). . . .

The Love of God

"The Lord did not set His love upon you, nor choose you, because you were larger than any other people — for you were the smallest of the peoples! It was because the Lord loved you, and because He meant to keep His oath which He swore to your fathers, that the Lord brought you out by great strength, and redeemed you from slavery, from the power of Pharaoh, king of Egypt. Know, therefore, that the Lord your God is a faithful God, who keeps His Covenant with those who love Him and observe His commandments, for a thousand generations. . . .

The Power of God

"And you shall eat and be satisfied, and bless the Lord your God, for the good land He has given you. . . .

"When you have eaten and are satisfied, and have built goodly houses to live in; and when your herds and flocks multiply, and your silver and gold increase, do not become proud and forget the Lord your God, who brought you through the great and dreadful wilderness. Do not boast to yourselves, 'My power and the might of my hand have gotten me this wealth.' . . .

"You shall remember the Lord your God, for it is He who gives you power to prosper; that He may establish His Covenant which He swore to your fathers . . . .

The Justice of God

"After the Lord your God has driven the wicked nations out of the land before you, do not say to yourselves, 'For my righteousness the Lord has brought me in to possess this land!' Not for your righteousness, or for the uprightness of your heart, are you entering upon possession of their land; but for the wickedness of these nations the Lord your God drives them out from before you, and that He may fulfill the promise which the Lord made to your fathers, Abraham, Isaac and Jacob. Do not forget this; for you are a stiff-necked people . . . .

True Worship: Living God's Life

"And now, Israel, what does the Lord your God ask of you, but to reverence the Lord your God, to walk in all His ways, to love Him, to worship Him with all your heart and all your soul; and to obey the rules and regulations which I command you this day!

"You shall reverence the Lord your God; you shall worship Him; and you shall be loyal to Him. He is your glory; He it is whom you shall praise.

"Therefore, you shall love the Lord your God, and keep His commandments always." *(Deuteronomy 6–11)*

III.

THIRD ORATION:
THE REWARDS OF THE COVENANT

After Moses had summed up the laws of the Covenant and had described its spirit, he instructed the priests and the Levites how, when they entered Canaan, they should arrange the Israelites by tribes facing each other on Mount Gerizim and Mount Ebal, and should there teach them the rewards and the punishments of the Covenant. There at Mount Ebal and Mount Gerizim, the new Israel publicly entered into the Covenant made between their fathers and God.

MOSES now gave the people this charge:

"Keep silence, and hear, O Israel! Today you become a people to the Lord your God. Therefore, you must obey what the Lord your God orders, keeping His commands and rules which I set upon you this day . . . .

"When you have crossed the Jordan, the following shall stand on Mount Gerizim to bless the people: Simeon, Levi, Judah, Issachar, Joseph, and Benjamin; and on Mount Ebal the following shall stand to pronounce the curse: Reuben, Gad, Asher, Zebulun, Dan and Naphtali . . . .

The Punishments of God

"The Levites shall declare aloud to all the men of Israel:

'Cursed be the man who makes a graven or molten image — a thing which the Lord detests — the work of a craftsman's hands, and sets it up in secret!'

"And all the people shall say:

'Amen — so be it!'

'Cursed be the man who dishonors his father or his mother!'

"And all the people shall say:

'Amen — so be it!'

'Cursed be the man who removes his neighbor's landmark!'

"And all the people shall say:

'Amen — so be it!'

'Cursed be the man who makes the blind to go astray on the road!'

"And all the people shall say:

'Amen — so be it!'

'Cursed be the man who perverts the justice due to the stranger, fatherless, and widow!'

"And all the people shall say:

'Amen — so be it!'

'Cursed be the man who does not observe the words of this Covenant!'

"And all the people shall say:

'Amen — so be it!' . . .

The Rewards of God

"If you shall hearken diligently to what the Lord, your God, says, and observe to do all His commandments, all these blessings shall come upon you:

> 'Blessed shall you be in the city,
> Blessed shall you be in the country;
> Blessed shall be the fruit of your body,
> The produce of your soil, the offspring of your cattle;
> Blessed be the contents of your basket and
>   kneading-trough;
> Blessed shall you be in your coming,
> And blessed shall you be in your going. . . .'

Accept the Covenant!

"You are standing this day, all of you, before the Lord your God, the heads of your tribes, your elders, your officers, all the men of Israel, together with your children, your wives, and the strangers who live with you, that you should enter into the Covenant of the Lord which He makes with you today, that He may establish you this day as His own people, and that He may be to you a God, as He promised you and as He swore to your fathers, Abraham, Isaac and Jacob . . . .

Choose to live!

"See, I have set before you this day life and good, and death and evil. If you hearken to the commands of the Lord, to love the Lord your God, to walk in His ways, and to follow His orders and rules and regulations, then you shall live and multiply, and the Lord your God shall bless you in the land whither you go in to possess it. But, if your heart turn away, and you will not hearken, I tell you this day you shall not live long in the land which you are crossing the Jordan to enter and possess it.

"I call heaven and earth to witness against you this day, that I have set before you life and death, the blessing and the curse. Choose life, therefore, that you and your children may live, by loving the Lord your God and obeying His commandments; for this is your life and the length of your days . . . .

God does not ask the Impossible

"This commandment which I put before you today is not too hard for you, neither is it far off. It is not in heaven, that you should say, 'Who shall go up for us and bring it down to us and make us hear it that we may do it?' Neither is it beyond the sea, that you should say, 'Who shall cross the sea for us and bring it to us, and make us hear it that we may do it?'

"But the word is very near you, in your mouth, and in your heart, that you may do it." (*Deuteronomy 27–30*)

IV.

THE SONG OF MOSES

Moses bade farewell to his people in a lofty and noble poem. He called upon heaven and earth as witnesses to Israel's acceptance of the Covenant with God.

AND Moses said:
"Assemble all the elders of your tribes, and your leaders, that I may speak these words, and call heaven and earth to witness against you!"

Then Moses spoke the words of this song in the presence and hearing of the whole assembly of Israel:

"Give ear, O heavens, and I will speak;
And listen, O earth, to the words of my mouth.
May my message drop as the rain,
And my speech distill as the dew;
Like mists on the tender grass,
Like showers upon the herb.
For I will proclaim the name of the Lord;
O praise Him for His greatness! . . .

How God chose Israel

"Remember the days of old,
Consider the years of many generations;
Ask your father, and he will declare to you,
Your elders, and they will tell you,
How the Most High gave a heritage
To each of the nations,
When He made divisions among mankind;
How He gave each people its portion,
But Jacob became the Lord's portion,
Israel His very own.
He found them in a desert land,
A howling, empty wilderness.

Like an eagle stirring up her nestlings,
Fluttering over her brood,
Spreading her wings to catch them,
Carrying them on her pinions,
So the Lord alone was Israel's protector. . . .

God — Defender of Israel

"The Lord will defend His people,
He will take pity on His servants.
When it is asked, 'Where is their God,
The Rock in whom they sought shelter?'
Learn now that I, I am He,
And there is no god but Me;
I kill, and I make alive;
I have wounded, and I heal;
And there is none that can rescue out of My hand.
As I live for ever, My hand shall uphold justice. . . .

For the last time Moses looked over the vast throng before
him. He blessed each tribe separately; he lifted his hands
in his final blessing over all Israel.

"There is none like to God, O Jeshurun (Israel),
Enthroned in the heavens as your help.
The eternal God is your dwelling-place,
And underneath you are His everlasting arms!
And Israel dwells in safety.
Fortunate are you, O Israel;
There is no people like you!"   (*Deuteronomy 31, 32, 33*)

V.

THE UNKNOWN GRAVE

Moses reached the last moments of his life on earth. From Mount Nebo in Moab he saw the Promised Land afar off. But he was not to enter it. The great leader's soul took flight, borne aloft, said our sages, on the wings of God's kiss. To this day Moses lies in an unknown grave. His complete disappearance saved Israel from worshipping him as a kind of human god.

THE Lord said to Moses:

"Behold, your days approach when you must die. Call Joshua and present yourselves in the Tent of Meeting, that I may commission him."

Moses and Joshua went and presented themselves in the Tent of Meeting. The Lord appeared in a pillar of cloud which stood over the door of the Tent. And He spoke to Joshua, the son of Nun, saying:

"Be strong and of good courage: for you shall bring the Israelites into the land which I swore to give them; and I will be with you."

Then Moses addressed these words to all Israel:

"I am a hundred and twenty years old this day. I can no longer move about; and the Lord has told me, 'You shall not cross over this Jordan.' The Lord your God, He will go over before you. Be strong and of good courage, fear not; for the Lord your God goes with you; He will not fail you, nor forsake you."

The last Moment

And Moses went up from the plains of Moab to Mount Nebo, the headland of Pisgah, east of Jericho. There the Lord showed him all the land. And the Lord said:

"This is the land which I swore to Abraham, Isaac and Jacob, that I would give to their descendants. I have allowed you to look upon it, but you shall not enter it."

So Moses, the servant of the Lord, died in the land of Moab, as the Lord had said; and he was buried in a valley in the land of Moab; and no man knows his burial-place to this day.

All Israel mourns

Moses was one hundred and twenty years old when he died; but his sight was not dim, nor his natural vigor weakened. The Israelites mourned over the passing of Moses for thirty days.

When the days of mourning had come to an end, the Israelites turned to Joshua, the son of Nun, and obeyed him and carried out the orders given by the Lord to Moses.

And there has not arisen since in Israel a prophet like Moses, whom the Lord knew face to face.   (*Deuteronomy 31, 34*)

נְבִיאִים

THE PROPHETS

יְהוֹשֻׁעַ

JOSHUA

A NEW period of great achievements opened for Israel when Joshua became their leader. The great task ahead of Joshua and the Israelites was to enter the Promised Land, conquer its inhabitants, and then hold possession of the land upon which they settled. Did the Israelites have competent leadership? Did they possess the courage required to defeat their foes? Did they have the necessary patience and hardihood to suffer much before they finally possessed the land? What kind of nations would they have to overcome? Would the land be worth the struggles and sacrifices they had to undergo to possess it?

The Book of Joshua answers such questions.

The leader of Israel was Joshua, of the strong tribe of Ephraim, and the beloved lieutenant of Moses. He was an old, seasoned warrior, of tested courage. He had been one of the two spies who had been confident that Israel could conquer the land. His military ability had been proven. He had fought against the Amalekites and had defeated them.

Israel's faith in God and His Covenant with Israel gave them unfailing powers of endurance and kept their hopes of victory bright. They were not discouraged or daunted by the many years it took them to conquer the nations opposing them.

Many small nations lived in ancient Palestine with names that sound strange to us today, names such as Amorites and Canaanites. They were warlike peoples, who used weapons of iron and chariots drawn by horses. They lived in cities, many of them perched on the top of hills. The cities were surrounded by high, thick walls, which made them easy to defend, but hard to attack. Each city was under the rule of its own king. Nevertheless, at times these kings united their forces against a common enemy.

The Israelites, if successful, were to be rewarded with the possession of a wonderful land. To our ancestors, Palestine, or Canaan as it was then called, was a land "flowing with milk and honey." After their wanderings for many years in the hot, dry, merciless deserts, the Israelites found Canaan a fruitful paradise.

The wars and conquests of Joshua are described in the book which bears his name. The Book of Joshua is the first book in the second large division of the Bible called "The Prophets" (in Hebrew *Nebi'im*).

I.

JOSHUA TAKES COMMAND

When Joshua took command of the Israelites, God set loyalty
to the Law of Moses as the main condition of his leadership.
Joshua was a man of action. He immediately determined to
carry out his mission. He prepared to cross the river Jordan.

God's Charge to Joshua

AFTER the death of Moses, the Lord spoke to Joshua, his
successor, saying:

"Moses My servant is dead. Arise now, and cross the Jordan,↓
you and all this people, into the land which I give to the Israelites.
Every foot of ground you walk on, I give to you, as I promised
Moses.

"As I was with Moses, so I will be with you; I will not fail
you nor forsake you. Be strong and of good courage; for you
shall cause this people to possess the land which I swore to their
fathers to give them.

"Only be strong and very brave, ever mindful to observe all
the Law which Moses, My servant, commanded you. Turn not
from it to the right hand or to the left, that you may succeed
wherever you go. This book of the Law shall not depart out of
your mouth; you shall study it day and night, that you may be
mindful to observe all that is written in it; for then you shall
make your ways prosperous, and you shall have good success.

"Have I not commanded you, 'Be strong and of good courage!'
Be not affrighted, nor dismayed; for the Lord your God is with
you wherever you go."

The People's Pledge

Joshua thereupon commanded the officers of the people to
pass through the camp and give this command: "Prepare food
for yourselves; for within three days you are going to cross the
↓For archaeological note see Item 8, p. 551 in the back of the book.

Jordan, to go in to possess the land which the Lord your God gives you as your own."

When the officers had delivered their message, the people answered Joshua, and said:

"All that you have commanded us we will do, and wherever you send us we will go. As we obeyed Moses in all things, so will we obey you. Only the Lord your God be with you, as He was with Moses! Be strong and of good courage!"   (*Joshua 1*)

II.

THE TWO SPIES

When the Israelites looked across the Jordan Valley, they could see the city of Jericho, the strongly fortified gateway into Canaan. It was important to win Jericho, for from there the road wound up to the hills whence they could fan out, striking north against the Canaanites, and south against the Amorites. Jericho had walls so thick that houses were built on top of them. The city seemed unconquerable. Therefore, Joshua sent two spies to Jericho to find out the strength of the city and the attitude of the inhabitants towards the Israelites.

WHILE Joshua remained with the Israelites east of the Jordan opposite Jericho, he sent two spies to explore the land, especially Jericho.

When they arrived, they came into the house of a woman named Rahab, and stayed there.

The king of Jericho was told that two men of Israel had come in that night to search out the land. The king sent a message to Rahab and said:

"Bring out the two men who have come to you, who have entered your house, for they have come to search out all the land."

She, however, had hidden the two men under some stalks of flax which she had spread out on the roof. She said to the king's messengers:

"Yes, the men came to me, but I did not know where they came from, and just about the time for shutting the gate of the city, when it was dark, the men went out. I do not know where they went. Hurry and pursue them, and you will overtake them."

The pursuers left her home and took the road to the Jordan as far as the fords; and as soon as they had left Jericho the gate was shut. Before the two men had laid down on the roof Rahab came to them and said:

"I know that the Lord has given you this land and that the fear of you has fallen upon us, that all the inhabitants of the land are losing heart. We have heard how the Lord dried up the water of the Red Sea before you, when you came out of Egypt;

and what you did to the two kings of the Amorites, Sihon and
Og, who were on the other side of the Jordan. When we heard
it, our hearts melted, and no courage was left in anyone because
of you; for the Lord your God is God in heaven above and on
the earth beneath. Now, therefore, I beg you swear to me by the
Lord, since I have dealt kindly with you, that you will also deal
kindly with my family, and give me a true sign that you will
save alive my father, my mother, my brothers and my sisters,
and all that they have, and deliver us from death."

The men said to her:

"We are ready to give our life for yours, if you do not tell
what we are doing; and when the Lord gives us the land, we will
deal kindly and faithfully with you."

"Get away into the mountain," she then said to them, "that
the pursuers may not find you; hide yourselves there three days,
until they have returned. Afterwards, you may go your way."

Then the men said:

"Behold, when we come into the land, you shall tie this scarlet thread in the window through which you let us down; and
you shall gather into your house your father and mother, your
brothers and sisters, and all your family. Whoever goes out of
the doors of your house into the street, shall be responsible for
his own death, and we will be guiltless. Whoever stays with you
in the house, we will be responsible for his death if anyone lays
hands on him. If, however, you betray what we are doing, we
will be free from our solemn promise to you."

"Let it be as you say," she said.

She let them down by a rope through the window; for the
house, in which she dwelt, was upon the side of the wall.

After they had gone, she tied the scarlet thread in the window.

They went into the mountains and stayed there three days,
until the pursuers had returned. Their pursuers had sought them
in every direction. Then the spies returned from the mountain,
took the road to the river, crossed it, and came to Joshua to whom
they told all that had happened to them.

"The Lord has given the whole land into our power," they
said to Joshua, "and, moreover, the natives are losing heart before
us."   (*Joshua 2*)

III.

JERICHO AND AI CAPTURED

After Joshua heard the report of the spies, he set his campaign
in motion. With the Ark of the Covenant carried before them
by the priests, the Israelites crossed the Jordan. There Joshua
set up a monument of twelve stones, one for each of the tribes,
and called the place Gilgal. Later, after he had begun the
conquest of the land, Joshua built an altar of unhewn stones
on Mount Ebal, and wrote on the stones a copy of the Law of
Moses.

JERICHO had shut its gates against the Israelites; none left
the city, and none entered it. The Lord said to Joshua:
"I have given Jericho into your hand, with its king and all
its men of valor. You and all your warriors shall march around
the city once a day for six days, and seven priests shall carry
seven rams' horns in front of the Ark of the Covenant. On the
seventh day you shall march around the city seven times, and the
priests shall blow with the horns. Then all the people shall raise
a mighty shout; and the wall of the city shall fall down flat, and
every man shall march in, straight before him."

Joshua called the priests, and said to them:
"Take up the Ark of the Covenant, and let seven priests carry
seven rams' horns before the Ark of the Lord."

And he said to the Israelites:
"March around the city, and let the armed men pass before
the Ark of the Lord; let the seven priests with the seven rams'
horns go ahead in the presence of the Lord, blowing the horns,
and followed by the Ark of the Lord. Let the armed men march
before the priests who blow the horns, and let the rearguard follow the Ark, blowing the horns as they go."

However, Joshua cautioned them:
"You shall not shout the battle-cry, nor let your voice be
heard; not a word shall escape from your mouth until the day
I bid you shout the battle-cry; then shall you shout!"

Joshua had the Ark of the Lord carried around the city once;
then they returned to the camp and passed the night there. The

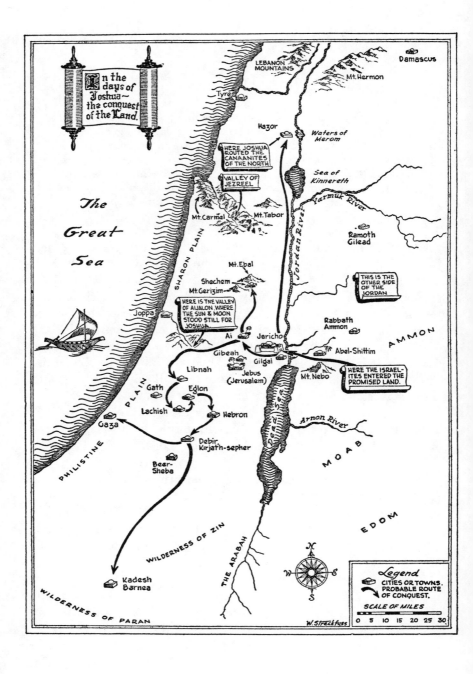

In the days of Joshua — the conquest of the Land.

Damascus

LEBANON MOUNTAINS

Mt. Hermon

Tyre

Hazor

Waters of Merom

HERE JOSHUA ROUTED THE CANAANITES OF THE NORTH.

Sea of Kinnereth

VALLEY OF JEZREEL

Yarmuk River

Mt. Carmel

Mt. Tabor

Ramoth Gilead

THE The Great Sea

SHARON PLAIN

Mt. Ebal

Shechem

Mt. Gerizim

THIS IS THE OTHER SIDE OF THE JORDAN

HERE IS THE VALLEY OF AIJALON, WHERE THE SUN & MOON STOOD STILL FOR JOSHUA.

Joppa

Rabbath Ammon

Ai

Jericho

AMMON

Abel-Shittim

Gibeah

Gilgal

Libnah

Jebus (Jerusalem)

Mt. Nebo

HERE THE ISRAELITES ENTERED THE PROMISED LAND.

Gath

Eglon

Lachish

Hebron

Dead Sea

Arnon River

Gaza

Debir, Kirjath-sepher

Beer-Sheba

MOAB

PLAIN

PHILISTINE

WILDERNESS OF ZIN

THE ARABAH

EDOM

Kadesh Barnea

WILDERNESS OF PARAN

N W E S

Legend

CITIES OR TOWNS.
PROBABLE ROUTE OF CONQUEST.

SCALE OF MILES

0 5 10 15 20 25 30

W. Streckfuss

second day they also marched around the city once and returned to the camp. This they continued to do for six days. On the seventh day, they arose at dawn and marched around the city seven times. At the seventh time, when the priests blew the horns, Joshua said to the Israelites:

"Shout, for the Lord has given you the city. The city, and all that is in it, shall be doomed; only Rahab, and those who are with her in her house, shall be spared, because she hid the messengers whom we sent."

When the Israelites shouted the battle-cry, and the priests blew the horns, the wall fell flat, and they went into the city and captured it.

Joshua spared the lives of Rahab, her father's family and all that she had, because she had hidden the messengers whom Joshua sent to explore Jericho.

Ai is taken by Ambush

Then Joshua with all his soldiers arose and started off for Ai. When he approached the city he selected thirty thousand of the bravest troops and sent them forth by night with this command:

"You shall lie in ambush to the west of the city in the rear. Do not go too far away, but all of you be ready. I, and all the soldiers who are with me, will approach the city, and when they come out against us, we will flee before them. They will come out after us, until we have drawn them away from the city, for they will think that we are fleeing from them. Then, as we run away, you shall rise up from the ambush and seize the city. When you have captured it, you shall set it on fire."

Joshua sent them away; and they went to the place of ambush.

Joshua spent the night in the valley. He rose early the next morning and gathered the Israelites; then, together with the elders of Israel, he led them against Ai. They marched up close to the city, and encamped on the north of Ai.

When the king of Ai saw this, his men went out to fight the Israelites, the king not knowing that Joshua's troops were hiding in ambush behind the city to attack his forces in the rear.

Joshua and his soldiers pretended to be beaten and fled toward the wilderness; and all the people that were in Ai were called out to pursue them. They pursued the Israelites, and left the city unguarded. Then Joshua's troops, who were hiding' in ambush, seized the city and set it on fire.

When the men of Ai looked back, they saw the smoke of the burning city rising up to heaven. They had no chance to escape in any direction; for the Israelites who had been fleeing to the wilderness, turned upon their pursuers. Meanwhile, the Israelites in Ai came out of the city to fight against them; they were surrounded by the Israelites, who let none of the people of Ai escape.   (*Joshua 6, 8*)

IV.

THE CRAFTY GIBEONITES

The capture of Jericho and Ai by the Israelites sent a wave
of terror among the remaining peoples of Canaan. The people
of Gibeon, an important city-state about five miles north of
Jerusalem, tricked the Israelites into making peace with them.
Later Joshua discovered their deception, but kept his promise
to the Gibeonites. After this, Joshua fought against and
conquered the other powerful kings of Canaan.

WHEN the inhabitants of Gibeon heard what Joshua had
done to Jericho and Ai, they thought they would act craftily.
They pretended to be ambassadors; they took old sacks on their
donkeys, as well as old, torn, patched wine-skins. They put old,
patched sandals on their feet, and worn garments on their backs;
and saw to it that the bread for their provisions was dry and
crumbled. Then they went to Joshua, who was camping at Gilgal, and said to him and the men of Israel:

"We have come from a far country. Now then make a treaty
with us."

Joshua said:

"Who are you, and where do you come from?"

To which they replied:

"Your servants have come from a very far country, because
of the name of the Lord your God. We have heard the fame of
Him, and all that He did in Egypt, and all that He did to the
two kings of the Amorites beyond the Jordan. Our elders and
all the inhabitants of our country told us: Take provisions for the
journey, and go and meet them, and say, 'We are your servants;
now then make a treaty with us.' This our bread we took hot
for our provisions out of our houses on the day that we left to
come to you; and now, behold, it is dry and crumbled. These
wine-skins were new, when we filled them, and now, behold, they
are torn. And these our garments and sandals are worn out from
the very long journey."

Joshua made a treaty with them to spare their lives; and the
leaders of the Israelites approved it by an oath.

Three days after they had made the treaty with them, the Israelites learned that the Gibeonites were their neighbors and that they dwelt in the same country. Whereupon, the Israelites journeyed and came to their cities on the third day. They did not kill them, because Joshua and their leaders had sworn not to do so.

Joshua then called them, and said to them:

"Why have you deceived us by saying, 'We live very far away,' when you dwell among us? Because you have deceived us, you shall never cease providing us with slaves, hewers of wood and drawers of water, for the house of my God!"

They said to Joshua:

"Your servants were told that the Lord your God had commanded His servant Moses to give you the whole land and to destroy all its inhabitants. Therefore, we were afraid for our lives because of you, and we did this thing. Here we are then in your power; do to us whatever you think right and proper."

This was what Joshua did to them. He saved them from the angry Israelites; but that day he made them hewers of wood and drawers of water for the Israelites, and for the altar of the Lord.

Battle of Gibeon

When the kings of Canaan heard that the Gibeonites had made peace with Israel, they gathered together to besiege Gibeon.

Joshua then made a surprise attack upon the kings of Canaan by marching his forces all night from Gilgal. It was on this day, when the Lord put these kings at the mercy of the Israelites, that Joshua spoke to the Lord, and in the presence of Israel said:

"Sun, stand thou still upon Gibeon;
And thou, Moon, in the valley of Aijalon!"

And the sun stood still, and the moon stayed, until the nation had avenged itself of its enemies. Is not this written in the Book of Jashar?* The sun stood still in the midst of heaven, and did not

*According to some scholars, there seems to have been an ancient literature, now lost, from which some portions of our Bible were taken. Besides *The Book of Jashar* mentioned here, there are other lost books, such as *The Book of the Wars of the Lord* (*Numbers 21.14*), *The Book of the Acts of Solomon* (*I Kings 11.41*), and others.

hasten to go down about a whole day. Never before or since has there been a day like that, when the Lord listened to the voice of a man; for the Lord fought for Israel.

Then Joshua, and his troops, returned to camp at Gilgal.

And Joshua captured all the cities of those kings, as well as the kings themselves. All the spoil of those cities and the cattle, the Israelites took as their booty.

As the Lord had commanded Moses, His servant, so did Moses command Joshua; and so had Joshua done; he left nothing undone of all that the Lord had commanded Moses.

Then the land had rest from war.   (*Joshua 9, 10.5–15, 11.12–23*)

V.

DIVISION OF THE LAND

After Canaan had been conquered, Joshua divided it among the tribes of Israel. Only seven divisions are mentioned here, because the tribes of Reuben and Gad had already received their share; the tribes of Judah and Ephraim remained where they were; and the tribe of Levi was not to receive any land. The division of the land was made by the casting of lots, which took place in the city of Shiloh, the religious center of the tribes. The Levites were given cities to live in; and cities of refuge were established. Each of the tribes settled down upon that portion of the land of Canaan that had been allotted to it. Thus, the Israelites began their new life in the Promised Land.

JOSHUA was old, and well along in years, when the Lord said to him:

"You are old, and very much of the land still remains to be conquered. Meanwhile, however, divide the land among Israel for an inheritance, as I have commanded you."

The Land is divided

The whole community of Israel assembled together at Shiloh and set up the Tent of Meeting. And Joshua said to them:

"Appoint three men for each tribe; and I will send them that they may explore the land. They shall map it out according to the inheritance of each, and then they shall report to me. They shall divide it into seven portions; Judah shall remain in its territory in the south, and the tribe of Joseph (Ephraim) in its territory in the north. I will cast lots for you here before the Lord."

The men did this; then they reported to Joshua at the camp in Shiloh. And Joshua cast lots for the Israelites before the Lord in Shiloh; and there Joshua divided the land among the Israelites, each receiving his share.

Joshua receives Timnath-serah

When the distribution of the land had been completed, the Israelites gave Joshua an inheritance among themselves. In accordance with the command of the Lord they gave him the city for which he had asked, namely, Timnath-serah, in the hill-country of Ephraim.

The Cities of Refuge

Then the Lord said to Joshua:

"Speak to the Israelites as follows: 'Assign cities of refuge for yourselves concerning which I spoke to you through Moses, so that if a man kills another man by accident, he may flee there. They shall serve you as places of refuge from the next of kin who might seek to avenge the dead man's blood. If the avenger of blood should pursue him, the elders shall not deliver him to the avenger; for he killed his fellowman accidentally.' "

And the Israelites accordingly set aside six cities in various parts of Canaan as cities of refuge.

The Levites' Cities and Fields

Then in Shiloh the heads of families among the Levites came to Eleazar, the priest, Joshua, and the heads of families in the other tribes of Israel, and said:

"The Lord gave command by Moses to give us cities to dwell in, together with their pasture-lands for our cattle."

The Israelites, in accordance with the command of the Lord, gave the Levites some of their own inheritance. The total number of cities given to the Levites was forty-eight, together with the pasture-lands adjoining these cities.

Thus the Lord gave Israel all the land which He had sworn to their fathers to give them. They possessed it, and settled down in it, and the Lord gave them peace on every side.   (*Joshua 13–21*)

VI.

JOSHUA'S FAREWELL ADDRESS

Before his death, Joshua caused the people to assemble together in the city of Shechem and, like Moses, renewed the
solemn Covenant between the Israelites and God.

A LONG time afterwards, when the Lord had given Israel
rest from all their enemies around them, and Joshua had
become old, he called together all Israel to Shechem and said to
them:

Loyalty to the Law

"I am old and well advanced in years. You have seen all
that the Lord your God has done for you to all these nations;
for it is the Lord your God who has fought for you. Be very courageous then to keep and to do all that is written in the book of
the Law of Moses, and turn not aside from it to the right hand
or to the left.

Beware of Idolatry!

"Do not mix with the heathen nations, those that are still
left with you. You shall not call upon the names of their gods,
nor swear by them, nor serve them, nor worship them. But you
shall cleave to the Lord your God, as you have done up to this
day. Take great care, therefore, that you love the Lord your God.

"If you in any way prove yourselves disloyal to your God,
and join yourselves with these nations, and make marriages with
them, and associate with them and they with you, know for a
certainty that the Lord your God will no longer drive these nations
out of your sight. They shall be a snare and a trap for you, until
you perish from off this good land which the Lord your God has
given you.

God also punishes

"Behold, this day I am going the way of all the earth. Consider therefore with all your heart and soul that not one of the good promises which the Lord your God made concerning you has failed. Hence, as every good promise has come to pass for you, so shall the Lord bring on you every punishment, until He has destroyed you from off this good land which the Lord your God has given you.

"Whenever you transgress the Covenant of the Lord your God, and go and serve alien gods, and worship them, then shall the anger of the Lord be kindled against you, and you shall perish quickly from off the good land which He has given you."

> After having reviewed the history of Israel from the days of Abraham, through their escape from Egypt, their wanderings in the Wilderness and their victories over their foes in Canaan, Joshua continued:

"Thus says the Lord, the God of Israel: 'I gave you a land on which you have never labored, and cities to dwell in which you did not build and vineyards and olive-groves to eat from that you did not plant. Therefore, worship the Lord, and serve Him faithfully and loyally.'

"You cannot serve the Lord and alien gods at the same time."

"No," the people said to Joshua, "it is the Lord we will serve."

Then Joshua said:

"Hereby you witness against yourselves that you have chosen the Lord to serve Him."

And they said, "We are witnesses."

Thus Joshua made a Covenant between God and the people that day. He made statutes and ordinances for them at Shechem. And Joshua wrote these words in the book of the Law of God. And, taking a large stone, he set it up under the sacred oak that was by the Sanctuary of the Lord. And Joshua said to all the people:

"Behold, this stone shall be a witness against us; for it has heard all the words that the Lord has spoken to us; it shall be a witness against you, lest you deny your God."

Then Joshua dismissed the people, each man to his own inheritance.

The Death of Joshua

After these events Joshua, the servant of the Lord, died. They buried him in the border of his own inheritance in Timnath-serah. (*Joshua 23–24*)

שׁוֹפְטִים

JUDGES

THE death of Joshua left no one to take his place. Without a strong leader to hold them together, the tribes soon lost their feeling of being a united people, Israel. Each tribe, dwelling on its own piece of land, had to struggle alone against its hostile neighbors. It had little or no interest in the welfare of the other tribes. Only when they were compelled to face a common enemy, and a leader of extraordinary ability rose up among them, did they unite, but only for the time necessary to ward off the common danger.

The period of the Judges recalls the early history of the thirteen American colonies, when each colony ruled itself and sometimes joined another colony against a common enemy like the Indians or the French. A long time passed before the thirteen colonies overcame their jealousies and united under one leader and were governed by one law. Very similar was the experience of the twelve tribes of Israel in their "colonial period," the days of the Judges.

The judges were local Israelite warriors. They were heroes of the sword, who helped to deliver their tribes from the power of their oppressors — the Moabites, Ammonites, Amalekites, Midianites, and, most powerful of all, the Philistines. After a victory on the battlefield, a tribe would accept this leader as ruler or judge, to lead it in times of peace. Some of the Israelites, even in the days of the Judges, began to understand the evil results of the lack of unity among the tribes and of the fact that "every man did what was right in his own eyes." They slowly began to realize the benefit of having one leader to unite, rule and lead them all as in the days of Moses and Joshua. But the time had not yet come for the rebirth of a united nation.

The chief events of this "colonial period" in Jewish history are recorded in the Book of Judges, which might also be called "The Book of Heroes."

171

I.

DISLOYALTY — PUNISHMENT — PEACE

In Canaan, the Israelites began to imitate the religious practices of the pagan peoples about them. The most common form of worship was that of Baal and Astarte, the gods of fertility, who were supposed to provide the land with water and to help it produce its grains and fruits. The Israelites soon adopted the worship of Baal and Astarte, which consisted of disgusting and horrible ceremonies. Had the Israelites not stopped these idolatrous practices, they would have become like the peoples about them and would have disappeared. God prevented this by raising up oppressors to punish them. When the people remembered the Covenant, and turned back from their idolatry, God sent them a powerful leader, a judge, who saved them from their oppressors. Then they enjoyed a period of peace.

WHEN Joshua had sent the people away, the Israelites went back, each to his own inheritance, to take possession of the land. Joshua died. In time, all that generation were gathered to their fathers. And another generation came that knew nothing about the Lord or the work He had done for Israel.

Israel begins to sin

The Israelites then did what was evil in the sight of the Lord and served the Baals. They forsook the Lord, the God of their fathers, who had brought them from the land of Egypt. They ran after alien gods, the gods of the peoples that surrounded them, and bowed down to them. They forsook the Lord and sacrificed to Baal and Astarte.

Israel is punished

The anger of the Lord was kindled against Israel, and He delivered them into the power of those who oppressed them; and He gave them into the power of their enemies around them. Wherever they marched, the hand of the Lord was against them for evil, as the Lord had threatened. They were in sore distress.

Champions of Israel

Then the Lord raised up judges to rescue them from their oppressors; but they did not listen even to their judges. They went astray after alien gods; they turned quickly from the path of their fathers who had obeyed the commands of the Lord.

When the Lord raised up judges for them, the Lord would be with His judges and would rescue the Israelites from the power of their enemies during all the lifetime of the judges. For the Lord was moved to pity by their groaning under the oppression of their tyrants and oppressors. But, when the judge died, they returned to their bad ways, and behaved worse than ever. They would not abandon any of their practices or stubborn ways.

Again the anger of the Lord was kindled against Israel, and He said:

"Because this nation has transgressed My Covenant which I formed with their fathers, and has not listened to My commands, I will no longer drive out of their way any of the nations that Joshua left when he died."

The Test of the Lord

The Lord left those nations to test Israel by means of them, to see whether they would keep the commands of the Lord as their fathers had done.   (*Judges 2*)

II.

DEBORAH — MOTHER IN ISRAEL

Deborah lived in Ephraim and was known for her great wisdom. In her days, Jabin, the Canaanite king, and Sisera, his general, made war on the Israelites. They were very powerful, for they had chariots of iron. Deborah sent for Barak and appointed him general over the united forces of Ephraim, Benjamin, Issachar, Zebulun and Naphtali. Together they defeated Jabin and Sisera and won a great victory on the slopes of Mount Tabor. After the battle, Deborah wrote her Song of Triumph. She described the dangerous times in which the Israelites lived; the battle in the midst of a terrific storm that flooded the river and helped to defeat Jabin by sweeping away his chariots; how the Kenite woman killed Sisera; and how Sisera's mother pathetically waited for him in vain. The Song of Triumph is a magnificent poem of stirring power and beauty.

THE Israelites did what was evil in the sight of the Lord, so the Lord gave them into the power of Jabin, the king of Canaan, who ruled in Hazor. The captain of his army was Sisera. The Israelites cried to the Lord; for Jabin had nine hundred iron chariots, and he had oppressed the Israelites cruelly for twenty years.

Now Deborah, a prophetess, the wife of Lappidoth, was judge in Israel at that time. She held court under the palm-tree of Deborah between Ramah and Beth-el, in the hill-country of Ephraim. The Israelites came to her for judgment.

She summoned Barak, the son of Abinoam, and said to him:

"The Lord, the God of Israel, commands you to march to Mount Tabor with ten thousand men from Naphtali and Zebulun, saying, 'I will draw Sisera, Jabin's captain, to meet you at the brook Kishon with his chariots and his troops, and I will put him into your power.' "

Barak said to her:

DEBORAH, A PROPHETESS

"The Israelites came to her for judgment."

(*Judges 4.5*)

see page 174

"If you will come with me, I will go; but if you will not come with me, I will not go."

She answered:

"I will surely go with you. Only the glory of the expedition will not be yours; for the Lord will give Sisera into the hand of a woman."

Then Deborah went with Barak to Kedesh. Barak called the men of Zebulun and Naphtali to Kedesh. Ten thousand Israelites followed him; and Deborah also marched with him.

Now Heber the Kenite had left the Kenites, the tribe of Jethro, and had pitched his tent as far north as the oak near Kedesh.

When Sisera learned that Barak had marched to Mount Tabor, Sisera gathered his nine hundred iron chariots and all his forces at the brook Kishon.

Deborah said to Barak:

"To the attack! This is the day when the Lord puts Sisera into your power. Does not the Lord march before you?"

Then Barak, with ten thousand men, charged down Mount Tabor. At the attack of Barak's swordsmen, the Lord put to flight Sisera, his chariots and all his forces. Sisera got down from his war-chariot and fled on foot. Barak pursued the chariots and the forces; and all the army of Sisera fell by the sword; there was not a man left.

When Sisera fled away on foot, he went to the tent of Jael, the wife of Heber the Kenite; for there was peace between Jabin, the king of Hazor, and the house of Heber the Kenite.

Jael went out to meet Sisera, and said to him:

"Turn in, my lord, turn in to me; fear not."

And he went with her into the tent. As she covered him with a rug, he said:

"Give me, I beg you, a little water to drink; for I am thirsty."

She gave him milk to drink, and he fell fast asleep.

Then Jael took a tent-pin, and a hammer in her hand, and went softly over to him and smote the pin into his temples and he died.

So God subdued on that day Jabin, the king of Canaan, before the children of Israel.

The Song of Triumph

On that day, Deborah sang with Barak, the son of Abinoam:

"Hear, O you kings! Give ear, O you rulers!
I will sing to the Lord,
I will sing praise to the Lord, the God of Israel.

The Enemy's Oppressions

In the years gone by, the highways were unused,
And travellers kept to the byways;
The villages in Israel were deserted,
Until I, Deborah, arose,
I arose, a mother in Israel.
They chose new gods;
Then was war in the gates.
But Israel had no armor-makers;
Armed men were lacking in the city.
Was there a shield or a spear to be seen
Among forty thousand in Israel?

The Battle-Cry sounds

The people of the Lord
Went down to the gates, crying:
'Awake, awake, Deborah;
Awake, awake, with your war-cry!
Arise, arise, O Barak,
Capture your oppressors, O son of Abinoam!'

Furious Battle is waged

They marched down against the warriors,
The Lord's people against the mighty.
The kings came, they fought;
Then fought the kings of Canaan.
They fought from heaven,
The stars in their courses fought against Sisera.
The brook Kishon swept them away,

That ancient brook, the brook Kishon.
The hoofs of the horses struck down
Their warriors by their furious plungings.
Bless, O my soul, the power of the Lord!

How Jael kills Sisera

Blessed above women shall Jael be,
The wife of Heber the Kenite,
Blessed above women!
Sisera asked for water, and milk she gave him;
In a lordly bowl she brought him curds.
She put her hand to a tent pin,
And her right hand to a workman's hammer.
She struck Sisera, crushing his head,
She smashed him, she crashed his temple in.
He sank at her feet, he fell, he lay;
Where he sank, there he fell down dead!

Vainly a Mother waits for her Son

Through the window she looked out and peered,
The mother of Sisera, through the lattice:
'Why is his chariot so long in coming?
Why tarry the wheels of his chariot?'
Then the wisest of her ladies replied —
Nay, she herself answered the question —
'They must be dividing the spoils they have taken,
A maiden or two for each warrior,
For Sisera a spoil of dyed garments,
A spoil of dyed garments embroidered,
And pieces of lace for his neck!'

God's Enemies shall perish

So perish all Thine enemies, O Lord!
But those who love Thee shall be as the sun,
Rising up, and going forth in his splendor."

And the land enjoyed peace for forty years.   (*Judges 4, 5*)

III.

GIDEON — THE MAN WHO REFUSED TO BE KING

Gideon, the son of Joash, of the clan of Abiezer, lived in the little village of Ophrah in Manasseh. In his time, the Midianites marched across Manasseh's borders, plundering and destroying, coming "as locusts — for multitude." Gideon was a strange and remarkable man. He had great powers of leadership. He was eager to save his people from their attackers. He was a man of deep humility, and always relied upon signs and omens, visions and dreams to guide his actions. When he triumphed over the Midianites, Gideon modestly attributed the victory to God.

THE Israelites again did what was evil in the sight of the Lord, and the Lord put them in the power of the Midianites for seven years. Because they feared the Midianites, the Israelites made hiding-places for themselves in the mountains, the caves, and other natural strongholds. And the Midianites destroyed the produce of the earth, and they left no food in Israel, neither sheep nor oxen. They came into the land to destroy it. Israel was brought very low through Midian. And the Israelites cried unto the Lord.

Gideon's Vision

Now the angel of the Lord came and sat down under the sacred tree at Ophrah, which belonged to Joash, the Abiezrite. His son, Gideon, was beating out some wheat inside the wine-press, to hide it from the Midianites. And the angel of the Lord appeared to him and said:

"The Lord is with you, you mighty man of valor!"

Gideon said:

"O, my lord, if the Lord is with us, why then has all this happened to us? Where are all His wonderful acts of which our fathers told us. Now the Lord has cast us off and put us into the power of the Midianites."

The angel, who was really the Lord, turned to him and said:

"With what strength you have, go and save Israel from the Midianites. Do I not send you?"

But Gideon said to Him:

"O Lord, how am I to save Israel? Behold, my family is the weakest in Manasseh, and I am the least in my father's house."

The Lord said to him:

"I will surely be with you, and you shall defeat the Midianites to a man."

The Dew and the Fleece

Now the Midianites assembled themselves together and they encamped in the Valley of Jezreel.

The spirit of the Lord entered into Gideon, and he sounded the war trumpets, and the Abiezrites gathered together under his leadership. He sent messengers throughout Manasseh, and to Asher, Zebulun, and Naphtali, and they came to join him. Then Gideon said to the Lord:

"If Thou wilt rescue Israel by my power, as Thou hast said — behold, I will put a fleece of wool on the threshing-floor; if there is dew on the fleece only, while it is dry on the ground around it, I shall know that Thou wilt rescue Israel by my power, as Thou hast said."

And this did happen. When he arose next morning, he wrung the fleece, and he squeezed out of the fleece a bowlful of water. Then Gideon said to the Lord:

"Let not Thine anger be kindled hotly against me, and I will speak just once more. Let me make trial, I pray Thee, but this once with the fleece; let it now be dry on the fleece only, but on all the ground around it let there be dew."

The Lord did so that night; the fleece alone was dry but on all the ground there was dew.

Selecting the best Men

Gideon and his men rose up early and encamped beside the spring of Harod; and the Midianite camp lay north in the valley.

Then the Lord said to Gideon:

"You have too many men with you. If I give the Midianites up to the Israelites, they will boast, 'We have saved ourselves.' Therefore proclaim to your people, 'Whoever is afraid may go home.' "

So Gideon put them to this test, and twenty-two thousand of the men went home, but ten thousand stayed. Then the Lord said:

"The men are still too many. Bring them down to the water, and let Me test them there for you. Every one of whom I say to you, 'This one shall go with you,' shall go with you; and every one of whom I say to you, 'This one shall not go with you,' shall not go."

Gideon brought the men down to the water. And the Lord said to him:

"Every one who laps up the water with his tongue like a dog, place on one side; and everyone who kneels down to drink, place on the other side."

The number of those who lapped with their tongue, putting their hand to their mouth, were three hundred men; but all the rest of the men knelt down on their knees to drink. And the Lord then said to Gideon:

"By the three hundred men who lapped will I save you and deliver the Midianites into your hands. Let all the rest of the men go home."

Gideon sent all the rest of the Israelites home, each to his tent, keeping only the three hundred men.

Now the camp of Midian was beneath the Israelites in the valley.

That same night the Lord said to Gideon:

"Go down into the camp of the Midianites secretly; for I am putting them into your hands. Take with you your servant Purah, and hear what they are saying; and after that you shall have the courage to attack the camp."

With his servant Purah, he went to the outposts of the soldiers that were in the camp of the enemy. Just as Gideon came near, one of the soldiers told his comrade:

"I just had a dream," he said, "that a cake of barley bread

tumbled into the camp of Midian and struck a tent so hard that it fell down and lay flat."

"That," his comrade explained, "is nothing other than the sword of Gideon, the son of Joash, an Israelite. The Lord is putting Midian into his power."

Gideon's Strategy

When Gideon heard the dream told and its interpretation he knelt in worship. Then he returned to the camp of Israel, and proclaimed:

"Up! The Lord is about to give the camp of Midian into your hands!"

Gideon divided his three hundred men into three companies. Into the hands of all of them he put trumpets and empty pitchers, and in each pitcher a torch. And he said to them, "Look at me, and do as I do. When I reach the outskirts of the camp, and when I blow on the trumpet and all the others with me, then you also shall blow your trumpets on every side of the camp and cry, 'For the Lord and for Gideon!' "

Gideon and the three hundred men he led reached the outskirts of the camp at the beginning of the middle watch, just when the guards had been posted. They blew their trumpets and smashed the pitchers in their hands. The other two companies also shattered their pitchers, blew their trumpets, and holding the torches in their left hands and the trumpets in their right, they shouted, "For the Lord and for Gideon!"

Gideon and his small army stood where they were, and the whole Midianite army awoke, sounded the alarm, and with wild cries fled.

When peace had come again, the Israelites said to Gideon:

"Rule over us, you and your son and your son's son, for you have saved us from the Midianites."

But Gideon said:

"I will not rule over you, nor shall my son rule over you. The Lord alone shall rule over you."   (*Judges 6–8*)

IV.

ABIMELECH — THE LITTLE MAN WHO WOULD BE KING

When Gideon died, Abimelech, his son by a Canaanite woman, persuaded the men of Shechem to make him their king. He began his reign by murdering all his brothers, except the youngest, Jotham, who escaped. While Abimelech was being crowned king, Jotham suddenly appeared and stood on a hill, a safe distance away, and told the assembled people a story about the trees. This tale has come to be known as "Jotham's Fable." Abimelech was the first man who tried to be a king among the Israelites; he failed, for he was not the right man. But his action showed that there was a growing need for unity among the tribes, a unity that expressed itself in wanting a king.

As SOON as Gideon died, the Israelites again went astray after the Baals. They forgot the Lord their God, who had saved them from all their foes on every side.

Abimelech, the son of Gideon, went to his mother's family and to his kinsmen in Shechem and spoke to them, saying:

"Ask the men of Shechem whether it is better for them to have seventy men ruling over them, all the sons of Gideon, or to have one man? Also, remind them that I am their own flesh and blood."

His kinsmen on his behalf repeated all this to the men of Shechem. Their hearts moved them to follow Abimelech. "He is our brother," they said; and they even gave him silver money from the temple of Baal, with which Abimelech hired worthless and reckless followers. He went to his father's house at Ophrah and there, upon one stone, he slew his brothers, the sons of Gideon. Only Jotham, the youngest son of Gideon, escaped; for he had hidden himself.

Jotham's Fable

All the men of Shechem gathered together beside the sacred tree connected with the sacred pillar in Shechem, and made Abimelech king. When they told it to Jotham, he went and stood on top of Mount Gerizim, and lifted up his voice and said:

"Hearken to me, men of Shechem, so that God may hearken to you! Once upon a time the trees set out to anoint a king over them. They said to the olive tree:

'Reign over us.'

But the olive tree said to them:

'Should I leave my rich olive oil, with which gods and men are honored, that I should rule over trees?'

Then the trees said to the fig-tree:

'Come you, and reign over us!'

But the fig-tree answered:

'Should I leave my sweetness and good fruit, that I should rule over trees?'

Then the trees said to the vine:

'Come you, and reign over us!'

But the vine said to them:

'Should I leave my juice which cheers gods and men, that I should rule over trees?'

Finally, all the trees said to the bramble:

'Come you, and reign over us!'

And the bramble said to the trees:

'If you anoint me king in good faith, come and take refuge in my shadow; and if not, let fire blaze from the bramble to burn up the very cedars of Mount Lebanon!' "

Then Jotham continued:

"Now then, if you have dealt truly and uprightly in making Abimelech your king, if you have acted fairly towards Gideon and his family, and treated him as he deserved — for my father fought for you and risked his life to rescue you from Midian, and you have risen against my father's family this very day, and killed his sons, seventy of them, upon one stone, and anointed Abimelech, the son of his slave-girl, king over the men of Shechem because he is your kinsman — if, I say, you have dealt truly and uprightly towards Gideon and his family, then rejoice in Abimelech, and let him rejoice in you. But if not, let fire blaze from Abimelech and burn up the men of Shechem; and let fire blaze from the men of Shechem and burn up Abimelech."

Then Jotham ran away and went to the village of Beer and dwelt there for fear of his brother, Abimelech. (*Judges 8, 9*)

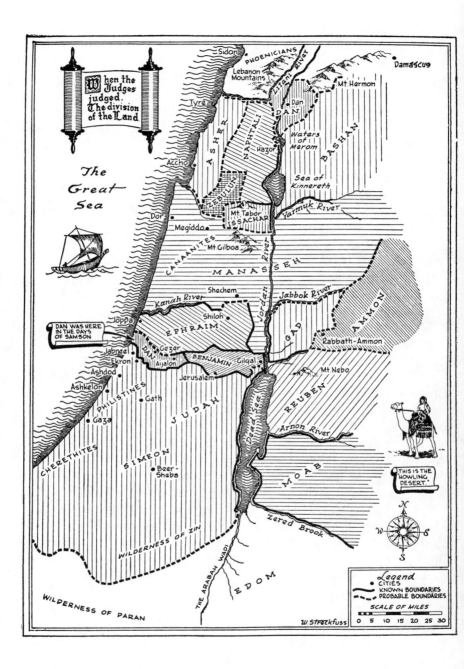

When the Judges judged. The division of the Land

The Great Sea

Sidon
PHOENICIANS
Lebanon Mountains
Litani River
Damascus
Mt Hermon
Tyre
Dan
Waters of Merom
Hazor
BASHAN
Accho
ASHER
NAPHTALI
ZEBULUN
Sea of Kinnereth
Dor
Mt Tabor
ISSACHAR
Yarmuk River
Megiddo
Mt Gilboa
CANAANITES
MANASSEH
Jordan River
Shechem
Kanah River
Jabbok River
Joppa
Shiloh
GAD
AMMON
DAN WAS HERE IN THE DAYS OF SAMSON
EPHRAIM
Rabbath-Ammon
Gezer
Jabneel
DAN
BENJAMIN
Gilgal
Ekron
Ajalon
Ashdod
Jerusalem
Mt Nebo
Ashkelon
REUBEN
PHILISTINES
Gath
Dead Sea
Arnon River
Gaza
JUDAH
CHERETHITES
SIMEON
Beer-Sheba
MOAB
THIS IS THE HOWLING DESERT.
Zered Brook
WILDERNESS OF ZIN
THE ARABAH WADI
EDOM
WILDERNESS OF PARAN

Legend
• CITIES
—— KNOWN BOUNDARIES
--- PROBABLE BOUNDARIES
SCALE OF MILES
0 5 10 15 20 25 30

W. Strackfuss

V.

SAMSON — A BRAVE MAN WHO USED HIS STRENGTH FOOLISHLY

Samson, the son of Manoah of the tribe of Dan, was a man of tremendous physical strength. But in intelligence and behavior he was like a child. In his days, the chief enemy of the Israelites were the Philistines, from whose name "Palestine" is derived. The Philistines were strongly organized into a League of City-States: Ekron, Ashdod, Ashkelon, Gath and Gaza. Samson, despite his great strength, did not rally the tribes, nor even the people of his own tribe to throw off the yoke of the Philistines. He used his strength to get personal vengeance on those who did him harm. Yet, in spite of his many faults, Samson is admired because he had the courage to fight an enemy of Israel all alone. Later, the oppression of the Philistines compelled the Israelites to set up a king to unite them, and lead them against their common foe.

THE Israelites again did what was evil in the sight of the Lord; so this time the Lord delivered them into the power of the Philistines.

Samson's Birth is surrounded with Wonders

Now there was a certain man of Zorah, of the tribe of Dan, named Manoah. He and his wife had no children. But an angel of the Lord appeared to the woman and said:

"Behold, you have no children; but now you shall bear a son. Therefore, be careful not to drink any wine or strong drink, and do not eat anything unclean. For he is to be a Nazirite to the Lord, that is, no razor shall be used upon your son's head, for from birth the boy shall belong to God. And he shall begin to save Israel from the Philistines."

The woman bore a son, and he was named Samson. The boy grew up, and the Lord blessed him; and the spirit of the Lord moved within him.

Samson develops remarkable Strength

One day Samson went to the village of Timnah, and there saw a Philistine woman. When he came back, he told his father and mother:

"I saw a woman at Timnah, one of the Philistine women; get her as a wife for me."

They said to him:

"Is there no woman in your own tribe, or among all our people, that you must marry a wife from among the heathen Philistines?"

Samson answered his father:

"Get her for me; for she pleases me well."

Samson went with his father and mother to Timnah. And as they approached the vineyards of Timnah, a young lion came roaring toward him. The spirit of the Lord came upon Samson and, although he had nothing in his hand, he tore the beast in two as one tears a kid. He did not tell his father and mother what he had done, for they had gone a little ahead of him and did not see what had happened.

Samson continued on his way and talked with the woman he had seen at Timnah; and his parents made arrangements for the wedding.

After a while he returned to marry her; and he turned aside to see the carcass of the lion; and there was a swarm of bees in the body of the lion, and honey. He scraped the honey into his hands and ate it as he went. He came to his father and mother and he gave some to them, and they also ate it; but he did not tell them that he had scraped the honey out of the carcass of the lion.

Samson's Riddles

At the time of his marriage in Timnah, Samson gave a feast; for so bridegrooms used to do. When the Philistines saw him, they provided thirty companions to be with him. And Samson said to them:

"Let me now tell you a riddle. If you can tell me what it means within the seven days of the feast, I will give you thirty fine linen robes and thirty suits of clothes; but if you cannot tell me, then you shall give me thirty fine linen robes and thirty suits of clothes."

They said to him:

"Tell your riddle, that we may hear it."

And he said to them:

> "Out of the eater came forth food,
> And out of the strong came forth sweetness."

For three days they could not solve the riddle. On the fourth day they said to Samson's wife:

"Coax your husband to give us the answer, or we will burn you and your father's house. Did you invite us here to make us poor?"

Samson's wife wept on his shoulder and said:

"You only hate me and do not love me at all! You have told a riddle to my fellow-countrymen and not told me what it is."

He said to her:

"See, I have not told it to my father and mother, and shall I tell you?"

She complained before him as long as the feast lasted, and on the seventh day he told her. She then told the riddle's answer to her fellow-countrymen. On the seventh day before the sun went down, the men of the city said to him:

> "What is sweeter than honey,
> And what is stronger than a lion?"

And he said to them:

> "If with my heifer you did not plow,
> You had not solved my riddle now."

Samson became angry. He was suddenly given divine strength, and he went to Ashkelon and smote thirty of their men, and took the spoil from them, and gave the suits of clothes to those who had guessed the riddle. But he was still angry, and he went away to his father's house.

*Fearing the Philistines, the Men
of Judah gave Samson up to them*

The Philistines then went and camped in Judah and made a raid on the village of Lehi. And the men of Judah said:

"Why have you come up against us?"

They replied:

"We have come up to bind Samson, to do to him what he has done to us."

Then three thousand men of Judah went down to the cavern in the cliff of Etam where Samson was hiding, and said to him:

"Do you not know that the Philistines are rulers over us? What are you doing to us?"

"As they did to me," he replied, "so have I done to them."

They said:

"We have come down to bind you and take you prisoner, that we may turn you over to the Philistines."

Samson said to them:

"Swear to me that you will not attack me yourselves."

"No," they replied, "we will bind you fast and deliver you to them; but we will not kill you."

They bound him with two new ropes and took him up from the cliff.

When his captors took him to Lehi, the Philistines greeted him with loud shouts. Samson was again suddenly given divine strength, and the ropes that were on his arms became like flax that had been burned in the fire, and his bonds melted from his hands. He found a fresh jaw-bone of an ass and, using it as a weapon, he killed a thousand men. Then Samson said:

"With the jaw-bone of an ass have I piled them
        mass on mass;
A thousand warriors have I slain with the jaw-
        bone of an ass."

And Samson judged Israel in the period of the Philistines for twenty years.

*Delilah discovers that Samson's Strength
lies in his being a Nazirite*

After these happenings, Samson fell in love with a woman in
the valley of Sorek, whose name was Delilah. The lords of the
Philistines came to her and said:

"Entice him and find out where his great strength lies and
how we can overpower him, that we may bind him and torture
him. We will each give you eleven hundred pieces of silver."

Delilah then said to Samson:

"Tell me, where does your great strength lie and how can
you be bound helpless?"

Samson said:

"If they bind me with seven fresh bowstrings that have not
been dried, I shall become weak and be like any other man."

The lords of the Philistines brought her seven fresh bowstrings
that had not been dried, and she bound him with them. She had
men lying in wait in the inner room, but when she shouted to
him, "The Philistines are on you, Samson!" he snapped the bowstrings as easily as a piece of yarn is snapped when it touches the
fire; so that they did not find out the secret of his strength.

Delilah then said to Samson:

"You have deceived me and lied to me; now tell me, I beg
you, with what you can be bound fast."

He said:

"If they only bind me with new ropes that have not been used,
I shall become weak and be like any other man."

Delilah took new ropes and bound him with them. Then she
shouted to him, "The Philistines are upon you, Samson!" Again
men were lying in wait in the inner room; but he broke the ropes
from his arms like a thread.

Then Delilah said to Samson:

"Hitherto you have deceived me and lied to me; tell me now
truly with what can you be bound fast?"

He said:

"If you weave the seven locks of my head with the web."

While he was asleep she took the seven locks of his hair and
wove them with the web, and shouted to him, "The Philistines

are upon you, Samson!" And he awoke out of his sleep, and pulled away the pin of the beam, and the web.

She said to him:

"How can you say, 'I love you,' when you do not trust me? You have deceived me these three times and have not told me the secret of your great strength."

At last, after she had daily begged and urged him, he was so wearied to death, that he told her the secret.

"No razor has ever touched my head," he said to her, "for I have been a Nazirite (that is, I have belonged to God) from my birth. If I were to be shaved, my strength would leave me; I should become weak like any other man."

When Delilah learned from him his secret, she sent for the lords of the Philistines and said:

"Come at once, for he has told me all his secret."

The lords of the Philistines came to her and brought the money with them. After she had put Samson to sleep, she called for a man, and had him shave off the seven locks of Samson's head. Then she shouted, "The Philistines are upon you, Samson!" He awoke out of his sleep and thought, "I will get up as I have done at other times and shake myself free." But he did not know that the Lord had left him.

Then the Philistines came into his room and seized him, and put out his eyes. They brought him to Gaza and bound him with chains of brass, and then he was set to grinding corn in prison. But his hair began to grow again soon after his head had been shaved.

Samson meets his Death in the Temple
of Dagon, a God of the Philistines

Now, the lords of the Philistines had gathered to offer a great sacrifice to Dagon, their god, and to rejoice; for they said, "Our god has delivered Samson our enemy into our power." When the people saw Samson, they shouted in honor of their god:

"Our god has laid low our foe,
He who brought our country woe,
He who slew us with many a blow!"

When their hearts were merry they said:

"Call Samson, that he may make us sport!"

They brought Samson from the prison, and he made sport for them. They then placed him between the pillars of the Temple.

Samson said to the young man who held him by the hand:

"Place me so that I can feel the pillars on which the building rests, that I may lean against them."

The building was full of men and women; and all the lords of the Philistines were there; and on the roof there were about three thousand men and women who had been looking on while Samson made sport for them. Then Samson called on the Lord and said:

"O Lord God, remember me, I pray Thee, and give me strength only this once, O God, that by one act I may avenge myself on the Philistines for my two eyes."

Samson then took hold of the two middle pillars upon which the building rested, one with his right hand and the other with his left, and while he leaned against them, he said:

"Let me die with the Philistines!" Then he bent with all his might against the pillars and the Temple fell upon the lords and upon all the people who were in it.

Thus, the dead that he slew at his death were more than those that he slew in his life.

And his brothers and all his family came and took him away and buried him in the burying-place of Manoah, his father.

The Tribe of Dan moves North

In those days the tribe of the Danites sought for themselves a new territory to dwell in, for until then no land had been allotted them among the tribes of Israel. The Danites sent five men of their tribe, men of valor, from Zorah and Eshtaol, to explore and examine the country. The five men departed and came to Laish and saw the people living there in perfect security; for there was no one in the land, possessing authority, who might put them to shame in anything, and they were far from the Phoenicians and had no dealings with any man.

When these men returned to their brothers in Zorah and Eshtaol, their brothers said to them:

"What is your report?"

They said:

"Arise, let us go up to Laish! We have seen the land, and it is very good. Do not sit idle here. Let us lose no time in entering and occupying the land. You shall come to a people that is secure, and a land that is large. God has given it into your hand, a place where there is no want and which has everything that is in the earth."

Thereupon, six hundred fully armed men of the tribe of Dan set out from Zorah and Eshtaol. They marched up and encamped at Kiriath-jearim in Judah. From there they moved on to the hill-country of Ephraim. They came to Laish and captured it.

They settled in the city, and called it Dan, after the name of Dan their ancestor.   (*Judges 13–16, 18*)

רוּת

RUTH

THE story of Ruth, of Moab, is one of the most beautiful
in all literature. It describes the friendship, the love and
the devotion of two women — Ruth and Naomi. It praises
loyalty — loyalty to one's family. This loyalty plants in human
beings the seed of confidence and faith in each other. And out
of the seed of loyalty in human beings to each other grows the
sturdy loyalty of man to God. As long as men live, they will
thrill to the words of Ruth to Naomi:

"Entreat me not to leave thee,
And to return from following after thee:
For whither thou goest, I will go;
And where thou lodgest, I will lodge;
Thy people shall be my people,
And thy God my God . . ."

The story of Ruth is all the more charming because it presents
a sharp contrast with the stormy times of the Judges, in which
it is placed, times so dark with war and cruel deeds. But, there
were years in that period when the Israelites were not engaged in
war, when they harvested in their fields and toiled patiently in
their little villages. The plain folk often suffered famine and
sorrow and the separation of families, and even death. Without
faithfulness and loyalty to each other to sustain them, life would
have been far more difficult for them, perhaps even impossible.
The rich helped the poor, moreover, by leaving the corners of the
field and whatever fell out of the hands of the reapers for the poor
to gather, that is, to glean for themselves. The right to glean was
commanded by biblical law.

This story, so full of peace and beauty, glows with the sun-
light of Palestine. The sweet smell of the earth is in it. We can

see the wheat and the waving corn in the fields, and hear the gleaners sing as they wield their scythes in the brilliant sunshine.

The Book of Ruth is read in Synagogue during the Shabuot festival which celebrates the in-gathering of the first fruits of the harvest. It recalls the ancient days of our people on the soil of Palestine, and some of their quaint customs. At the end it tells how David, the ideal king of Israel, was descended from lovely Ruth, the Moabitess.

In the Bible, the Book of Ruth is found among "The Writings." It is placed here, however, since the background of its story is that of the period of the Judges.

I.

RUTH'S LOYALTY

IT came to pass in the days when the judges judged, that there was a famine in the land. A certain man of Beth-lehem in Judah took his wife and two sons to live in the land of Moab. His name was Elimelech and that of his wife Naomi, and his two sons were Mahlon and Chilion. After they had been living in Moab for some time, Elimelech died, and Naomi was left with her two sons. They married Moabite women, named Orpah and Ruth. About ten years later, Mahlon and Chilion both died, and Naomi was left without husband or children.

Naomi wishes to return to Judah.
Ruth's beautiful Words of Loyalty.

Bereft of her two children as well as of her husband, Naomi set out with her daughters-in-law from the land of Moab to return to Judah, for she had heard that the Lord had remembered His people and had given them food. As they were setting out on the journey to Judah, Naomi said to her daughters-in-law:

"Go, return each of you to the home of your mother. May the Lord be kind to you as you have been kind to the dead and to me. The Lord grant that each of you may find peace and happiness in the house of a new husband."

She kissed them good-bye; but they began to weep aloud and said to her:

"No, we will go back with you to your people."

But Naomi said:

"Go back, my daughters; why should you go with me? Can I still have sons who might become your husbands? Go back, my daughters, go your own way, for I am too old to have a husband. Even if I should say, 'I have hope,' even if I should have a husband tonight and should have sons, would you wait for them until they were grown up? Would you remain single for them? No, my daughters! I am sorry for you, for the Lord has afflicted me."

They again wept, and Orpah kissed her mother-in-law good-bye, but Ruth clung to her.

Naomi said:

"See, your sister-in-law is going back to her own people and to her own gods; go along with her!"

But Ruth answered:

"Entreat me not to leave thee, and to return from following after thee; for whither thou goest, I will go; and where thou lodgest, I will lodge; thy people shall be my people, and thy God my God; where thou diest, will I die, and there will I be buried. The Lord do so to me, and more also, if aught but death part thee and me."

When Naomi saw that Ruth had made up her mind to go with her, she ceased urging her to return.

They travelled on until they came to Beth-lehem in Judah at the beginning of the barley harvest.

RUTH

"... thy people shall be my people, and thy God my God ..." (*Ruth 1.16*)

see page 196

SAMUEL ANOINTS SAUL

"The Lord has anointed you to be a prince
over His people . . ."   (*I Samuel 10.1*)

see page 214

II.

THE MEETING OF RUTH AND BOAZ

Naomi was related through her husband to Boaz, a very wealthy man of the family of Elimelech.

One day Ruth, the Moabitess, said to Naomi:

"Let me now go to the fields and glean among the ears of corn after him in whose sight I shall find favor."

"Go, my daughter," said Naomi to her.

She went, and came and gleaned in the field after the reapers; and it was her good fortune to glean in that part of the field which belonged to Boaz.

Just then Boaz returned from Beth-lehem. He greeted the reapers and said to his servant who had charge of them:

"Whose maiden is this?"

The servant replied:

"It is the Moabite maiden who came back with Naomi from the land of Moab; and she said, 'Let me glean, I beg you, and gather sheaves after the reapers.' So she came, and has continued from the morning until now, and she has not rested a moment in the field."

Ruth the Gleaner

Then Boaz said to Ruth:

"Listen, my daughter. Do not glean in any other field nor leave this place, but stay here with my maidens. I have told the young men not to trouble you. When you are thirsty, go to the jars and drink of that which the young men have drawn."

Ruth bowed low and said to him:

"Why are you so kind to me, to take interest in one who comes from another land?"

Boaz replied:

"I have heard what you have done for your mother-in-law. May the Lord repay you for what you have done, and may you be fully rewarded by the God of Israel, under whose wings you have come to take refuge."

She said:

"I trust I may please you, my lord, for you have comforted me and spoken kindly to your servant, although I am not really equal to one of your own servants."

At noonday Boaz said to her:

"Come here and eat some of the food and dip your piece of bread in the sour wine."

She sat beside the reapers; and she ate until she had had enough and had some left. When she rose to glean, Boaz gave this order to his young men: "Let her glean even among the sheaves and do not disturb her."

So she gleaned in the field until evening. Then she beat out that which she had gleaned; and it was about a bushel of barley. She took it up and went into the city, where she showed her mother-in-law what she had gleaned. She also gave Naomi what she had left from her meal after she was satisfied.

Naomi said to Ruth:

"Where did you glean today and where did you work?"

Ruth told her where she had worked, and said:

"The name of the man with whom I worked today is Boaz."

Naomi said to her daughter-in-law:

"The man is a near relative of ours."

And Ruth, the Moabitess, said:

"Yes, he said to me, 'You must keep near my young men until they have completed all my harvest.' "

Naomi said to Ruth:

"It is best, my daughter, that you should go out with his maidens and that no one should find you in another field."

So Ruth gleaned with the maidens of Boaz until the end of the barley and wheat harvest; and she lived with her mother-in-law.

Naomi advises her Daugher-in-Law

And Naomi said to Ruth:

"My daughter, shall I not try to find a home for you where you will be happy and contented? Is not Boaz a relative of ours? This very night he is going to winnow barley on the threshing-floor. So you prepare yourself and put on your best clothes and go down to the threshing-floor; but do not make yourself known to Boaz until he is through eating and drinking. Then when he lies down, you mark the place where he lies."

Ruth said to her:

"I will do as you say."

She went to the threshing-floor and did just as her mother-in-law told her. When Boaz was finished eating and drinking and was in a happy mood, he went to lie down at the end of a heap of grain. Then Ruth came to him softly. And Boaz said:

"Who are you?"

She answered:

"I am Ruth your servant; take me in marriage, for you are a near relative." *

Boaz replied:

"May you be blessed by the Lord, my daughter. Have no fear; I will do for you all that you ask; for all my townsmen know that you are a good woman. Now it is true that I am a near relative; yet there is one nearer than I. If he will marry you, let him do so. But if he, being your nearest relative, will not marry you, then as surely as the Lord lives, I will do so."

When Ruth came to her mother-in-law, Naomi said:

"Is it you, my daughter?"

Ruth told Naomi all that the man had done for her. She said:

"He gave me these six measures of barley; for he said, 'Do not go to your mother-in-law empty-handed.' "

Naomi said:

"Wait quietly, my daughter, until you know how this will turn out, for Boaz will not rest unless he settles it all today."

---

*Ruth's appeal to Boaz was based on an ancient Israelite custom. The brother of a man who died without leaving an heir had to marry the widow. The purpose of this custom was to perpetuate the name of the dead man and to keep his property within the family. Although Boaz was not a brother, nor an immediate kinsman, he had the right to marry Ruth, because the kinsman more closely related to the dead husband refused to do so. This custom must be remembered, to understand why Naomi advised Ruth to go to Boaz.

III.

RUTH'S MARRIAGE TO BOAZ

Meanwhile Boaz went to the city gate and sat down. The near relative of whom Boaz had spoken came along.

Boaz called to him:

"Ho, sir! Turn aside and sit down here."

He turned aside and sat down.

And Boaz said to him:

"Naomi, who has come back from the country of Moab, is offering for sale a piece of land which belonged to our relative Elimelech, and I thought that I would lay the matter before you, and ask you to redeem it in the presence of these elders who sit here. If you will redeem it and so keep it in the family, do so; but if not, then tell me, that I may know; for no one but you has the right to redeem it, and I am next to you."

He said:

"I will redeem it."

Then Boaz said:

"On the day that you redeem the field from Naomi, you must also marry Ruth, the Moabitess, the widow of Mahlon, that a son may be born to bear his name and to receive this field."

Boaz buys the Field from Naomi

The near relative said:

"I cannot redeem it for myself, for fear that I should lose what already belongs to me. You may take my right of redeeming it as a relative, for I cannot do so."

Now in those days this was the custom in Israel concerning redeeming and concerning exchanging: to make a valid agreement between two men, the one drew off his shoe and gave it to the other.

So the near relative said to Boaz:

"Buy it for yourself."

And he drew off his shoe.

Then Boaz said to the elders and to the people present:

"You are my witnesses at this time that I have bought all that was Elimelech's and all that was Chilion's and Mahlon's from Naomi.   Moreover, I have secured Ruth, the Moabitess, the widow of Mahlon, to be my wife so that she may have a son who will receive this land and carry on Mahlon's name, and the name of the dead be not cut off from among the people. You are witnesses this day."

Then the elders and the people who were at the city gate said:

"We are witnesses. May the Lord make the woman who is coming into your house like Rachel and Leah, the two who built up the house of Israel, and make you also famous in Beth-lehem. May your house be like the house of Perez, whom Tamar bore to Judah, through the children which the Lord shall give you by this young woman."

Boaz married Ruth, and in time the Lord gave her a son.

And the women said to Naomi:

"Blessed be the Lord who has not left you at this time without a near relative, and may his name be famous in Israel. This child will bring back your strength and take care of you in your old age; for your daughter-in-law who loves you, who is worth more to you than seven sons, has a son!"

Ruth, the Ancestress of David

Naomi took the child in her arms and she became its nurse.

The women of the neighborhood also said:

"Naomi has a son!"

They named him Obed. And he became the father of Jesse, who was the father of David.

Because the great King David was descended from Ruth and Boaz, the story of his ancestry is given here.

> Perez* was the father of Hezron.
> Hezron was the father of Ram.
> Ram was the father of Amminadab.

*Perez was the son of Judah, who was the son of Jacob.

Amminadab was the father of Nahshon.
Nahshon was the father of Salmon.
Salmon was the father of Boaz.
Boaz was the father of Obed.
Obed was the father of Jesse.
And Jesse was the father of David.*

---

*Throughout the Bible, genealogies, lists of ancestral names like this one, are frequently found. The modern reader does not always find them interesting; but they furnish Bible scholars with much valuable information, and often help them to identify certain characters, trace obscure relationships, and in general to learn a great deal about the ancient world of the Bible. The Israelites were proud of their family histories, and loved to trace them back.

שְׁמוּאֵל א׳–ב׳

SAMUEL

HOW was the first Jewish kingdom established? Who were the men who laid its foundations?

When the period of the Judges closed, the tribes of Israel were divided one from the other; moreover, they were harshly oppressed by the Philistines. Each of the tribes fiercely loved its independence, and that very love of independence prevented them from becoming one, united nation.

The Philistines were a shrewd, strong, and well-led foe. They were united in a federation, and were well trained in the arts of war. They had set up a fortress in Gibeah, in the very heart of the tribe of Benjamin. They had disarmed the neighboring Jewish tribes; they forbade blacksmiths from making tools, and armormakers from forging weapons for Israel. They had even destroyed the religious capital of the tribes, the city of Shiloh.

How was Israel to overcome this powerful enemy and become a free people again?

At this time, God brought forward an inspiring religious leader in Samuel, the son of Elkanah. Samuel, unlike the judges before him, was not a hero of the sword. He was judge, teacher, and prophet to *all* Israel.

Samuel travelled from Ramah his birthplace to Mizpah, Gilgal, and other centers of worship, as a judge, to settle the people's disputes and quarrels. He assembled them in public places to discuss with them current Jewish affairs and to conduct religious worship. Samuel acted as priest, but he did not wait for the people to come to him; he went to seek out and teach the people. He spoke to them about their God, and their Covenant with God. He explained to them the Law of Moses, and the common religion which bound them together. He stirred up in them old memories of their eventful past.

Samuel was a prophet, or, as such men were called in those days, a "seer." The early seers were considered very much like fortune-tellers. They were consulted about articles that had been lost, animals that went astray, the success of journeys, the outcome of wars, and other important matters. But Samuel was more than that kind of seer. He was a teacher of righteousness who reminded the Israelites that their God was mainly concerned with their conduct. Samuel was a leader who wanted his people to enjoy a new and a better future.

What was most outstanding in Samuel was that he worked not for his tribe alone, but for *all* Israel. Since he could not do all this work himself, he trained a group of young men to become his assistants. Like Samuel, they travelled about the country, not singly, however, but in enthusiastic bands. They used novel methods to attract the attention and the interest of the people. They sang songs, chanted, and played on musical instruments. They told of the might and glory of the God of *all* Israel and called upon the people to worship Him, and in return He would deliver them from the power of the Philistines as He had delivered their ancestors from the Egyptians. When they sang, their enthusiasm grew until it reached such excitement that they began to dance.

These young men, through their preaching, and teaching and exhortations, aroused hope, courage and faith in the heart of the people. The people called them "*nebi'im*," prophets, for they believed that the spirit of God was within them. Samuel inspired these young men with his own patriotic feelings which they in turn communicated to the people. These religious patriots were the first of a great succession of religious leaders — the Hebrew prophets. They were truly heroes of the spirit, courageous teachers of the Covenant of God to *all* Israel, and mankind.

The Books of Samuel — First and Second Samuel — tell the story of those exciting days, and describe vividly how Samuel, King Saul and King David played heroic roles in the establishment of the first Jewish kingdom.

I.

THE BIRTH OF SAMUEL

IN the city of Ramah, in the hill country of Ephraim, lived a man named Elkanah. He had two wives: the name of one was Hannah, and that of the other Peninnah. Peninnah had children, but Hannah had no children.

The childless Hannah

Elkanah used to go each year to Shiloh to worship and sacrifice to the Lord of hosts. The priests of the Lord at Shiloh were Eli and his two sons, Hophni and Phinehas. When the day came for Elkanah to offer a sacrifice, he gave portions to his wife Peninnah and to all her sons and daughters; but because he loved Hannah, he gave her a double portion, although the Lord had given her no children. Peninnah vexed Hannah and mocked her, for she was childless. Elkanah did this year after year; but when Hannah went to the temple of the Lord, Peninnah so vexed her that she wept and would not eat. Elkanah said to her:

"Hannah, why do you weep? And why do you not eat? Why is your heart so troubled? Am I not better to you than ten sons?"

One day after they had eaten in Shiloh, Hannah went to the temple of the Lord; and Eli, the priest, was there beside the door-posts of the temple. Her heart was sad, and she prayed to the Lord and wept bitterly. She made this solemn promise:

"O Lord of Hosts!
If Thou wilt indeed look on my affliction,
And remember me, and not forget Thy servant,
But wilt give Thy servant a man-child,
Then I will give him unto Thee,
All the days of his life."

Hannah prayed a long time before the Lord, and Eli watched her mouth. She was speaking to herself; only her lips moved, but her voice could not be heard. Therefore, Eli thought that she was drunk, and he said to her:

"How long will you be drunken? Put away your wine, and leave the presence of the Lord."

But Hannah replied:

"No, my lord, I am an unhappy woman; I have not drunk wine nor any strong drink, but I have poured out my heart before the Lord. Do not think that your servant is a wicked woman, for I have spoken until now out of my great grief and vexation."

Eli said:

"Go in peace, and may God grant what you have asked of Him."

She said:

"May your servant find favor in your sight!"

Hannah went away. Her face was no longer sad.

Early the next morning she and her husband rose; and after they had worshipped the Lord, they returned to their home in Ramah.

Samuel is born

When the time had come, Hannah had a son and named him Samuel, saying, "I have asked him of the Lord."

Elkanah and all his house again went to offer the yearly sacrifice to the Lord. But Hannah did not go with him, for she said to her husband:

"When the child is weaned, I will bring him, that he may go to the Lord's temple and live there for ever."

Elkanah said to her:

"Do what seems best to you; wait until you have weaned him; only may the Lord help you to carry out your promise."

Hannah nursed her son until she weaned him. On a later pilgrimage she went with Elkanah to Shiloh.

She took Samuel with her, with three bullocks, a bushel of flour, and a bottle of wine, and brought him to the temple of the Lord. After the bullock had been sacrificed, Hannah brought the child to Eli and said:

"Oh, my lord, as surely as you live, I am the woman who stood by you here, praying to the Lord. For this child I prayed. The Lord has granted what I asked of Him. Therefore I have given him to the Lord; as long as he lives he belongs to the Lord."

Samuel serves the Lord

Elkanah and Hannah returned to their home in Ramah, but the boy remained at the temple to serve the Lord under the guidance of Eli the priest. Samuel, dressed in his linen robe, ministered before the Lord in the temple. His mother made him a little robe, and from year to year brought a new one to him when she came up with her husband to offer the yearly sacrifice. And the boy Samuel grew up in the temple of the Lord.

Now, the sons of Eli were wicked men. They cared nothing for the Lord, and they despised the offerings which were brought to the temple for Him. Eli was very old; and he heard what wrongs his sons were doing, and he said to them:

"Why do you do such things? For I hear of your wicked deeds from all this people. No, my sons; it is not a good report that I hear the people of the Lord spread about you."

They did not heed the voice of their father.

As the boy Samuel grew older, he won favor both with the Lord and also with men. He continued to serve the Lord under the guidance of Eli. In those days not many messages came from the Lord; there was no frequent vision.

Samuel's Vision

It came to pass one day, when Eli lay in his room — his eyes had begun to wax dim so that he could not see — while the lamp of God was still burning, and Samuel lay down to sleep in the temple of the Lord, wherein the Ark of God was kept, that the Lord called:

"Samuel! Samuel!"

"Here am I!" he said.

He ran to Eli and said:

"Here am I; for you called me."

"I did not call," Eli said, "go back and lie down."

He went and lay down. Then the Lord called again:

"Samuel! Samuel!"

Again Samuel arose and went to Eli and said:

"Here am I; for you called me."

"I did not call, my son," he said, "go back and lie down again."

Samuel did not yet know the Lord nor had a message from the Lord ever been given to him. So when the Lord called Samuel again the third time, he rose and went to Eli and said:

"Here am I; for you called me."

Then Eli perceived that the Lord was calling the boy. Therefore, he said to Samuel:

"Go, lie down; and if you are called again, you shall say, 'Speak, Lord; for Thy servant heareth.' "

Samuel went and lay down in his place. And the Lord came and called as at other times:

"Samuel! Samuel!"

Samuel answered:

"Speak, for Thy servant heareth."

The Lord said to Samuel:

"See, I am about to do a deed in Israel that will make the ears of everyone who hears it tingle. On that day I will do to Eli all that I have said that I would do to his house from the beginning even to the end; for they did not do what God commanded, and he did not stop them."

Samuel lay until morning; then he rose and opened the doors of the temple of the Lord. He feared to tell the vision to Eli. Then Eli called Samuel and said:

"Samuel, my son."

"Here am I," he answered.

"What was it," Eli asked, "that the Lord told you? Keep nothing, I beg you, from me! May God do to you whatever He will, if you hide anything from me of what He said to you!"

Samuel told him everything and hid nothing from him.

"It is the Lord," Eli said. "Let Him do what is good in His sight."

And Samuel grew, and the Lord was with him.

All Israel knew that Samuel was chosen to be a prophet of the Lord, since the Lord had revealed Himself to Samuel.

And the word of Samuel came to all Israel.   (*I Samuel 1–4*)

II.

ISRAEL'S RUTHLESS ENEMY —
THE PHILISTINES

IN those days the Philistines assembled their armies to war
against Israel. Israel went out against the Philistines to battle;
but they were defeated. And when the people returned to their
camp, the leaders of Israel said:

"Why has the Lord defeated us today before the Philistines?
Let us bring the Ark of the Covenant from Shiloh, that God may
go out with us and deliver us from our enemies."

The leaders sent to Shiloh, and they brought the Ark of the
Lord from the temple. When it came to the camp, all the Israelites shouted so loud that the earth rang. When the Philistines
heard the noise of the shouting, they asked:

"What does the noise of this great shouting in the camp of
the Israelites mean?"

When they learned that the Ark of the Lord had been brought
to the camp, they were afraid, for they said:

"God has come into their camp. Woe to us! for it has never
been so before. Be strong, and be real men, O Philistines, lest
you become slaves to the Israelites."

The Philistines capture the Ark

The Philistines fought, and Israel was defeated. The Israelites
fled in confusion, every man to his tent. The slaughter was very
great. The Ark of the Lord was taken; and the two sons of Eli,
Hophni and Phinehas, who had come along with those who had
brought the Ark, were slain.

A Benjaminite ran from the battle-line and came to Shiloh.
His clothes were torn and earth was on his head. When he arrived,
Eli was sitting by the gate watching the road, for his heart trembled
for the safety of the Ark of God.

When the man told the people of Shiloh of the defeat of the
Israelites, they all cried out; and when Eli heard the noise of the
outcry, he said:

"What is the meaning of this uproar?"

The man came quickly and told Eli:

"I am the man who came from the battle, for I fled from the army."

Eli asked:

"How did the battle go, my son?"

The messenger answered:

"Israel fled before the Philistines, and there has been a great slaughter, and your two sons are dead, and the Ark of the Lord has been taken."

When he mentioned the capture of the Ark of the Lord, Eli fell off his seat, his neck was broken and he died.

Samuel judges Israel

After their defeat by the Philistines, the Israelites grieved sorely. They turned to Samuel for his counsel and help. Samuel said to them:

"If you put away the foreign gods and Astartes from your midst, and turn to the Lord with all your heart and serve Him alone, He will deliver you out of the power of the Philistines."

The Israelites put away the Baals and the Astartes, and served the Lord alone. Then Samuel said:

"Gather all Israel to the city of Mizpah, and I will pray on your behalf to the Lord."

The Israelites gathered in Mizpah, made a sacrifice, and fasted on that day, saying:

"We have sinned against the Lord."

And Samuel judged the Israelites in Mizpah.

When the Philistines heard that the Israelites were gathered together in Mizpah, they again gathered to war against Israel. The Israelites heard of this, and they were afraid. And Samuel cried out to the Lord on behalf of Israel, and the Lord answered him. For just as he was burning up the sacrifice, the Philistines attacked Israel; but the Lord that day thundered with a great thunder upon the Philistines, and threw them into confusion; whereupon, Israel overcame them.

Samuel judged Israel all the days of his life. He went around each year to Beth-el, and Gilgal, and Mizpah; and he judged Israel in all those places. And he returned always to Ramah, for there was his home; there, too, he judged Israel; and he built there an altar for the Lord.

The People demand a King: Samuel's Warning

When Samuel was old, the elders of Israel came to him at Ramah, and they said to him:

"You are old, and your sons do not follow in your footsteps; now make a king for us to rule us like all the nations."

Then Samuel warned them and said:

"This will be the manner of the king who shall reign over you. He will take your sons and appoint them to be his horsemen, and to be his captains, and to plow his land, and to reap his harvest, and to make his instruments of war. He will take your daughters to be cooks and bakers. He will take your fields and your vineyards and your olive-groves. He will take the tenth of your flocks. And you shall become his servants."

But the people refused to follow the advice of Samuel; and they said:

"No, but there shall be a king over us. We want to be like all the nations, that our king may judge us and go out before us and fight our battles."

When Samuel heard the words of the people, he repeated them in the presence of the Lord. And the Lord said to Samuel:

"Hearken to the voice of the people, and give them a king."

(I Samuel 4–8)

III.

SAUL — FIRST KING OF ISRAEL

THERE was a man of Benjamin named Kish, a man of wealth, who had a son whose name was Saul. Saul was in the prime of life, strong and handsome. There was not a man among the Israelites more handsome than he was; he was a head taller than any of the people.

Samuel meets Saul

Now some asses of Kish had been lost. Kish told Saul to take one of the servants with him and go off in search of the asses. They went through the hill-country of Ephraim, but the asses were not there. They also went through the land of Benjamin, and failed to find them. When they reached the land of Zuph, Saul said to his servant:

"Come, let us return, lest my father cease caring for the asses and become anxious about us."

The servant said to him:

"Behold, now there is a man of God in this city, a man who is held in honor; whatever he says surely comes to pass. Let us go there; perhaps he can tell us concerning the journey we are on."

Saul replied to his servant:

"But, if we go, what shall we bring the man? Our sacks are empty of bread; there is no present to bring the man of God. What have we?"

The servant answered:

"I have with me a quarter of a silver shekel. I will give it to the man of God that he may tell us about our journey."

Saul said to his servant:

"Good, come and let us go!"

They went to the city where the man of God was.

As they went up the ascent to the city, they met some young women going out to draw water, and asked them:

"Is the seer here?"

They answered them:

"He is; behold, he is before you; he has just come into the city this moment, for the people have a sacrifice today on the hilltop. Go, then, for you will meet him this moment."

They went into the city. Just as they entered the gate, Samuel came out towards them, on his way up to the hilltop.

Now, the day before Saul arrived, the Lord had told Samuel:

"About this time tomorrow I will send you a man out of the land of Benjamin, and you shall anoint him to be prince over My people Israel; he shall save them from the power of the Philistines; for I have seen the suffering of My people, and their cry has reached Me."

When Samuel saw Saul, the Lord reminded him:

"Behold the man of whom I told you: this man shall have authority over My people."

Saul drew near to Samuel and said:

"Tell me, I beg you, where the seer's house is."

And Samuel answered Saul:

"I am the seer. Go up to the hilltop before me, for you shall eat with me today; in the morning I will let you go, and will tell you all that is in your mind. As for the asses that were lost three days ago, do not worry about them; they have been found. But the honor to lead Israel, to whom does it belong? Is it not for you and your father's house?"

Saul answered:

"Am I not a Benjaminite, of the smallest tribe in Israel? Is not my family the least of the tribe of Benjamin? Why then, do you speak to me in this manner?"

Samuel anoints Saul

Samuel took Saul and his servant and brought them into the dining-hall, where he made them sit at the head of the guests. And Saul ate with Samuel that day.

When, after having gone to the hilltop and sacrificed, they came down to the city, a couch was spread for Saul upon the roof, and he lay down to sleep.

At daybreak Samuel called to Saul:

"Arise, that I may send you on your way."

Saul arose, and he and Samuel went into the street. They were walking to the limits of the city, when Samuel said to Saul:

"Tell the servant to go on ahead; but stop here yourself, that I may cause you to hear the message from God."

Then Samuel took a vial of oil and poured it over Saul's head and kissed him, and said:

"The Lord has anointed you to be a prince over His people Israel. You shall rule over the Lord's people and save them from the hands of their enemies. This shall be the sign that the Lord has appointed you to be prince over His people; when you have departed from me today, you shall find two men at Rachel's tomb; and they will tell you, 'The asses you went to seek have been found; and your father has ceased to care about the asses but is anxious concerning you.'

"Later you shall come to the hill of God. As you come to the city, you will meet a band of prophets coming down from the high-place with lutes, drums, flutes and lyres playing before them; and they will prophesy. And the spirit of the Lord will suddenly inspire you, and you shall prophesy along with them and become a changed man."

What happened to Saul

After Saul had left Samuel, God changed his spirit. And all those signs occurred that day.

When he reached the hill, a band of prophets met him. The spirit of God inspired him, and he prophesied along with them. When the people who knew him before saw him prophesying along with the prophets, they said to each other:

"What has come over the son of Kish? Is Saul also among the prophets?"

And when he had finished prophesying, Saul went home.

Saul's uncle asked him and his servant:

"Where have you been?"

"To seek the asses," he answered, "and when we saw that they were not found, we came to Samuel."

Saul's uncle asked:

"Tell me, I beg you, what Samuel said to you."

Saul said:

"Why, he told us plainly that the asses had been found!"

But about the matter of the kingdom, of which Samuel spoke, Saul said nothing.

Saul, unknown to the Israelites,
meets the Test of military Leadership
by defeating the Ammonites

About a month later, Nahash the Ammonite came and besieged the town of Jabesh in Gilead, and the men of Jabesh-gilead said to Nahash:

"Make a treaty with us and we will serve you."

Nahash the Ammonite replied:

"I will make a treaty with you on this condition, that every man's right eye be gouged out. So shall I set disgrace upon all Israel."

The elders of Jabesh then said to him:

"Give us seven days that we may send messengers through all the land of Israel. If there is no one to deliver us, then we will come out to you."

The messengers came to Saul's town of Gibeah and told their story to the people. The people wept aloud; and as Saul was coming home behind the oxen from the field, he said:

"What ails the people, why are they weeping?"

They told him what the men of Jabesh had said. The spirit of the Lord inspired Saul, when he heard this; and his anger was kindled greatly. He took a pair of oxen, and cut them in pieces, and sent the pieces through all the land of Israel by messengers, saying:

"Whoever does not come forward after Saul and Samuel, so shall it be done to his oxen!"

The dread of the Lord fell upon the people, and they came out as one man. Saul told the messengers to tell the men of Jabesh:

"You will be rescued tomorrow by the time the sun grows hot."

The messengers went and told the men of Jabesh, and they were glad.

The men of Jabesh then said to Nahash:

"We will come out to you tomorrow, and you can do to us whatever seems good to you."

On the morrow Saul divided the people into three companies. They made their way into the camp of the enemy early in the morning and fought against the Ammonites until noon. The survivors were so scattered that no two Ammonites were left together.

Saul is elected King by the People.
Samuel demands Obedience to the God
of Israel from the King and People.

The people then went to Gilgal and there, before the Lord, made Saul their king.

Samuel said to the people:

"I have listened to your voice, in all that you said to me, and I have made a king over you. Now, the king walks before you; but as for me, I am old and gray-headed, and my sons are grown-up men among you. I have walked before you from my youth to this day. Here I am! Testify against me in the presence of the Lord and of His anointed king! Whose ox have I taken? Or whose animal have I taken? Whom have I mistreated? Or whom have I cheated? From whom have I accepted a bribe to blind my eyes with it? Testify against me, and I will restore it to you."

The people cried out:

"You have never cheated us, nor oppressed us, nor accepted a bribe from anyone."

Samuel said:

"The Lord is witness and the anointed king is witness this day against you, that you have not found anything to accuse me of!"

And they said, "He is witness."

Samuel continued:

"Behold, the Lord has set a king over you! If you will reverence the Lord, and serve Him, and hearken to His voice and not rebel against the commandments of the Lord, if both you and the king who reigns over you are followers of the Lord your God, well and good. But if you will not hearken to the voice of the

Lord, if you rebel against the commandments of the Lord, then shall the hand of the Lord be against you, and against your fathers. Only fear the Lord, and serve Him in truth with all your heart. If you persist in doing wrong, both you and your king will be swept away."

Thus did Samuel explain to the people the methods of the kingdom; he wrote them on a scroll in the presence of the Lord.

Then all the people shouted aloud:

"Long live the king!"

And they offered sacrifices there to the Lord; and Saul and all the men of Israel were very happy. (*I Samuel 9–12*)

IV.

SAUL — THE REJECTED

THE Philistines gathered once more to fight against Israel with thirty thousand chariots, six thousand cavalry, and infantry as numerous as the sand on the seashore. They assembled and encamped at Michmas, east of Beth-aven. When the men of Israel saw they were in great danger, the people hid themselves in caves, in thickets and in pits. Some crossed the Jordan into the land of Gad and Gilead. Saul was still at Gilgal, and the people were deserting him, because of their fear of the outcome.

Saul's Disobedience

Saul waited seven days, according to the time set by Samuel, but the prophet did not come to Gilgal; and meantime the people scattered from him. Saul said:

"Bring the sacrifices here to me!"

He offered up the sacrifice.

No sooner had he finished offering the sacrifice than Samuel arrived.

Saul went to meet and greet him, but Samuel said:

"What have you done?"

Saul answered:

"I saw that the people scattered from me, and that you had not come at the time set, and that the Philistines had gathered at Michmas. I thought that the Philistines would come down upon us at Gilgal, and I had not sought the favor of the Lord. I forced myself therefore, and offered the sacrifice."

Then Samuel said to Saul:

"You have done foolishly. Had you obeyed the command of the Lord your God, then the Lord would have established your kingdom over Israel for ever. But now your kingdom shall not continue. The Lord has sought a man after His own mind, and He has appointed him to be prince over His people, because you have not obeyed what the Lord commanded you."

Then Samuel arose and went on his way from Gilgal.

Jonathan's brave Deed

Saul now numbered the people who were present with him, about six hundred men. Saul, and Jonathan his son, and the people with them remained at Gibeah; but the Philistines encamped at Michmas.

One day Jonathan said to his young armor-bearer:

"Come, let us go over to the Philistines' garrison on the other side."

He did not tell his father. Nor did the people know that Jonathan had gone.

Between the passes where Jonathan planned to go over to the Philistines' garrison, there was a rocky crag on the one side and a rocky crag on the other.

When the two of them showed themselves to the Philistines' garrison, the Philistines said:

"Behold, the Israelites are creeping out of their holes where they had hidden themselves!"

The men of the garrison called out to Jonathan and his armor-bearer:

"Come to us, and we will show you something!"

Then Jonathan said to his armor-bearer:

"Come, follow behind me; for the Lord has put them into the hand of Israel."

Jonathan climbed up on his hands and feet, his armor-bearer after him. About twenty of the men of the garrison fell before Jonathan and his armor-bearer. This caused a panic to spread in the camp of the Philistines.

Saul's watchman in Gibeah noticed the camp of the Philistines swaying hither and thither, and Saul said to the troops with him:

"Search, and see who has gone from us!"

When they searched, Jonathan and his armor-bearer were not to be found. Meanwhile the tumult in the camp of the Philistines went on and increased. Then Saul and all the troops with him gathered together and went into battle. There was such confusion that every Philistine's sword was turned against his fellow, and they were soon in flight. When all the men of Israel who were hiding in the hill-country of Ephraim heard that the Philistines had fled, they too pursued them. Thus the Lord saved Israel that day.

The People plead for Jonathan

On that day Saul held the people to strict obedience with an oath:

"Cursed be the man who eats any food until it be evening, and I be avenged on my enemies."

So none of the people tasted food. And all the people came into the forest; and there was honey on the ground. But no man put his hand to his mouth, for the people feared the oath. But Jonathan had not heard his father give that command to the people. And he put forth the end of the rod that was in his hand and dipped it in a honeycomb; he put the honey in his mouth; and his eyes brightened. Then one of the people spoke and said:

"Your father charged the people with an oath, saying: Cursed be the man who eats food this day."

Jonathan said:

"I am quite ready to die."

Then Saul said, "Jonathan, you shall surely die."

But all the people said to Saul:

"Shall Jonathan die? Jonathan who won this great victory for Israel? Never! As the Lord lives, not a hair of his head shall fall to the ground; for he has conquered by God's help this day."

Thus the people saved Jonathan from being put to death.

Destroy the Amalekites!

Samuel said to Saul:

"The Lord sent me to anoint you king over His people, Israel. Now listen to the voice of the Lord. This is what the Lord of hosts says, 'I intend to punish the Amalekites for what they did to Israel when they opposed them on their way up from Egypt. Go and defeat the Amalekites and Agag their king; destroy Agag and all that belongs to him.' "

Saul summoned his troops. And Saul smote the Amalekites with the edge of the sword. But Saul and the people spared Agag their king, and the best of the sheep and of the oxen, and the lambs, though they destroyed whatever other property was common and worthless.

A message from the Lord came to Samuel:

"I am sorry that I set up Saul to be king, for he has turned back from following Me; he has not obeyed My commandments."

Samuel grieved, and he cried to the Lord all night.

In the morning Samuel arose early and went to meet Saul. When they met, Saul said:

"May the Lord bless you! I have carried out the commandment of the Lord."

"Then," Samuel asked, "what is this bleating of sheep in my ears? What is this lowing of oxen that I hear?"

And Saul said:

"They have taken them from the Amalekites; the people spared the best of the sheep and the oxen to sacrifice to the Lord your God; the rest we have utterly destroyed."

"Silence!" said Samuel, "let me tell you what the Lord told me this night."

"Speak on," said Saul.

Samuel continued:

"Though you may be little in your own sight, are you not head of the tribes of Israel? The Lord anointed you king over Israel, and the Lord sent you on a mission to destroy the Amalekites. Why then, have you not obeyed the voice of the Lord? Why have you taken the spoil and done wrong in the eyes of the Lord?"

Saul said to Samuel:

"I have obeyed the voice of the Lord. I have gone on the mission which the Lord sent me. I have caught Agag, king of Amalek, and I have destroyed the Amalekites. But the people took the spoil, the sheep and oxen, to sacrifice to the Lord your God."

Then Samuel said:

"Does the Lord find delight in burnt-offerings and sacrifices, as He does in obedience to His word? Behold, to obey is better than sacrifice, and to hearken than the fat of rams. Because you have rejected the word of the Lord, He has also rejected you from being king."

The rejected King

Saul then said to Samuel:

"I have done wrong; I have broken the command of the Lord and your instructions. It was because I was afraid of the people, that I did what they demanded. Pray pardon my sin; come back with me that I may worship the Lord."

But Samuel said:

"No, I will not return with you, for you have rejected the word of the Lord, and the Lord has rejected you from being king over Israel."

As Samuel turned about to go away, Saul laid hold on the skirt of his robe, and it tore. And Samuel said to him:

"The Lord has torn the kingdom of Israel from you, and has given it this day to another, who is a better man than you."

Samuel then went to Ramah; and Saul returned to his house in Gibeah. And Samuel never saw Saul again until the day of his death; but Samuel mourned for Saul. And the Lord repented that He had made Saul king over Israel.   (*I Samuel 13–15*)

V.

DAVID — THE SHEPHERD BOY

*Samuel secretly anoints David
to be King over Israel*

THE Lord said to Samuel:
"How long will you mourn over Saul, since I have rejected him from being king over Israel? Fill your horn with oil and go to Jesse in Beth-lehem; for I have provided for Myself a king among his sons."

Jesse had eight sons, and David was his youngest.

Samuel did what the Lord told him. When he arrived at Beth-lehem, the elders of the town trembled as they came forward to meet him. They said:

"Does your visit mean peace?"

"Yes," he replied, "I have come to sacrifice to the Lord. Sanctify yourselves and come with me to the sacrifice."

He sanctified Jesse and his sons and invited them to the sacrifice.

Then Jesse caused seven of his sons to walk past Samuel. And Samuel said to Jesse:

"The Lord has not chosen these."

Samuel asked Jesse:

"Are all your sons here?"

He answered:

"There remains yet the youngest, but he is a shepherd tending the sheep."

"Send and bring him," said Samuel, "for we will not sit down to our banquet until he is here."

Jesse sent for David, and he came home. He was a lad with fine eyes, a ruddy complexion, and was handsome of appearance. Then the Lord said:

"Arise, and anoint him; this is the man!"

Samuel took the horn of oil and anointed him; and from that day the spirit of the Lord inspired David strongly. Then Samuel rose, and went to Ramah.

Saul, rejected by Samuel, is troubled.
Gloom and Bitterness grow within him.

Now the spirit of the Lord had departed from Saul, and an evil spirit troubled him. Saul's servants said to him:

"An evil spirit is troubling you. Let your servants find a skillful player on the harp; then whenever the evil spirit comes on you, he shall play music, and you shall be well."

Saul answered:

"Find me a man who plays well, and bring him to me."

One of them said:

"I have seen a son of Jesse of Beth-lehem who is a skillful player, a brave man, a good soldier, prudent in affairs, a man of good presence, and the Lord is with him."

Saul sent messengers to Jesse, requesting:

"Send me your son David, who is with the sheep."

Jesse loaded a donkey with bread, and a bottle of wine, and a kid, and sent them by his son David to Saul. And when David came to Saul and presented himself, Saul loved him greatly and made him his armor-bearer. Then Saul sent to Jesse, and said:

"Let David remain in my service, I beg you, for I am well pleased with him."

Whenever the evil spirit came upon Saul, David would take the harp and play; so Saul found relief; then all would be well, and the evil spirit would depart from him.

The Philistines attack again.
David accepts Goliath's Challenge.

The Philistines again gathered their forces for war, and they camped between Socoh and Azekah. Saul and the men of Israel assembled and pitched camp in the valley of Elah; and they were prepared for battle against the Philistines.

The Philistines stood on one side of a hill, and the Israelites stood on a hill opposite; and there was a valley between them. From the ranks of the Philistines, Goliath of Gath, one of their champions, walked forward. He was about ten feet tall. He had a bronze helmet on his head, and he wore a bronze breastplate of scales, weighing about two hundred pounds. The shaft of his spear was like a weaver's beam. And his shield-bearer went before him.

Goliath stood and shouted to the forces of Israel:

"Why set up in line of battle? Am I not a Philistine, and you servants of Saul? Choose a man for yourselves, and let him come down to me. If he be able to fight with me and kill me, then we will be your slaves; but if I overcome him and kill him, then you shall be our slaves and serve us."

And the Philistine added:

"I taunt the forces of Israel today! Give me a man, that we may fight together!"

When Saul and the Israelites heard those words of the Philistine, they were dismayed, and greatly afraid. For forty days the Philistine champion came forward and issued his challenge, morning and evening.

Then David said to Saul:

"Let no man's courage fail him; your servant will go and fight this Philistine."

Saul said:

"You are not able to fight this Philistine; you are only a youth, and he has been a warrior from his youth."

But David replied:

"Your servant kept his father's sheep; and when a lion or a bear came and seized a sheep from the flock, I went out after him and struck him and rescued the sheep from his mouth; when he turned against me, I caught him by his throat and killed him with a blow. Your servant has killed both lion and bear. And this heathen Philistine shall be like one of them, for he has taunted the armies of the living God. The Lord who saved me from the paw of the lion and the paw of the bear will save me from the hand of this Philistine."

Then said Saul to David:

"Go, and may the Lord be with you."

David conquers Goliath

Saul clad David with his own apparel, and he put a bronze helmet on his head, and he clad him in a coat of mail. David buckled his sword over his apparel, and tried to walk, but he could not, for he was not used to such armor. Then David said to Saul:

"I cannot go with these; I am not used to them."

David took them off. He took his club in his hand, and chose five smooth stones out of the brook and put them in the shepherd's bag; he took his sling in his hand; and he drew near to the Philistine.

When the Philistine looked at the champion of the Israelites and saw David, he despised him; for he was but a youth. The Philistine said to David:

"Am I a dog that you come against me with a club?"

And the Philistine cursed David by his god. And he said:

"Come to me, and I will give your flesh to the birds of the air and the beasts of the field."

David answered the Philistine:

"You come to me with a sword and a spear and a javelin, but I come to you in the name of the Lord of hosts and of the God of the armies of Israel whom you have insulted this day. The Lord will deliver you into my hands. And all the world will know that Israel has a God, and all here present know that the Lord does not save by sword and spear; for the battle is the Lord's, and He will put you into our hand."

When the Philistine started forward to attack David, David hurried forward to meet the Philistine. David put his hand into his bag, and took out a stone, put it in his sling and slung it; and it struck the Philistine on his forehead, and he dropped on his face to the ground. David ran over to where the Philistine had fallen, and drawing his sword from its sheath, he slew Goliath.

When the Philistines saw their champion dead, they fled.

Then the armies of Saul raised their battle-cry and pursued the Philistines as far as the entrance to Gath and the gates of Ekron.　(*I Samuel 16, 17*)

VI.

SAUL AND DAVID

*Saul, jealous of David, begins to
fear, then to hate him. David
weds the Princess Michal.*

WHEN the Israelites and David returned from dispersing and slaying the Philistines, the women came out of the cities of Israel, singing and dancing, to meet King Saul with cries of rejoicing and with cymbals. As they danced, the women sang:

"Saul has slain his thousands,
And David his ten thousands."

Saul was very angry, for their words displeased him; and he said:

"To David they ascribe ten thousands, but to me only thousands; what else does he lack but the kingdom itself?"

Saul eyed David from that day forward. He was afraid of David, and he did not let him stay near him. He removed David from him, and made him commander over a thousand men; and David went out and came in before the people. In all that he did David had great success; and the Lord was with him. When Saul saw that David had great success, he became still more afraid of him. But all Israel and Judah loved David; and they saw him going about and attending to his own business.

Michal, Saul's daughter, was in love with David; and they told Saul and it pleased him. For Saul thought, "I will give her to him in order to ensnare him, that the Philistines may capture him."

Saul commanded his servants to speak privately with David and tell him: "The king is delighted with you, and all his servants love you; now, then, become the king's son-in-law "

When Saul's servants told this to David, he said:

"Do you think it a light matter for a poor man, a man of no position, to become the king's son-in-law?"

When Saul's servants told him David's answer, he replied:

"You must tell David that the king does not desire any dowry for the bride except the proof that he has killed a hundred Philistines." Saul hoped to make David fall by the hand of the Philistines.

David went with his men and killed two hundred Philistines. Thereafter, Saul gave him his daughter Michal as his wife; and Michal loved David. Saul saw and knew that the Lord was with David; and Saul became still more afraid of David, and was David's enemy continually.

Jonathan and David become Friends. Saul's Fear of David increases. He begins to persecute David. Jonathan's Friendship put to the Test.

Saul thereupon ordered Jonathan and his officers to kill David. But Jonathan and David had become fast friends; and Jonathan loved David as himself. Jonathan made a compact with David, and he stripped himself of his robe and gave it to David, together with his sword and his bow. So Jonathan told David:

"My father Saul seeks to slay you. Now, take care tomorrow morning, and stay in some secret place and hide yourself. I will go out and stand beside my father in the field where you are; and I will speak with my father about you and if I learn anything, I will tell you."

Jonathan spoke favorably of David to Saul his father.

"Let not the king sin against his servant David," Jonathan said, "for he has not wronged you. He has acted most faithfully to you. Why, then, will you sin against innocent blood to slay David for no reason?"

Saul listened to Jonathan and solemnly promised:

"As the Lord lives, he shall not be put to death."

Jonathan called David, and Jonathan told him all this; and Jonathan brought David to Saul, and David attended him as before.

Then war broke out again; and David went out and fought with the Philistines and defeated them with heavy losses. An evil spirit came upon Saul, as he sat in his house with his spear in his hand. While David was playing music nearby, Saul tried to pin David to the wall with the spear; but David slipped away so that Saul drove the spear into the wall; and David fled and escaped that night.

Saul sent messengers to David's house to watch him and to slay him in the morning. But Michal warned him saying:

"If you do not save your life tonight, you will be a dead man tomorrow."

Michal let David down through the window; and he went, and fled, and escaped. When Saul sent messengers to seize David, Michal said:

"He is sick."

Saul sent back the messengers to see David, with the command: "Bring him here to me in his bed, that I may slay him."

When the messengers returned, there was the household god which Michal had put in David's bed with a pillow of goat's hair under its head. Saul said to Michal:

"Why have you deceived me like this, and let my enemy go free?"

Michal answered Saul:

"He said to me, 'Let me go! Why should I slay you?'"

So David escaped; and he came to Samuel at Ramah, and told him all that Saul had done. Then he and Samuel went and dwelt in Naioth.

David appeals to Jonathan.
Jonathan's Love for David.

Later David returned from Naioth and came to Jonathan, to whom he said:

"What have I done? What is my iniquity? What wrong have I done to your father, that he seeks my life?"

"Far from it," replied Jonathan, "you shall not be put to death. My father does nothing, great or small, without letting me know; and why should my father hide this from me? He surely will not."

But David answered:

"Your father knows well that you are fond of me, so he says to himself, 'Jonathan must know nothing of this, lest it grieve him.'

But as the Lord lives and as you live, there is but a step between me and death."

Jonathan then said:

"What do you desire me to do for you?"

David answered:

"Tomorrow is the new moon festival, when I should sit at the table with Saul. Let me go and hide myself in the field until evening. If your father misses me, then say, 'David asked permission of me to go to Beth-lehem, his city, for the yearly sacrifice is there for all his family.' If he says, 'Good,' then it is well with your servant; but if he be angry, then know that he is determined to harm me."

Jonathan said:

"Far be it from you! If I should learn that my father is determined to do you harm, I will tell you."

When David said to Jonathan:

"Who will tell me if your father answers you roughly?" Jonathan replied:

"I swear by the Lord, the God of Israel! About this time tomorrow I will find out how my father feels. I will let you know that you may get away safely. May the Lord be with you as He has been with my father. And may you, not only while I live, show me the kindness of the Lord; but, if I should die, you must never cease to be kind to my family."

Jonathan caused David to make a solemn promise to him, because he loved him; for Jonathan loved David as much as he loved his own life.

And Jonathan said to David:

"Tomorrow is the new moon festival; and you will be missed, for your seat will be empty. On the third day, when you will be greatly missed, go to the place where you hid yourself when my father attacked you, and sit down there beside the stone, Ezel. I will shoot three arrows on one side of it, as though I shot at a mark. I will send the boy, saying, 'Go, find the arrows!' If I call to the boy, 'See, the arrows are on this side of you; pick them up,' then come forward; all is peace with you, and as the Lord lives, there is nothing to fear. But if I tell the boy, 'See, the arrows are beyond you,' then go, for the Lord sends you away. And as for the promise you and I have made, the Lord is witness between you and me for ever."

So David hid himself in the field.

When the new moon festival came, the king sat down at the table to eat. The king sat in his place as at other times, on his seat beside the wall; and Jonathan sat opposite him, and Abner, his general, sat beside Saul; but David's place was empty. Saul, however, did not say anything.

But on the next day, when David's place was again empty, Saul said to Jonathan:

"Why has not the son of Jesse come to the table, yesterday or today?"

Jonathan answered:

"David earnestly asked leave of me to go to Beth-lehem, for he said, 'Let me go, for we have a family sacrifice in the city, and my brothers have commanded me to be there.' Therefore, he has not come to the king's table."

Saul's anger was aroused against Jonathan, and he said to him:

"You son of rebellion! Do I not know that you have chosen the son of Jesse as your friend, to your own shame and the shame and disgrace of your mother? As long as the son of Jesse lives on the earth, you shall not be safe nor your kingdom. Send now and bring him to me, for he deserves to die."

Jonathan answered Saul his father and said:

"Why should he be put to death? What has he done?"

Saul cast his spear at him. Jonathan then knew that his father had determined to put David to death.

Next morning, Jonathan went out to the field, at the time appointed with David, and a little boy was with him. He said to the boy:

"Run, and find the arrows which I shoot."

As the boy ran, he shot an arrow beyond him. When the boy came to the place where the arrow which Jonathan had shot lay, Jonathan called to him:

"Is not the arrow beyond you? Make speed, hasten, stay not!"

Jonathan's boy gathered up the arrows and came to his master.

The boy knew nothing about the signal. Only Jonathan and David understood.

Jonathan gave his weapons to the boy and told him to carry them to the city.

As soon as the boy had gone, David arose from beside the stone, Ezel, and bowed himself to the ground. And they kissed one another, and they wept.

Jonathan then said:

"Go in peace! As for what we have sworn in the name of the Lord, the Lord shall be between me and you, and between my descendants and your descendants for ever."

David departed.

And Jonathan went to the city.   (*I Samuel 18–21*)

VII.

DAVID — REFUGEE FROM SAUL

After David had escaped from Saul's attempt to kill him, he had to live the life of an outlaw for many years and was compelled to flee from place to place. Saul was kept informed by spies where David was, and, whenever he was free from his wars against the Philistines, Saul pursued David. In the Cave of Adullam, David gathered together many discontented men, rebels and outcasts, and organized them into a loyal band of followers. David during these years of his outlawry showed himself to be a just, able and brave leader. In spite of Saul's enmity against him, David was always generous to Saul, and though he had the opportunity many times to kill Saul, David refused to harm "the Lord's anointed" king.

DAVID fled to the Cave of Adullam. When his brothers and all his father's house heard it, they went there to him. Everyone who was in distress, and everyone who was in debt, and everyone who was discontented, gathered round him. He became their leader; and he had about four hundred loyal followers.

David went to Mizpeh, in Moab, and said to the king of Moab:

"Let my father and mother be with you, till I see what God will do for me."

He brought his parents and left them with the king of Moab, and they stayed with him all the time that David remained in his stronghold.

The Priests of Nob

One day Saul was seated in Gibeah under a tamarisk-tree, with his spear in his hand, and his officers were standing around him. And Saul said to his officers:

"Hear now, you Benjaminites! Will the son of Jesse give each of you fields and vineyards, or will he make you all commanders of regiments and captains of companies — that you have all schemed against me? No one tells me when my son makes a compact with the son of Jesse; no one has pity enough for me to tell me that my son has stirred up my servant to be my enemy, as he is this day!"

Then Doeg the Edomite, the driver of Saul's mules, said:

"I saw the son of Jesse come to the village of Nob, to Ahimelech the son of Ahitub. As a priest, he consulted the Lord for him, and gave him food, and gave him the sword of Goliath the Philistine."

The king sent for Ahimelech the priest, and for his father's house, the priests of Nob. They came to the king, and Saul said:

"Why have you conspired against me, you and the son of Jesse? You gave him bread and a sword, you consulted God for him, that he should rise against me as an enemy, which he does this day."

Ahimelech replied:

"Who of all your officers is so trusted as David, the king's son-in-law, the captain of your bodyguard, and honored in your house? Is this the first time I have consulted God for him? No! Let not the king accuse his servant or any of my father's house; your servant has not the slightest knowledge of this affair."

The king then said:

"Die you must, Ahimelech, you and all your father's house!"

And the king said to his guard:

"Turn, and slay the priests of the Lord! They were in league with David too; they knew he was running away, and they never told me!"

But the king's officers would not lift their hands to strike down the priests of the Lord. So the king said to Doeg the Edomite:

"Turn, and strike the priests down!"

Doeg the Edomite turned, and he struck the priests down, and slew that day eighty-five men. He also captured Nob, the city of the priests, giving no quarter, but killing men and women, children and infants, oxen, donkeys and sheep.

Only Abiathar, a son of Ahimelech, escaped. He fled to David, and when he told David that Saul had slain the priests of the Lord, David said to him:

"I knew that day, when Doeg the Edomite was there, that he would surely tell Saul; I am to blame for the death of all your father's house. Stay with me, do not fear; whoever seeks your life must seek my life; you are in safety with me."

In the Wilderness of En-gedi

When he returned from his pursuit of the Philistines, Saul was told that David was in the Wilderness of En-gedi. Saul took three thousand chosen men and went to seek David and his men. On his way he came to some sheepfolds, where there was a cave. And Saul went inside the cave.

David and his men were seated in the innermost parts of the cave; and David's men whispered to him:

"Behold the day on which the Lord promised that He would put your enemy in your power and let you do what you like to him."

But David said:

"The Lord forbid that I should do this to Saul, to the Lord's anointed! — that I should lift my hand against him, when he is the Lord's anointed!"

David checked his men and would not let them attack Saul. But David got up and secretly cut off the skirt of Saul's robe, though afterwards David was sorry because he had done so.

Saul left the cave and was going on his way, when David, who had followed him, called to Saul:

"My lord, the king!"

When Saul looked back, David bowed to the ground, and said:

"Why do you listen to men who tell you that David seeks to injure you? You see for yourself today that the Lord put you in my power inside the cave; but I refused to kill you, I had mercy on you; I said, 'I will not lift my hand against Saul, for he is the Lord's anointed.' Moreover, my father, look here at the skirt of your robe in my hand! I cut off the skirt of your robe, and I did not kill you. May the Lord judge between you and me! May the Lord avenge me upon you! But my hand shall never strike you!"

When David had finished, Saul said:

"Is this your voice, David my son?"

And Saul wept aloud.

"You are more righteous than I," he said to David. "You have done good to me, but I have done evil to you. Now I know that you shall surely be king, and that the kingdom of Israel is to be yours. Promise me then, by the Lord, that you will not cut off my descendants after me, that you will not destroy my name out of my father's house."

David promised this to Saul.

And Saul went home; but David and his men returned to his stronghold.

Abigail, the Woman of good Sense

David now went into the wilderness of Maon, where Nabal, a very wealthy man, lived with Abigail, his wife. He was rough and ill-mannered, while she was beautiful and sensible. He owned three thousand sheep, that he sheared at Carmel, and a thousand goats.

When David learned in the wilderness that Nabal was shearing his sheep, he sent ten of his young men with the command:

"Get you up to Carmel, and go to Nabal's house, and greet him in my name. You shall say to him and to his family: 'Peace be to you, and peace to your family, and peace be to all you have. I have heard that you have sheep-shearers. Your shepherds have been with us, and we did not harm them, and nothing of theirs was missing all the while they were in Carmel. Ask your young men, and they will tell you. Let my young men, therefore, find favor with you, for we have come on a feast day. Give also whatever you have at hand in the way of food to your servants and to David.' "

When David's young men came to Carmel, they spoke to Nabal for David as they had been told, and waited. But Nabal answered David's young men gruffly.

"Who is David? And who is the son of Jesse? There are many slaves nowadays that break away from their masters! Shall I then take my bread and my wine, and the meat I have killed for my own shearers, and give them to men from — I know not where?"

David's men thereupon left him and returned to David, and told him how his request had been met. David said to his men:

"Every man buckle on his sword!"

They buckled on their swords; and David also buckled on

his sword. About four hundred men were ordered to follow him, and two hundred remained with the baggage.

Meanwhile, one of the young shepherds had told Abigail, the wife of Nabal:

"David sent messengers from the wilderness to greet our master; but he insulted them. The men were very good to us, and we have not been harmed, nor have we missed anything, as long as we went with them in the open fields. All the time we were tending the sheep, they were a protection to us, night and day. Now know and consider what you should do, for there is trouble coming against our master and all his house; he is such an ill-tempered creature that one cannot speak a word to him."

Abigail made haste, and took two hundred loaves of bread, two bottles of wine, five roasted sheep, two bushels of parched grain, a hundred clusters of raisins, and two hundred fig cakes, and she put these supplies on donkeys. And she told her young men to go before her, and she would follow. But Abigail said nothing about the matter to her husband Nabal.

She was riding on her donkey down the side of the hill, when she met David and his men coming towards her.

When Abigail saw David, she alighted quickly and bowed down before him. She fell at his feet, and said:

"Upon me, my lord, upon me the blame. Let your servant speak to you, and listen to her words. Let not my lord pay any attention to Nabal, for he is like his name. 'Fool' is his name, and foolishness rules him. But I, your servant, did not see the young men of my lord, whom you sent."

David replied:

"Blessed be the Lord, the God of Israel, who sent you to meet me this day! Blessed be your discretion for saving me this day from the guilt of bloodshed and from avenging myself with my own hand. For as the Lord, the God of Israel, lives, who has kept me from doing you harm, had you not hurried to meet me, Nabal would not have had a single man left him by the morning!"

David then accepted the gifts she brought him. And he said to her:

"Go back in peace to your house. I have listened to your voice and granted your desire."

And Abigail returned to Nabal; he held a feast in his house like the feast of a king. Nabal's heart was merry within him for he was quite drunk; so Abigail did not tell him anything till daybreak. In the morning, when the effects of the wine had left him, his wife told him what she had done. His heart died within him, and he became like a stone. About ten days later he had a stroke, and he died.

When David heard that Nabal was dead, he said:

"Blessed be the Lord who has punished Nabal's evil-doing to me and has kept me from doing wrong; for the Lord has returned Nabal's crime upon his own head."

David then sent messengers to Abigail to ask her to become his wife. When his messengers came to Abigail and told her: "David has sent us to you to take you to him to be his wife," she rose and bowed to the earth and said:

"Behold, your humble servant here is a slave, ready to wash the feet of my lord's servants."

Abigail hastened and quickly mounted her donkey; and five of her maids accompanied her. She went with his messengers to David and became his wife.

On the Hill of Hachilah

One day the Ziphites came to Saul at Gibeah and said:

"David is hiding on the Hill of Hachilah."

Saul, accompanied by picked men, went to the desert of Ziph to search for David. He camped on the Hill of Hachilah. David had been keeping to the desert, and when he learned that Saul was pursuing him, he sent out spies who discovered where Saul had camped. Then David went close to where Saul and his men were.

David looked at the place where Saul had camped, with Abner in command of his army. Saul's tent was well within the camplines, and his troops were posted about it. David then called for volunteers, and said:

"Who will come down with me to Saul, to the camp?"

Abishai, the brother of Joab, who was captain of David's forces, said:

"I will go down with you."

David and Abishai picked their way through the lines of Saul by night, and found Saul asleep, with his spear stuck in the ground at his head; and Abner and the troops lay around him!

Then Abishai said to David:

"God has put your enemy into your hand today. Let me strike him, I beg you, to the earth with his own spear! Just one stroke, for I will not need to strike him twice!"

But David answered:

"Do not destroy him; for who can lay hands on the Lord's anointed and be innocent?" And he added:

"As the Lord lives, the Lord shall smite him; his day shall come to die; or he shall go into battle and be swept away. The Lord forbid that I should put out my hand against the Lord's anointed! But now take the spear at his head and the cruse of water, and let us go!"

David took the spear and the cruse of water at Saul's head; and they went away; no one saw them, no one knew anything, no one awoke; for they were all asleep; because a deep sleep from the Lord had overcome them.

David went over to the other side and stood on the top of a hill at some distance, with a wide space between. And David called to Abner:

"Abner, will you not answer?"

Abner replied:

"Who is calling?"

And David said:

"Are you not a valiant man? Who in Israel is like you? Why then have you not kept watch over your lord the king? Someone came in to murder the king your lord! This thing is not good that you have done. As the Lord lives, you deserve to die for failing to keep watch over your king, over the Lord's anointed! And now, see where the king's spear is, and the cruse of water that was at his head!"

Saul recognized David's voice; and he said:

"Is that your voice, my son David?"

David said:

"It is my voice, my lord, O king."

And David went on:

"Why does my lord pursue after his servant? What have I done? What evil stains my hands? For the king of Israel has come out to seek my life like a hunter seeking a partridge in the hills."

Saul said:

"I have done wrong; return, David my son, I will never hurt you again, since you held my life precious this day. I have played the fool and erred exceedingly."

David answered:

"Here is the king's spear! Let one of the young men come over and get it."

Then Saul said to David:

"Blessed are you, my son David! You shall do great things, and you shall surely prevail."

So David went his way, and Saul returned to his place.

David thought to himself:

"I shall one day be killed by Saul. The best thing for me to do is to escape to the land of the Philistines. Then Saul will give up hope and search for me no more in all the land of Israel; and so I shall escape from him."

So David arose and marched across country, with his six hundred men, and they came to Achish, king of Gath. And David and his men dwelt with Achish at Gath, each man with his family.

When Saul was told that David had fled to Gath, he sought for him no longer.   (*I Samuel 22–27*)

VIII.

THE DEATH OF SAUL AND JONATHAN

The curtain fell on the strange, exciting, yet sad life of King Saul. He was a man of generous nature, who really loved Samuel and David. His jealousy, suspicion and hatred were undoubtedly due to mental sickness, "the evil spirit." Although Saul did not conquer the Philistines, he taught the Israelites to stand up to them. David later built on what Saul had accomplished and was able to destroy the power of the Philistines for ever. Saul will always be remembered as the king who united Israel and held its loyalty to the end of his life.

After Samuel's Death

SAMUEL died and was buried in his own city of Ramah; and all Israel mourned for him. And Saul ordered the mediums and those who divined by the spirits of the dead to be driven out of the land.

Now, the Philistines came again to wage war and pitched their camp at Shunem. Saul gathered all of his armed forces and encamped at Gilboa. But when Saul saw the army of the Philistines, he was afraid, and his heart trembled greatly. When he asked of the Lord whether he should go against them, the Lord did not answer him either by dream or by lot or by the prophets. Then Saul said to his servants:

"Seek me a woman who divines by a spirit, that I may go and ask through her."

His servants said to him:

"Behold, there is such a woman at En-dor."

The Witch of En-dor

Saul disguised himself, and put on other clothes and went to En-dor, taking two of his men with him. They came to the woman by night. He said:

"Divine for me by a departed spirit, and bring up for me the one whom I shall name."

The woman said to him:

"You know what Saul has done, how he has driven from the land the mediums and those who divine by the spirits of the dead. Why then do you lay a trap to catch me, to cause me to die?"

But Saul swore to her by the Lord, saying:

"As the Lord lives, no punishment shall come to you for this thing."

Then the woman said:

"Whom shall I bring up to you?"

Saul said:

"Bring me up Samuel."

The woman looked at Saul and screamed; and she said to him:

"Why have you deceived me? You are Saul!"

Saul replied:

"Have no fear; what do you see?"

She said:

"I see a spirit coming up out of the earth."

He asked:

"What does he look like?"

She said:

"An old man comes up; and he is covered with a robe." Saul knew it was Samuel; and he bowed with his face to the earth.

And Samuel said to Saul:

"Why have you disturbed me, to bring me up?"

Saul answered:

"I am in deep distress; the Philistines make war against me, and God has departed from me. He answers me no more, either by prophets or by dreams. Therefore I have called you to make known to me what I should do."

And Samuel said:

"Why do you ask of me, since the Lord has departed from you to side with your enemy? He has taken the kingdom from your hand and given it to another, even to David. Tomorrow you and your sons shall be with me; and the Lord will deliver the army of Israel into the power of the Philistines."

The words of Samuel filled Saul with fear, and he fell at full length upon the earth. He had no strength in him, for he had not eaten any food all that day and night. When the woman saw that Saul was in great fear, she said to him:

"Behold, I have taken my life in my hand and have done what you asked me. Now, therefore, listen also to my voice and let me set before you a little food, that you may eat it and get strength for your journey."

Saul refused and said:

"I will not eat."

But his servants together with the woman urged him; and he listened to their voice. He arose from the earth and sat upon the bed. She placed a meal before Saul and his servants, and they ate. Then they rose up and went away that night.

The Battle of Gilboa. Saul
and Jonathan die.

The Philistines fought against the forces of Saul. The Israelites fled and many of them fell down slain upon Mount Gilboa. And the Philistines closely pursued Saul and his sons. They slew Jonathan, Abinadab and Malchi-shua, the sons of Saul. Then Saul, after he had been severely wounded, said to his armor-bearer:

"Draw your sword and thrust me through with it, so that these heathen Philistines may not come and make mock of me."

But his armor-bearer would not; for he was sore afraid. Saul, therefore, took his own sword and fell upon it. When his armor-bearer saw that Saul was dead, he also fell upon his sword and died. So Saul died, and his three sons, and his armor-bearer, on the same day together.

When the men of Israel on the other side of the valley, and the people beyond the Jordan, learned that the men of Israel had fled and that Saul and his sons were dead, they forsook their cities and fled; and the Philistines came and dwelt in them.

On the next day, when the Philistines came to spoil the slain, they found Saul and his three sons fallen on Mount Gilboa. They cut off Saul's head and stripped off his armor. They sent messengers all round the Philistine country to carry the tidings to their idols and to the people. And they fastened his body and his sons' bodies to the walls of Beth-shan, and put his armor in the temple of Astarte.

When the inhabitants of Jabesh in Gilead — whom Saul had once rescued from the Ammonites — heard what the Philistines had done to Saul, their valiant men assembled and marched all night to Beth-shan. They unfastened the bodies of Saul and his sons from the walls of Beth-shan and brought them to Jabesh and mourned over them there. Then they took their bones and buried them under the tamarisk tree in Jabesh, and fasted seven days.

David, in Ziklag, on hearing the News of the Death of Saul and Jonathan, writes his "Song of Sorrow"

David meanwhile waged war on the Amalekites from the city of Ziklag which Achish, king of Gath, had given him. Three days after David had come back from his defeat of the Amalekites, a man came from Saul's camp with his clothes torn and with earth upon his head.

When he came into the presence of David, he fell to the ground before him. David said to him:

"Where do you come from?"

He answered:

"I have escaped from the camp of Israel."

David asked:

"How did the battle go? Tell me."

He answered:

"The people fled from the battlefield, all of them have fallen, and Saul and Jonathan are dead!"

Then David and all the men with him tore their clothes, and mourned and wept and went without food until evening, for Saul and Jonathan, his son, and the people of the Lord who had fallen by the sword.

And David chanted this lamentation over Saul and his son Jonathan:

> "Thy beauty, O Israel, upon thy high places is slain!
> How are the mighty fallen!
>
> Tell it not in Gath,
> Publish it not in the streets of Ashkelon!
> Ye mountains of Gilboa,
> Let there be no dew nor rain upon you;
> For there the shield of the mighty
>   was vilely cast away,
> The shield of Saul, not anointed with oil.
>
> Saul and Jonathan were lovely and pleasant in
>   their lives,
> And in their death they were not divided.
> They were swifter than eagles,
> They were stronger than lions.
>
> I am distressed for thee, my brother Jonathan.
> Very pleasant hast thou been to me.
> Thy love to me was wonderful.
> How are the mighty fallen,
> And the weapons of war perished!"

(I Samuel 28, 31; II Samuel 1)

IX.

FROM SHEPHERD BOY TO KING

David goes to Hebron in Judah.
He becomes King of Judah.

AFTER the death of Saul, David asked the Lord:
"Shall I go to any of the cities of Judah?"
The Lord answered:
"Go."
David asked:
"To which shall I go?"
He said:
"To Hebron."

So David went to Hebron with his wives, Ahinoam and Abigail. And David also brought his faithful followers with him, every man with his household; and these dwelt in the villages about Hebron.

Then the men of Judah came to Hebron, and they anointed David king over the house of Judah.

David rewards the Men of Gilead
for their Kindness to Saul

And David was told about the men of Jabesh-gilead who had buried Saul; and he sent messengers to the leading men of Jabesh-gilead and said:

"Blessed are you of the Lord, because you have shown this kindness to your master Saul and buried him! May the Lord be kind and true to you! And I will repay you your kindness, for having done this thing. Be brave, then, and be strong! Saul your master is dead, and the people of Judah have anointed me king over them."

The House of Saul wars against the
House of David for the Kingship

Now Abner, commander of Saul's army, had taken Saul's son Ish-bosheth to Mahanaim, where he made him king over all Israel. But the house of Judah followed David.

Abner and the followers of Ish-bosheth marched from Mahanaim to Gibeon.⌄ Meanwhile, Joab, David's commander, and his
followers had also marched out, and they met at the pool of
Gibeon. They encamped, one on one side of the pool and the other
on the other side.

That day the fight that followed was very fierce, but Abner
and the men of Israel were beaten by the followers of David.

Then Abner called to Joab and said:

"Shall the sword devour for ever? Do you not know that the
outcome will be bitter? How long will it be then before you bid
the people return from pursuing their fellow-countrymen?"

"As God lives!" said Joab, "had you not spoken the word,
not one of the men would have stopped pursuing his fellow until
morning."

The war between the house of Saul and the house of David
went on for a long time; but David grew stronger and stronger,
while the house of Saul became weaker and weaker.

Then Abner sent messengers to David, saying:

"Make a treaty with me, and you will get my help in bringing
all Israel over to your side."

"Very well," said David, "I will make a treaty with you. But
I make one demand upon you: do not appear before me unless
you bring Saul's daughter, Michal, when you come to see me."

And so Abner returned Michal to David her husband.

David becomes King of all Israel

Now Abner communicated with the leaders of Israel, saying:

"In times past you wanted to make David your king; now
then do it! The Lord has promised, 'By the hand of My servant
David I will save My people Israel from the power of the Philistines and from the power of their enemies!'"

Abner then came to Hebron to tell David all that Israel had
determined to do. When Abner arrived at David's house, accompanied by twenty men, David held a feast for Abner and his
men. Abner said to David:

"I will arise and go, and will gather all Israel to my lord the
⌄For archaeological note see Item 9, p. 551 in the back of the book.

king, that they may make a treaty with you, and that you may reign over all as you desire."

David dismissed Abner; and he went in peace.

Just then Joab and soldiers of David returned from a raid, bringing rich spoil with them. When Joab was told that Abner had come to the king, and that the king had sent him off in peace, Joab went and said to David:

"What have you done? Why have you sent him away and let him go in peace? You should know that Abner came to deceive you, to note your movements, to find out all you were doing!"

Joab left David and sent messengers after Abner, who was brought back to Joab. David knew nothing of this. When Abner was brought back to Hebron, Joab took him aside to the town-gate for a quiet talk. While they talked, Joab stabbed Abner. Thus he paid with his life for having shed the blood of Asahel, Joab's brother.

When David afterwards heard of this, he said:

"I and my kingdom are guiltless before the Lord of the murder of Abner. May the doom fall on Joab's head and on all his father's house!"

Then David ordered Joab and all his troops to put on sack-cloth, and mourn in front of Abner's body. King David followed the funeral procession. They buried Abner in Hebron; and the king wept aloud at Abner's grave, as did the people.

When Saul's son, Ish-bosheth, heard that Abner had died at Hebron, he lost courage, and all the Israelites, who were his followers, became frightened. Two men who were captains of his troops, one named Baanah and the other Rechab, of the tribe of Benjamin, went to the palace of Ish-bosheth, where he was taking his rest at noon. The door-keeper of the palace was asleep; so Rechab and Baanah slipped into the palace and stabbed Ish-bosheth to death as he lay in bed.

Then all the tribes of Israel came to David at Hebron and said:

"Behold, we are your bone and your flesh! In times past, when Saul ruled over us, it was you who led the armies of Israel; and the Lord said to you, 'You shall shepherd My people Israel, and you shall be prince over Israel.' "

Then all the leading men of Israel came to David at Hebron, and he made a covenant with them before the Lord; and they anointed David king over all Israel. And David was thirty years old when he began to reign, and he reigned forty years. In Hebron he reigned over Judah seven years and six months; and in Jerusalem he reigned thirty-three years over all Israel and Judah. (*II Samuel 2–5*)

X.

JERUSALEM — THE CITY OF GOD

David captures Jerusalem.
He makes it his Capital.

DAVID assembled all the picked men of Israel, thirty thousand of them. And the king and his men went to Jerusalem against the Jebusites, the inhabitants of that city.

The Jebusites told David:

"You will never come in here; even blind men and cripples could drive you off!"

They thought: David cannot come in here. But David did capture the stronghold of Zion. David's orders for the day were:

"Whoever strikes down a Jebusite is liable to death! David wages no war against 'blind men and cripples'!"

David dwelt in the stronghold. He called it "the City of David," and he built a wall round the city. And David became greater and greater, for the Lord the God of hosts was on his side.

And Hiram, king of Tyre, sent messengers to him, with cedarlogs and carpenters and masons, and they built a palace for David.

David brings the Ark of the Lord
to Jerusalem

David consulted with the chief men of Israel, and he said to the assembly of Israel:

"If it seem good to you and acceptable to the Lord our God, let us send quickly to all our people in the land of Israel, that they may join us in bringing back the Ark of the Lord; for during the reign of Saul we did not seek it."

And all the assembly said that they would do so, for the plan seemed right to the people. So David gathered all Israel together in order to bring the Ark from Kiriath-jearim in Judah.

As the Ark of the Lord was carried into the City of David, King David danced before the Lord.

DAVID BRINGS THE ARK TO JERUSALEM

"... David danced before the Lord."

(II Samuel 6.14)

see page 250

SOLOMON AND THE QUEEN OF SHEBA

"It was a true report I heard . . . of your wisdom!"

(*I Kings 10.6*)

see page 272

After bringing in the Ark of the Lord, they put it inside the tent pitched for it by David. He offered burnt-offerings and sacrifices to the Lord. He then blessed the people in the name of the Lord of hosts. Then all the people returned home.

When David went to greet his family, Michal, his wife, met him and said:

"Fine honor did the king of Israel gain for himself today, uncovering himself before the people, as any loose fellow would!"

David said to Michal:

"It was before the Lord that I danced and made merry."

This was how David and the house of Israel brought up the Ark of the Lord to the City of David.

David forbidden to build a Temple

After the king had taken up residence in his palace, the king said to the prophet Nathan:

"Here I live in a house of cedar, while the Ark of the Lord is inside the curtains of a tent!"

That night the word of the Lord came to Nathan, the prophet, saying:

"You shall say to My servant David: 'I took you from the pasture, from tending sheep, that you should be king over My people Israel. I have been with you wherever you went, to destroy all your enemies before you, and I will make you a name like that of the great in the earth. But, you are not to build Me a Temple to dwell in. When your life is ended and you are buried with your fathers, I will raise up your son after you, and I will make his rule strong. Your son shall build a Temple for My name, and I will establish the throne of his kingdom for ever."

(*II Samuel 5–7; I Chronicles 13, 17*)

XI.

NATHAN — THE PEOPLE'S CONSCIENCE

King David's Sin

ONE DAY at sunset, while Joab was besieging Rabbah, the royal city of the Ammonites, David rose from his couch and walked upon the roof of the royal palace. From the roof he saw a woman who was very beautiful. David sent and inquired after the woman; and someone said:

"Is she not Bathsheba, the wife of Uriah the Hittite?"

And David sent messengers to bring her. She came to him. And later she returned to her home.

He wrote a letter to Joab and sent it by Uriah. He wrote in the letter:

"Place Uriah in the front line where there is the fiercest fighting, then draw back from behind him, that he may be struck down and die."

Joab posted guards over the city, and sent Uriah to the place where he knew that brave men had been placed by the enemy. When the men of the city went out to fight against Joab, some of the soldiers of David fell, and Uriah the Hittite was killed.

Then Joab sent to tell David all about the war, and he gave this command to the messenger:

"When you have finished telling the king all about the war, if he is angry and says to you, 'Why did you go so near to the city to fight? Did you not know that they would shoot from the wall? Why did you go so near the wall?' then shall you say, 'Your servant Uriah the Hittite is dead also!' "

The messenger went to Jerusalem and told David all that Joab commanded him. And David told the messenger:

"Say to Joab, 'Let not this thing trouble you, for the sword devours in one manner or another. Go on fighting against the city and capture it.' "

When Bathsheba heard that Uriah her husband was dead, she mourned for him. When the mourning was past, David sent and took her to his house, and she became his wife, and in time she bore him a son.

Nathan the Prophet
tells a Parable

What David had done displeased the Lord, and He sent the prophet Nathan to David.

Nathan went to him and said:

"There were two men in one city: the one rich and the other poor. The rich man had many flocks and herds; but the poor man had nothing but a single ewe lamb which he had bought. He fed it and it grew up with him and with his children. It used to eat of his own food and drink out of his own cup, and it lay in his bosom and was like a daughter to him.

"Now a traveller came to the rich man; and the rich man spared his own flock and herd and did not take an animal from it, to make ready for the traveller who had come to him, but took the poor man's lamb and prepared it for the guest who had come."

David's anger was kindled furiously against the man, and he said to Nathan:

"As the Lord lives, the man who has done this deserves to die; he shall repay the value of the lamb fourfold, because he did this and had no pity!"

And Nathan said to David:

"Thou art the man!"

And Nathan continued:

"The Lord, the God of Israel declares: 'I made you ruler over Israel and I delivered you out of the hand of Saul. I gave you the house of Israel and of Judah. If that were too little I would add so much more. Why have you despised the word of the Lord to do what is wrong in His sight? You have struck down Uriah the Hittite with the sword, and have taken his wife to be your wife, and have killed him with the sword of the Ammonites. Now, therefore, the sword shall never depart from your house!' "

And David said:

"I have sinned against the Lord."

Then Nathan said to David:

"The Lord has pardoned your sin. You shall not die. Yet,

because by this deed you have shown irreverence for the Lord, the child that is born to you shall surely die."

And Nathan returned to his house.

King David's Sorrow

And the Lord struck the child that Bathsheba bore to David, and it was very sick. David prayed to God for the child and ate no food, but went in and lay all night in sackcloth upon the earth. The older men in his house stood over him to raise him from the earth; but he would not rise nor eat with them.

On the seventh day the child died. The servants of David were afraid to tell him that the child was dead, for they said:

"While the child was yet alive, we spoke to him and he would not listen to us. How can we tell him that the child is dead. He will do some harm to himself."

When David saw that his servants were whispering together he knew that the child was dead, and he said to his servants:

"Is the child dead?"

They replied:

"He is dead."

David rose from the earth, washed and changed his clothes and went into the house of the Lord and worshipped. After that he went to his own house; and he asked for bread, and when they set it before him, he ate.

His servants said to him:

"What is this you have done? You ate no food and cried for the child while it was alive; but when the child died, you rose and ate bread."

He replied:

"While the child was yet alive, I ate no food and cried aloud, for I said, 'Who knows whether the Lord will have mercy, so that the child will live?' But now that he is dead, why should I eat no food? Can I bring him back again? No, I shall go to him; but he will not return to me."

David consoled his wife, Bathsheba.

Later Bathsheba bore David another son whom he named Solomon. And the Lord loved Solomon.   (*II Samuel 11–12*)

XII.

"ABSALOM, MY SON! MY SON!"

David's family increased and quarrels broke out in the royal
household. Each of his wives, jealous of the others, wanted
to obtain the throne for her son. David's sons also quarreled
bitterly with each other. His eldest son Amnon committed a
crime against Tamar, the sister of his half-brother Absalom.
Absalom in revenge killed Amnon and fled to his grandfather,
the king of Geshur, where he lived for three years in exile.
Later Absalom was permitted to return to Jerusalem and was
restored to royal favor. But the young prince secretly nursed
a grudge against his father David. Absalom conspired against
King David, and revolted against him. This incident came to be
known as "Absalom's Rebellion."

ANOTHER son of David was named Absalom. In all Israel
there was no man so much praised for his beauty as Absalom.
From the soles of his feet to the crown of his head there was not
a blemish in him. And he had a magnificent head of hair which
grew thick and heavy.

Because of the anger of David, Absalom had fled to the village
of Geshur, after he had ordered his servant to kill his brother,
Amnon, who had wronged Absalom's sister, Tamar. On his
return from Geshur, Absalom lived in Jerusalem for two years
without meeting or going to see his father David. Then Joab
told the king that Absalom was in Jerusalem, and he summoned
Absalom. When Absalom came into his presence, David kissed
Absalom.

Absalom seeks popular Favor

Some time later Absalom prepared a chariot and horses and
fifty men to run before him. He used to rise up early and stand
beside the gate of the city; and, whenever any man came with
a case for the king to decide, Absalom would say to him:

"What city do you belong to?"

When the man replied, "Your servant belongs to one of the
tribes of Israel," Absalom would say:

"Your case is good and just; but the king has not appointed anyone to hear you. O that I were made judge in the land, so that every man who has any complaint or cause might come to me! I would see that he received justice!"

Whenever a man came near to bow before him, he put out his hand and took hold of him and kissed him. In this way Absalom treated the Israelites who came to David for justice. Thus, Absalom stole the hearts of many of the men of Israel.

Conspiracy at Hebron

A few years later Absalom said to his father:

"I would like to go to Hebron and keep my promise which I made to the Lord. When I was staying at Geshur, your servant made this vow, 'If the Lord restores me to Jerusalem, I will offer worship to the Lord in Hebron.' "

David said to him:

"Go in peace!"

He arose and went to Hebron. And Absalom sent messengers to all the tribes of Israel, saying:

"As soon as you hear the sound of the trumpet, you shall cry: 'Absalom is king in Hebron!' "

With Absalom went two hundred men from Jerusalem, who went innocently; they knew nothing at all of what he intended to do. Absalom also sent for Ahithophel, David's counsellor, and the uncle of Bathsheba, who still grieved over what David had done to Uriah.

The conspiracy grew stronger, and the number of people who joined Absalom increased.

David flees from Jerusalem

A messenger came to David, saying:

"The hearts of the men of Israel are with Absalom."

David said to his officers around him:

"Let us be up and flee; else we shall never escape from Absalom! Quick, away, lest he overtake us suddenly and bring harm upon us and kill the people of the city!"

The officers answered:

"Your servants are ready to do whatever our lord the king decides."

So David left Jerusalem, and the people after him; and they halted in Beth-merhak.

The Battle of the Forest of Ephraim

Absalom, accompanied by his troops, crossed the Jordan. He had placed Amasa in command of his army.

David mustered his troops and appointed commanders of regiments and captains of companies. He divided the troops into three armies, one to be commanded by Joab, one by Abishai, and one by Ittai the Gittite. The king said to the soldiers:

"I will surely go with you myself."

The soldiers replied:

"You shall not. If we run away, they will not care for us; or if half of us die, that will not matter to them; but you — you are worth ten thousand of us. Besides, the right thing for you is to send us reinforcements from the city."

Then the king said:

"I will do what you think best."

He stood beside the gate, while the troops marched out. The king commanded Joab, Abishai, and Ittai, saying:

"Deal gently, for my sake, with young Absalom!"

The troops heard the king giving the generals this command concerning Absalom.

David's army took the field against Absalom. And the battle was fought in the Forest of Ephraim. The army of Absalom was defeated there by David's forces. The slaughter was heavy; about twenty thousand fell. The battle spread over the surrounding country; but the deep forest devoured more people than did the sword.

Tragic Death of Absalom

When Absalom met David's soldiers, he was riding on his mule. As the mule passed under the thick boughs of a great oak, the hair of his head caught fast in the oak, and he was pulled off his mule and hung in the air, between heaven and earth. The mule that was under him darted away.

A man told Joab:

"I saw Absalom hanging in an oak."

Joab said to the man:

"You saw him! Why did you not strike him to the ground? I would have given you ten pieces of silver and a belt."

But the man said:

"Though I should receive a thousand pieces of silver, I would not lay my hand on the king's son. We heard the king ordering you and Abishai and Ittai saying, 'Pray be careful of young Absalom, for my sake!' If I had taken his life, nothing would have been hidden from the king of Israel, and you yourself would not have tried to save me."

Joab answered:

"I will not waste time with you."

He called to some of his men to follow him to the oak tree, caught up three spears, and drove them into Absalom's heart. Then ten of Joab's armor-bearers gathered around and struck down Absalom till he died. His body was cast into a deep pit within the forest, and a great heap of stones was piled upon him.

Then Joab blew the trumpet, and the troops came back from their pursuit of the enemy.

David's Grief

Joab then said to a Cushite (Ethiopian):

"Go and tell the king what you have seen."

The messenger bowed before Joab and ran off. But Ahimaaz, the son of Zadok, said to Joab:

"Let me also run after the messenger."

Joab said:

"My son, why will you run? You will not get any payment for your news."

He answered:

"Come what may, I am going to run."

"Well," said Joab, "run!"

Ahimaaz ran by way of the Jordan valley; and he overtook the messenger.

David was sitting between the gates. The watchman had gone up to the roof of the gateway at the wall and, when he looked, he saw a man running. The watchman shouted to tell the king

The king said:

"If he is alone, he has good news to tell."

Meanwhile he kept on drawing nearer. Then the watchman saw another man running; and the watchman shouted down into the gate-house:

"Here is another man running!"

The king said:

"He also is bringing good news."

The watchman replied:

"I notice that the first man runs like Ahimaaz the son of Zadok."

"A good man," said the king, "he comes with good news."

Then Ahimaaz came up and said to the king:

"Hail!"

He bowed before the king, and said:

"Blessed be the Lord your God, who has handed over the men who rebelled against my lord the king!"

The king said:

"Is young Absalom safe?"

Ahimaaz replied:

"When Joab sent your servant off, I noticed a great uproar, but I do not know what it was."

The king said:

"Step aside and stand here."

He stepped aside, and said nothing more. Whereupon the first messenger sent by Joab cried:

"News for my lord the king! The Lord this day has avenged you on all who rose against you!"

The king asked him:

"Is young Absalom safe?"

The messenger answered:

"May the enemies of my lord the king and all who rise to harm you meet the fate of that young man!"

The king then knew that Absalom was dead.

He went up to the room over the gate and wept.

As he wept he cried:

"O my son Absalom! my son, my son Absalom! O that I had died instead of you, Absalom, my son, my son!"

Joab rebukes David

Joab was told that the king was weeping and mourning for Absalom. Indeed, the victory of that day appeared to have been turned into mourning, for when the troops heard that the king was bewailing the death of his son, they stole into the city like soldiers ashamed of having run away from battle. Joab went to the king and said:

"You have shamed this day the troops who have saved your life and the lives of your household, because you love your enemies and you hate those who love you! You have declared this day that officers and soldiers are nothing to you! I see plainly that if Absalom had lived today, and we had died, you would have been quite pleased. Come, get up and go out, and encourage your troops."

Then the king arose, and sat in the gate. And when the troops heard that the king was sitting in the gate, they came into the presence of the king.

David returns to Jerusalem

As for Israel, every man went to his home.

The king returned, and came to the Jordan. David passed over it and went to his palace in Jerusalem.* (*II Samuel 14–19*)

---

*For King David as composer of religious poetry, see the Book of Psalms, pages 421 ff.

KINGS

EVERYONE knows the story of the American Civil War. The original thirteen colonies won their freedom from England and succeeded in forming a Union, the United States of America. They adopted the Constitution which was the law by which they governed themselves. For about seventy-five years the American nation grew in strength, power, and influence, and its people were prosperous and happy.

Then came a terrible crisis. All that the American people had built was about to be destroyed. The southern states wanted to withdraw from the Union and form a separate government for themselves. The northern states, however, sought to maintain the Union. A long and bloody war was fought and the Union was preserved. Much of the credit for saving the Union belongs to Abraham Lincoln, one of the noblest and wisest leaders who ever lived.

When we read the history of the first Jewish kingdom, we are reminded of the American Civil War, but with one difference. Unfortunately for the Jewish people, they had no wise and understanding Lincoln who could keep the twelve tribes united in one national Union, and thus preserve the United Kingdom.

From the times of the Judges, through the years of Samuel, King Saul and King David, down to the last days of King Solomon (about whom we shall soon read), the tribes struggled to form a more perfect Union. Under King David they had actually become the United Kingdom of Israel.

But the tribes had not forgotten their ancient jealousies. Moreover, the many buildings built by Solomon caused hardships in the form of heavy taxes and even "forced" labor. Wealthy classes and poor classes appeared among the people of Israel. Injustice grew with prosperity, and the United Kingdom began to fall apart. Through the reigns of David and his son, Solomon, the kingdom remained united, though a brief revolt had broken out against the latter. Had a wise king followed Solomon, some-one in spirit like Solomon himself, perhaps the Jewish kingdom might have remained united. But the young Prince Rehoboam who succeeded his father, Solomon, as king, was short-sighted, lacked wisdom, and acted harshly towards his people.

Civil War then broke out in Israel. The Jewish people became divided into two kingdoms; the northern kingdom was known as Israel, and the southern kingdom was known as Judah. Each, until it was destroyed, had its own kings.

Thus weakened, the two kingdoms could not well stand up against the powerful foes that attacked them. In time the north-ern kingdom of Israel, whose capital was Samaria, was defeated by the Assyrians, and its tribes disappeared; and later the southern kingdom of Judah, consisting of two tribes, was conquered by the Babylonians. Jerusalem, its capital, was burned, its land was laid waste, and the people of Judah were forced to leave the Land of Israel and go into exile in far-off Babylonia. Thus, the first Jewish kingdom came to a sad and unhappy end.

During those stormy and tragic days, God did not leave His people without guidance. He raised up a number of remarkable men whom all mankind reveres to this day. They were the Hebrew prophets, courageous teachers and preachers of God's message. The prophets were inspired Jewish patriots who contended against ignorance, superstition and idolatry, and against wrong and injus-tice. They helped to educate the Jewish people to cast off the worship of idols and to accept as their God the Creator of the universe, the Father of all mankind, the God of the whole world. They taught that God wanted people to live honest, just and righteous lives; that He sought from them truth, love and mercy. They warned them that God would punish even His people Israel, if they did not live in accordance with His Law. But they prom-ised that God would strengthen and protect Israel, if they obeyed the laws of His Covenant. They held out hope for the coming of a Great Peace over the whole earth, when all wars would cease from among mankind. Unfortunately, the Jewish people did not listen to the voices of their prophets, but blindly pursued injustice

and wrong until they suffered severe punishments, and their kingdoms were destroyed.

The earlier prophets, like Elijah and Elisha, did not write down
their fiery speeches. They are known as the Former Prophets (in
Hebrew, *Nebi'im Rishonim*); the others, who left us their written
sermons and prophecies, are called the Latter Prophets (in Hebrew,
Nebi'im Aharonim).

The story of this period of Jewish history is told in the two
Books of Kings. The Books of Chronicles are also quoted here,
because they, too, contain much information about the Jewish
rulers not found in the Books of Kings. The Books of Chronicles
were written much later than the Books of Kings.

I.

SOLOMON ASCENDS THE THRONE

Solomon anointed King

KING David was an old man, well advanced in years. The king commanded:

"Call Bathsheba."

When she came before him, David said:

"As the Lord lives, even as I promised you, 'Assuredly Solomon, your son, shall reign after me and succeed to my throne,' so will I do this very day."

Bathsheba bowed to the ground, and cried:

"May my lord King David live for ever!"

King David had Zadok the priest, Nathan the prophet, and Benaiah, the son of Jehoiada, his captain of the guard, summoned to his presence. When they appeared before him, the king said to them:

"Take your king's personal troops, mount my son Solomon upon my own mule, and bring him down to Gihon; and let Zadok the priest, and Nathan the prophet, anoint him there as king over Israel. And blow a trumpet blast and proclaim, 'Long live King Solomon!'

"Then march behind him, and let him come and sit upon my throne, for he is to succeed me. I have appointed him to be king over Israel and Judah."

So Zadok the priest, Nathan the prophet, and Benaiah the son of Jehoiada, together with the foreign bodyguard, mounted Solomon upon King David's mule and took him to Gihon, where Zadok took the vial of oil from the sacred Tent and anointed Solomon. They then blew the trumpet, and the people shouted:

"Long live King Solomon!"

Solomon to build a Temple

David called for Solomon his son, and when he appeared, charged him to build a Temple for the Lord, the God of Israel, saying:

"My son, it was in my heart to build a Temple for the Lord my God. But the word of the Lord came to me, saying:

" 'You have shed blood abundantly, you have waged great wars; you shall not build a Temple to My name. No, a son shall be born to you who shall be a man of peace; I will give him rest from all his enemies. His name shall be Solomon (Peaceful), and during his reign I will give Israel peace and quietness. He shall build a Temple for My name and I shall be a father to him and establish his royal throne over Israel for ever.'

"Now, my son, the Lord be with you and prosper you, and build the Temple of the Lord your God, as He has spoken concerning you!"

When David's time to die drew near, he called Solomon to him and gave him this further charge:

"I am going the way of all the earth. Be strong then, and show yourself a man. Keep the commandments of the Lord your God and obey His orders. Follow the Law of Moses so that, whatever you do and wherever you turn, you may have success. Then the Lord will fulfill His promise to me that, if my children are careful how they live, I shall never lack a man upon the throne of Israel."

David died in a ripe old age, having had life and riches and honor to the full. He was buried in Jerusalem, the City of David, where he slept with his fathers. Solomon his son ascended the throne of David, and his kingdom was firmly established.

(*I Kings 1–3; I Chronicles 22, 29*)

II.

"A WISE AND UNDERSTANDING HEART"

Solomon's Dream and Wish

SOLOMON loved the Lord. One day he went to sacrifice at Gibeon, for there was a chief shrine in that city. He offered upon that altar a thousand sacrifices.

While he was at Gibeon, the Lord appeared to Solomon in a dream, and said:

"Ask what I shall give you."

Solomon answered:

"Thou hast shown unto David, my father, great kindness. Now, O Lord my God, Thou hast made me king in the place of David, my father. I am still but a youth who does not know how to rule. Give Thy servant, therefore, an understanding heart to judge Thy people, that I may know the difference between right and wrong. For who is able to rule this Thy great people?"

The Lord was pleased that Solomon had asked this; and the Lord said to him:

"Because you have asked this and have not asked for yourself long life nor riches nor death to your enemies, but have asked for yourself understanding to know what is right, I have now granted what you ask; I have given you a wise and understanding heart. I also give you what you have not asked, both riches and honor."

Then Solomon awoke and, behold, it was a dream! And he returned to Jerusalem.

The Case of the two Women

One day two women came before the king. One woman said:

"O, my lord, I and this woman dwell in one house; and in the house I had a child. Three days later this woman also had a child; and we were together; there was no stranger with us in the house. While we two were alone, this woman's child died in the night, because she lay upon it.

"Then she rose at midnight and took my son from beside me, while I slept, and laid it in her bosom, and laid her dead child in my bosom. When I rose in the morning to nurse my child, behold, it was dead; but when I looked at it closely in the morning, behold, I found that it was not my son."

The other woman said:

"No; the living is my son, and the dead is your son!"

Thus they spoke before Solomon.

Solomon thought: "One says, 'This living son is mine, the dead belongs to you;' the other says, 'No; the dead son is yours, mine is the living one.'"

Then the king said, "Bring me a sword."

They brought a sword to Solomon.

He commanded:

"Divide the living child in two, and give half to the one, and half to the other."

Then the woman who was the mother of the living child exclaimed — for she yearned for her son with all her heart:

"O, my lord, give her the living child, and in no way put it to death."

But the other said:

"No, divide it; it shall be neither yours nor mine."

Then Solomon said:

"Give the first woman the living child, and in no way put it to death. She is its mother!"

All Israel heard of the judgment which the king gave, and they had great respect for him. For they saw that he had in him God's own wisdom for doing justice.

Solomon's Fame for Wisdom

God gave Solomon wisdom and understanding and largeness of heart like the broad sea-sands. Solomon's wisdom surpassed the wisdom of all the peoples of the east and all the wisdom of Egypt. He was wiser than all men, and his fame spread to all the nations round about.

He composed three thousand proverbs; and his songs numbered a thousand and five.

He spoke of trees, from the cedar in Lebanon to the hyssop that springs out of the wall. He spoke also of animals, birds, reptiles and fishes. People came from every nation, sent by all the kings in the world, who had heard of Solomon's wisdom, in order to gain understanding. (*I Kings 3, 5.9–14*)

III.

SOLOMON BUILDS THE TEMPLE

KING Solomon reigned over a united Israel. The people of
Judah and Israel were numerous as the sand on the seashore;
they ate and drank and enjoyed themselves. Judah and Israel
dwelt safely, every man under his vine and under his fig-tree,
from Dan to Beer-sheba, all the days of Solomon. He ruled wisely,
and peace was enjoyed on every side. He lived by the laws laid
down by his father David; only, he sacrificed and burned incense
at the shrines. The people also sacrificed at the shrines, because
no Temple had yet been built in honor of the Lord.

The Building of the Temple

When Hiram, king of Tyre, heard that Solomon had become
king upon the death of his father David, he sent his officers to
Solomon; for Hiram had always been friendly to David.

Solomon sent this message to Hiram:

"You know that my father David could not build a Temple
in honor of the Lord his God, because of the wars which he had
to wage. The Lord my God has now given me peace on every
side; and I intend to build a Temple. Now, therefore, give orders
that cedar-trees be felled for me on Lebanon. My servants shall
join your servants, and I will pay you any wage you fix for your
servants; for you know we have no one with the skill to fell timber
like the Phoenicians."

When Hiram heard what Solomon said, he rejoiced greatly.
He said:

"Blessed be the Lord the God of Israel for giving David a
wise son to rule over this great people!"

And Hiram sent this message to Solomon:

"I have heard your message; I will do all you desire concerning timber of cedars and firs. My servants shall bring the timber
down from Lebanon to the sea; and I will make the logs into rafts
to go by sea to any place you decide upon; there I will have them
broken up for you to take away. You will meet my wishes by
providing the food for my servants."

Hiram gave Solomon all the cedar and fir timber that he desired. And Solomon gave Hiram wheat and beaten oil as food for his servants — such was Solomon's gift to Hiram year by year. Solomon then raised a labor force from Israel, thirty thousand men, whom he sent to Lebanon in divisions of ten thousand a month. And Adoniram was in charge of this labor force.

Solomon and Hiram were at peace; and the two men made an alliance with each other.

In the fourth year of Solomon's reign over Israel he began to build the Temple of the Lord. The Temple was built with stone made ready at the quarry; neither hammer nor axe nor any tool of iron was heard in the Temple while it was in building.

In the eleventh year of Solomon's reign, the Temple was completed in every part, exactly as planned. He was seven years in building it.

The Dedication of the Temple

Solomon then assembled the leaders of Israel in Jerusalem to bring the Ark of the Lord to the Temple at the time of the autumn festival, which is the Festival of Tabernacles.

When all the leaders of Israel had assembled, the priests took up the Ark. And they brought up the Ark of the Lord, and the Tent of Meeting, and all the sacred vessels that were in the Tent. The priests brought the Ark of the Lord to its proper place, in the Sanctuary of the Temple. There was nothing in the Ark except the two Tables of the Law which Moses had placed there at Mount Sinai. When the priests came out of the Sanctuary, a cloud so filled the Temple of the Lord that the priests were unable to stand and perform their service, for the glory of the Lord filled His Temple.

Solomon's Prayer

Then spoke Solomon:

"I have built Thee, O Lord, a lofty Temple to dwell in,
   A settled place for Thee to abide in for ever."

He then spread out his hands toward heaven, and prayed:

"O Lord, God of Israel, there is no God like Thee in heaven above or on earth below.

"But will God really dwell on the earth? Behold, heaven and the heaven of heavens cannot contain Thee. How much less this Temple that I have built! Nevertheless, listen to the prayer of Thy servant and of Thy people Israel; hear Thou in Thy home, in heaven; and when Thou hearest, forgive!"

Then Solomon blessed all the community of Israel:

"Blessed be the Lord, who has given rest to His people Israel, as He promised. May He maintain the cause of His people Israel, as every day shall require; so that all the nations of the earth may know that the Lord, He is God; there is none else."

The Sacrifice and the Feast

Then Solomon and all the people with him offered sacrifice before the Lord. And they held a feast for seven days and seven days. Thus the king and the people dedicated the Temple of the Lord.

Then Solomon sent the people away. They blessed the king and returned home, joyful and glad of heart for all the goodness that the Lord had shown to His servant David, to Solomon, and to His people Israel.

The Lord's Warning

When Solomon had completed building the Temple of the Lord, the Lord appeared to Solomon a second time, as He had appeared to him at Gibeon, and said to him:

"I have heard your prayer, and I have done for you all you desire. If you live with upright heart and integrity, to do as I have commanded and to keep My laws, then I will establish your throne over Israel for ever. But if you turn away from following after Me, you or your children, if you do not keep the commands I have set before you, then I will uproot Israel out of the land I gave them, and cast out of My sight this Temple which I have hallowed for My name; and Israel shall become a proverb among all nations."

(*I Kings 4–8; II Chronicles 7*)

IV.

SPLENDOR, FAME AND TROUBLE

The Splendor of Solomon

WHEN Solomon began his reign over Israel, he divided the country into twelve districts, each governed by an officer, and the twelve officers were under a single chief.

Solomon married the daughter of the Pharaoh of Egypt, and took her to the City of David till he finished his own palace and the Lord's Temple, and the wall around Jerusalem.

Solomon took thirteen years to finish the building of his own palace. He also built the Hall of Justice where he judged the people. He made a palace, too, similar to this Hall, for Pharaoh's daughter. All these buildings were made of costly stones, hewn according to measurements.

And Solomon gathered together chariots and horsemen. He had one thousand four hundred chariots and twelve thousand horsemen. These he stationed in chariot cities↓ and at Jerusalem.

King Solomon also made a navy of ships on the shore of the Red Sea at Ezion-geber near Eloth↓ in the land of Edom. And Hiram sent his men, expert seamen, to man the fleet along with the men of Solomon. They sailed to Ophir and brought back from there four hundred and twenty bars of gold for King Solomon.

King Solomon made three hundred shields of beaten gold; three pounds of gold went to each shield. Moreover, the king made a great throne of ivory, which he overlaid with the finest gold. Such a throne had never been made in any kingdom. King Solomon's drinking-vessels were of gold, and all the vessels in the house called "The Forest of Lebanon" were of pure gold; none of silver — silver was thought not worth using in Solomon's day. The king had at sea a navy which sailed with the navy of Hiram; once every three years this navy brought home gold and silver, ivory, and apes, and peacocks.

In wealth and in wisdom King Solomon exceeded all the kings of the earth. And all the earth came to visit Solomon, and everyone brought him presents.

↓For archaeological note see Item 10, p. 552 in the back of the book.

The Fame of Solomon

When the Queen of Sheba heard of the fame of Solomon, she came to prove him with hard questions. She brought with her a very great train of servants, and her camels carried spices and much gold and precious stones. When she had an audience with Solomon, she told him all that was in her heart. And Solomon gave her the correct answers to all her questions; none had been too difficult for him to answer.

When the Queen of Sheba realized the wisdom of Solomon, had seen the palace that he had built, had eaten the food of his table, looked over the housing of his officers, noticed the way his servants attended him, their clothing, his cupbearers, and the sacrifices which he offered in the Temple of the Lord, she was greatly surprised. She said to Solomon:

"It was a true report I heard in my own country of your acts, and of your wisdom! But I did not believe it, until I came, and I saw for myself. And, behold, the half was not told me; you have wisdom and prosperity far greater than what was reported to me."

She presented the king with a hundred and twenty bars of gold, a wealth of spices, and jewels; no supply of spices ever again came to him as rich as the Queen of Sheba's present to King Solomon.

King Solomon in turn gave the Queen of Sheba whatever she asked, besides what he gave her out of his royal bounty.

Then she returned to her own land.

Dark Shadows begin to fall

Now King Solomon had married many foreign women, besides the daughter of Pharaoh — Moabites, Canaanites, Edomites, Hittites, and Ammonites.* He had seven hundred wives of royal birth. When he grew old, his wives influenced Solomon to worship their gods, and he did not remain loyal to the Lord his God. Solomon built a palace of worship for Chemosh, the god of Moab,

---

*It was the custom then for the head of a country to marry the daughter of the king with whom a treaty or alliance had been made. These foreign princesses brought with them into the capital city their religious shrines and priests.

on the mount opposite Jerusalem, and for Moloch, the god of the Ammonites. He did the same for all his foreign wives, who offered sacrifices to their gods.

The Lord was angry with Solomon for straying from Him, the God of Israel. The Lord said to Solomon:

"Since you have not obeyed My Covenant and My laws which I have commanded you, I will surely rend the kingdom from you and give it to your servant. Nevertheless I will not do this during your lifetime, for the sake of David your father; I will rend it out of the hand of your son."

Solomon suppresses a Revolt

Now Jeroboam, son of Nebat, of the tribe of Ephraim, was in the service of Solomon. He was a man of great ability. When Solomon saw that the young man was industrious, he placed him over all the men of the tribe of Ephraim who were working for the king. He had charge of all the labor-gangs.

It came to pass one day, when Jeroboam went out of Jerusalem, that the prophet Ahijah of Shiloh met him on the way, and took him aside. They two were alone in the open field. Ahijah then took the new garment which he wore, and rent it into twelve pieces. And he said to Jeroboam:

"Take ten pieces for yourself; for this is the message of the Lord, the God of Israel: 'I will rend the kingdom out of the hand of Solomon and will give ten tribes to you, but he shall have only one tribe.' "

Jeroboam rebelled against Solomon.

Solomon, therefore, sought to kill him. But Jeroboam fled to Egypt, where he remained until the death of Solomon.

Solomon dies

Solomon reigned in Jerusalem over Israel forty years. Then Solomon was buried in the City of David, where he slept with his fathers. (*I Kings 4-11*)

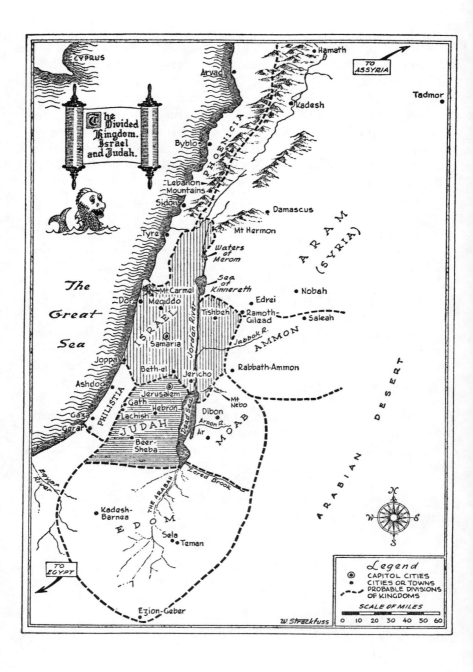

V.

THE HOUSE IS DIVIDED

When King Solomon died, the United Kingdom of Israel came to its end; it broke up into two separate kingdoms. The Kingdom of Judah, with its capital city Jerusalem, had as its first king Rehoboam, son of King Solomon. The Kingdom of Israel, with its capital later at Samaria, had Jeroboam, son of Nebat, as its first king. Jeroboam introduced the worship of the Bull, the symbol of fertility, the Mazeboth (Pillars) and the Asheroth (Sacred Trees) in honor of the pagan goddess Astarte. Thus, Jeroboam brought back the lower religion of the heathen peoples of ancient Palestine, and for this he and all the kings who imitated him were bitterly condemned by the prophets.

REHOBOAM, the son of Solomon, reigned after him. When Jeroboam, who was still in Egypt, heard that Solomon had died, he came back to his native town, Zeredah, in the highlands of Ephraim (Israel). The people sent for Jeroboam, and he, with the assembled Israelites, came to speak to Rehoboam in Shechem, where he had come to be crowned king. They told Rehoboam:

"Your father's burden upon us was heavy; lighten the heavy burden your father laid upon us and his crushing service, and we will serve you."

King Rehoboam said to them:

"Go away for three days; then come back to me."

The people went away. Then Rehoboam asked advice from the old men who had been in the service of Solomon his father. He inquired what answer they would advise him to give the people.

They said to him:

"If you will serve this people now, give them a favorable answer, they will be your servants for ever."

But he did not heed the advice of the old men and asked the young men who had grown up with him and had been in his service.

He asked them what answer they would advise him to give to the demand of the people that Solomon's burdens should be lightened.

The young men said to him:

"Make this answer to them: 'My little finger is thicker than my father's thigh! Whereas my father burdened you with a heavy yoke, I will make your yoke still heavier; my father chastised you with whips, but I will chastise you with scorpions (whips studded with spikes).' "

When the people returned to Rehoboam on the third day, as he had directed, he answered them harshly. He did not follow the advice which the old men had given him, but spoke to them as the young men had advised, saying:

"My father made your yoke heavy, but I will make your yoke still heavier; my father chastised you with whips, but I will chastise you with scorpions."

So Rehoboam paid no attention to the people.

When Israel saw that he paid no attention to their demands, they gave him this answer:

> "What portion have we in the house of David?
> We are done with Jesse's son!
> To your tents, O Israel!
> Look out for your own house, O David!"

And they went away.

When King Rehoboam sent Adoniram, who had charge of the labor-gangs, to them, the Israelites stoned him to death. Thereupon, Rehoboam quickly mounted his chariot and fled to Jerusalem.

Thus Israel rebelled against the house of David. It was brought about by the Lord, that He fulfill His promise which He had made through Ahijah to Jeroboam.

Jeroboam becomes King of Israel

When the Israelites heard that Jeroboam had returned from Egypt, they made him their king. None remained loyal to the house of David, except the tribe of Judah and the tribe of Benjamin.

On reaching Jerusalem, Rehoboam gathered all the men of Judah and Benjamin to attack Israel in order to recover his kingdom. But this message came from the Lord to Shemaiah, a man of God:

"Give this message from the Lord to Rehoboam, king of Judah, and to all the men of Judah and Benjamin, and to the rest of the people: 'You shall not march or fight against your brothers in Israel. Return home, every man of you! What has happened I have caused to happen!'"

They listened to this message from the Lord and returned home, as the Lord had bidden them.

Jeroboam fortified Shechem in the highlands of Ephraim, and lived there. Then Jeroboam thought:

"The kingdom will go back to the house of David, if these people go up to sacrifice at the Temple of the Lord in Jerusalem. Their heart will turn to their lord again, to Rehoboam the king of Judah."

Whereupon he took counsel, and he made two golden bulls and said to the people:

"You have gone up long enough to Jerusalem; behold your gods, O Israel, the gods that brought you out of the land of Egypt!"

One of them he placed in Beth-el, and the other in Dan.

He also turned some shrines into temples, and made priests from among all sorts of people. This proved a sin for the house of Jeroboam, and led to its being swept off the face of the earth, and destroyed. (*I Kings 12, 13*)

VI.

ELIJAH — THE PROPHET

After Rehoboam and Jeroboam died, many kings ruled in Judah and Israel. The kings had great power, but the spokesmen for the oppressed people were the prophets. The greatest of the earlier prophets was Elijah. He first appeared in the reign of King Ahab, son of Omri, king of Israel, who had married Jezebel, the daughter of the king of Phoenicia. Queen Jezebel sought to make her religion of Baal the religion of the Royal Court and of the people. Elijah fought to keep the nation from accepting this religion with its cruel practices. Numerous legends have gathered about the life of Elijah the Tishbite, for he had made a deep impression on the heart and mind of Israel. To this day the Cup of Elijah graces the *seder* table each Passover.

Samaria, the northern Capital

OMRI, king of Israel, bought the hill of Samaria from a man named Shemer; and he built a city on the hill and named it Samaria, after Shemer, its former owner.

Omri did what was evil, and displeased the Lord.

When Omri died, his son Ahab ruled over Israel. Ahab married Jezebel, the daughter of Ethbaal, king of the Zidonians, and then began to worship the Phoenician god, Baal. He reared up an altar for Baal in the temple of Baal, which he caused to be built in Samaria. Ahab also made an image of Astarte. Ahab displeased the Lord, the God of Israel, more than all the kings of Israel before him.

Elijah appears suddenly and declares the
Drought a Punishment sent by God

Now, Elijah came from Tishbeh in Gilead to tell Ahab:

"As surely as the Lord, the God of Israel, lives, whom I serve, there shall be neither dew nor rain these years except as I command it."

Then this message of the Lord came to Elijah:

"Go from here and hide yourself near the brook Kerith, east of the Jordan. And you shall drink from the brook; and I have commanded the ravens to feed you there."

Elijah went in obedience to the command of the Lord; he dwelt by the brook Kerith east of the Jordan. The ravens brought him bread and meat in the morning and bread and meat in the evening; and he drank from the brook. After a while the brook dried up, because there was no rain in the land.

Then this message of the Lord came to Elijah:

"Arise, go to the city of Zarephath, which belongs to Zidon, and live there. I have commanded a widow there to give you sustenance."

So he arose and went to Zarephath.

The Widow of Zarephath

When he came to the gate of the city, the widow was there gathering sticks. He called to her and said:

"Bring me, I beg you, a little water in a vessel, that I may drink."

As she was going to get it, he called to her:

"Bring me, I beg you, also a bit of bread."

She replied:

"As surely as the Lord your God lives, I have nothing baked, only a handful of meal in the jar and a little oil in the cruse. Now I am gathering a few sticks, that I may go in and prepare it for myself and my son, that we may eat it and thereafter starve."

Elijah said to her:

"Fear not; go and do as you have said; but first make me a little cake, and bring it to me; and afterward make some for yourself and your son. For the Lord the God of Israel declares, 'The jar of meal shall not be empty, nor the cruse of oil fail, until the day the Lord sends rain upon the land.'"

She went and did as Elijah directed; and she and her child, as well as Elijah, had food to eat for many days.

Now, some time later, the woman's son fell sick; and his sickness was so severe that he stopped breathing. She said to Elijah:

"What have I to do with you, O man of God? Have you come here to remind God of some sin of mine and to take the life of my son?"

He said to her:

"Give me your son."

He took him out of her hands, and carried him up into the upper chamber, where he was staying, and laid him on his own bed. Then he prayed to the Lord and said:

"O Lord, my God, hast Thou also brought misfortune upon this widow with whom I sojourn, by slaying her son? Pray, let this child's life come back to him!"

He stretched himself upon the child three times, and again prayed to the Lord and said:

"O Lord, my God, I pray Thee, give back this child's life to him again."

The Lord listened to Elijah's prayer; and when the life of the child came back to him, he sat up. Then Elijah took the child and brought him to his mother; and he said:

"See, your son lives!"

And the woman said:

"Now I know that you are a man of God, and that the message of the Lord that you speak is truth."

King Ahab seeks Elijah—The faithful Obadiah

In the third year of the drought this word of the Lord came to Elijah:

"Go, show yourself to Ahab, and I will send rain on the land."

Elijah went on his mission to show himself to Ahab.

The drought was severe in Samaria. And Ahab had called Obadiah, the overseer of the palace, who was very loyal to the Lord. Indeed, when Queen Jezebel ordered the prophets of the Lord to be killed, he hid a hundred of them in caves, and kept them supplied with bread and water. And Ahab said to Obadiah:

"Come, let us go through the land to all the springs and to all the brooks; perhaps we may find grass, so that we can save the horses and mules alive, and not lose all the beasts."

They divided the land between them to survey it: Ahab went one way by himself, and Obadiah another.

While Obadiah was on his way, Elijah suddenly met him. And Obadiah knew him, and bowed himself to the ground, and said:

"Is it you, my lord Elijah?"

He answered:

"It is I. Go, and tell your master, 'Elijah is here.' "

But Obadiah said:

"What sin have I done that you would give your servant over to Ahab to kill me? As surely as the Lord your God lives, there is no nation or kingdom where my lord has not sent to seek you; and when they said, 'He is not here,' he made each of the kingdoms and nations take an oath that no one had found you. Now you say, 'Go, tell your master, Elijah is here!' But as soon as I have left you the spirit of the Lord will carry you whither I know not, so that when I come and tell Ahab and he cannot find you, he will slay me, although I, your servant, have been loyal to the Lord from my youth."

Then Elijah said:

"As the Lord of hosts lives, before whom I stand, I will surely show myself to Ahab today."

Elijah warns King Ahab

Obadiah went to meet Ahab and gave him the message of Elijah. And Ahab went to meet Elijah. When Ahab saw Elijah, he said to him:

"Is it you, you troubler of Israel?"

He answered:

"I have not troubled Israel; but you and your father's house are the trouble-makers, because you have forsaken the commands of the Lord and have run after the Phoenician Baal."

Elijah shows the Power of God over Baal and his Priests at Mount Carmel

And Elijah continued:

"Send messengers, and gather to me at Mount Carmel all the Israelites and the four hundred and fifty prophets of Baal who eat at Jezebel's table."

Ahab sent to all the Israelites and gathered the prophets of Baal together at Mount Carmel. Then Elijah came near to the people and said:

"How long will you halt between two opinions? If the Lord be God, follow Him; but if Baal, then follow him."

The people were silent.

Then Elijah said to the people:

"I, even I only, am left a prophet of the Lord; but there are four hundred and fifty prophets of Baal. Let us take two bullocks. Let them choose one bullock for themselves, and cut it in pieces, and lay it on the wood, and put no fire under; and I will dress the other bullock, and lay it on the wood, and put no fire under. Then you call on your god, and I will call on the Lord. And the god who answers by fire is the true God!"

All the people cried:

"It is a fair test."

Elijah then said to the prophets of Baal:

"Choose one bullock for yourselves, and dress it first; for you are many; and call on your god, but put no fire under."

They took the bullock which was given them and dressed it, and called on Baal from morning till noon, crying:

"O Baal, answer us."

There was no voice or answer, although they danced in halting manner about the altar.

When it was noon, Elijah mocked them and said:

"Call loudly, for he is a god; either he is thinking, or he has gone out, or he is on a journey, or perhaps he sleeps and must be awakened!"

They cried aloud and cut themselves, as was their custom, with swords and lances until the blood gushed out upon them. When midday was past, they cried out in frenzy till the time of the offering of the evening sacrifice. But there was neither voice, nor any to answer, nor any that paid attention to their cry.

Elijah then said to all the people:

"Come near to me."

All the people drew near to him, and he repaired the altar of the Lord that had been thrown down. Around the altar he made a trench that would hold about two bushels of seed. He placed the pieces of wood in order and cut the bullock in pieces and laid it on the wood. Then he said:

"Fill four jars with water, and pour it on the sacrifice and on the pieces of wood."

He said:

"Do it a second time."

They did it a second time.

"Do it a third time."

And they did it a third time, so that the water ran around the altar. The water also filled the trench.

When it was time to offer the evening sacrifice, Elijah the prophet came near and said:

"O Lord, God of Abraham, of Isaac, and of Israel, let it be known this day that Thou art God in Israel, that I am Thy servant, and that I have done all these things at Thy command. Hear me, O Lord, hear me, that this people may know that Thou, the Lord, art God, and that Thou mayest win back their hearts."

Then a fire of the Lord consumed the sacrifice and the wood, the stones and the dust, and licked up the water that was in the trench. When all the people saw it, they bowed to the ground and cried:

"The Lord, He is God! The Lord, He is God!"

Elijah then commanded them:

"Take the prophets of Baal; let not one of them escape!"

They took the prophets of Baal to the brook Kishon and there put them to death.

Elijah turned to Ahab and said:

"Go, eat and drink. There are signs of abundance of rain."

Ahab went to eat and drink. But Elijah went up to the top of Mount Carmel and bowed himself down upon the earth. And he said to his servant:

"Go up now, look toward the sea."

He went up and looked and said:

"There is nothing."

Seven times Elijah said:

"Go again."

The servant went back seven times, and at the seventh time he said:

"Behold, a cloud as small as a man's hand is rising out of the sea."

Then Elijah said:

"Go, say to Ahab: 'Make ready your chariot; go down, that the rain may not stop you.' "

In a little while the heavens grew black with clouds and wind, and there fell a great rain.

Ahab rode for the Valley of Jezreel.

And Elijah was given divine strength; and he tightened his belt, and ran before Ahab to the entrance of Jezreel.

Jezebel, angry at the Death of the Priests of Baal, threatens Elijah's Life

When Ahab told Jezebel that Elijah had put the prophets of Baal to death, she sent a messenger to Elijah, saying:

"As surely as you are Elijah and I am Jezebel, may the gods kill me and worse if by this time tomorrow I do not make your life as the life of one of the prophets of Baal."

When Elijah heard this, he fled.   (*I Kings 16–19*)

ELIJAH IN THE CAVE

"And after the fire there came a still, small
voice." (*I Kings 19.12*)

see page 285

ELIJAH ACCUSES AHAB

"Because you have given yourself to do what is evil in
the sight of the Lord, I will bring evil on you . . ."

(I Kings 21.20–21)

see page 288

VII.

ELIJAH DEFENDS THE COMMONER

In the incident of Naboth's vineyard Elijah championed a
commoner against the scheme of King Ahab and Queen Jezebel.
In those days a man could not be forced to part with his ancestral land even by a king. King Ahab knew this; but Jezebel,
being a foreigner, did not respect this Jewish tradition. She
invented a charge of treason against Naboth and had his possessions taken from him. The people were secretly enraged, but
Elijah publicly denounced the king and queen.

WHEN Elijah reached Beer-sheba, which is in Judah, he
left his servant there. But he himself travelled a day's journey into the wilderness. He sat down under a juniper tree, and
he prayed that he might die. He cried:

"I have had enough. O Lord, take away my life now, for I
am not better than my fathers."

He lay down under the juniper tree and fell asleep. And behold, an angel touched him and said to him:

"Rise and eat!"

He saw beside his head a cake baked on hot stones, and a
cruse of water. He ate and drank and lay down again.

The angel of the Lord came again and said:

"Rise and eat, or else the journey will be too much for you."

He rose and ate and drank, and went by the strength of that
food forty days and forty nights to Horeb (Sinai), the mountain
of God.

God renews Elijah's Spirit

There Elijah went into a cave for shelter.

Suddenly, the Lord passed by, and a great and strong wind
rent the mountains and broke in pieces the rocks before the Lord.
But the Lord was not in the wind. After the wind an earthquake;
but the Lord was not in the earthquake. After the earthquake
there came a fire; but the Lord was not in the fire. And after
the fire there came a still, small voice.

When Elijah heard it, he wrapped his face in his mantle and went out and stood at the entrance of the cave. Then he heard a voice saying:

"What are you doing here, Elijah?"

He replied:

"I have been very zealous for the Lord the God of hosts; for the Israelites have forsaken Thy Covenant, thrown down Thine altars, and slain Thy prophets with the sword; and I, even I only am left; and they seek my life."

The Lord said to him:

"Go back; take the wilderness road to Damascus. When you arrive there, anoint Hazael to rule over Aram, and Jehu the grandson of Nimshi to be king over Israel; and Elisha, the son of Shaphat, to succeed you as prophet."

Elijah went back, as the Lord commanded him.

Elijah appoints Elisha

On the way Elijah came upon Elisha, the son of Shaphat, as he was plowing behind twelve yoke of oxen. When Elijah went to him and threw his mantle upon him, Elisha left the oxen and ran after him and said:

"Let me, I beg you, kiss my father and my mother, and then I will follow you."

Elijah said:

"Go, but consider what I have done to you!"

Elisha turned back and took one pair of oxen and offered them as a sacrifice and, using the wooden plows and yoke as fuel, boiled their flesh, and gave it to the people to eat.

Then he followed Elijah and served him.

Naboth's Vineyard

Now Naboth, the Jezreelite, had a vineyard in Jezreel, near by the palace of Ahab who ruled in Samaria. Ahab said to Naboth:

"Give me your vineyard, that I may have it as a garden of herbs because it is near my palace; and I will give you a better vineyard for it; or, if it is more pleasing to you, I will pay you its worth in money."

Naboth replied:

"The Lord forbid that I should give the inheritance of my fathers to you!"

Ahab returned to his palace sullen and displeased because of what Naboth had said to him. He lay down on his bed, and turned away his face, and would eat no food.

Jezebel his wife came to him and wanted to know:

"Why are you so sullen that you will not eat?"

He replied:

"Because I spoke to Naboth: 'Give me your vineyard for money; or else, if it please you, I will give you another vineyard for it.' But he answered: 'I will not give you my vineyard.' "

Jezebel said:

"Do you not govern the kingdom of Israel? Rise, and eat, and let your heart be merry. I will give you the vineyard of Naboth."

Jezebel's Scheme

So Jezebel wrote letters in Ahab's name, sealed them with his seal, and sent the letters to the leaders and nobles who lived in the city along with Naboth.

In the letters she wrote:

"Proclaim a fast, and put Naboth in front of the people. Set up two evil men before him, and let them witness this charge against him: 'You cursed God and the king.' Then carry him outside the city and stone him, that he die!"

The leaders and nobles of Naboth's city did as Jezebel commanded in her letters to them. They proclaimed a fast and put Naboth in front of the people. Two evil men came and sat before him; and the evil men in the presence of the people said:

"Naboth cursed God and the king."

Naboth was carried out of the city and was stoned so that he died. And Jezebel was told:

"Naboth has been stoned and is dead."

As soon as Jezebel heard that Naboth had been stoned and was dead, she said to Ahab:

"Rise, take the vineyard of Naboth which he refused to sell you, for Naboth is not alive, but dead."

Ahab then went to the vineyard of Naboth to take possession of it.

Elijah's terrible Warning

Meanwhile this command came from the Lord to Elijah, the Tishbite:

"Rise, go down to meet Ahab, king of Israel, who lives in Samaria. Behold, he is now in the vineyard of Naboth, where he has gone to take possession of it. Say to him, 'This is the message of the Lord: Have you killed and also taken possession? In the place where the dogs licked the blood of Naboth, they shall also lick your blood.' "

Elijah then went to Naboth's vineyard, where Ahab met him. Ahab said to Elijah:

"Have you found me out, O my enemy?"

He answered:

"I have found you out. And the Lord has declared: 'Because you have given yourself to do what is evil in the sight of the Lord, I will bring evil on you. And the dogs shall eat Jezebel in the moat by the wall of Jezreel.' "

When Ahab heard these words, he tore his clothes, put on sackcloth and ate no food. He fasted and repented of his crime. And he went about softly.

Then a message of the Lord came to Elijah:

"Do you see how Ahab humbles himself before Me? Because he humbles himself before Me, I will not bring the evil in his days; but in his son's days will I bring the evil upon his house."

Elijah disappears in a Whirlwind of Flame.
Elisha inherits the Mantle of Prophecy.

It came to pass, when the Lord was about to take up Elijah to heaven in a whirlwind, that Elijah went with Elisha from Gilgal. Elijah said to Elisha:

"Stay here, for the Lord has sent me as far as Beth-el."

And Elisha said:

"As surely as the Lord lives and as you live, I will not leave you."

Both continued on their way to Beth-el.

The disciples of the prophets at Beth-el came out to Elisha and said:

"Do you know that today the Lord will take away your master from you?"

He said:

"Yes, I know it; hold your peace."

Elijah then said to him:

"Elisha, stay here, I beg you; for the Lord has sent me to Jericho."

But he said:

"As surely as the Lord lives and as you live, I will not leave you."

They came to Jericho.

The disciples of the prophets at Jericho came near to Elisha and said:

"Do you know that today the Lord will take your master from you?"

He answered:

"Yes, I know it; hold your peace."

Elijah then said to Elisha:

"Stay here, I beg you; for the Lord has sent me to the Jordan."

He replied:

"As surely as the Lord lives and as you live, I will not leave you."

And they two went on together.

Fifty disciples of the prophets went and stood opposite them afar off; and they two stood by the Jordan. Then Elijah wrapped up his mantle, and with it struck the waters; and they were divided, so that they two went over on dry ground. When they had gone over, Elijah said to Elisha:

"Ask what I shall do for you, before I am taken from you."

Elisha said:

"Let a double portion of your spirit be upon me."

He replied:

"You have asked a hard thing; but if you see me when I am taken from you, it shall come to you; but if you do not, it shall not come."

As they were going on their way talking, suddenly a chariot of fire drawn by horses of fire separated the two of them; and Elijah went up by a whirlwind into the heavens.

As Elisha saw this, he cried out:

"My father! my father! the chariots of Israel and its horsemen!" *

When he saw Elijah no more, Elisha took hold of his own garments, and tore them in two pieces. Then lifting the mantle of Elijah which had fallen from the prophet, he returned and stood on the bank of the Jordan.

When the disciples of the prophets who were at Jericho some way off saw Elisha, they exclaimed:

"The spirit of Elijah rests on Elisha!"

The Death of King Ahab

Now, Ahab, king of Israel, and Jehoshaphat, king of Judah, made war on Aram. Ahab said to Jehoshaphat:

"I shall go into the battle in disguise. But you can put on your kingly robes."

Ahab disguised himself and went into battle.

The king of Aram, meanwhile, had ordered the captains of his chariots to fight with no one, young or old, except Ahab, king of Israel. Upon nearing Jehoshaphat, the chariot-captains thought he was the king of Israel, so they surrounded him. But upon seeing that he was not the king of Israel, the chariot-captains stopped pursuing him.

Then an archer shot an arrow, and by chance it struck Ahab, king of Israel, between the breastplate and the lower part of his armor.

---

*Elijah is considered to be Israel's greatest protector, comparable to an army in himself.

Ahab cried to the driver of his chariot:

"Wheel about and carry me out of the battle, for I am wounded."

As the fighting grew fiercer that day, Ahab remained to face the Aramaeans till night fell. While he was propped up in his chariot, the blood from his wound poured into the bottom of his chariot.

That evening Ahab died.

Then a cry went through his camp:

"Back to your towns, back to your country, every man of you, for the king is dead!"

His followers left the battlefield and returned to Samaria, where they buried Ahab.

When his chariot was washed at the pool of Samaria, the dogs licked up his blood. So the prophecy of Elijah came true.

And Ahab slept with his fathers, and Ahaziah, his son, reigned after him.   (*I Kings 19–22* and *II Kings 2*)

VIII.

ELISHA — ONE WHO LOVED HIS FELLOWMEN

Elisha followed his master Elijah in his loyalty to the God of Israel. Elisha was a strange person. He won the love of people through his kindness, his eagerness to help the poor, the afflicted and the sick. Through all the stories and legends about the wonders and miracles he performed runs the golden thread of his helpfulness to Gentiles as well as to Jews. In this way Elisha made people feel that God Himself was helpful also. He brought God's spirit home to people in the midst of their worries, struggles, sorrows, joys, hopes and fears.

The Widow's Cruse of Oil

NOW, a certain woman of the wives of the disciples of the prophets cried to Elisha, saying:

"Your servant, my husband, is dead. You know that your servant worshipped the Lord. Now a creditor has come to take my two children and make them his bond-slaves."

Elisha asked:

"What shall I do for you? Tell me what do you have in the house?"

She replied:

"Your humble servant has nothing in the house at all, except a pot of olive-oil."

He said:

"Go, borrow vessels from all your neighbors, empty vessels, and plenty of them. Then shut yourself into the house, you and your sons, and pour the oil into all those vessels, and set aside that which is full."

She went away and shut herself and her sons inside the house. They brought the vessels to her, and she poured out the oil. When the vessels were full, she said to her son:

"Bring me another vessel."

He said to her:

"There is not another vessel."

Then the oil stopped flowing.

When she went and told the man of God, he said: "Go, sell the oil, and pay your debts, and live, you and your sons, on the rest."

The Shunammite Woman

It happened one day that Elisha went to Shunem, where a rich lady who lived there made him take some food. Thereafter, he used to go in for a meal whenever he passed there. So she said to her husband:

"Behold, I see that this is a holy man of God, who passes by us continually. Come, let us make a little guest-chamber for him on the roof, with a bed and a table and a stool and a candlestick, so that whenever he comes to us he can stay here."

One day Elisha came, and he turned into the little chamber and rested there. He said to his servant Gehazi:

"Call this Shunammite."

When she stood before him, he told Gehazi to ask her:

"What is to be done for you, since you have taken so much trouble for us? Shall we say a word for you to the king or to the captain of the army?"

She said:

"No, I dwell among my own people."

He then asked Gehazi what was to be done for her; and Gehazi replied:

"She has no son, and her husband is old."

Elisha said:

"Call her."

When she came to the door, he said,

"This time next year you shall embrace a son."

She answered:

"No, my lord, you man of God, do not deceive your humble servant!"

Next year, however, when the time came around, the woman had a child, as Elisha had said to her. When the boy grew up, he went out one day to his father among the reapers. And he called to his father:

"My head! my head!"

The father ordered his servant to carry the boy to his mother. And when he was brought to his mother, he sat on her lap till noon; and then died.

She carried him up, and laid him on the bed of the man of God, and shut the door upon him, and went to her husband and said:

"Send me one of the servants and one of the donkeys, that I may speed to the man of God and come back again quickly."

He asked:

"Why go to him today? It is neither new moon festival nor the Sabbath."

She said:

"I have a good reason."

She saddled the donkey and told her servant:

"Drive ahead, don't slacken the pace, till I tell you to stop."

So she went to the man of God at Mount Carmel.

When the man of God saw her afar off, he said to his servant Gehazi:

"Behold, there is the Shunammite! Run to meet her and ask: 'Are you well? Is your husband well? Is the child well?' "

She answered:

"It is well."

And she came to the man of God upon the hill, and grasped his feet. Gehazi came near to push her away, but the man of God said:

"Let her alone; she has a troubled heart; and the Lord has not told me. He has hidden it from me."

Then she cried:

"Did I ask my lord for a son? Did I not say, 'Do not deceive me'?"

Then Elisha told Gehazi:

"Gird up your loins, take my staff in your hands, and go your way; if you meet anyone, do not greet him; and if anyone greets you, do not stop to reply. Lay my staff on the face of the child."

The mother said to Elisha:

"As the Lord lives and as you live, I will not go home without you."

He arose and went with her. Gehazi had gone before them, and laid the staff on the face of the child; but, there was not a sound or sign of life. Then he came back to tell Elisha that the child had not wakened. When Elisha came into the house, there was the child lying dead upon his bed!

Elisha went in, therefore, and shut the door upon the two of them, and prayed to the Lord. Then he laid himself upon the child, and put his mouth on the child's mouth, his eyes on the child's eyes and his hands on the child's hands, and, as he stretched himself upon the child, its flesh grew warm. Elisha rose up, walked to and fro, and then went and again stretched himself upon the child; and the child opened his eyes.

Then Elisha called to Gehazi and ordered him to summon the Shunammite. When she came in, at his bidding, he said:

"Take up your son."

Then she went in and fell at his feet, bowing herself to the ground. She lifted up her son and went away.

Naaman the Leper

Now, Naaman, captain of the army of the king of Aram, was a great man, highly honored by his king, and famous, because by him the Lord had given victory to Aram. But, he was a leper.

On one of their raids in the land of Israel, the Aramaeans had carried off captive a little girl. She had become servant to Naaman's wife. And she said to her mistress:

"Would that my lord were with the prophet who lives at Samaria! He would cure my lord of his leprosy."

When Naaman heard this, he went in and told the king what the Israelite girl had said.

The king of Aram replied:

"Go now, and I will send a letter to the king of Israel."

So Naaman departed, and took with him many valuable gifts. And he brought the king of Israel the letter, which read:

"With this letter, I send you my servant Naaman that you may cure him of his leprosy."

When the king of Israel read the letter, he tore his clothes and cried:

"Am I God, to kill and to make alive, that this man sends to me to cure a man of leprosy? Consider and see how he is trying to pick a quarrel with me!"

When Elisha the man of God heard that the king of Israel had torn his clothes in despair, he sent this message to the king of Israel:

"Why have you torn your clothes? Let the man now come to me, and he shall know there is a prophet in Israel."

Naaman then drove his chariots and horses to the door of Elisha's house. Elisha sent out word to him:

"Go and wash in the Jordan seven times, and your body shall once more be well and clean."

Naaman was angry, and went away, muttering:

"I expected he would come out to me and call upon the Lord his God, and wave his hand over the place and cure the leper. Are not Amanah and Pharpar, the rivers of Damascus, better than all the waters of Israel? Could I not wash in them and be clean?"

And he turned and drove away in a rage.

But his servants came near to him and said:

"If the prophet had told you to do some great thing, would you not have done it? How much rather, then, when he only tells you: Wash, and be clean?"

At this Naaman went down and dipped seven times in the Jordan, as the man of God had ordered. His body became once more like a child's body, and he was clean. Then, he returned to the man of God, he and all his retinue, and he stood in his presence, and said:

"Behold, now I know there is no God in all the earth except in Israel! Accept a present, I beg you, from your humble servant."

But Elisha said:

"As surely as the Lord lives whom I serve, I will accept nothing."

Naaman urged him, but he refused. Then said Naaman:

"Well, let your servant at least have two mules' load of earth; for after this your servant will offer neither burnt-offering nor sacrifice to other gods but to the Lord.

"And may the Lord pardon me in this: when my master, the king, enters the house of the god Rimmon to worship there, and he leans on my arm, and I bow myself in the house of Rimmon when he bows in the house of Rimmon, may the Lord pardon your servant!"

Elisha said to him:

"Go in peace!"

He left.

Kindness to Enemies

Once when the king of Aram warred against Israel, he took counsel with his servants, saying:

"In such and such a place shall be my camp."

But Elisha the man of God sent word to the king of Israel, saying:

"Beware that you do not pass such a place, for the Aramaeans are hiding there."

The king of Israel sent soldiers to the place about which the man of God warned him, and saved himself. This happened more than once. It greatly troubled the king of Aram. He summoned his officers and asked them:

"Will you not tell me who has betrayed us to the king of Israel?"

One of his officers replied:

"No one, my lord, O king; but Elisha, the prophet in Israel, tells the king of Israel the words that you speak in your bedchamber."

The king said:

"Go and see where he is, that I may send and seize him."

They told the king:

"Behold, Elisha is now in Dothan."

The king sent a large force from his army to Dothan. They came at night and surrounded the city. When the man of God rose early the next morning and went out, an army with horses and chariots had enclosed the city. His servant said to Elisha:

"Alas, my master! What shall we do?"

He answered:

"Fear not: for they who are with us are more than they who are with them."

And Elisha prayed, and said:

"Lord, I pray Thee, open his eyes, that he may see."

The Lord opened the eyes of the young man; and he saw; and, behold, the mountain round about Elisha was full of horses and chariots of fire.

When the enemy came down to him, Elisha prayed to the Lord, and said:

"Make, I pray Thee, this people blind."

And the Lord made them blind as Elisha asked.

Elisha then said to them:

"This is not the way, neither is this the city. Follow me and I will bring you to the man you seek!"

He led them to Samaria.

As soon as they came to Samaria, Elisha said:

"O Lord, open the eyes of these men, that they may see."

And the Lord opened their eyes, so that they could see, and there they were in Samaria. When the king of Israel saw them, he said to Elisha:

"My father, shall I strike them down?"

Elisha answered:

"You shall not strike them down; would you strike down those whom you have not taken captive with your sword nor with your bow? Set bread and water before them, that they may eat and drink, and go to their master."

He had a great feast spread for them, and after they had eaten and drunk, he sent them away to their master.   (*II Kings 4–6*)

IX.

ELISHA DESTROYS THE HOUSE OF OMRI

As kindly as Elisha was towards all men, so stern was he with those he considered the enemies of the Lord. Like Elijah, he struggled to rid Israel of Baal-worship and its evils. He was convinced that the ruling house founded by Omri — King Ahab and his descendants — was the source of this evil, because they were worshippers of Baal. He, therefore, determined to destroy the house of Omri. When the time was ripe, he secretly anointed Jehu, a young captain in the army, as the king of Israel, for Jehu was vigorous in action and ruthless against Baal-worship. These events later came to be known as "The Revolt of Jehu." Shortly thereafter Elisha died.

WHEN Joram, the son of Ahab,↓ was king of Israel, Ahaziah began to reign as king of Judah. Ahaziah followed the ways of the house of Ahab, for he had married a wife of that family.

King Ahaziah went with King Joram to war against Hazael, king of Aram, at Ramoth-gilead. There the Aramaeans wounded Joram. And Joram went to the Valley of Jezreel to recover from his wounds. King Ahaziah went down to visit Joram at Jezreel, where he lay ill.

Elisha anoints Jehu King

At this time Elisha the prophet called one of the disciples of the prophets and said to him:

"Gird up your loins, take this vial of oil in your hand and go to Ramoth-gilead. When you arrive there, look for Jehu, the son of Jehoshaphat, take him to an inner room, away from those who are with him. Then take the vial of oil, and pour it on his head, and say: 'The Lord declares, I have anointed you king over Israel.' Then open the door and leave without delay."

The young man went to Ramoth-gilead. When he arrived, the officers of the army were sitting together. He said:

"Captain, I have a message for you."

↓For archaeological note see Item 11, p. 552 in the back of the book.

Jehu said:

"For which of us?"

He replied:

"For you, Captain."

Jehu rose and went into the house; and the young man poured the oil on his head and said to him:

"The Lord, the God of Israel, says: 'I have anointed you king over the Lord's people, even over Israel!' "

Then he opened the door and hurried away.

When Jehu came out to the officers of the king, they asked him:

"Is all well? Why did this mad fellow come to you?"

He answered:

"You know the man and his message."

They said:

"You are deceiving us. You must tell us."

Jehu replied:

"He said this to me: 'The Lord says, I have anointed you king over Israel.' "

Each then hastened to take his garment, and lay it at Jehu's feet on the stairs, and blew the horn, saying:

"Jehu is king of Israel!"

Thus Jehu plotted against Joram.

He said to the officers:

"If you are on my side, let no one escape from the city to bring the news to Jezreel."

Then Jehu rode off in a chariot to the Valley of Jezreel, where Joram lay ill. It chanced that Ahaziah, king of Judah, had come down at that time to visit King Joram.

Now a watchman was standing on the tower of Jezreel, and he spied a cloud of dust made by Jehu as he rode; and he said:

"I see a company of men."

King Joram said:

"Send a horseman to meet them, and let him say: 'Is it peace?' "

The horseman went out to meet them, and said:

"The king of Israel asks: 'Do you come in peace?' "

Jehu replied:

"What have you to do with peace? Turn and follow me."

And the watchman said to Joram:

"The messenger went to them, but does not return."

Joram sent out a second horseman who came to Jehu and said:

"The king of Israel asks: 'Do you come in peace?'"

Jehu answered:

"What have you to do with peace? Turn and follow me."

The watchman again said to Joram:

"He also went to them but does not return; however, the driving is like the driving of Jehu, for he drives furiously."

Then Joram said:

"Get my chariot ready."

When it was ready, he went to meet Jehu and found him in the field of Naboth the Jezreelite. When Joram saw Jehu, he said:

"Do you come in peace, Jehu?"

And Jehu answered, "What peace, so long as the wickedness of your mother, Jezebel, and her witchcrafts are so many?"

Then Joram turned and fled. But Jehu drew his bow with his full strength and sent an arrow at Joram which went through his heart, and he died in his chariot.

Jehu turned to Bidkar, his charioteer, and said:

"Take him up and throw him into the field of Naboth the Jezreelite, for I well remember that, as you and I rode together after Ahab his father, the Lord pronounced this sentence upon him: 'Surely I saw yesterday the blood of Naboth and his sons, and I will punish you on this same piece of land.' Now therefore take and cast him into this piece of land, as the Lord has said."

Then Jehu continued on his way and arrived at Jezreel.

When Jezebel heard of all this, she painted her eyes, arranged her hair, and looked out of the window. As Jehu entered in at the gate, she said:

"Is it peace, you traitor, you murderer of your master?"

He looked up to the window and cried:

"Who is on my side? Who?"

Two or three officers looked down on him, and he commanded:

"Throw her down!"

They threw her down; and the horses trampled on her; and some of her blood was sprinkled on the wall.

When Jehu had something to eat and drink, he gave this command:

"Look after this cursed woman and bury her, for she is a king's daughter."

But when they went to bury her, they found no more of her than the skull, the feet and the hands. When they went back and reported this to Jehu, he said:

"This is what the Lord declared by his servant Elijah when he said, 'On the piece of land at Jezreel shall the dogs eat the flesh of Jezebel, and her body shall be as refuse on the face of the field, so that no one may say: This is Jezebel.' "

The Death of Elisha

Now, Elisha fell ill with the disease of which he was to die. And Jehoash, king of Israel, went to him and grieved over his illness, crying:

"My father! my father! the chariots of Israel and its horsemen!"

Elisha said to him: "Take bow and arrows." Then he said: "Draw the bow."

And Elisha laid his hands on the king's hands. He opened the window towards the east. Then Elisha said:

"Shoot."

He shot his arrow; and Elisha cried:

"The Lord's arrow of victory! Victory over Aram! You shall smite the Aramaeans at Aphek and wipe them out."

Then Elisha died. (*II Kings 8–9, 13.14–20*)

X.

ATHALIAH — THE BLOODY QUEEN

Athaliah, daughter of King Ahab and Queen Jezebel, was a worshipper of the Baal religion, like her Phoenician mother. She wanted to establish the Baal religion in the heart of Jerusalem, the capital city. Her chance came when Jehu↓ killed her son, King Ahaziah. Athaliah seized the throne of Judah and made herself Queen. She was a strong-willed, cruel woman, who put all but one of the king's sons to death. The sister of Ahaziah rescued little Prince Joash from the hands of Athaliah. About six years later, Jehoiada, the High Priest of the Temple, organized a revolt against Athaliah's rule. He placed the young Joash on the throne of Judah.

Athaliah as Queen of Judah

WHEN Athaliah, the mother of King Ahaziah, learned that her son was dead, she put to death all of Ahaziah's children. But Jehosheba, the sister of Ahaziah, had secretly taken Joash, the son of Ahaziah, and placed him with his nurse. In this way she hid him from Athaliah, and saved him from being slain. For six years the boy was hidden in the Temple of the Lord; and Athaliah reigned over the land.

Athaliah and her priests caused the Temple of the Lord to be violated and plundered, and gave to Baal all the offerings in the Temple of the Lord.

Jehoiada plans the Revolt

In the seventh year of her reign, Jehoiada, the High Priest, called together the captains of the royal guard and brought them into the Temple of the Lord. After he had made them take a solemn oath, he showed them Ahaziah's son; and he gave them these commands:

"This is what you shall do: A third part of you, those who come in on Sabbath to guard the palace, along with the two other divisions who come in on Sabbath to guard the Temple of the Lord, shall all surround Joash, each man with his weapons in his hand. Any stranger in the ranks is to be slain. You must guard Joash, when he goes out of the Temple and comes into the palace."

The captains carried out the orders of Jehoiada; each brought
↓For archaeological note see Item 12, p. 552 in the back of the book.

his men to Jehoiada the priest, those who were off duty on Sabbath and those who were to come on duty. And the priest handed the captains the spear and shields that had been King David's, which were in the Temple of the Lord. And the men stood guard.

Then Jehoiada brought out the king's son, and put upon him the crown and the royal ornaments. They proclaimed Joash king over Judah, anointed him with oil, and they clapped their hands and shouted:

"Long live the king!"

When Athaliah heard the cheers of the guard and of the people, she came to them in the Temple of the Lord. She looked, and she saw the king standing on the platform, as was the custom, with the captains and the trumpeters beside him, and the people present rejoiced and blew with trumpets.

Then Athaliah tore her clothes in grief, and shouted:

"Treason! Treason!"

Jehoiada ordered the captains and the army commanders:

"Bring her forth between the ranks, and kill with the sword anyone who follows her."

The priest forbade her to be slain inside the Temple of the Lord.

They seized her, and as she went through the place for the horses' entry to the palace, she was slain.

Jehoiada made a solemn agreement between the Lord and the new king and the people, that they should be the Lord's people.

King Joash cleanses the Land
and renovates the Temple

Joash was seven years old when he began to reign. He reigned forty years in Jerusalem. Joash did what was right in the eyes of the Lord all his days, since Jehoiada, the priest, instructed him.

The people went to the temple of Baal and destroyed it, and smashed his altars and images to pieces.

Then Joash hired builders and masons, and brought timber and stone to repair the Temple of the Lord.

Afterwards, some officers conspired against King Joash, and killed him as he was going down to Beth-millo. So he died, and they buried him with his fathers in the City of David.

(II Kings 11, 12; II Chronicles 24)

XI.

THE KINGDOM OF ISRAEL ENDS

Jeroboam II, the great-grandson of Jehu, ruled over Israel.*
When he died, confusion broke out and kings came and went,
one after the other, until Israel's prosperity and glory faded
away. Finally, Hoshea son of Elah, came to the throne.**
He was the last king of Israel. During his reign the Empire of
Assyria became very powerful. Its ruler, King Shalmaneser,
demanded tribute of King Hoshea, and when the king of
Israel refused, Shalmaneser besieged Samaria, capital of Israel.
After three years Assyria took the city↓ and destroyed the King-
dom of Israel.

HOSHEA, the son of Elah, reigned over Israel, and he did
what was evil in the eyes of the Lord.

And Shalmaneser, king of Assyria, marched against him, and
Hoshea became his vassal and brought him tribute. But the
king of Assyria discovered Hoshea was conspiring against him
(for Hoshea sent messengers to the king of Egypt instead of bringing tribute to Shalmaneser, as he had done each year), and so he
took him prisoner.

Shalmaneser marched up through the land, and laid siege to
Samaria, the capital city, for three years. In the ninth year of
Hoshea's reign, the king of Assyria took Samaria, and carried
large numbers of the Israelites away to Assyria, and settled them
in Halah, and in Habor, on the river of Gozan, and in the cities
of Media.

And the king of Assyria brought some of his own people from
Babylonia and other places, and settled them in Samaria instead of
the Israelites. These people took possession of Samaria and dwelt
in its cities.

---

*During his reign the prophet Amos preached his great sermons. For Amos'
prophecies see pages 323 ff.

**During his reign the prophet Hosea delivered his great sermons. For Hosea's
prophecies see pages 337 ff.

↓For archaeological note see Item 13, p. 553 in the back of the book.

When they began to live there, they did not worship the Lord; therefore the Lord sent lions among them, which killed some of them. And they spoke to the king of Assyria, saying:

"The nations which you have carried away and settled in the cities of Samaria do not know the customs of the God of the land. Therefore, He has sent lions among them, and they slay them, because the people do not know the customs of the God of the land."

Then the king of Assyria commanded:

"Send there one of the priests whom I carried away from Samaria and let him go and dwell there, and let him teach them the customs of the God of the land."

One of the priests, who had been carried away to Assyria from Samaria, was sent back to Israel and he dwelt in Beth-el, and he taught the people how they should obey and why they should fear the Lord. Thus they learned why to fear the Lord, but they also continued to serve their own gods, according to the custom of the nations from which they had been carried away.*

Why Israel was destroyed

Now all this came about because the Israelites had sinned against the Lord their God, who brought them out of the land of Egypt. They had worshipped other gods and followed the customs of the nations whom the Lord had cast out to make room for the Israelites. But the Israelites had done what was evil in the sight of the Lord their God, and had set up shrines in all their cities, and had sacrificed there like the nations before them. And they had served idols about which the Lord had said to them: "You shall not do this thing."

The Lord had warned Israel and Judah by all His prophets saying:

"Turn from your evil ways, and keep My commands and laws which I gave your fathers and which I sent to you by My messengers the prophets."

*Later, this mixture of peoples came to be known as Samaritans; they were half-Jews.

However, they would not listen; they were as stubborn and as stiff-necked as their fathers. They refused to observe the laws and the Covenant which He had made with their fathers, and the warnings He had given them. They went after false gods to become false like them.

They made idols, worshipped the stars and honored Baal. They even passed their children through fire like the worshippers of Moloch. They practiced magic and consulted witches. They gave themselves to do other things, evil in the eyes of the Lord.

Thus the Lord was very angry with Israel and removed them from His sight. So Israel was carried away out of their own land to Assyria.

Only the kingdom of Judah was left.   (*II Kings 17*)

XII.

HEZEKIAH — THE GOOD KING

The destruction of the northern Kingdom of Israel greatly frightened the people of the southern Kingdom of Judah, as well as its king, Hezekiah. Hezekiah was a good king. In his time a new power was rising in the far east beyond Assyria. It was Babylonia. Its emperor sought allies, and he urged Judah to join Babylonia against Assyria. Isaiah the prophet warned King Hezekiah against Babylonia, for he did not believe Babylonia was any more to be trusted than Assyria.* In those days, Micah, the prophet of the countryside, also preached to the people.

IT WAS in the third year of Hoshea, the last king of Israel, that Hezekiah the son of Ahaz, began to reign in Judah. He did what was right and ruled justly in the eyes of the Lord, exactly as David his ancestor had done. He trusted in the Lord, the God of Israel; there was no king of Judah like him, before or afterwards. He cleaved to the Lord, and obeyed the commands given by the Lord to Moses. The Lord was with him, and in all his ventures he prospered.

The Temple and the Passover

In the first year of his reign Hezekiah opened the doors of the Temple of the Lord and repaired them. He summoned the priests and the Levites, and said to them:

"Hear me, O Levites; purify yourselves and purify the Temple of the Lord, the God of your fathers, and remove the idols out of the holy place."

The priests went inside the Temple of the Lord to cleanse it. They went to King Hezekiah in the palace and reported that they had cleansed all the Temple of the Lord, the altar and all its vessels, and the table of the showbread, with its vessels; they

---

*For Isaiah's sermons and prophecies see pages 345 ff. Isaiah delivered his great prophecies during the reigns of King Uzziah, King Ahaz and King Hezekiah; it is said that he was put to death during the cruel reign of King Manasseh.

also restored and sanctified all the vessels which King Ahaz had cast aside.

Hezekiah then sent letters to all Israel (although their kingdom had been destroyed, some Israelites still remained in the land) and to Judah, that they should come to the Temple of the Lord at Jerusalem to celebrate the Passover in honor of the Lord, the God of Israel. Couriers carried these letters from the king and his nobles all over Israel and Judah.

There was a large gathering at Jerusalem to celebrate the Festival of Unleavened Bread. For seven days the Israelites who had come to Jerusalem celebrated the festival with great delight.

Then the priests arose and blessed the people. Their voice was heard by the Lord; and their prayers came up to heaven.

Micah the Prophet

In those days, the Lord spoke to His people through the prophet Micah, who lived in Moresheth near the border of the Philistines. He said:

"With what shall I come before the Lord,
And bow myself before God on high?
Shall I come before Him with burnt-offerings,
With calves of a year old?
Will the Lord be pleased with thousands of rams,
With ten thousands of rivers of oil?
Shall I give my first-born for my transgression,
The fruit of my body for the sin of my soul?
It hath been told thee, O man, what is good,
And what the Lord doth require of thee:
Only to do justly, and to love mercy,
And to walk humbly with thy God." (*Micah 6.6–8*)

Hezekiah's Illness

Now King Hezekiah became very sick, near to death. And Isaiah, the prophet, came to him and said:

"Thus says the Lord: 'Set your house in order, for you shall die, and not live.' "

Hezekiah turned his face to the wall and prayed and wept.

And Isaiah left his presence.

Before Isaiah had gone out of the middle court of the city, this word of the Lord came to him:

"Return and say to Hezekiah, the prince of My people, that the Lord, the God of his father David, declares:

'I have heard your prayers, I have seen your tears; behold, I will heal you. I will rescue both you and this city from the king of Assyria. I will defend this city for My own sake and for the sake of My servant David.'"

Soon after this Hezekiah recovered.

Hezekiah was held in the greatest of honor, and he had enormous wealth. He built treasuries to hold silver, gold, jewels and spices, arsenals for shields, and all kinds of beautiful articles. He also had storehouses for grain, wine and oil, and barns for large numbers of cattle, and pens for sheep; he acquired great numbers of flocks and herds, for God gave him great possessions.

Hezekiah also built a pool↓ and an aqueduct which brought water into the City of David.

And he succeeded in all that he undertook.

Hezekiah, relying on Babylonia,
rebels against Assyria

Now, Hezekiah rebelled against Sennacherib, the new emperor of Assyria, and refused to pay him tribute.

In the fourteenth year of King Hezekiah, Sennacherib, emperor of Assyria, marched against all the fortified cities of Judah and took them. And Hezekiah, king of Judah, sent this message to the emperor of Assyria:

"I have done wrong; withdraw, and I will pay any fine you demand."

The emperor of Assyria fixed the fine at three hundred bars of silver and thirty bars of gold. Hezekiah gave him all the silver to be found in the Temple of the Lord and in the treasuries of the king's palace. Hezekiah also cut off the gold from the doors of the Temple of the Lord, and from the door-posts, to give tribute to the emperor of Assyria.

↓For archaeological note see Item 14, p. 553 in the back of the book.

The emperor of Assyria then sent his commander-in-chief, Rab-shakeh, from the town of Lachish, where the emperor was, to Jerusalem with a great army. When they came to Jerusalem, they took up their position outside the wall of the city by the conduit of the upper pool.

Rab-shakeh stepped forward, shouting aloud in the Hebrews' language:

"Hear you this word from the great emperor of Assyria! 'Do not listen to Hezekiah, when he persuades you that the Lord will save you. Has any one of the gods of the nations yet saved his land from the hand of the emperor of Assyria? Where are the gods of Samaria? Have they saved Samaria from me? What gods of all the gods of the countries have saved their country from me, that the Lord should now save Jerusalem from me?' "

The inhabitants of the city held their peace. They made no reply. The king had commanded them not to answer him.

Sennacherib forced to withdraw.
Isaiah encourages the King and
the People.

When Hezekiah heard these boastful words, he tore his clothes, put on the sackcloth of mourning, and went into the Temple of the Lord. He sent Eliakim and Shebna and the elders of the priests, robed in sackcloth, to the prophet Isaiah. They gave him this message from Hezekiah:

"This is a day of trouble, of chastisement, and of shame. It may be that the Lord your God will hear all that Rab-shakeh has said, whom his master, the king of Assyria, has sent to insult the living God; it may be that the Lord your God will have some answer for the words He has heard. Pray, then, for the remnant of this people."

When the messengers from the king came to Isaiah, he gave them this message from the Lord for their king:

"Do not be afraid of the words you have heard from these officers of the king of Assyria who have blasphemed Me. I will make him hear a rumor, so that he shall go back to his own country and fall by the sword in his own land.

"The Lord declares that the emperor of Assyria shall never come to this city. 'I will defend this city to save it, for My own sake, and for My servant David's sake,' says the Lord."

That very night the angel of the Lord went to the Assyrian camp and struck down a hundred and eighty-five thousand men.

Sennacherib then departed and returned to Assyria and dwelt at Nineveh. As he was worshipping in the temple of Nisroch his god, his sons slew him with the sword.

And Hezekiah slept with his fathers.

(II Kings 18, 19, 20; II Chronicles 29, 30, 32; Isaiah 37, 38)

XIII.

KING JOSIAH — RESTORER OF THE COVENANT

Hezekiah was followed by his son, Manasseh, who persecuted the prophets. After his death and the death of his son, Amon, the young Prince Josiah became king of Judah. In the reign of King Josiah, Babylonia came to its full power after conquering Assyria. Meanwhile, the prophets Zephaniah, Nahum and Habakkuk were active among the people. And the great prophet Jeremiah, about whom we shall read later, now came upon the scene.* A most important event took place in the early years of Josiah's rule. A book had been found while the Temple was being renovated. Some believe it was the Five Books of Moses; others hold that it was only the Book of Deuteronomy. King Josiah was profoundly moved when it was read to him. He started a series of reforms in its spirit.

JOSIAH was eight years old when he commenced his reign, which lasted for thirty-one years. He did what was right in the eyes of the Lord, and followed in the footsteps of his ancestor David.

> *Zephaniah, the Prophet, condemns the People for their Idolatry and the Leaders for their Corruption*

At this time the prophet Zephaniah warned the people of the evils in their midst. He cried:

"Silence before the Lord God,
For the day of the Lord is near at hand!
I will stretch out My hand against Judah,
Against all the inhabitants of Jerusalem.
I will cut off the Baal from this place,
And the young priests, with the old priests,
And those who bow themselves upon the housetops

---

*For the prophecies and sermons of Jeremiah see pages 377 ff.

To the hosts of heaven,
Who give up following the Lord.
I will punish the princes and the royal house,
Who by their violence and fraud enrich the palace."

(*Zephaniah 1.4–9*)

Repairing the Temple

In the eighteenth year of his reign, Josiah sent Shaphan, the scribe, to the Temple of the Lord with the command:

"Go to Hilkiah, the High Priest, and see that, when he has taken the money that is brought into the Temple of the Lord, he give it to the workmen who have charge of the Temple of the Lord. Let him give it to the carpenters, the builders, and the masons who are in the Temple of the Lord, to repair the breaks in it and to buy timber and cut stone to restore it."

Finding the Book of the Law

Now, Hilkiah, the High Priest, said to Shaphan:

"I have found a book of the Law in the Temple of the Lord."

Hilkiah gave the book to Shaphan, and he read it. Shaphan then went to King Josiah and told him:

"Your servants have taken the money that was found in the Temple and have turned it over to the workmen who have charge of the Temple of the Lord."

And then Shaphan said:

"Hilkiah, the priest, has given me a book."

And Shaphan read the book to the king.

When Josiah heard the words of the book of the Law, he tore his clothes in grief. He commanded Hilkiah, Achbor the son of Micaiah, Shaphan and Asaiah his servant:

"Go, inquire of the Lord for me, and for the people, and for all Judah about the words of this book that has been found; for the Lord must be very angry with us, because our fathers have not listened to the words of this book nor done all that we are there commanded to do."

Hilkiah, the priest, and Ahikam and Achbor went to Huldah, the prophetess, who lived in Jerusalem, and talked with her. She said to them:

"This is the message of the Lord, the God of Israel: Tell the man who sent you to me that the Lord says, 'I am now about to bring evil upon this place and upon its people, even all that is written in the book which the king of Judah has read.' But you shall say to the king of Judah who sent you to inquire of the Lord that the Lord, the God of Israel, declares, 'Because you have repented and humbled yourself before the Lord and have wept before Me, your eyes shall not see all the evil which I am about to bring upon this place.' "

They told Josiah what she had said.

At the king's command, they summoned all the leaders of Judah and Jerusalem. And Josiah went to the Temple of the Lord, and with him the men of Judah and the people, including the children.

Josiah read to them all the words of the book of the Covenant which had been found in the Temple of the Lord. And he stood by the pillar and made a solemn promise before the Lord to obey all the commands and carry out all the commandments written in this book. And all the people also agreed to do this.

Josiah's Reformation

Josiah then commanded Hilkiah, the High Priest, and the second priest and the gate-keepers to bring out from the Temple of the Lord all the things that were made for Baal and for Astarte and for all the host of heaven. He burned them outside Jerusalem in the fields by the river Kidron, and carried their ashes to Beth-el. He also put down the idolatrous priests, whom the kings of Judah had appointed to offer sacrifice at the shrines on the high places in the cities of Judah and in the places around Jerusalem; those idolatrous priests also who offered sacrifices to Baal, the sun, the moon, and the planets and all the host of heaven.

He destroyed Topheth, which is in the Valley of Ben-Hinnom, so that no man might make his son or daughter pass through the fire to Moloch. He removed the horses at the entrance of the Temple of the Lord, which the kings of Judah had given to the sun, and burned the chariots of the sun. Josiah broke down and crushed in pieces the altars that were on the roof, which the kings had made.

Josiah also broke down the altar and the old temple at Beth-el This was the high place which Jeroboam, the son of Nebat, had made, and he burned the Asherah there. He also removed the shrines on the high places that were in Samaria.

The Great Passover

Then Josiah gave this order to the people:

"Keep the Passover to the Lord your God, as is commanded in this book of the Covenant."

Such a Passover as this had not been kept from the days of the Judges who had judged Israel and during the period of the kings of Israel and Judah. This Passover was kept in honor of the Lord in Jerusalem for the first time in the eighteenth year of Josiah's reign.

Josiah was the first ruler who turned to the Lord with all his heart, with all his soul, and with all his might. Nor were any of the kings who followed like him.

News comes at this Time also that Assyria has been conquered by Babylonia, and Nineveh, its hated Capital, has been destroyed. Nahum, the Prophet, voices the general Rejoicing.

Nahum the prophet, when Nineveh was destroyed, proclaimed:

"Behold upon the mountains the feet of the messenger,
That bringeth good tidings, and announceth peace!
O, Nineveh, the destroyer has come up against you!
O, city soaked with blood!

'Ruined is Nineveh,' they say;
There is none to lament her.
All who are told of your fate
Loudly clap their hands;
For whom have you not wronged?"   (*Nahum 2.1, 3.7, 19*)

Pharaoh-necoh marches north against
Assyria. Josiah, suspecting an Attack
on Judah, orders his Army to meet him.

At this time, Pharaoh-necoh, king of Egypt, rebelled against the king of Assyria and marched out against him. Josiah went out to meet him, but Pharaoh-necho sent his ambassadors to him with this message:

"What have you to do with me, O king of Judah? I march against your ancient foe, and not against you. Stop interfering with God, who is on my side, lest He destroy you."

The Battle of Megiddo. The
Death of King Josiah.

But Josiah would not trust Pharaoh-necoh and he directed his forces to attack Pharaoh's. The battle opened in the Valley of Megiddo. The archers of the enemy aimed at King Josiah and their arrows struck him; and Josiah cried to his men:

"Take me away, for I am badly wounded."

His men lifted him out of the chariot in which he had been wounded, put him into his reserve chariot, and they drove him to Jerusalem. There he died; and he was buried in the tombs of his fathers.

All Judah and Jerusalem mourned for Josiah.

(*II Kings 22, 23; II Chronicles 34, 35*)

XIV.

ZEDEKIAH — LAST KING OF JUDAH

Zedekiah, son of King Josiah, was a man of good intentions but of weak character. He promised not to rebel against Nebuchadnezzar, the mighty emperor of Babylonia, but he was persuaded to break his promise. The Babylonians marched against Jerusalem, besieged the city, and starved it into submission. Jeremiah saw the destruction of the Kingdom of Judah, her nobility and her people,* but his last message was one of comfort and hope. With the end of the Kingdom of Judah, the great adventure which began in the days of Samuel and Saul came to an end. And the people of Judah went weeping into exile in Babylonia.

ZEDEKIAH, son of Josiah,↓ reigned eleven years in Jerusalem, and did what was evil in the eyes of the Lord.

Jeremiah's Advice to Zedekiah

In the fourth year of Zedekiah's reign, Jeremiah the prophet spoke to Zedekiah and said:

"Submit to the yoke of the emperor of Babylonia, and serve him and his people that you may live! Why should you and your people die by sword, famine, and pestilence?

"Do not listen to the words of the prophets who say to you, 'You shall not serve the emperor of Babylonia!' For it is a lie which they are prophesying to you."

Jeremiah also spoke to the priests and to the people, and said:

"Thus says the Lord, 'Do not listen to the words of your prophets who prophesy to you; for it is a lie which they are prophesying to you.' "

Zedekiah, disregarding Jeremiah's
Advice, rebels against Babylonia

But Zedekiah rebelled against the emperor of Babylonia. And Zedekiah sent ambassadors to Egypt, that they might help him with horses and troops.

---

*Tradition holds that the Book of Lamentations was written by Jeremiah on the destruction of Jerusalem. See pages 483 ff.

↓For archaeological note see Item 15, p. 553 in the back of the book.

In the ninth year of Zedekiah's reign, Nebuchadnezzar, emperor of Babylonia, attacked Jerusalem with all his army; they pitched camp and ran a wall around it, and besieged the city.

The word of the Lord came to Jeremiah:

"Thus says the Lord, the God of Israel: Go to Zedekiah, king of Judah, and say to him, 'Thus says the Lord: Behold, I am giving this city into the power of the emperor of Babylonia, and he shall burn it; and you yourself shall not escape, but shall most certainly be captured and you shall see the emperor of Babylonia face to face; and to Babylonia shall you go.' "

Jeremiah arrested and put in Prison for the Duration of the War. A Negro Youth saves Jeremiah from Death.

The princes heard the words of Jeremiah that he spoke to the people of the city. And the princes said to the king:

"Have this man, we beg you, put to death; for he is disheartening the soldiers that are left in the city, and the people as well, by speaking such words to them; for this man is seeking not the welfare of this people, but their ruin."

Zedekiah said:

"Behold, he is in your hands; for the king can do nothing against you."

They took Jeremiah, and cast him into the cistern of Malchiah, the royal prince, which was in the guard-court, letting Jeremiah down with ropes. As there was no water in the cistern, but only mud, Jeremiah sank in the mud.

Ebed-melech, the Ethiopian, in the service of the palace, heard that they had put Jeremiah in the cistern. He went to the king and told him:

"My lord the king, these men have done wrong in treating Jeremiah as they have done, casting him into the cistern to die there of hunger, because there is no more bread in the city."

The king commanded Ebed-melech:

"Take with you three men from here, and draw Jeremiah out of the cistern before he dies."

Ebed-melech took the men and went to the wardrobe of the palace, and took from there some torn and tattered rags, and let them down by ropes to Jeremiah in the cistern. Then Ebed-melech, the Ethiopian, called down to Jeremiah:

"Put these torn and tattered rags, I beg you, below your armpits under the ropes."

Jeremiah did so, and then they drew Jeremiah up with the ropes out of the cistern.

And Jeremiah then was imprisoned in the palace of the king.

Zedekiah, fearing for his own Life, again asks Jeremiah for Advice. A secret Meeting between King and Prophet.

King Zedekiah sent for Jeremiah, and said to him:

"I am going to ask you a question, and you must conceal nothing from me."

Jeremiah listened to what the king asked, and he said to Zedekiah:

"If I tell you the truth, are you not sure to put me to death? And if I give you advice, you will not listen to me."

King Zedekiah swore an oath in secret to Jeremiah:

"As the Lord lives who made this life of ours, I will neither put you to death, nor hand you over to the men who are seeking your life."

Jeremiah said to Zedekiah:

"Thus says the Lord, the God of hosts, the God of Israel:

'If you but surrender to the officers of the emperor of Babylonia, your life shall be spared, and this city shall not be burned; both you and your household shall be spared. But if you do not surrender to the officers of the emperor of Babylonia, this city shall be handed over to the Chaldeans (Babylonians), who shall burn it; and you yourself shall not escape from their hands.' "

Then the king said to Jeremiah:

"Let no one know of our conversation, on pain of death."

And Jeremiah was taken back to his prison, and was kept there until the day that Jerusalem was captured.

*Jerusalem destroyed on the ninth Day
of the Month of Ab—Tish'ah be-Ab*

Jerusalem was besieged↓ by the Babylonian army until the eleventh year of King Zedekiah. In that year, on the ninth day of the fourth month, Jerusalem was taken. An opening had been made through the walls, and the officers of the emperor of Babylonia came to the middle gate.

When Zedekiah, the king, and his warriors saw them, they fled and left the city by night by the way of the royal garden. But the army of the Chaldeans followed them and captured Zedekiah on the plains of Jericho. They brought him to Nebuchadnezzar, who was then at Riblah in the land of Hamath. Nebuchadnezzar killed the sons of Zedekiah before his eyes. He put to death all the nobles of Judah. Then he blinded Zedekiah's eyes, bound him in chains, and had him taken to Babylonia. There he remained in prison until he died.

The Temple in Ruins

Nebuzaradan, an officer of Nebuchadnezzar, burned the Temple of the Lord, the royal palace, and all the houses in Jerusalem. Then the soldiers of the Chaldeans broke down the walls around Jerusalem. The rest of the inhabitants who were left in the city, Nebuzaradan carried away captive. However, he left some of the poorest of the people to take care of the vineyards and farms.

All the vessels that were in the Temple of the Lord the Chaldeans broke in pieces, and they carried the brass from them to Babylonia. All the other vessels of brass, and of gold, and of silver, Nebuzaradan took away.

He also carried away Seraiah, the High Priest, and Zephaniah, the second priest, and the three gate-keepers and brought them to Nebuchadnezzar at Riblah.

And the people of Judah who did not live in Jerusalem were also carried away captive from their own land.

↓For archaeological note see Item 16, p. 554 in the back of the book.

Jeremiah—torn between Sorrow and Hope

And Jeremiah, the prophet, wept:

"My heart is sick within me,
For the wound of the daughter of my people.
I am wounded with grief;
I walk in mourning;
Horror has seized me.
O, that my head were waters,
And my eyes a fountain of tears,
I would weep day and night
For the slain of the daughter of my people!"

(*Jeremiah 8.18–9.1*)

Then the word of the Lord came to Jeremiah saying:

"Behold, days are coming when I will make a new Covenant with the house of Israel and the house of Judah; not like the Covenant that I made with their fathers on the day that I took them from the land of Egypt. This is the Covenant that I will make with the house of Israel: I will put My Law within them. I will write it on their hearts. I will be their God, and they shall be My people. As once I watched over them to root up and pull down, to destroy and to overthrow, and to afflict, so will I watch over them to build and to plant."

"There is hope, O Israel, for your future!"

(*II Kings 24, 25; II Chronicles 36; Jeremiah
27, 29, 31, 34, 37, 38, 39, 52, 31.17*)

עָמוֹס

AMOS

AMOS, the prophet, was born in the little village of Tekoa, which lay in the hill country of Judah, about eighteen miles south of Jerusalem. Little is known about Amos' life except that he was a shepherd and eked out his living by tending sycamore trees. He was a simple, strong, stern man who lived close to nature and to God.

Amos attacked evil-doing and falsehood, wrong and oppression, and he hated deceit in religion. He observed the wickedness of the northern kingdom, Israel, when he came to its cities to sell his sheep and fruits; he brooded over what he saw, and he was greatly distressed.

It was about the middle of the reign of King Jeroboam II, who ruled from 785 to 745 B. C. E. Jeroboam had conquered all his enemies, and they paid him vast amounts of tribute. The roads of commerce were filled with caravans laden with rich merchandise, and the merchants of Israel became very wealthy.

The city of Beth-el had been elevated to the principal religious center of Israel; it had become like Jerusalem in the southern kingdom. A temple had been set up there, with a large body of priests headed by a chief priest named Amaziah. To Beth-el, especially on festival days, people came from all parts of the kingdom to offer sacrifices. They enjoyed peace with their neighbors, and their prosperity made their horizon seem bright.

But, in spite of the apparent prosperity and religious observance, the masses of the people lived in crushing poverty. Only the rich benefited from the national prosperity; and they spent their easily acquired wealth for luxuries. The poor were continually in debt. The workers in the city ofttimes had to pawn their possessions to buy grain for food. The farmers had to borrow money and mortgage their land, even their homes. If the crops

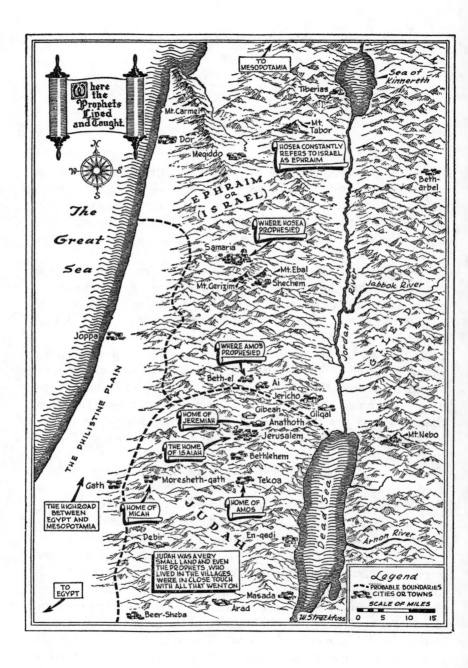

failed, they lost their livelihoods, and, with nothing left, were compelled to sell themselves or their children into slavery.

The rich enjoyed great influence in high places. They controlled the appointments to all public offices, so that officials feared to refuse their wishes. Even the judges in the courts were under their thumbs and often took bribes that corrupted justice. It was an evil time.

Amos was not consoled by the fact that similar evil conditions existed among other nations. He believed that Israel should be better than the other nations, for God had chosen Israel to be His people. This gave Israel no special privileges that should make them arrogant. It meant rather that a greater responsibility rested upon them. It meant living a purer, more just personal and national life.

The gods of the pagan religions were not concerned with justice among men. They sought sacrifices that were really bribes for their favors. The God of Israel, taught Amos, did not desire bribes. The God of Israel demanded justice as a natural right of man. He hated oppression. He despised idleness and luxury. He had laid down His laws of righteous conduct in His Covenant of the Law. Hence, if Israel sinned, Israel's punishment would be more severe than that of other peoples.

Amos, moreover, saw how God intended to punish Israel. He discerned a cloud rising in the northern sky, soon to spread over the land to make it dark with war and suffering and death. That cloud was Assyria. Amos believed that God would use Assyria as His agent to punish the wickedness of Israel and the other nations.

And so, because he loved his people, Amos answered the call in his heart to speak against their wrongdoing, to plead with them to rid their national life of evil, and to do justice and righteousness, and, in this way, to prevent the punishment that threatened them.

The prophecies that Amos delivered he later wrote down, and they have been preserved for us to this day. Amos is known as the first of the "writing" prophets. His prophecies form part of a book known as "The Twelve" because the book includes the speeches of twelve prophets. These twelve are called the Minor

Prophets, not because they are less important, but because we have fewer of their speeches than we have of the Major Prophets — Isaiah, Jeremiah and Ezekiel — and, in the Bible, they are placed after the Major Prophets.

The Minor Prophets as they appear in the Bible are: Hosea, Joel, Amos, Obadiah, Jonah, Micah, Nahum, Habakkuk, Zephaniah, Zechariah, Haggai and Malachi.

Amos in order of time came first.

I.

THE PROPHET OF DOOM

Amos thought about the evil doings of Israel for a long time. A voice seemed to speak in his heart; it was the voice of God, calling him to warn Israel. Amos, his heart filled with sorrow and pity, obeyed the voice of God. He had been shown many visions of the northern kingdom's destruction, but each time he had pleaded with God to spare "little Jacob." Each time God's compassion had saved Israel, but now the time had come when Israel was doomed.

THE WORDS OF AMOS, WHO WAS AMONG THE HERDSMEN OF TEKOA, WHICH HE SAW CONCERNING ISRAEL IN THE DAYS OF UZZIAH, KING OF JUDAH, AND IN THE DAYS OF JEROBOAM THE SON OF JOASH, KING OF ISRAEL, TWO YEARS BEFORE THE EARTHQUAKE.

The Vision of the Locusts

THE Lord showed me this sign: He showed Himself to me forming a brood of locusts, just as the spring crops were coming up, after the king's crop had been mowed.

They devoured all the green growth, and I cried:

"O Lord God, forgive, I pray; how can Jacob recover?— He is so small."

Then the Lord relented, and the Lord said:

"It shall not be."

The Vision of the Fire

Then the Lord showed me this sign: He showed Himself to me calling down fire to consume the great oceans, to burn up the tilled land.

I cried:

"O Lord God, cease, I pray; how can Jacob recover?— He is so small."

Then the Lord relented, and the Lord said:

"Neither shall it be."

The Vision of the crooked Wall

Then the Lord God showed me this sign: He showed Himself to me standing beside a wall, a plumb-line in His hand.

The Lord said to me:

"What do you see, Amos?"

I said:

"A plumb-line."

Then the Lord said:

"Behold, with a plumb-line I test My people, as a builder tests a wall. If it be crooked, it must fall. So never again will I pardon Israel. The high places of Isaac shall be laid waste, the shrines of Israel shall be ruined, and I will rise up against the house of Jeroboam with the sword." *(Amos 7.1–9)*

II.

GOD AGAINST ISRAEL

Amos went to Beth-el and announced God's complaints against Israel. He listed the wrongs committed by the surrounding nations, and described how God would punish Aram, Philistia, Edom, Ammon, Moab and Judah. When the people heard of the coming downfall of their enemies, they naturally rejoiced, though they became uneasy when Amos mentioned Judah. Then Amos declared that God's justice would also punish Israel for their wrongdoings.

THUS says the Lord:
    "For three transgressions of Israel,
Yea, for four, I will not prevent their punishment.
Because they sell honest people for money,
And the needy for a pair of shoes.
They trample on the heads of the poor,
And they prevent the humble from getting justice.
They lay themselves down beside the altar
Upon clothes taken from the poor in pledge.
And in the house of their God the priests drink
The wine of them that have been fined."

God will punish Israel

"So now I will cause you to collapse and fall,
As a cart collapses heavily laden with sheaves.
Even the swift-footed shall not escape by flight,
And the strong shall not use his strength,
And the warrior shall not save himself.
The archer shall not stand his ground,
Nor shall he who rides upon horseback escape.
The stoutest of heart among the warriors
Shall flee away naked on that day,"
Says the Lord.   (*Amos 2.6–16*)

III.

WICKED SAMARIA

Amos went to Samaria, the political capital of the northern kingdom, and accused the wrongdoers who were destroying Israel from within — the dishonest businessmen, the pleasure-mad rich, the corrupt judges and the selfish, vain women. He warned the Israelites that their evil deeds were bringing the nation to its ruin.

L ISTEN to this charge of the Lord against you,
O children of Israel,
Against the whole family,
Which I brought up out of the land of Egypt, saying:
You alone, of all mankind, have I cared for;
Therefore — I will punish you for all your misdeeds.

Dishonest Businessmen

Listen to this,
You men who crush the humble,
And oppress the poor, muttering:
"When will the new moon be over,
That we may sell our grain?
When will the Sabbath be done,
That our corn may be on sale?"
You make your measures small,
And your weights heavy,
You cheat by tampering with the scales —
And all to buy up innocent people,
To buy up the needy for a pair of shoes,
To sell the very refuse of your grain.
The Lord has sworn by the pride of Jacob:
"Never will I forget what you have done!"

Pleasure-mad Rich

Woe to them that are at ease in Zion,
And self-confident on the mount of Samaria,
The nobles and the leaders of the nation!

They lie upon their beds of ivory,
They stretch themselves out upon couches,
They eat lambs from the flock,
And calves from the midst of the stall.
They croon to the music of the lyre,
And compose songs like David himself,
And lap up wine by the bowlful,
And use for ointment the best of oil —
With never a single thought
For the bleeding wounds of the nation.

Corrupt Judges

You turn justice to wormwood,
And trample down righteousness to the earth,
And hate a man who exposes you,
And loathe him who is honest with you!
I know how countless are your crimes,
And how innumerable your misdeeds;
You browbeat honest men,
And accept bribes,
And cheat the poor of justice.

Selfish and vain Women

Listen to this, you cows of Bashan,
You women on the mountain of Samaria,
You who cheat the poor and are hard on the needy,
Who tell your husbands:
"Let us have wine to drink!"
"As sure as I am God," the Lord Almighty swears,
"Your day is coming,
When you will be dragged out of the city with hooks,
The very last of you with fish-hooks!
Out shall you go through breaches in the walls,
Each of you headlong,"
Thus says the Lord!

"Prepare to meet your God!"

The Lord God has sworn by Himself:
"I loathe the pride of Jacob,
His palaces I hate.
I will destroy the city and everything in it."
Behold, the Lord is about to command
That the great house shall be smitten into ruins,
And the small house into fragments.
"Lo, I will raise up a nation against you,
O house of Israel,
And they shall crush you.
And because I will do this to you,
Prepare to meet your God, O Israel!"

(*Amos 3.1–2, 8.4–6, 6.1–6, 5.7–13, 4.1–3, 6.8–14, 4.12*)

IV.

THE GOD OF JUSTICE

The climax of Amos' life came in the sacred city of Beth-el. The magnificent religious ceremonies of a great holiday had been completed. The people, led by their priests, had finished the Temple services. What more could God want? Suddenly, Amos appeared in the public square. He began to speak in the sad, mournful tones of a funeral dirge.

Funeral Song

FALLEN, never to rise again,
    is the virgin of Israel!
Prostrate on her own soil,
    with none to raise her up!

Worship or Sinning?

"Come to Beth-el, and — sin!
  Bring your sacrifices every morning,
  And after three days your tithes!
  Burn a thank-offering of leavened bread,
  And declare your free-will offerings!
  For so *you* love to do, O house of Israel."

"But *I*, I hate, I despise your feasts,
  And I take no pleasure in your festal gatherings.
  Even though you offer Me burnt offerings,
  And your grain-offerings, I will not accept them.
  And the thank-offerings of your fatted beasts
  I will not look upon.
  Take away from Me the noise of your songs,
  To the melody of your lyres I will not listen."

What does God want?

"Let justice well up as waters,
  And righteousness as a mighty stream."

"Seek *Me*, that you may live;
  But seek not Beth-el.
  Seek good and not evil, that you may live;
  And so the Lord, the God of hosts,
  Will be with you, as you say.
  Hate the evil, and love the good,
  And establish justice in the gate.
  And then perhaps the Lord, the God of hosts,
  Will be gracious
  To a remnant of Israel."

(Amos 5.1–2, 4.4–5, 5.21–24, 5.4–5, 5.14–15)

PRIEST AGAINST PROPHET

"You visionary! Be off to the land of Judah..."

(Amos 7.12)

see page 335

"MY FRIEND HAD A VINEYARD"

"Judge, I pray you, between me and my vineyard!"

(Isaiah 5.3)

see page 351

V.

THE PRIEST EXPELS THE PROPHET

When Amos finished his prophecy, the chief priest, Amaziah, clad in the majestic robes of his office, with his priestly crown on his head, came before Amos. He turned angrily on the shepherd-prophet and ordered him to leave Beth-el and never return. Because Amos was forbidden to speak in public, he wrote his prophecies for people to read.

Amaziah condemns Amos

"**Y**OU visionary! Be off to the land of Judah,
   And earn your living there!
Play the prophet there,
But prophesy not any more at Beth-el,
For this is the king's sanctuary,
The royal shrine!"

Amos answers the Priest

And Amos replied:

"I am no prophet, neither am I a prophet's son.
I am a shepherd, and a dresser of sycamore-trees;
And the Lord took me from following the flock,
And the Lord said to me:
'Go, prophesy to My people Israel.'
Now then, listen to what the Lord says.
You say: 'Prophesy not against Israel,
And preach not against the house of Isaac.'
But *the Lord* says:
'Your wife shall suffer shame in the city,
Your sons and daughters shall fall by the sword,
Your land shall be divided up,
And you yourself shall die in a foreign land.
For Israel is indeed to be led off into exile,
Far from their own country.' "   (*Amos 7.12–17*)

VI.

AMOS' FINAL HOPE

Amos still hoped that Israel would be saved from complete destruction, and that Judah, his native country, also would survive in the days to come. Amos dreamed of a future age of peace and happiness.

"IN THAT day I will raise up
    The hut of David that is fallen;
I will wall up its ruins,
And close up its breaches,
And I will rebuild it as in the days of old . . .
I will bring back
The exiles of My people Israel,
And they shall build the waste cities, and dwell in
    them,
And they shall plant vineyards, and drink their wine;
They shall also make gardens, and eat their fruit.
And I will plant them upon their land,
And they shall no more be uprooted
From the land which I have given them,"
Says the Lord,
Your God.   (*Amos 9.11, 14-15*)

הוֹשֵׁעַ

HOSEA

ABOUT fifteen years after Amos' appearance at Beth-el, a new voice was heard in Israel. It was the voice of Hosea.

Unlike Amos, Hosea was born in the northern kingdom. He could not easily pronounce upon Israel the sentence of doom for their misdeeds. His naturally tender nature was filled with sorrow and love and pity for his people.

The times had worsened since Amos had prophesied.

Assyria, at first like a gray mist on the horizon, now loomed like a thunder-cloud, threatening terrible storms over the land. The kings of Israel, in their madness, played politics with Assyrian and Egyptian monarchs, and had to pay them tribute.

Murder and assassination removed one king after another from the throne of Israel. Since Jeroboam II's death, six kings, in about twenty-three years, ruled the shaking throne, four of them murderers of their predecessors.

The people fell back into their ancient sin of idolatry. They continued to crowd their sacred shrines at Beth-el and Gilgal, but they worshipped images of the Golden Bull, and they sacrificed to the Baals, the nature deities, who, they foolishly thought, made the land fertile and produced grain and fruit, and oil and wine.

Even the priests were not loyal to their tasks. They multiplied in number, but they neglected the people's education; they gave Israel no instruction in the true knowledge of God. They raised no voice against the evils and wrongdoings that filled the land with violence and injustice.

Thus, Israel, beset by powerful enemies outside, was collapsing from within. The end of the kingdom of Israel actually came at the hands of Assyria in 722 B. C. E.

In those stormy times, Hosea, the prophet, lived and felt him-self called upon to preach the word of God. One day, he relates, he heard God speaking to him in his heart, summoning him to be His prophet:

"Set the trumpet to your lips,
Like a watchman, over the house of the Lord!"

(Hosea 8.1)

As God's watchman, Hosea's task was to warn his people of the dire punishments that must follow their evil practices. His voice carried no scorn or angry threat. He spoke of Israel's repentance, and God's love and healing mercy. To Hosea God was not only the God of justice, as Amos had taught. He was also the God of mercy. If Israel would but mend their ways and return to paths of uprightness and decency, God would forgive them and help them to live.

How did Hosea discover the meaning of God's love for Israel?

A tragic, marital experience had changed the whole course of Hosea's personal life. He had married a woman, named Gomer, whom he loved deeply. With her he had three children. He thought he had achieved a perfect, happy home. But, Gomer proved herself unfaithful to him, and sought the company of de-ceitful "lovers" who gave her gifts. Hosea drove her from his house. But he was unable to uproot his love for her out of his heart. Because of his great love for her, he searched her out, and when he found her in the slave-market where she had been sold by her "lovers," he purchased her. He made her live by herself for a short time, not so much to punish her, as to give her time to repent her evil deeds and redeem herself. Then he took her back into his home once more.

Hosea's personal suffering led him to understand what God's feelings for Israel must be like. He expressed God's relationship to Israel through the symbol of marriage. As Hosea had loved Gomer, so God loved Israel. God was the "husband" of Israel; Israel was the "wife" of God. As Gomer had forsaken Hosea for her "lovers" who gave her gifts, so Israel had abandoned God for the nature Baals who, they believed, gave them water, grain, wool, flax, oil and wine. But, as Hosea could not abandon the wife he loved, though she proved faithless, and he wooed her back to him, so God sought to win Israel back to their old loyalty and their old purity. As Gomer had to be set apart until she redeemed herself, so God would take Israel out into the wilderness of exile, not to destroy them, but to cleanse them of their evil ways. Then He would restore them to their rightful place as God's people.

History records that Israel did not heed the pleadings of Hosea. The nation walked its evil path to destruction and death as a people. Conquered by Assyria, Israel was deported from Palestine, and forever disappeared. Thereafter, they became known to history as "the lost ten tribes of Israel."

The Book of Hosea, which contains the sorrowful prophet's prophecies, is placed first in the Book of the Twelve, but in time Hosea came after Amos.

I.

FRUITS OF UNFAITHFULNESS

Hosea was saddened by the wrongs he saw, and felt deep grief at the harm they brought Israel. These evils were the bitter fruits of unfaithfulness, and they rotted the national life "like a moth" that destroys a garment. Tirelessly, Hosea pleaded with Israel to change their ways, and to do what God wanted in His service.

THE WORD OF THE LORD THAT CAME TO HOSEA, THE SON OF BEERI, IN THE DAYS OF UZZIAH, JOTHAM,↓ AHAZ, AND HEZEKIAH, KINGS OF JUDAH, AND IN THE DAYS OF JEROBOAM, THE SON OF JOASH, KING OF ISRAEL.

Crime follows Crime

HEAR the word of the Lord, O Israelites!
The Lord has a quarrel with the inhabitants of the
    land,
Because there is no truth, nor mercy,
Nor knowledge of God in the land.
Swearing and lying and murder and stealing and unfaith-
    fulness!
They break out, and one crime follows hard upon another.
Therefore the land mourns
And everything that dwells in it languishes,
Even the beasts of the field, and the birds of the air,
And the very fish of the sea are perishing.

The wicked Priests

"With you is My quarrel, O priest!
My people are destroyed for want of knowledge.
And because you have rejected knowledge,
I will reject you from being My priest.
Since you have forgotten the Law of your God,
I will likewise forget your children.
↓For archaeological note see Item 17, p. 554 in the back of the book.

The more the priests were increased,
The more they sinned against Me.
I will change their glory into shame.
They fatten on the sins of My people.
So has arisen the proverb —'Like people, like priest.'
I will punish the priest for his misdeeds,
And will repay them for the wrongs they do."

The silly Politicians

"Israel has become like a silly dove, without understanding;
Their leaders call to Egypt, they go to Assyria.
As they go, I will spread My net over them;
I will bring them down as the birds of the air.
Woe to them! For they have wandered away from Me!
Ruin to them! For they have rebelled against Me!
For they sow the wind,
And they shall reap the whirlwind.
I shall cause your destruction, O Israel!
Who can help you?
Where now is your king,
That he may rescue you?
And all your princes
That they may rule you,
Of whom you said:
'Give me a king and princes!'
I give you a king in My anger,
And I take him away in My wrath.
Samaria shall bear her guilt;
For she has rebelled against her God."

(*Hosea 4.1–9, 7.11–13, 8.7, 13.9–16, 14.1*)

II.

THE GOD OF LOVE

Hosea admired family life so much, and the love and kindness that should be found there, that he used family expressions to describe how he thought God acts towards Israel. Hosea's father loved him tenderly and Hosea was grateful for that love. Therefore, he occasionally compared God's love for Israel (or Ephraim, as Hosea poetically called Israel) to that of a fond father who loves his son. Amos thought of God as the spirit of strict justice; but Hosea discovered in God tenderness and pity and love.

"WHEN Israel was a child, I came to love him,
And out of Egypt I called him.
But the more I called him,
The more he went away from Me.
He sacrificed to the Baals,
And made offerings to idols.
Yet it was I, I who taught Ephraim to walk.
I took him up in My arms.
But he did not know that I cared for him.
With human lines I led him,
With loving words I guided him.

"Now the sword shall fall upon his cities,
And shall break down his gates and destroy
them,
Because of his evil counsels.

"How shall I give you up, O Ephraim!
How shall I surrender you, O Israel!
My heart is turned within Me;
My compassions are kindled together.
I will not carry out the fierceness of My anger;
I will not return to destroy Ephraim.
For I am God and not man,
The Holy One in the midst of you.
I will not destroy!" (*Hosea 11.1–6, 8–9*)

III.

THE NEW BETROTHAL

Hosea believed that as he had taken back his erring wife, after she had suffered and repented, so God would woo Israel in the wilderness of exile, and take them back to Him, purified through suffering. And "in the end of days" Israel would know true faithfulness and enjoy its rewards.

God's Call to repent

RETURN, O Israel, to the Lord, your God;
    For you have stumbled because of your sins.
Take with you words of sincere repentance,
And return to the Lord.

God's Forgiveness

"I will heal their backsliding,
I will love them freely.
Now My anger has turned away from them.
I will be as the dew to Israel;
They shall blossom like a lily.
I will bring them into the wilderness,
And there I will tenderly woo them,
And speak lovingly to their heart.
Then shall they respond to Me there,
As in the days of their youth,
When they came up out of the land of Egypt.

The new Betrothal

"And on that day it shall come to pass,
That you shall call Me, 'My Husband,'
And you shall no more call Me, 'My Baal.'
For I will remove the names of the Baals
From your mouth;
They shall never be mentioned again.

And I will betroth you to Myself for ever.
Yea, I will betroth you to Myself
In righteousness and justice,
In lovingkindness and in mercy.
I will betroth you to Myself
In faithfulness;
And you shall know the Lord.

Peace, Security and Happiness

"And on that day I will make a covenant for Israel
With the beasts of the field, and with the birds of the air,
And with the reptiles of the ground;
And the bow and the sword and battle will I wipe out of the land;
And I will make them to lie down in safety.
I will speak to the heavens,
And they shall respond to the earth with rain;
And the earth shall respond with its grain, its wine, and its oil;
And they shall respond to Jezreel (the fertile valley).
And I will repeople Israel in the land,
And I will have mercy on them that had not obtained mercy;
And I will say to them that were not My people:
'You are My people.'
And My people shall say:
'Thou art our God.' "   (*Hosea 14.2, 3, 5, 2.18–25*)

יְשַׁעְיָה

ISAIAH

ISAIAH, son of Amoz, lived and prophesied in Judah, the southern kingdom. He has been called the prophet-statesman. Like Amos and Hosea before him, Isaiah was a great preacher who interpreted to the people what God wanted of them. He was a child when Amos spoke at Beth-el, and he was a young man when Hosea pleaded with Israel to return to the Lord. His own teachings reveal that he learned much from both these prophets.

Isaiah was a native of Jerusalem, and he so loved his native city that he poetically called it "the daughter of Zion." He was sorely grieved to see it filled with vices and evils that would bring about its ruin. Jewish tradition represents Isaiah as a member of the royal family, for he was influential with the rulers and the political leaders of his country. Even the king turned to him occasionally for counsel.

He was married to a woman whom he called "the prophetess." We know that he had at least two sons to whom he gave names symbolic of the ideas he believed in. To one son he gave a long, strange name — *Maher-shalal-hash-baz*, "Speed-booty-hasten-prey." It was a name that carried a terrible threat and a warning. Assyria, he warned by this name, a cruel and powerful foe, was hastening to loot Judah, and would pounce upon her like a hungry lion on its prey. Another son he called *Shear-Yashub* — "A remnant shall return," to express his faith that, no matter what disasters might overtake Judah, its worthy part, though a mere remnant, would survive.

Isaiah lived in times of great national crises. During those days, Assyria dominated the eastern part of the world. Isaiah had witnessed the destruction of Israel, the northern kingdom, by Assyria. He felt it as a stunning blow to his Jewish pride. He looked upon it as a warning of what might happen to Judah and his beloved Jerusalem. Little Judah was caught in the whirlpool of international politics, thrust about by Assyria to the north and by Egypt to the south. Nearer Judah to the north were both Israel and Aram; and on her eastern and western boundaries were smaller nations. The most important question of his times was: How should Judah guide herself so as to maintain her independence and find security?

The kings of Judah, especially King Ahaz and King Hezekiah, used the usual methods of kings and politicians. Sometimes they made an alliance with Egypt against Assyria; at times they fawned upon Assyria and paid her great tribute; at other times they conspired with the smaller nations to rebel against Assyria; occasionally they even attempted to try the hazards of war. Isaiah was opposed to all such schemes.

Because of the active part he took in the affairs of Judah over a period of about forty years (740 to 700 B.C.E.), Isaiah is regarded as a statesman. He never held any office in the government. But he gave advice to his king and people on grave decisions that involved the very life and future of his country. His counsel was more often rejected than heeded, but, unlike other prophets who merely preached lofty ideals, Isaiah sought to embody them in the daily conduct of his people.

What was Isaiah's counsel to Judah?

Isaiah's policy for Judah was like that of Washington's many centuries later for the United States, then a young and weak republic: Keep free of all entangling alliances with foreign powers. Isaiah knew that Assyria and Egypt were not concerned about Judah's welfare. They wanted to control Palestine which lay between them, because Palestine meant rich tribute to its conqueror. It also stood as a barrier-state between them; and, above all, it meant a market where the ruling power could sell its merchandise. Spoils, security and trade were the reasons why Assyria and Egypt each wanted to rule Palestine. But, Isaiah stood for complete neutrality. He believed that, if Judah's national life was inwardly pure and healthy and righteous, it could keep out of the wars of that age. He was convinced that this was best for Judah's welfare. Furthermore, since alliances in those days meant bringing foreign religions, their idols, their priests, their worship and their heathen ways of life into Jerusalem, Isaiah feared that these alliances would undermine the pure religious life of the people of Judah. Thus, concern for the religious health of his people also counselled no entangling alliances.

All Isaiah's teachings flowed from his belief in the holiness of God. God's holiness was to be found wherever men practiced mercy and love, purity and goodness, righteousness and justice, and where they made these the most important and worth-while values in life. God was not to be worshipped merely by sacrifices; He did not seek material power and wealth. God sought goodness in the human heart, and right conduct among men and nations.

So strong was Isaiah's faith in God's holiness that, in the midst of a greedy and corrupt generation and in the midst of a cruel and warlike world, he dared to dream of a Golden Age in the days to come, when all injustice and wrong would be swept away. He hopefully used the expression, "And it shall come to pass at the end of days." In that Golden Age, the remnant of the Jewish people, God's holy people, would return to the holy city of Zion, where a perfect king, filled with the spirit of holiness, would rule them. And the whole world would know holy peace. It is because of these teachings that Isaiah is known as the prophet of holiness.

Isaiah lived to an old age. We have no record of the date or manner of his death. There is a Jewish tradition that he was put to death in a very cruel manner in the reign of Manasseh, son of King Hezekiah.

The Book of Isaiah consists of the prophecies of the first of the three Major Prophets, the other two prophets being Jeremiah and Ezekiel. It is not only a collection of Isaiah's prophecies, but also contains chapters which describe the historical events of his times. It consists of sixty-six chapters. According to tradition Isaiah wrote all these chapters, the last twenty-six of which forecast events that would occur in the future.

Many scholars, however, believe that the latter part of the book (chapters 40 to 66) was written later by another prophet whose name is unknown, but who probably lived in Babylonia shortly before that country was conquered by Cyrus the Persian about 545 B.C.E.

I.

ISAIAH'S VISION — THE GOD OF HOLINESS

After a brilliant reign of forty years, King Uzziah of Judah died. His death left the people of Judah, and among them the youthful Isaiah, worried about the future. We can imagine Isaiah walking the streets of the city, his mind on the effect of the disease which had recently stricken the king to death. He was reminded of the moral diseases, the spiritual uncleanness and the wrongs of Jerusalem, the city he loved. Would death come to the city because of its sickness, as death had come to the king? Full of these unhappy thoughts, Isaiah turned into the Temple to seek the comfort of God's presence, who was always thought to be dwelling there. In that sacred place, Isaiah's thoughts moved away from the wickedness, corruption and evil of men to the pure and clean holiness of God. As in a trance, he saw the vision and heard the call that made him a prophet of God.

THE VISION OF ISAIAH, THE SON OF AMOZ, WHICH HE SAW CONCERNING JUDAH AND JERUSALEM, IN THE DAYS OF UZZIAH, JOTHAM, AHAZ, AND HEZEKIAH, KINGS OF JUDAH.

IN the year that King Uzziah died I saw the Lord sitting on a high and lofty throne; and the train of His robe filled the Temple. Above Him stood the seraphim (guardian angels). Each had six wings, one pair to cover the face, another to cover the feet, and another with which to fly. And they called to one another:

"Holy, holy, holy, is the Lord of hosts;
The whole earth is full of His glory."

The foundations of the thresholds trembled at the voice of those who called, and the Temple was filled with smoke.

*God's Holiness makes Isaiah
aware of his own Uncleanness*

I said:

> "Woe to me! for I am undone;
> Because I am a man of unclean lips,
> And I dwell among a people of unclean lips;
> For my eyes have seen the King,
> The Lord of hosts."

Isaiah is purified and called to be a Prophet

Then one of the seraphim flew to me with a glowing coal in his hand, which he had taken from off the altar; and he touched my mouth with it and said:

> "See! this has touched your lips;
> Your iniquity is removed,
> And your sin is forgiven."

Then I heard the voice of the Lord, saying:

> "Whom shall I send,
> And who will go for us?"

Then I said:

> "Here am I! Send me."

And He said:

> "Go and say to this people:
> 'You shall hear, but understand not;
> And you shall see, but perceive not!'
> Make the heart of this people fat,
> Dull their ears, and make their eyesight poor,
> That they may not see with their eyes,
> Nor hear with their ears,
> Nor understand with their hearts,
> Lest they return, and be healed."

*Surprised and disappointed that
God seeks to punish Judah, the
Prophet asks: How long?*

Then I said:

"Lord, how long?"

And He said:

"Till cities lie waste, without inhabitant,
And houses without man;
And the land be left utterly waste,
And the Lord have removed men far away,
And the forsaken places be many
In the midst of the land.

*After the fiery Punishment passes,
the Holy Seed, the Remnant of
Judah, will remain, purified*

"Even if a tenth remain in it,
This must pass through the fire again,
Like a terebinth, or like an oak,
Whose stump remains when it is felled,
So the holy seed shall be the stump that remains."

(Isaiah 6)

II.

GOD'S VINEYARD: A PARABLE

Isaiah appeared one day in a public place, perhaps in the dress of a minstrel, and recited the parable or story of his friend's vineyard. When he had won the attention of the crowd, and their sympathy for his friend who destroyed his vineyard, Isaiah turned upon his listeners with the warning that they, Judah, were the vineyard of the Lord of hosts.

L ET me sing a song of my Friend,
 A love-song regarding His vineyard.

My Friend had a vineyard
On a very fruitful hill;
He dug it, and cleared it of stones,
And planted it with the choicest vines;
He built a watchtower in the midst of it,
And hewed out a wine-vat in it;
And he expected it to bring forth grapes,
But it brought forth wild grapes.

Now, you inhabitants of Jerusalem,
And you men of Judah,
Judge, I pray you, between me and my vineyard!
What could have been done more for my vineyard,
Than what I have done for it?
Why then, when I looked that it should
  bring forth good grapes,
Brought it forth only wild grapes?

So now come, let me tell you
What I will do to my vineyard:
I will take its hedge away, and it shall be
  eaten up;
I will break through its fence, and it shall
  be trampled down;

Yes, I will lay it waste, unpruned and unhoed,
And there shall spring up in it briers and thorns;
And I will command the clouds
That they rain no rain upon it.

For the vineyard of the Lord of hosts
Is the house of Israel, *
And the men of Judah
The plantation in which He delighted.
He looked for justice,
But there was only violence;
For righteousness,
But there was only the cry of the wronged!   (*Isaiah 5.1–7*)

---

*The prophets of the southern kingdom referred to their people by the name of Judah; but sometimes they used the name of Israel for the whole Jewish people. However, they always spoke of God as the God of Israel, meaning the God of *all* the Jewish people in both the northern and southern kingdoms.

III.

VINTAGE OF WILD GRAPES

The successful reign of Uzziah had brought into the country, together with prosperity, all the evils and wrongs which Amos and Hosea had denounced in the northern kingdom. These were the "wild grapes," poisonous and destructive, in God's vineyard, Judah. Judah had to suffer for these "wild grapes." The unfaithful vineyard of the Lord had to undergo shame, suffering and exile. Assyria was the agent of God's wrath, and Assyria hastened like a ferocious lion to leap upon its prey. Judah turned to Egypt for help against Assyria, but in vain. And soon Ariel, Isaiah's poetic name for Jerusalem, was reduced to cold, dead ashes in a burned-out hearth.

HOW has she suffered shame,
   the once faithful city;
She that was full of justice,
And righteousness lodged in her,
But now murderers!

A rebellious and sinful Nation

Hear, O heavens, and give ear, O earth!
For the Lord has spoken:
"I have reared and brought up children,
But they have rebelled against Me!
The ox knows its owner,
And the donkey its master's crib;
But Israel does not know,
My people shows no understanding."
Ah, sinful nation, a people whose guilt is heavy,
A brood of evil-doers, children who deal corruptly;
They have forsaken the Lord,
They have turned away from the Holy One of Israel!

The Land is desolate

Why will you earn fresh blows,
   by continuing to revolt?
Your whole head is sick,
   your whole heart is faint;

From the sole of the foot to the head
      no part is sound;
Your country lies desolate, your cities are burned,
Foreigners ravage your land under your very eyes.
The daughter of Zion is left all alone
Like a booth in a vineyard,
As a shed in a cucumber field,
Like a besieged city.
Had not the Lord of hosts left us a very small remnant,
We should have become like Sodom, no better than
      Gomorrah.

The Egyptians shall fail Judah

Woe to those who go down to Egypt for help,
And rely on horses;
Those who trust in chariots, because they are many,
And in horsemen, because they are mighty;
But they look not to the Holy One of Israel,
Nor seek the Lord!
Yet He is the wise one, and brings calamity,
And does not withdraw His words.
He will rise against the house of those who do evil,
And against the help of them who work mischief.
The Egyptians are men, and not God,
And their horses are flesh, and not spirit.
So, when the Lord shall stretch out His hand,
The helper shall stumble, and the helped one shall fall;
And they all shall perish together.

God summons Assyria as the Agent
of His Wrath, the Rod of His Anger

Therefore, the anger of the Lord is kindled against
      His people,
And He has stretched out His hand against them,
And He has smitten them,
So that the mountains quaked;
And their dead bodies lay as refuse in the streets.

His anger has not yet stopped,
And His hand is stretched out still.
And He will raise a signal to a nation from afar,
He will whistle to it from the end of the earth.
And lo, speedily, swiftly shall it come,
None weary, none stumbling in its ranks;
None shall slumber nor sleep;
Not a belt slack, not a shoe-string broken,
Arrows sharpened, bows all bent,
Horses' hoofs as hard as flint,
Chariot wheels like whirlwinds;
Roaring like a lion, growling like young lions,
Gripping its victim with a snarl,
Bearing it off, with none to rescue.

Woe to you, Ariel, Ariel,
The city where David encamped!
(Isaiah 1.21, 2-9, 31.1-3, 5.25-29, 29.1)

IV.

NOT SACRIFICE BUT HOLINESS

Isaiah believed that Judah sinned because the people had a wrong notion of what God wanted, of what religion really was. They thought that religion was merely the performance of certain rituals — prayers, sacrifices, ceremonials. But Isaiah, like Amos and Hosea, condemned this kind of religion. Not that they sought to abolish the Temple or the sacrifices, but they believed that religion must also teach responsibility for right and wrong conduct. Because God is holy, God wants those who worship Him also to be holy, that is, they should live just and good lives, clean from all the base and ugly evils of men and the world.

HEAR the word of the Lord,
    you rulers of Sodom;
Give ear to the Law of our God,
    you people of Gomorrah!
"What care I for all your lavish sacrifices?"
    says the Lord;
"I am sick of slaughtered rams, of fat
    from well-fed beasts;
The blood of bullocks and of lambs
    is no delight to Me.
Who asks this of you,
    when you gather in My presence?
Who demands this of you —
    the trampling of My courts?
Bring no more worthless offerings!
    the smoke of sacrifice is vain, I loathe it;
Your gatherings at the New Moon and on Sabbath,
    I cannot endure them.
Your fasts and festivals,
    My soul hates them;
They are a burden to Me,
    I am weary to bear them.

You may stretch out your hands,
    but I will hide My eyes from you,
And when you offer many prayers,
    I will not hear;
Your hands are full of bloodshed.

"Wash you, make yourselves clean,
Put away your evil-doings from My sight.
Cease to do wrong,
Learn to do right,
Seek justice, relieve the oppressed,
And put a check on violence.
Let orphans have their rights,
Plead the cause of the widow."

"Come now, and let us reason together,"
    says the Lord;
"Though your sins be as scarlet,
    They shall be as white as snow;
Though they be red like crimson,
    they shall be white as wool.
If only you are willing to obey . . . ."   (*Isaiah 1.10–19*)

V.

"KEEP CALM! HAVE NO FEAR!"

Isaiah first showed himself a statesman when Pekah, the king of Israel, and Rezin, the king of Aram, made war on Judah to compel Judah to join their conspiracy against Assyria. When they besieged Jerusalem, King Ahaz of Judah and his people were frightened, and the king determined to appeal to Assyria for help. Isaiah learned of this and came before the king to oppose his plan. He mocked the dying strength of Israel and Aram, calling them "stumps of smoking firebrands." He warned the king that, if Judah accepted help from Assyria, Judah would become Assyria's vassal. It also showed a lack of faith in God. As Isaiah beautifully put it: They rejected "the gently flowing waters of Shiloah" (the quiet help of God) for "the mighty and many waters of the Euphrates" (the warlike aid of Assyria). Isaiah's advice, however, was disregarded.

IN the days of Ahaz, king of Judah, Rezin, king of Aram, and Pekah, son of Remaliah, king of Israel, went up to Jerusalem to war against it; but they could not prevail against it. When it was reported to the house of David that the Aramaeans had joined with the forces of Israel, the heart of King Ahaz and of his people trembled as the trees of the forest tremble before the wind.

Isaiah and Shear-Yashub

The Lord said to Isaiah:

"Go out with your son, Shear-Yashub, to meet Ahaz at the end of the conduit of the upper pool, on the road to the Fullers' Field; and say to him: 'Keep calm; have no fear; do not lose courage because of these two stumps of smoking firebrands, because of the fierce anger of Rezin, king of Aram, and Pekah, son of Remaliah. They have formed this evil plot against you, to march against Judah and terrify and overpower it, and to set up as puppet ruler the son of Tabeel.'

But the Lord declares:

"Their plot shall not stand, it shall not succeed . . .
But if you will not have faith, surely you shall
not be established."

Immanuel — "The Lord is with us"

The Lord spoke to Ahaz, saying:

"Ask a sign of the Lord your God; ask that it be performed either in the nether world or in the heaven above."

But Ahaz replied:

"I will not ask, nor put the Lord to the test."

Then Isaiah said:

"Listen now, O house of David! I am weary of you! Will you insist on making my God weary as well as myself? The Lord Himself shall give you a sign. There is a young woman with child, who shall bear a son and shall call his name 'Immanuel,' 'The Lord is with us.' He shall eat curds and honey, but before the child knows good food from bad, the land whose two kings you dread shall be desolate."

And again the Lord spoke to me, saying:

"Since this people has rejected the gently flowing waters
        of Shiloah,
And are overwhelmed with fear of Rezin and the son
        of Remaliah,
I shall bring upon them the mighty and many waters
        of the Euphrates,
Even the king of Assyria and all his proud hosts.
And it shall rise above all its channels and overflow
        all its banks;
It shall sweep through Judah, a rushing flood, reaching
        up to the neck."

And Isaiah added:

"But His (God's) wings will be outstretched, and shall protect your land from side to side; for 'Immanuel' — 'The Lord is with us.' "

Isaiah's Faith in his Message

Then said Isaiah:

"I will seal up my message, and commit my counsel to the safekeeping of my disciples; then I will wait for the Lord who now hides His face from the house of Israel; I will hope for Him. I and the children whom the Lord has given me are signs and omens set in Israel by the Lord of hosts, who dwells on Mount Zion." *(Isaiah 7.1–8, 8.16–18)*

VI.

"THE END OF DAYS"

Isaiah dreamed of a Golden Age in the days to come. It is all the more remarkable that he should have held such high hopes for the future, because his times were so warlike and cruel, so without easy hope and promise. It was an age of vast chaos. Yet, for Isaiah, beyond the chaos and darkness the light of God's spirit shone, and it promised the coming of a better and happier world. It was Isaiah's faith in God's holiness that strengthened him and enabled him to dream heroic dreams for Zion, for Israel, and for all mankind.

THE message that Isaiah received concerning Judah and Jerusalem.

Jerusalem the holy

It shall come to pass in the end of days,
That the mountain of the Lord's house shall be
Established as the highest mountain,
And shall be exalted above the hills.
All the nations shall flow to it,
And many peoples shall go and say:
"Come, let us go up to the mountain of the Lord,
To the house of the God of Jacob,
That He may teach us of His ways,
And we will walk in His paths."
For out of Zion shall go forth the Law,
And the word of the Lord from Jerusalem.

Universal Peace

He shall judge between the nations,
And shall decide for many peoples;
And they shall beat their swords into plowshares,
And their spears into pruning hooks;
Nation shall not lift up sword against nation,
Neither shall they learn war any more.

The ideal Ruler — A great human Leader

There shall come forth a shoot out of the stock
    of Jesse,
And out of his roots a twig shall grow forth.
And the spirit of the Lord shall rest upon him,
The spirit of wisdom and understanding,
The spirit of counsel and might,
The spirit of knowledge and of the fear of the Lord.

He shall not judge by sight only,
Nor render decisions on hearsay,
But with righteousness shall he judge the poor,
And with equity decide for the needy.
By the rebuke of his mouth shall he smite the ruthless,
By the breath of his lips shall he slay the wicked.
The girdle on his loins shall be righteousness,
And the band on his waist faithfulness.

All Nature at Peace

The wolf shall dwell with the lamb,
And the leopard lie down with the kid;
The lion shall eat straw like the ox,
The calf and young lion graze together,
And a little child shall lead them.
The cow and the bear shall be friends,
And their young shall lie down together.
The infant shall play on the hole of the asp,
And the young child put his hand in the basilisk's den.
They shall not hurt nor destroy
Throughout all My holy mountain;
For the earth shall be full of the knowledge of
    the Lord,
Even as the waters cover the seas.

The Remnant shall return

It shall come to pass in that day
That the root of Jesse,
Who will be standing as a signal to the peoples —

To him will the nations go,
And his resting-place will be glorious.
And it shall come to pass in that day
That the Lord will once more raise His hand
To recover the remnant of His people
From Assyria and from Egypt,
From Pathros and Ethiopia, from Elam and from
    Shinar,
From Hamath and from the islands of the sea.
He will raise a signal to the nations,
And will assemble the dispersed of Israel;
And the scattered of Judah will He gather together
From the four corners of the earth.

And a highway shall there be and a road,
Which shall be called The Way of Holiness.
The unclean shall not pass over it;
But the redeemed shall walk on it,
The ransomed of the Lord shall return by it.
They shall come to Zion with singing,
And everlasting joy shall be upon their heads;
They shall obtain gladness and joy,
And sorrow and sighing shall flee away.

(Isaiah 2.1–4, 11.1–12, 35.8–10)

ISAIAH OF THE EXILE

The following chapters are attributed by some modern scholars to the other Isaiah, the one of the Exile. The occasion when this Isaiah delivered them was about the time when Cyrus, king of Persia, announced that the Jews could return to Palestine to rebuild their Temple and nation. Because these writings were similar to Isaiah's in grandeur of ideas and in beauty of language, they were added to the original book of Isaiah. This unknown author has come to be called "The Second Isaiah," "The Great Unknown," or "Isaiah of the Exile."

I.

"BID JERUSALEM TAKE HEART!"

Isaiah of the Exile saw glowing visions of the return of the Jewish people to Palestine. He described the exiles gathering from all lands, streaming across plains, mountains and deserts, and joyfully coming home to Jerusalem. His words are rich in beauty and tenderness. They brought comfort and encouragement to his saddened and weary people.

God has pardoned Israel

"BE comforted, O be comforted, My people,"
    says your God;
"Bid Jerusalem take heart;
    and proclaim to her,
That her time of service is ended,
    that her guilt is paid in full,
That she has received of the Lord's hand
    double for all her sins."

The Highway of God

Hark! a voice calls:
"Clear the way of the Lord in the wilderness,
Make straight in the desert a highway for our God.
Every valley shall be raised up,
And every mountain and hill shall be brought low;
And the uneven ground shall become a plain,
And the rugged heights a valley.
Then shall the glory of the Lord be revealed,
And all flesh shall see it together;
For the mouth of the Lord has spoken."

Good Tidings for Zion

O messengers of good news to Zion,
Get up on a high mountain!
O messengers of good news to Jerusalem,

Lift up your voice with strength!
Lift it up, fear not;
Say to the cities of Judah:
"Behold your God!"
How beautiful upon the mountains
    are the feet of the messenger of good tidings,
Who announces peace,
    and news of salvation;
Who says to Zion:
    "Your God is King."
Hark! your watchmen! they lift up the voice,
    together they sing;
For they shall see eye to eye,
    when the Lord restores Zion.
Break forth into joy, sing together,
    you waste places of Jerusalem!
For the Lord has comforted His people,
    He has redeemed Jerusalem.

The Exiles on the March

"Fear not, for I am with you;
I will bring your children from the east,
And I will gather you from the west;
I will say to the north, 'Give up your captives!'
And to the south, 'Keep them not back!'
Bring My sons from afar,
And My daughters from the end of the earth;
Every one who is called by My name,
Whom I have created to glorify Me.

A new Heaven and Earth

"For behold, I create new heavens
And a new earth;
And the former things shall not be remembered,
Nor come to mind.

"Be glad and rejoice forever
In what I create.
And I will rejoice in Jerusalem,
And take joy in My people;
And the voice of weeping shall be no more heard
    in her,
Nor the sound of crying . . .

Glory and Peace

"They shall build houses, and inhabit them;
And they shall plant vineyards, and eat the fruit
    of them.
They shall not build, and another inhabit,
They shall not plant, and another eat;
For as the days of a tree shall be the days of
    My people,
And My chosen one shall long enjoy the work of
    their hands.
And all your children shall be taught of the Lord;
And great shall be the peace of your children."

(*Isaiah 40.1–9, 52.7–9, 43.5–7, 65.17–22, 54.13*)

MESSENGER OF PEACE

"How beautiful upon the mountains are the feet of
the messenger of good tidings, who announces
peace . . ." (*Isaiah 52.7*)

see page 365

JEREMIAH SAVED FROM THE MOB

"This man does not deserve to die; he has
spoken to us in the name of the Lord our
God." (*Jeremiah 26.16*)

see page 389

II.

CYRUS — THE LORD'S SHEPHERD

King Cyrus of Persia freed the Jewish exiles after he had conquered Babylonia.* Because of his great justice and kindness to the Jewish people, Isaiah of the Exile considered him the instrument or agent of God's plan to restore Israel to their ancestral land. The prophet, however, emphasized the gratitude that the Jews owed to God, the source of their redemption, who selected Cyrus to bring it about.

Cyrus the victorious

THUS says the Lord to His anointed,
　　To Cyrus, whose right hand He has grasped,
To subdue nations before him,
And to ungird the loins of kings,
To open the doors of cities before him,
And that their gates may not be shut:
"I will go before you,
And make the crooked places straight.
The doors of bronze will I break in pieces,
And the gates of iron I will cut asunder;
I will give you treasures hidden away in dark places,
The hidden riches of secret places;
That you may know that I am the Lord,
That I, who have called you by your name,
Am the God of Israel.
For the sake of Jacob My servant,
And Israel My chosen one,
I have called you by your name,
I have honored you, though you knew Me not.
I am the Lord, and there is none else,
Beside Me there is no God.
I will strengthen you, though you knew Me not;
That men may know from the rising of the sun,

*For Cyrus' Proclamation see page 531; and for the story of the return to Palestine read the Books of Ezra-Nehemiah, pages 529 ff.

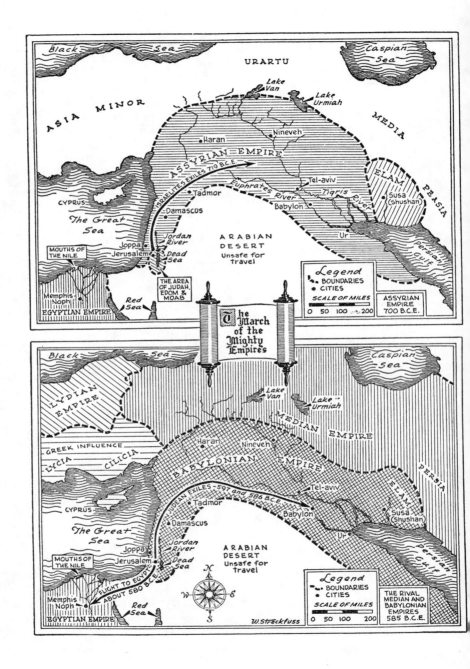

The March of the Mighty Empires

Top map:

Black Sea

Caspian Sea

URARTU

ASIA MINOR

Lake Van

Lake Urmiah

MEDIA

Haran

Nineveh

ASSYRIAN EMPIRE

ISRAELITES EXILES 719 B.C.E.

PERSIA

Tadmor

Euphrates River

Tel-aviv

Tigris River

ELAM

Damascus

Babylon

Susa (Shushan)

CYPRUS

The Great Sea

Jordan River

Joppa

Jerusalem

Dead Sea

ARABIAN DESERT
Unsafe for travel

Ur

Persian Gulf

MOUTHS OF THE NILE

THE AREA OF JUDAH, EDOM & MOAB

Legend
BOUNDARIES
CITIES
SCALE OF MILES
0 50 100 200

ASSYRIAN EMPIRE 700 B.C.E.

Memphis-Noph

EGYPTIAN EMPIRE

Red Sea

Bottom map:

Black Sea

Caspian Sea

LYDIAN EMPIRE

Lake Van

Lake Urmiah

MEDIAN EMPIRE

GREEK INFLUENCE

Haran

Nineveh

LYCIA

CILICIA

BABYLONIAN EMPIRE

PERSIA

CYPRUS

The Great Sea

JUDEAN EXILES - 597 and 586 B.C.E.

Tadmor

Tel-aviv

Babylon

ELAM

Susa (Shushan)

Damascus

Joppa

Jordan River

Jerusalem

Dead Sea

ARABIAN DESERT
Unsafe for travel

Ur

Persian Gulf

MOUTHS OF THE NILE

FLIGHT TO EGYPT ABOUT 580 B.C.E.

Memphis Noph

EGYPTIAN EMPIRE

Red Sea

Legend
BOUNDARIES
CITIES
SCALE OF MILES
0 50 100 200

THE RIVAL MEDIAN AND BABYLONIAN EMPIRES 585 B.C.E.

W. Streckfuss

And from the west,
That there is none beside Me.
I am the Lord, and there is none else;
I form the light and create darkness;
I make peace, and create evil;
I am the Lord, who does all these things."

Cyrus called by the Lord

"I am the Lord who says of Jerusalem:
'She shall be inhabited;'
And of the cities of Judah:
'They shall be built,
And their ruins will I raise up;'
Who says to the deep: 'Be dry!
And all your rivers will I dry up;'
Who says of Cyrus:
'He is my shepherd,
And shall perform all My wishes;'
Who says of Jerusalem:
'She shall be built,'
And of the Temple:
'Your foundations shall be laid.' "

(Isaiah 45.1–7, 44.26–28)

III.

"THE SERVANT OF THE LORD"

Isaiah of the Exile believed that Israel's sufferings had a meaning, namely, they were to make the Jewish people worthy of being God's messenger to the rest of mankind. He called Israel "the suffering servant of God." Israel had a great purpose in the world: To teach mankind about God, how He distinguished between right and wrong in the world, and wanted men always to choose the right.

L ISTEN, O isles, to me,
And hearken, you peoples, from afar!

Sword and Arrow of the Lord

The Lord called me from birth,
He made my mouth like a sharp sword.
In the shadow of His hand He hid me;
He made me like a polished arrow,
In His quiver He concealed me.

Israel the chosen Servant

He said to me: "You are My servant,
Israel, through whom I will show forth My glory."
But I said, "I have labored in vain,
I have spent my strength for nought and vanity;
Nevertheless the Lord will do me justice,
My God will see to my reward."

A Light to the Nations

And now says the Lord,
Who formed me at birth to be His servant,
He will bring back Jacob to Himself,
And Israel shall be gathered to Him —
For I am honorable in the eyes of the Lord
And my God has become my strength —

And He says: "It is too slight a thing
Merely to gather the tribes of Jacob again
And restore the children of Israel;
I will also make you a light to the nations,
That My salvation may reach to the end of the earth."

Let Israel not fear

"But you, Israel, My servant,
Jacob whom I have chosen,
The descendants of Abraham My friend;
Whom I have brought from the ends of the earth,
And called from its uttermost parts,
To whom I said, 'You are My servant,
I have chosen you, and have not rejected you;'
Fear not, for I am with you,
Be not dismayed, for I am your God!
I will strengthen you, I will help you;
I will uphold you with My victorious right hand."

The Mission of the Servant

"Behold! My servant, whom I uphold;
My chosen one, in whom I delight.
I have put My spirit upon him,
He shall make the right to go forth to the nations.
He shall not fail nor be crushed,
Till he establish the right in the earth;
And the isles shall wait for his teaching."

(*Isaiah 49.1–6, 41.8–10, 42.1–4*)

IV.

GOD OF THE WHOLE WORLD

More clearly and fully than any of the other great prophets, Isaiah of the Exile taught that God is the Creator and Guide of the whole world and of all nations and peoples, and that He is also found in the heart and spirit of each human being. Because God is the God of the whole world, all mankind is really one universal family. Isaiah's great teaching that God is the universal Father of mankind has influenced and shaped the minds and thoughts of men about God and man throughout the ages.

THUS says the Lord:
 "The heaven is My throne,
And the earth is My footstool;
Where is the house, then, that you can build for Me?
And where is the place that may be My resting-place?
My hand made all these things,
And so all these things are Mine,"
Says the Lord;
"Yet I will look on this man,
On him who is humble and contrite in spirit,
And who trembles at My word."

God's infinite Greatness

Who has measured the waters in the hollow of His hand,
And ruled off the heavens with a span,
And inclosed in a measure the dust of the earth,
And weighed the mountains in scales,
And the hills in a balance?
Who has measured the spirit of the Lord,
And instructed Him as His counsellor?
With whom took He counsel for His enlightenment,
And who taught Him the path of right?
Who taught Him knowledge,
And showed Him the way of understanding?
Behold, the nations are like a drop from a bucket,

Like fine dust in the scales are they counted.
Behold, the isles weigh no more than a grain;
And Lebanon itself is not sufficient for fuel,
Nor are its beasts enough for burnt-offerings;
All the nations are as nothing before Him;
He considers them as things of nought, and vanity.

The Foolishness of Idols

To whom, then, would you liken God?
Or what likeness would you compare to Him?
An idol!
The smelter casts it,
And the goldsmith overlays it with gold,
And the silversmith fastens it with silver chains.
Each one helps his fellow,
And says to his comrade, "Have courage!"
The smelter cheers on the goldsmith,
He that smooths with the hammer
Him that strikes on the anvil,
Saying of the riveting, "It is good!"
As he fastens it with nails,
So that it cannot be moved.

God's infinite Might

Do you not know? Do you not hear?
Has it not been told you from the beginning?
Have you not understood the foundations of the earth?
It is He who sits enthroned
Above the circle of the earth,
So high that its inhabitants
Are like grasshoppers;
Who stretches out the heavens
Like a curtain,
And spreads them out like a tent to dwell in;
Who brings princes to nothing,
And makes the rulers of the earth
As a thing of nought.

Hardly have they been planted,
Hardly have they been sown,
Hardly has their stock taken root in the earth,
When He blows upon them,
And they wither,
And the whirlwind carries them away
Like stubble.
"To whom, then, would you liken Me,
That I should be equal?"
Says the Holy One.
Lift up your eyes on high,
And see! Who created these (the hosts of the heavens)?
He who brings out their host by number,
He calls them all by name;
Through the greatness of His might,
And the strength of His power
Not one is missing.

God's infinite Love

Why do you complain, O Jacob,
Why do you cry, O Israel:
"My fate is hidden from the Lord,
My right is disregarded by my God?"
Have you not known? Have you not heard?
The Lord is a God everlasting,
The Creator of the ends of the earth.
He does not faint, nor grow weary;
His understanding is past searching out.
He gives power to the faint;
And to him that has no might He increases strength.
Though the youths faint and grow weary,
Though the young men utterly fall,
They that wait for the Lord shall renew their
        strength;
They shall mount up with wings like eagles;
They shall run, and not be weary;
They shall walk, and not be faint.

God's Providence

Seek the Lord while He may be found,
Call upon Him while He is near;
Let the wicked forsake his way,
And the man of iniquity his thoughts;
And let him return to the Lord,
And He will have compassion upon him,
And to our God, for He will abundantly pardon.
"For My thoughts are not your thoughts,
Neither are your ways My ways," says the Lord.
"For as the heavens are higher than the earth,
So are My ways higher than your ways,
And My thoughts than your thoughts.
As the rain comes down and the snow from heaven,
And return not there,
Until they water the earth,
And make it bring forth and bud,
And give seed to the sower and bread to the eater;
So shall My promise be that goes out of My mouth:
It shall not return to Me fruitless,
But shall accomplish that which I please,
And make the thing to which I sent it prosper.
For you shall go out with joy,
And be led forth with peace;
The mountains and the hills
Shall break forth before you into singing,
And all the trees of the field
Shall clap their hands."

All Mankind shall worship God

"Turn to Me, then, and be saved,
All ends of the earth!
For I am God, and there is none else.
Indeed, I have taken an oath —
A word has gone out of My mouth in righteousness,,

And shall not come back —
That to Me every knee shall bow,
Every tongue shall swear,
And say: 'Only in the Lord
Is victory and strength.' "

(*Isaiah 66.1–2, 40.12–31, 41.6–7, 55.6–12, 45.22–25*)

יִרְמְיָה

JEREMIAH

JEREMIAH, the prophet, was born in the little village of
Anathoth, situated a short distance northeast of Jerusalem.
He was the son of Hilkiah and came from a priestly family. Jeremiah received his early education from his parents. He studied
the writings of Amos, Isaiah, and Micah. Especially did he love
the tender words of Hosea by whom he was strongly influenced.

Jeremiah was a shy, sensitive man, of gentle and loving nature.
He was easily wounded and hurt. He was of an intensely religious
temperament. He was not at all fond of the excitements of public
life. He disliked contention and controversy. He might have
lived a quiet, sheltered life, for his family was well-off, owning
land in Anathoth. But he heard the voice of God speaking in his
heart. Against his will, he felt compelled to answer the voice,
though this meant giving up the normal experiences of life — he
never married — and personal happiness.

Tragic, indeed, was the life of this "man of sorrows"!

Jeremiah had to endure the very opposite of what his nature
and temperament would normally have desired. He became a
man of contention and controversy. He found himself the object
of scorn and hatred. He was publicly whipped and condemned to
death. He saw his beloved Judah swallowed up in a sea of flame
and blood. He met his death in a foreign land.

The times Jeremiah lived in were dark and evil. The follies
of idolatry had grown to such proportions, the injustice and
cruelty of man towards his fellows had become so intolerable,
the blind leaders — kings, priests, nobles and prophets — so corrupt that Judah, his beloved Judah, was like an apple which,
though outwardly sound, was inwardly rotten to the core.

The larger world, moreover, outside Judah, was going through vast changes. Assyria was decaying and was falling before the armies of the new, vigorous power of Babylonia, whose mighty emperor, Nebuchadnezzar, soon came to dominate that age and world. To the south of Judah, Egypt, ever jealous of Assyria and then of Babylonia, kept stirring up trouble among the small nations, to use them, and especially Judah, for her advantage against Babylonia. The kings of Judah, one after the other, became puppets, placed on the throne not by the will of the people but by Egypt or Babylonia.

In this confused and stormy age, Jeremiah's destiny was to witness the coming doom of his people. The ones he loved, he had to condemn. He was like a minister who walks to the gallows with the one about to die. He preached, unheeded by the common people; he was hated by the priests and the false prophets; his writings were burned by the king; and he himself was wrongly suspected of being a traitor to his country.

As prophet of God, Jeremiah was torn between his desire to save his people, and his duty to tell them his message of doom and destruction. Jeremiah's spirit was laden with a grief so great that the inner sufferings of this noble and saintly man still bring tears to one's eyes.

We know more about Jeremiah than about the other prophets because Jeremiah had a devoted and loyal friend named Baruch, the son of Neriah. Baruch was not only companion and friend to Jeremiah, he was also his secretary who wrote down Jeremiah's sermons, and added a biography in which he laid bare the very soul of the sorrowing prophet.

At first, Jeremiah's ideas were similar to those of Isaiah. He, too, believed that Judah should keep free from all alliances. When, however, Babylonia conquered Assyria, he recognized the growing power of Babylonia, saw that in time it would dominate the world, and urged Judah to make peace with it. He opposed both king and nobles who yielded to the persuasion and promises of Egypt to help in the conspiracy against Babylonia and revolt. To the very end, Jeremiah preached submission to Babylonia, and strict faithfulness to the treaties that bound Judah to Nebuchadnezzar. That way he believed lay peace and security for the little kingdom.

This policy, unpopular with the king and the nobles, brought upon him their anger and persecution.

Jeremiah, like all the other prophets, also contended against the hideous idolatry which filled the land. Under King Manasseh (692 B.C.E. to 638 B.C.E.), due to alliances with foreign nations, Assyrian and Egyptian idolatry flooded Judah. The ancient Baals were once more worshipped on every hilltop; the Queen of Heaven and the stars were worshipped under every tree; and even the sacrifice of children to the fire-idol Moloch was practiced.

In the reign of King Josiah (638 B.C.E. to 609 B.C.E.) the High Priest Hilkiah, during repairs in the Temple, discovered a book; it may have been the Book of Deuteronomy. It was read to King Josiah, and it made a profound impression on him. He realized how far his people had strayed from the Covenant of God. King Josiah, who was a good king, instituted the Great Reformation. The land was cleansed of the idols and "high places," and Jerusalem was held to be the only proper place of worship.*

This happened about five years after Jeremiah became prophet. Undoubtedly, Jeremiah was encouraged by this action of the king. It was successful as far as it went, but it did not entirely satisfy Jeremiah. The Reformation was merely external; it did not move into the hearts of the people and change them. Jeremiah could not accept outer form and ceremony without inwardness of spirit. He believed that God demanded right attitudes of mind, a heart sensitive to standards of goodness, and the practice of justice and righteousness in the national life.

Jeremiah, therefore, attacked the Temple worship as useless, even dangerous, for it gave the people a false sense of security at a time when they needed every ounce of spiritual health, to face the outer world of storm and uncertainty. His attacks on false religion brought down upon him the hatred of its priests and its prophets. They even went so far as to have him flogged in public and put on trial for his very life.** Even his kinsmen of Anathoth turned against him and once tried to assassinate him.

Jeremiah was left alone with his God.

*For Josiah's Reformation, see page 315.
**For the attacks on Jeremiah, see page 319.

After the death of King Josiah, his younger son, Jehoahaz, friendly to Babylonia, ruled only three months. He was compelled to abdicate his throne by Pharaoh-necho, who carried him off to Egypt and elevated his older brother, Jehoiakim, to the throne. It was during King Jehoiakim's reign that the great battle of Carchemish (605 B.C.E.) was fought, in which the Babylonians under Nebuchadnezzar completely defeated the forces of Egypt, and Babylonia became the supreme ruler of Western Asia. Nebuchadnezzar kept King Jehoiakim on the throne of Judah as his vassal. Three years later King Jehoiakim rebelled against Babylonia. He was killed probably resisting the Babylonians, and his son, Jehoiachin, ruled after him and continued the rebellion. After three months he was captured. Nebuchadnezzar carried him and the chief men of the nation, the nobles and the priests, into exile to Babylonia. This came to be known as the First Captivity.

Zedekiah, the youngest son of the old King Josiah, was placed on the throne by Nebuchadnezzar. He was a weak and uncertain man. He held Jeremiah in high esteem, almost in superstitious awe; but public opinion was hostile to Jeremiah, and public opinion had to be considered. Moreover, King Zedekiah resented from the beginning the supremacy of Babylonia, and when a new Pharaoh came to the throne of Egypt, a secret alliance between them was formed, and King Zedekiah rebelled against Babylonia. Secretly, King Zedekiah summoned Jeremiah from his prison to consult with him. But Jeremiah's advice to submit to Babylonia did not please him.

Nebuchadnezzar besieged Jerusalem, and after eighteen months of famine and suffering the city fell. The king fled with his family, but he was captured. His sons were killed before his eyes. Then the king himself was blinded and carried captive to Babylonia. With this Second Captivity, the kingdom of Judah, in 586 B.C.E., came to its unhappy end.

Jeremiah survived the siege and was permitted to remain in Judah. Nebuchadnezzar set up Gedaliah, the son of Ahikam, as governor of the crushed community. A short time passed, and Gedaliah was assassinated. The people of Judah still in the land fled in terror to Egypt. Jeremiah pleaded with them in vain. They then carried him off with them to Egypt — the Egypt he hated throughout his life. There, according to tradition, still protesting against their idol-worship, the old prophet was stoned to death.

The Book of Jeremiah is the second book of the Major Prophets. It consists of fifty-two rather lengthy chapters. Due to the work of Baruch, son of Neriah, this book contains history, biography and prophecy. Much, if not all, of the prophecy was dictated to this faithful disciple by Jeremiah himself. The history and biography were undoubtedly written later by Baruch.

I.

THE PROPHET'S CALL

Jeremiah was a very young man when he received the call to be a prophet. He was dismayed; for he knew well the stubbornness of the people, and the fate of the previous prophets. But God had chosen him before he was born; he could, therefore, only obey. Jeremiah told two parables after his call. The parable of the Almond Branch (in old English, "waketree") expressed Jeremiah's confidence that God would fulfill His promise. Through the parable of the Boiling Pot, he warned his countrymen of danger reaching the boiling-point in the north. Jeremiah may have meant the outbreak of the wild, ferocious Scythians which took place about that time.

THE WORDS OF JEREMIAH, THE SON OF HILKIAH, OF THE PRIESTS THAT WERE IN ANATHOTH IN THE LAND OF BENJAMIN, TO WHOM THE WORD OF THE LORD CAME IN THE DAYS OF JOSIAH, THE SON OF AMON, KING OF JUDAH, IN THE THIRTEENTH YEAR OF HIS REIGN. IT CAME ALSO IN THE DAYS OF JEHOIAKIM, THE SON OF JOSIAH, KING OF JUDAH, UNTO THE END OF THE ELEVENTH YEAR OF ZEDEKIAH, THE SON OF JOSIAH, KING OF JUDAH, UNTO THE CARRYING AWAY OF JERUSALEM CAPTIVE IN THE FIFTH MONTH.

Appointed a Prophet

THE word of the Lord came to me saying:
"Before I formed you in your mother I knew you,
And before you were born I sanctified you;
I have appointed you a prophet to the nations."
Then I said:
"Ah, Lord God! I cannot speak;
For I am only a youth."
But the Lord said to me:
"Do not say, 'I am only a youth';
For to all to whom I send you, you shall go,
And whatever I shall command you, you shall speak.
Do not be afraid of them;
For I am with you to deliver you."

The Prophet's Task

Then the Lord stretched forth His hand and touched my mouth; and the Lord said to me:

"See! I have put My words in your mouth;
This day I give you authority over the nations
        and over the kingdoms,
To root up and to pull down, to destroy and
        to overthrow,
To build, and to plant."

Parable of the Almond Branch

Moreover, the word of the Lord came to me, saying:
"What do you see, Jeremiah?"
I said:
"I see a twig of an almond tree (waketree)."
Then the Lord said to me:
"You have seen well; for I am watching (wakeful) over My
word to perform it."

Parable of the Boiling-Pot

A second time the word of the Lord came to me, saying:
"What do you see?"
I said:
"I see a boiling-pot; and the face thereof is from the north."
Then the Lord said to me:
"Out of the north shall trouble boil over upon the inhabitants
of the land. For behold, I am summoning all the kingdoms of
the north; and they shall come, and they shall set up each his
throne at the entrance of the gates of Jerusalem, and against all
her walls round about, and against all the cities of Judah. And
I will pass sentence on all the wickedness of those who have forsaken
Me to offer sacrifice to other gods, and worshipped what their own
hands have made.

"Do not be afraid!"

"As for you, strengthen yourself, stand up and tell them all
I command you; do not be afraid of them, lest I make you afraid
before them. Behold, I have made you this day like a fortified
city, and an iron pillar and a bronze wall, against the whole land —
against the kings of Judah, its princes and priests, and its common
people. They shall fight against you, but they shall not overcome
you; for I am with you to deliver you." (*Jeremiah 1.4–19*)

II.

EVILS THAT DESTROY WITHIN

Jeremiah, in his early years, because of King Josiah's Reformation, hoped that the people would change their hearts and minds and return to their God. He pleaded with the people of Judah in tender and loving words, very much like those of Hosea. But, when he discovered the deep-rooted nature of their evils, he became convinced that it was too late for them to change. He could only warn them against the day of punishment coming.

THE word of the Lord came to me, bidding me go and proclaim this message from the Lord in the hearing of Jerusalem:

Israel's early Love for God

"I remember the affection of your youth,
　The love of your bridal days,
　How you followed Me through the wilderness,
　In a land that was not sown.
　Israel was set apart for the Lord,
　So dear to Him, so sacred,
　That her destroyers were all punished;
　And evil befell them."

Israel gone astray after Idols

"What did your fathers find wrong in Me
　That they went far from Me,
　And followed a thing of naught,
　And they themselves became naught?
　The priests never asked, 'Where is the Lord?'
　Those who handled the Law cared nothing for Me;
　The rulers rebelled against Me;
　The prophets prophesied by Baal, and sought
　　　useless idols.

God changed for a Nothing

"Has any nation changed its gods
    (gods that are no gods)?
But My people have changed their glory
For a useless thing!
Be astonished, O heavens, at this;
Be amazed, beyond words!
For My people have committed two evils:
They have forsaken Me, the fountain of living waters,
And hewed for themselves cisterns, broken cisterns,
That can hold no water."

Entangling Alliances

"What business had you to go to Egypt
    To drink the waters of the Nile?
What right had you to go to Assyria,
    To drink the waters of the Euphrates?"

Dishonest Wealth

"Wicked men are found among My people,
    Who set their snares to trap their fellowmen;
Like cages filled with birds,
    Their houses are filled with dishonest gains.
Thus they have become great and prosperous;
They grow fat, and have become sleek;
They go to any length in crime,
But make no move for justice.
They plead not the cause of the fatherless,
Nor defend the rights of the needy.
Shall I not punish them for these things?
Shall I not make such a nation pay for these
        iniquities?"

False Prophets and Priests

"High and low alike are all greedy for gain;
    Prophet and priest alike deal falsely,
    And they treat the wounds of My people lightly,

Saying: 'Peace, peace,' when there is no peace.
A horrible thing, an appalling thing,
Has happened in the land:
The prophets prophesy in the service of falsehood,
And the priests rule at their beck and call:
And My people love to have it so!"

Why does not Israel return?

"Do not men get up when they fall?
Do they not retrace their steps
After a wrong turning in the road?
Then why does this people continue in its path
When they have taken a wrong turning?
They hold fast to their falsehood,
They refuse to retrace their steps.
Yea, the very stork of the air
Knows when to migrate;
The dove, the swallow, and the crane
Observe the time of their coming;
But My people know not the ordinance of the Lord.
They have rejected the word of the Lord;
And what wisdom remains in them?"

Israel seems hopeless

"Can the Ethiopian (Negro) change his skin,
Or the leopard his spots?
Then may you also do good,
Who are accustomed to do evil.
Therefore, I will scatter you like straw
Driven by the wind of the wilderness;
Such is the fate I deal to you,
Your destiny,
Because you have forgotten Me,
And trusted in what is false."

(Jeremiah 2.1–5, 8, 11–13, 18; 5.26–29;
6.13–15; 5.30–31; 8.4–7; 13.23-25)

III.

"THE TEMPLE SHALL BE AS SHILOH!"

Jeremiah attacked the false faith of the people in the mere presence of the Temple in Jerusalem. He mocked the popular slogan, "The Temple of the Lord!" For side by side with the Temple, the people continued to worship idols and to practice injustice. Only right conduct, he pleaded, could please God. He reminded the people of the fate of the Tabernacle at Shiloh where God had once dwelt, but which was now destroyed. So God would destroy this Temple. For saying this Jeremiah might have been put to death, had not cooler heads than the priests intervened.

THE message that came to Jeremiah from the Lord: "Stand at the entrance-gate of the Lord's house, and make this proclamation there:

Not Temple Worship but Righteousness

'Hear the Lord's message, you men of Judah, who enter by these gates to worship the Lord! Here is what the Lord of hosts, the God of Israel, has to say: Amend your ways and your doings, that I may dwell among you in the Temple here. Trust not in false phrases like "The Temple of the Lord! The Temple of the Lord!" If you thoroughly amend your ways and doings; if you thoroughly see justice done between man and man; if you oppress not the stranger, the fatherless, and the widow, and shed not innocent blood in this place, and walk not after other gods to your own hurt; then will I allow you to remain in this place, in the land that I gave to your fathers, for ever and ever.

The Temple may become like Shiloh!

'What? Steal, murder, commit adultery, perjure yourselves, sacrifice to Baal, wander after other gods, and then come to present yourselves before Me in this house, which belongs to Me, thinking you are now quite safe — safe to go on with these evil practices! Is this house, My very own house, become a den of robbers in your eyes?

'Go to My sacred shrine at Shiloh, where I first established My tabernacle; see what I did to it, on account of the wickedness of Israel, My people! So now with you. Because you have done all these things, because you would not listen when I spoke to you eagerly and earnestly, because you would not answer My call, therefore, as I have done to Shiloh, so will I do to My very own house here, the house on which you rest your confidence, and to the place that I gave to you and your fathers. And I will cast you out of My sight, as I cast out your kinsmen, the whole people of Ephraim (Israel).' "

Jeremiah is arrested

When Jeremiah had finished saying all that the Lord had ordered him to say to the people, the priests and the prophets and all the people seized him. They shouted:

"You shall die! What do you mean by prophesying in the Lord's name that this Temple shall become like Shiloh and that this city is to be desolate, without an inhabitant?"

All the people gathered around Jeremiah in the house of the Lord. When the authorities of Judah heard these things, they came up to the house of the Lord from the royal palace; and they seated themselves at the entrance of the new gate of the Lord's house.

Then the priests and the prophets said to the authorities and to the people:

"This man deserves to die. He has been prophesying against this city — you have heard him with your own ears!"

Then Jeremiah said to the authorities and to the people:

"The Lord sent me to prophesy against this house and this city all the words that you have just heard. Now then, amend your ways and doings, and obey the voice of the Lord your God; and the Lord will relent, He will withhold the evil He has pronounced against you. As for myself, I am in your power; you can do with me as you think right and good. Only be sure of this, that if you put me to death, you bring the guilt of innocent blood upon yourselves, and upon this city, and upon its inhabitants; for it is a fact that the Lord has sent me to say all this in your hearing."

Freedom of Speech upheld.
Saved from the Mob.

The authorities and the people said to the priests and the prophets:

"This man does not deserve to die; he has spoken to us in the name of the Lord our God."

Then some of the elders of the land also rose to their feet and said to the popular assembly:

"When Micah of Moresheth prophesied during the reign of Hezekiah, king of Judah, he told all the people of Judah that this was the word of the Lord of hosts:

'Zion shall be plowed as a field,
And Jerusalem shall become a heap of ruins,
The Temple-hill a mere wooded height.'

"Did King Hezekiah and the people of Judah put him to death? Did they not reverently entreat the Lord, till the Lord relented and withheld the evil He had proclaimed against them? But as for us, we are about to bring evil on ourselves!"

Then Ahikam, the son of Shaphan, came to the aid of Jeremiah, and did not permit him to be handed over to the people so that they should put him to death. (*Jeremiah 7 and 26.7–19, 24*)

IV.

THE BURNING OF THE BOOK

King Jehoiakim, puppet of Egypt, wanted to revolt openly against Babylonia. He hated Jeremiah for his opposition to his plan. And Jeremiah was forbidden to speak in the Temple court. He now wrote his sermons down through Baruch, his faithful secretary and friend. When Jeremiah's book was brought to the attention of King Jehoiakim and read to him, the king angrily burned it page by page. He also ordered the arrest of Jeremiah and Baruch.

IN the fourth year of King Jehoiakim, the son of King Josiah of Judah, this message came to Jeremiah from the Lord:

Jeremiah dictates his Book

"Take a scroll and write upon it all that I have spoken to you against Jerusalem, and against Judah, and against all the nations, from the day when I first spoke to you in King Josiah's reign down to this day. It may be that the house of Judah will hear all the evil that I intend for them, and they will all give up their evil ways and receive My pardon for their sin and guilt."

Jeremiah called Baruch, the son of Neriah; and Baruch wrote upon a scroll, while Jeremiah dictated all that the Lord had said to him. Then Jeremiah told Baruch:

"I am forbidden to enter the Temple; therefore, you must go, and read aloud on a fast-day in the Temple the words of the Lord which you have written, at my dictation, on the scroll. The people are to hear them, and you shall also read them aloud to the people of Judah who come in from the small cities. It may be that, with humble entreaties to the Lord, they will all give up their evil ways; for fierce is the anger and fury with which the Lord has threatened this people."

Baruch reads Jeremiah's
Book to the People

Baruch, the son of Neriah, did all that the prophet Jeremiah told him. When the people of Jerusalem and all who came in to Jerusalem from the small cities of Judah were summoned to a fast before the Lord, Baruch read aloud Jeremiah's words. He read from the window of the side-room belonging to Gemariah, the son of Shaphan, the scribe.

Baruch is reported to the
Authorities

When Micaiah, the son of Gemariah, heard the words of the Lord read from the scroll, he went to the palace, where he found all the authorities seated in the scribe's room. After Micaiah had told them the words that he had heard Baruch read aloud from the scroll to the people, the authorities sent Jehudi, the son of Nethaniah, to tell Baruch to bring them the scroll. When Baruch appeared, scroll in hand, they told him to sit down and read it aloud.

The Authorities report Baruch
to King Jehoiakim

When they had heard all the words, they turned to one another in alarm, whispering:

"We must inform the king of this."

They asked Baruch:

"How did you come to write all this?"

Baruch answered:

"Jeremiah dictated it to me, and I wrote it down in ink upon the scroll."

Then the authorities said to Baruch:

"Go into hiding, you and Jeremiah; let no man know where you are."

After depositing the scroll in the room of Elishama the scribe, they went to the king's private chambers and told the king everything that had occurred.

The King burns Jeremiah's Book

The king sent Jehudi for the scroll; and when he brought it from the room of Elishama the scribe, he read it aloud to the king and all the authorities present.

The king was in his winter-house; and a brazier was burning before him. When Jehudi had read three or four leaves, the king would slash them off with a penknife and cast them into the fire in the brazier, till the whole of the scroll was consumed in the fire.

They were not afraid, nor did they rend their garments, neither the king, nor any of his ministers who heard all these words. The authorities entreated the king not to burn the scroll; but, he would not listen to them. Instead, the king ordered the royal prince, Jerachmeel, and two officers, to bring Jeremiah and Baruch to him.

But the Lord had hidden them.

After the king had burned the scroll, this word of the Lord came to Jeremiah:

"Take another scroll, and write upon it all the words that were on the former scroll, which Jehoiakim, the king of Judah, burned."

Jeremiah writes again

Then Jeremiah took another scroll and gave it to Baruch who wrote upon it, at Jeremiah's dictation, all the words of the book that Jehoiakim, king of Judah, had burned; and there were added besides many similar words.   (*Jeremiah 36*)

V.

JEREMIAH'S LETTER

The situation in Judah went from bad to worse. King Jehoiakim treacherously rebelled against Babylonia. Nebuchadnezzar attacked Jerusalem in 597 B.C.E. After a siege of three months, he captured the city. Then he returned to Babylonia and took with him ten thousand of the best people of Judah, and great treasure. This was the First Captivity. Nebuchadnezzar placed Zedekiah, youngest son of King Josiah, on the throne of Judah as his vassal. To the exiles of the First Captivity, Jeremiah wrote a letter in which he gave them sound advice. He urged them to become good citizens of Babylonia. He also taught them a new truth about their religion: Their religion was not bound to Temple or country. It could be practiced in Babylonia as well as in Palestine. In teaching this, Jeremiah helped the Jewish people to survive later, when their Temple was destroyed and they were exiled from the Holy Land.

THESE are the words of the letter which Jeremiah, the prophet, sent from Jerusalem to the elders of the captivity, and to the priests, the prophets, and all the people whom Nebuchadnezzar had carried into exile from Jerusalem to Babylonia:

Be good Citizens!

"Thus says the Lord of hosts, the God of Israel, to all the captivity whom I have caused to be carried into exile from Jerusalem to Babylonia:

'Build houses and dwell in them, and plant gardens, and eat their fruits; marry wives and raise up families; take wives for your sons and husbands for your daughters; and multiply where you are — never let your numbers diminish. And seek the peace of the city whither I have sent you to be citizens. Pray to the Lord for it, for in the peace thereof shall you have peace.

Learn to seek God there!

'Do not let yourselves be deceived by the prophets and the seers among you; do not listen to their dreams; for they are prophesying falsely to you in My name — I have not sent them. As soon as Babylonia's seventy years have passed, I will remember you and carry out My promise to you, to cause you to return to this place. For I keep in mind My purpose for you, a purpose of good, not of evil, to give you a future and a hope. And you shall pray to Me, and I will answer you. And you shall seek Me, and find Me, when you shall search for Me with all your heart. And I will be found by you, says the Lord, and I will turn your captivity, and gather you from all the nations and from all the places whither I have driven you; and I will bring you back to the place whence I caused you to be carried away captive.' " *(Jeremiah 29.1–14)*

VI.

JEREMIAH'S ACT OF FAITH

King Zedekiah, in spite of all the warnings of Jeremiah, joined a conspiracy against Babylonia. Once more Nebuchadnezzar hastened to Jerusalem, this time determined to destroy the city. Jeremiah, as he attempted one day to walk out of the city gate to go to his native town of Anathoth, was arrested as a traitor, beaten, and thrown into prison. King Zedekiah, weak and uncertain, secretly summoned Jeremiah from prison and asked his advice. Jeremiah still counseled submission to Babylonia. Jeremiah then returned to prison. In that desperate hour, when Judah seemed lost, Jeremiah performed an act of great faith. He purchased a piece of land in Anathoth, and took special care to preserve the deed of purchase for years to come.

THE word of the Lord came to Jeremiah in the tenth year of Zedekiah, king of Judah, at the time when the army of the king of Babylonia was besieging Jerusalem. Jeremiah, the prophet, was a prisoner in the guard-house which was in the king of Judah's palace.

Family Inheritance

The Lord said to Jeremiah:

"Hanamel, the son of your uncle, shall come to ask you to buy his field at Anathoth; for you have the first right to purchase it."

Hanamel, my uncle's son, came to me in the guard-house, as the Lord had said. He said:

"Buy, I beg you, my field at Anathoth; for the right of inheritance is yours, and the right to redeem it is yours; buy it for yourself."

Jeremiah buys the Field

I bought the field at Anathoth from Hanamel, my uncle's son, paying him seventeen shekels of silver. I signed the deed, and sealed it, and had it witnessed, and paid him the money in full. Then I took the purchase deeds, the sealed document containing the terms and conditions, and that which was open, and handed them to Baruch, the son of Neriah, in the presence of the witnesses who signed the purchase deeds, before all the Jews who were seated in the guard-house.

Preserving the Deed of Sale

Before them, I gave this charge to Baruch:

"These are the words of the Lord of hosts, the God of Israel: 'Take these purchase-deeds, the sealed document and the one which is open, and put them in an earthen jar, that they may last many days. For,' says the Lord of hosts, the God of Israel, 'the time will come when houses and fields and vineyards shall yet again be bought in this land.' "

Jeremiah's Prayer

After I delivered the purchase-deeds to Baruch, the son of Neriah, I prayed thus to the Lord:

"Ah Lord God! The siege-mounds for storming the city have reached it. Because of the sword, the famine and the pestilence, the city is sure to fall into the hands of the Chaldean (Babylonian) besiegers! Thy threat has been fulfilled, as Thou seest. Yet it wast Thou, O Lord, who didst tell me to buy the field for money. I had the deeds written and sealed and witnessed, and here is the city falling into the hands of the Chaldeans!"

God answers Jeremiah

Then this word of the Lord came to me:

"I am the Lord, God over all men. Is anything too hard for Me? As surely as I have brought. all this great evil upon this people, so surely will I bring upon them all the good I promised them. In this land that you call desolate, stripped of men and cattle, handed over to the Chaldeans, fields shall again be bought. Men shall buy fields for money, deeds shall be subscribed and sealed and witnessed, in the land of Benjamin, and in the places about Jerusalem, and in the cities of Judah, in the highlands, in the lowlands, and in the south. For I will, indeed, cause them to return from their captivity."

(Jeremiah 32)

VII.

THE GOD OF THE INNER SPIRIT

What Jeremiah had foreseen happened in 586 B.C.E. Nebuchadnezzar captured Jerusalem↓ and reduced it to ashes. The kingdom of Judah came to its end and its people were forced into exile. This is known as the Second Captivity. During his ministry a new belief grew within Jeremiah. He believed that God would make a new Covenant with Judah and Israel, this time to be written on each one's heart. Through such men the Jewish people would be re-established and would survive. To Jeremiah, Israel was an eternal people.

"BEHOLD, the days come," says the Lord, "when I will sow the house of Israel and the house of Judah with the seed of man, and with the seed of beast. And as once I watched over them to pluck up and to break down, to destroy and to overthrow and to afflict, so will I watch over them to build and to plant. In those days they shall say no more:

'The fathers have eaten sour grapes,
And the children's teeth are set on edge.'

But every one shall die for his *own* iniquity — every man who eats the sour grapes, his *own* teeth shall be set on edge.

A new Covenant

"Behold, the days come, when I will make a new Covenant with the house of Israel and with the house of Judah; not like the Covenant that I made with their fathers when I took them by the hand to bring them out of the land of Egypt — that Covenant of Mine which they broke — but this is the Covenant that I will make with the house of Israel after those days:

"I will put My Law within them, and I will write it on their hearts; and I will be their God, and they shall be My people. And they shall teach no more every man his neighbor, and every man his brother, saying: 'Know the Lord'; for they shall all know Me, from the least of them to the greatest of them; for I will forgive their iniquity, and their sin will I remember no more."

↓For archaeological note see Item 18, p. 555 in the back of the book.

Israel — the redeemed

"Again will I build you, and you shall be built,
O virgin of Israel . . .
For there shall be a day,
When the watchmen shall call upon mount Ephraim:
'Arise, and let us go up to Zion,
Unto the Lord our God . . .'
And they shall come and sing in the height of Zion,
And shall flow to the goodness of the Lord;
And their souls shall be as a watered garden,
And they shall not pine any more at all.
Then shall the maiden rejoice in the dance,
And the young men and the old together.
For I will turn their mourning into joy,
And I will comfort them, and make them rejoice
        from their sorrow.
And My people shall be satisfied with My goodness."

Israel — the eternal People

Thus says the Lord:

"Who gives the sun for a light by day?
And who fixes the orbs of moon and stars
        for a light by night?
Who stirs up the sea till its waters
        roar?
The Lord of hosts is His name.
If ever these fixed orbs depart from My
        sight, says the Lord,
Only then shall the people of Israel cease
        from being a nation
Before Me for ever."

(*Jeremiah 31.4, 6, 12–14, 27–36*)

יְחֶזְקֵאל

EZEKIEL

E ZEKIEL, the son of Buzi, was born in Judah, and was of
high priestly family. He seems to have come under the
influence of Jeremiah, whom he may have known personally.
When a young man, he was exiled to Babylonia in the First Captivity that took place during the reign of King Jehoiachin, in
597 B. C. E. He was active as prophet in Babylonia about twenty-
two years. Herein he was different from the other Hebrew prophets, for he was the first to prophesy outside of Palestine.

Ezekiel took up his residence, together with the rest of the
exiles, in the village of Tel-aviv, south of the city of Babylon, by
a canal known as the River Chebar. He was married, and one
of his most solemn prophecies was delivered in connection with
his wife's death, which took place at the very time that Jerusalem
was destroyed.

It was Nebuchadnezzar's plan not to scatter a conquered
people throughout his kingdom, but to establish them in one
place as a community. Thus it happened that Ezekiel, a priest
without a Temple, could still practice his religious leadership
among his people. On Sabbaths and on holydays, the small exiled
Jewish community would gather in his home to worship God as
best they could in that foreign land, and, perhaps, to hear Ezekiel
read the Law and interpret it. He was, in truth, the founder of the
first Synagogue.

Ezekiel's task as spiritual leader to his people was a difficult
one. It was a time of great confusion. The Temple was in Jerusalem; that was God's dwelling-place. How could the people
worship God in a strange land? Ezekiel had to teach the exiles
that God could be found and worshipped even in Babylonia.

Furthermore, when Jerusalem was destroyed, many questioned
whether it was worth while worshipping a God who could be

vanquished by the gods of Babylonia. For, in those days, the common belief was that not only the nations fought, but their gods also joined in the battle. And the conquering god won the worship and loyalty of those whose god was conquered.

Still others believed that the exile would last for only a short time, though Jeremiah's letter discouraged that unfounded optimism.

All these questions Ezekiel had to face and answer. Ezekiel was deeply religious. His faith in God, despite all the misfortunes of his people, had not been broken.

Ezekiel's messages came during two periods. Some came before Jerusalem was destroyed. During that time, his words, like those of Jeremiah, were filled with the note of inescapable doom. He knew the idolatry of the people, the injustices of the princes, and the treachery of Judah's kings. He, too, like Jeremiah, believed that Nebuchadnezzar was God's agent to punish Judah. He therefore taught the small group of exiles that, when Jerusalem fell, it was not because God was weak or less strong than the gods of Babylonia, but, on the contrary, because God Himself, the God of justice, had used Babylonia to punish wicked Judah.

After the destruction of Jerusalem, Ezekiel changed the tone of his message from that of woe and lament to words of comfort, encouragement and hope. He taught that God could be worshipped outside of Palestine, for He was the God of the whole world. He held that the Jewish community could survive the national disaster by their common love of and faith in God, and by their common hope of returning to Palestine and building a new Israel. He believed that his immediate task was to prepare the Jews for that "far-off, divine event." So certain was Ezekiel of the restoration of his people to Palestine that he drew up detailed plans for the future Temple on the Hill of Zion.

Ezekiel was both prophet and priest. He combined the prophet's spiritual ideals and the priest's insistence on rites and ceremonies. He could not think of his Beloved Community of Israel without either. This union of prophetic spirit and priestly law was the special contribution Ezekiel made to the Jewish people. Ezekiel was, in a sense, the founder of the religious Jewish community in the Diaspora (the lands of dispersion), a community of Jews bound together by the bond of religion and the hope of national restoration.

Ezekiel had to overcome the exiles' fear that their situation was hopeless because of the sins of their fathers in Judah. He, therefore, emphasized what Jeremiah had already begun to teach — individual responsibility, that is, the sinner alone shall be punished for his sins. If the fathers were evil-doers, their children would not suffer, unless they followed in their father's footsteps. Therefore, the children of the evil-doers of Judah had no reason to despair. If they changed their attitude towards life, their standards and their conduct, they would find that God would forgive them, and give them a fresh start in life.

Ezekiel was subject to trances in which he saw visions. His visions were weird and strange, and through them God seemed to speak to him. He taught his messages by relating these visions. He also prophesied by means of parables and symbolic actions. He liked to use pet phrases which he repeated time and again, such as "a rebellious house," referring to the people of Judah, and "son of man," meaning mortal man, as referring to himself when God spoke to him.

For all time to come, Ezekiel will be remembered as the religious genius who helped his people, when disaster had swept everything away, to face steadfastly the unknown future. He brought into the black night of their exile the light of tender comfort and strong faith. Above all, in their moments of faint weakness, he taught by his very name — which in Hebrew was *Yechezke'el*, "God will strengthen" — that God Himself would give them the power and courage to overcome defeat and survive as a people.

The Book of Ezekiel is the third book of the Major Prophets.

I.

THE GOD OF POWER

Ezekiel was called to be a prophet in the midst of a vision he saw of storm-clouds and flashing lightnings, in which God appeared to him like a tremendous Power, and compelled him to undertake his difficult task. It is important to notice that God, who hitherto appeared only in the Temple in Jerusalem, now spoke to Ezekiel in Babylonia. Ezekiel, filled with the power of God's words — symbolically eaten in a scroll — was sent to bring God's message to his people.

IN THE FIFTH DAY OF THE MONTH, IN THE FIFTH YEAR OF THE EXILE OF KING JEHOIACHIN, THE WORD OF THE LORD CAME TO EZEKIEL, THE SON OF BUZI, BY THE RIVER CHEBAR; AND THE HAND OF THE LORD WAS THERE UPON HIM.

The Vision of the Lord

I LOOKED, 'and behold, a stormy wind came from the north, a great cloud, with fire flashing through it, and a radiance round about it, while out of the midst of it gleamed something with a luster like that of shining metal.

Out of the midst of it stood forth the likeness of four living creatures, and this was their appearance: their form was like that of a man. Each, however, had four faces and four wings.

Over the heads of the creatures was the likeness of a vault, and it glittered like transparent ice, and was stretched forth above their heads. Under the vault one pair of their wings touched those of the next creature, while the other pair covered the body. When they moved, the sound of their wings sounded to me like the sound of mighty waters, or like the voice of the Almighty.

Above the vault that was over their heads was the likeness of a throne, colored like sapphire; and upon the likeness of the throne was a likeness like that of a man sitting upon it.

From the appearance of his loins upward I saw something with a luster like that of shining metal; and from the appearance of his loins downward I saw something resembling fire, with a radiance round about it, resembling the bow that appears in the clouds on a rainy day.

Such was the likeness of the glory of the Lord, as it appeared to me. And when I saw it, I fell upon my face. Then I heard the voice of someone speaking.

The Prophet's Mission

And He said to me:

"Son of man, stand up and I will speak to you."

As He spoke, the spirit entered in me and made me stand upon my feet. I heard Him say:

"I am sending you to the children of Israel, that nation of rebels who have rebelled against Me; they and their fathers have sinned against Me down to this day. I am sending you to them, hard-faced and stubborn as they are, and you must tell them what the Lord says. And whether they listen or refuse to listen, for they are a rebellious house, they shall learn that there is a prophet among them.

"Son of man, fear them not, fear not what they say, although they defy and despise you — fear not what they say, dread not their angry looks, for they are a rebellious house. Tell them what I say, whether they will listen or refuse to listen."

The Scroll of the Lord

"And you, son of man, listen to what I say. Be not rebellious like this rebellious house. Open your mouth and eat what I now give you."

I looked, and there was a hand stretched out to me, holding a written scroll! When He unrolled it before me, it was written all over, outside as well as inside, with laments and dirges and woes. He said:

"Son of man, eat this scroll, then go and speak to Israel."

I opened my mouth and He made me eat the scroll, telling me:

"Son of man, swallow and digest this scroll I now give you."

When I ate it, the scroll tasted sweet as honey in my mouth.

The Prophet warned:
Be strong!

Then He said to me:

"Son of man, go to Israel and speak My words to them. It is to no people of a foreign tongue or a difficult language that you are sent, but to Israel. It is to no foreign nations whose language you cannot understand. No, if I sent you to them they would listen to you! But Israel will not listen to you, for they will not listen to Me.

"They are stubborn and defiant, every one of them. But I will make you as defiant and as stubborn. I will make your temper unyielding as adamant, harder than flint. Fear them not, dread not their angry looks, for they are a rebellious house."

He added:

"Son of man, attend and listen to all I tell you. Then go to the exiles, to the members of your people, and tell them what the Lord says, whether they will listen or refuse to listen."

Then a spirit picked me up, and I heard behind me a loud, rushing noise: "Blessed be the glory of the Lord from His place." It was the noise made by the wings of the creatures touching one another. And the spirit lifted me up and carried me away, and I went with my spirit in a fierce glow, and the hand of the Lord was strong upon me.

The Watchman of the Lord

I came to the exiles who dwelt at Tel-aviv, by the river Chebar. There I sat for seven days, overwhelmed. At the end of seven days this word from the Lord came to me:

"Son of man, I have appointed you a watchman to Israel; whenever you hear a word from Me, you must give them My warning." (*Ezekiel 1.1–3, 2–3.17*)

II.

EACH ONE IS RESPONSIBLE

The exiles in Babylonia questioned God's justice, for they believed themselves guiltless of Judah's sins, yet they suffered a sad fate. They repeated the words of a current proverb which said that children suffer for the sins of their parents. But this belief led to despair. Why should a man suffer for the wrongs done by another? Ezekiel denied the truth of this proverb, and he taught that each man was responsible for his own conduct.

THIS word of the Lord came to me, saying:

The false Proverb

"What do you mean by using this proverb in the land of Israel:

'The fathers have eaten sour grapes,
And the children's teeth are set on edge'?

"As I live, says the Lord, you shall never again use this proverb in Israel. All souls are Mine: the soul of the father as well as the soul of the son is Mine. Only the one who sins shall die.

The righteous man — his Reward

"If a man be righteous and do what is just and honorable, if he join not in the heathen feasts upon the hilltops, nor worship the idols of the Israelites, nor commit adulteries, nor wrong anyone; if he restore to the debtor his pledge, take nothing through robbery, give his bread to the hungry and clothe the naked, nor demand interest on a loan, nor exact usury; if he keep his hand from doing wrong, render just decisions between man and man, and follow My commands, he is righteous. He shall live."

The wicked Man — his Punishment

"The one who sins shall die. A son shall not be responsible for his father's guilt, nor a father for his son's guilt. The righteous man shall be credited with his own righteousness, and the wicked man with his own wickedness."

*Each is responsible for his
own Conduct*

"If a wicked man repent of all his sins which he has committed, and keep all My laws and do what is just and right, he shall surely live; he shall not die. None of the righteous deeds which he has done shall be forgotten; because he has done right, he shall live."

"If a righteous man give up being righteous and practice evil, doing every abominable thing that a wicked man does, none of his righteous deeds shall be remembered. For the sin of which he is guilty, he shall die."

God's Ways are just

"And yet Israel complains: The Lord is not acting fairly!

"My ways not fair, O Israel!

"Is it not rather your ways that are not fair and right?

"O Israel, I will deal with every one of you as he has lived. Repent and give up your transgressions, or they will be your ruin. Have done with all your sins against Me, and make a new heart and a new spirit for yourselves.

"O house of Israel, why will you die?

"I have no pleasure in the death of anyone who dies," says the Lord.

"Therefore, repent, and live!"   (*Ezekiel 18*)

III.

FOR GOD'S OWN HONOR

Ezekiel had to meet the accusation that God was powerless to save His people. Ezekiel taught the exiles that it was God Himself who had brought punishment on Israel. Moreover, Ezekiel pointed out that Israel would be restored not because they were worthy of it, but because God would thus vindicate His name and His sacred honor in the sight of the nations. They would see God's power to redeem and rebuild, provided they changed their conduct for the better.

THIS word of the Lord came to me, saying:

"Son of man, prophesy thus to the mountains of Israel, and say: Hear the word of the Lord! O Mountains of Israel, hear what the Lord God has to say to the mountains and to the hills, to the streams and to the valleys, to the waste places and the deserted cities, that have become a prey and a derision to the nations round about!

"I swear that the nations around you shall have to bear their shame when they are ruined!"

Restoration is coming!

"But you, O mountains of Israel, your forests shall put out their branches, they shall bear fruit for Israel, My people; for soon Israel will be coming back. I am for you, and I will care for you, and you shall be tilled and sown.

"I will multiply men upon you, even all the house of Israel, even all of it. And the cities shall be repeopled, and the waste places shall be rebuilt. I will make the men and beasts upon you numerous, and settle you as you used to be. I will do better for you than at the first, and you shall learn that I am the Lord."

For the sake of God's Name:
His Honor

"Son of man, when the Israelites lived in their own land, they defiled it with their practices; so I vented My fury upon them for drenching My land with bloodshed and defiling it with their idols. I scattered them among the nations, till they were dispersed over the world; I punished them for their practices.

"But it lowered My sacred honor to have them scattered thus among the nations. For the peoples sneered: 'These are the people of the Lord, and yet they are driven out of the land!' But I have great concern for My sacred honor, thus profaned by the dispersion of the house of Israel. Therefore, say to the house of Israel: Thus says the Lord God: It is not for your sake, O house of Israel, that I do this, but for the sake of My own sacred honor. I will uphold My high honor which has been lowered and profaned because you are scattered among the nations. And when I show them what I am, by My dealings with you, then, says the Lord, the nations shall know that I am the Lord."

A new Heart and a new Spirit

"I will gather you from among the nations and take you from all countries, and I will bring you back to your own land. Then will I sprinkle clean water over you, and you shall be clean from all your impurities, and you shall be cleansed from all your idols. A new heart also will I give you, and a new spirit will I put within you. I will take away the stony heart out of you and I will give you a heart of flesh. I will put My spirit within you, and I will cause you to live by My laws, and you shall obey and observe My commandments. You shall dwell in the land that I gave to your fathers.

"You shall be My people, and I will be your God."

The Land shall be rebuilt

"I will call to the grain and will increase it. And I will bring no famine upon you. I will make your fruit and your crops abundant, that you may no more be taunted by the nations with famine. Not for your sake will I act thus, says the Lord; be ashamed and humiliated for your wrongdoings, O house of Israel!

"I will cause the cities to be inhabited and the waste places shall be rebuilt. And men shall say, 'This land that was desolate is like the garden of Eden today; and the waste places and desolate cities are fortified and inhabited!'

"Then the nations round about shall know that I, the Lord, have rebuilt the ruined cities and replanted the desolate land. I, the Lord, have spoken it, and I will do it." (*Ezekiel 36*)

THE VALLEY OF DRY BONES

"Son of man, can these bones live?" (*Ezekiel 37.3*)

see page 409

DAVID THE PSALMIST

"I will sing praise to my God . . ." *(Psalms 104.33)*

see page 430

IV.

THE VALLEY OF DRY BONES

Ezekiel's faith in the power of God to bring new life into the Jewish people, seemingly dead, was dramatically expressed in the strange but fascinating vision he saw of the dead bones that sprang to life.

THE hand of the Lord was laid upon me.

And the Lord led me forth by His spirit and set me down in the midst of the valley, and it was full of bones. Then He made me pass around about them, and I saw that they were very many in the open valley.

He said to me:

"Son of man, can these bones live?"

I answered:

"O Lord God, only Thou knowest."

Again He said to me:

"Prophesy over these bones, and say to them: Dry bones, hear the word of the Lord. I will cause breath to enter into you, and you shall live. And I will lay sinews upon you, and clothe you with flesh, and cover you with skin, and put breath in you, that you may live again and know that I am the Lord."

So I prophesied as He commanded me. And as I spoke, there was a movement. And the bones came together, each into its place; and as I looked, sinews came upon them, and flesh clothed them, and skin covered them, but there was no breath in them.

Then He said to me:

"Son of man, prophesy to the breath, and say: The Lord commands, Come from the four winds, O breath, and breathe upon these slain, that they may live."

So I prophesied as He commanded me, and the breath came into them, and they lived and stood up upon their feet, an exceedingly vast multitude.

Then He said to me:

"Son of man, these bones represent the whole house of Israel. They say: Our bones are dried up, and our hope is lost; we are completely cut off."

Therefore prophesy, and say to them:

"Thus says the Lord God: I will open your graves, and raise you from them, O My people; and I will bring you into the land of Israel. Then, O My people, you shall know that I am the Lord. And I will put My spirit in you, and you shall live, and I will restore you to your own land; and you shall know that I, the Lord, have spoken and accomplished it, says the Lord." (*Ezekiel 37*)

יוֹנָה

JONAH

JONAH was a reluctant prophet. He refused to obey God's command that he go to the Gentiles in the city of Nineveh and bring them His promise of forgiveness, if they repented of their sins. Jonah did not believe them worthy of God's love, nor did he think they were capable of repenting. Hence, Jonah had to be taught the lesson of God's universal love for all mankind.

The Book of Jonah was not written by Jonah, but about him. According to tradition, its author was one of the "Men of the Great Synagogue" who lived during the days when the Jews returned from the Babylonian exile. It is understandable that, after the suffering and humiliation of the exile, many Jews became hostile to the non-Jewish world, because of their national tragedy. In their anguish they questioned whether the Gentiles were capable of receiving the lofty message of God's forgiveness, and perhaps even denied their worthiness to receive His love and compassion.

This attitude, however, was itself unworthy of the true Jew. For the whole spirit of Judaism, enlarged and enriched by the prophets of Israel, was that all men are God's children, and therefore are capable of knowing God and worthy of receiving His divine blessings. It was to teach this lesson that the Book of Jonah was written.

Why did the author take Jonah, the son of Amittai, as the hero of his tale? Probably because a prophet named Jonah, who lived in the reign of Jeroboam II (*II Kings 14.25*), had the reputation of being a very nationalistic patriot. As such, he symbolized the narrow and prejudiced spirit that the author of the book wished to oppose.

Some regard the Book of Jonah as a true description of an historical event. But others believe that it is a parable, that is, a tale told to teach a lesson. As a parable, we can understand better the incident of the fish that swallowed Jonah. Other peoples have legends in which their heroes were supposed to have been swallowed by dragons or huge sea-monsters, and later were saved from death and were brought out to safety. So, too, we find that the prophet Jeremiah (*Jeremiah 51.34, 44*) compared Babylonia to a great monster that swallowed Israel, but, from its belly (*Galut*, Exile) God delivered His people.

As Israel prayed for deliverance from the depths of the exile and was rescued, so Jonah was saved from the belly of the fish that he might continue on his mission to Nineveh.

So noble is the message of the Book of Jonah, that God is one and mankind is one, our Sages made it part of the Synagogue's service. On the Day of Atonement, at the afternoon service (*Minhah*), Jews throughout the world read how God's love and mercy are not confined to Israel but embrace all mankind.

I.

JONAH'S FLIGHT

The word of the Lord came to Jonah, the son of Amittai, saying:

"Arise, go to that great city, Nineveh, and proclaim against it; for their wickedness is known to me."

But Jonah started to flee to Tarshish from the presence of the Lord. He went down to Joppa and found a ship going to Tarshish; so he paid the fare and embarked on the ship to go in it to Tarshish from the presence of the Lord.

But the Lord caused a furious wind to descend upon the sea, and there was such a mighty tempest that the ship was in danger of breaking into pieces. The sailors became afraid, and each man cried for help to his own god; and they threw into the sea the wares that were in the ship, to lighten it. But Jonah had gone down into the innermost part of the ship; and he lay there, and was fast asleep. Then the captain of the ship came and said to him:

"How is it that you are asleep? Arise and call upon your God; perhaps God will think of us, so that we may not perish."

The Lot falls upon Jonah

They said to one another:

"Come, let us cast lots, that we may know on whose account this evil has come upon us."

They cast lots, and the lot fell upon Jonah. Then they said to him:

"Tell us, what is your occupation, and where do you come from? What is your country, and to what people do you belong?"

He said to them:

"I am a Hebrew, and a worshipper of the Lord, the God of heaven, who made the sea and the dry land."

Then the men were exceedingly afraid, and said to him:

"What is this you have done?"

For they knew that he was fleeing from the presence of the Lord, because he had told them.

They said to him:

"What shall we do to you, that the sea may be calm for us?" For the sea grew more and more stormy.

He said to them:

"Take me up, and throw me into the sea, and the sea will be calm for you, for I know that on account of me this great tempest has overtaken you."

The Humaneness of the Sailors

But the men rowed hard to get back to the land; they could not, however, for the sea grew more and more stormy ahead.

Therefore, they cried to the Lord and said:

"We beseech Thee, O Lord, we beseech Thee, let us not perish for this man's life, nor let us be guilty of shedding innocent blood, for Thou art the Lord; Thou hast done as it pleased Thee."

Then they took up Jonah and threw him into the sea; and the sea became calm. The men feared the Lord exceedingly, and they offered a sacrifice and made vows to Him.

II.

JONAH SWALLOWED BY THE FISH

Now the Lord had prepared a great fish to swallow Jonah; and Jonah was inside the fish three days and three nights. Then Jonah prayed to the Lord his God, saying:

> "Out of my trouble I called unto the Lord,
>   And He answered me;
> For Thou hast cast me into the depths,
>   Into the heart of the sea.
> I will sacrifice to Thee with the voice
>   Of thanksgiving;
> What I have vowed, I will pay.
> Deliverance belongeth unto the Lord!"

Then the Lord commanded the fish, and it threw Jonah out upon the dry land.

God's second Command

The word of the Lord came to Jonah a second time:
"Arise, go to that great city Nineveh, and proclaim to it the message that I bid you."
Jonah started for Nineveh, as the Lord commanded.
Nineveh was a great city, three days' journey across. And Jonah went through the city a day's journey, and he proclaimed:
"Forty days more and Nineveh shall be overthrown!"

Nineveh responds to God's Message

The people of Nineveh believed God; and they proclaimed a fast and put on sackcloth, from the greatest to the least of them. And when the word came to the king of Nineveh, he rose from his throne, took off his robe, dressed in sackcloth, and sat in ashes. And he made this proclamation and published it in Nineveh:

"By the decree of the king and his nobles!
Man, beast, herd and flock shall not taste
anything; let them not eat nor drink water;
but let both man and beast put on sackcloth, and let them cry earnestly to God,
and turn each from his evil way and from
the acts of violence which they are doing.
Who knows but that God may relent and turn away
His anger, that we may not perish."

When God saw that they turned from their evil ways, He relented of the evil which He said He would do to them, and did not do it.

III.

THE ANGRY PROPHET

This displeased Jonah exceedingly and he was angry. And he prayed to the Lord, and said:

"Ah, Lord, was not this that I said when I was still in my own country? It was what I wished to prevent by fleeing to Tarshish; for I knew that Thou art a God, gracious and merciful, patient, and abounding in love, and relenting of evil. Therefore, O Lord, take now, I beseech Thee, my life from me; for it is better for me to die than to live!"

But the Lord said:

"Are you doing right in being angry?"

Jonah's Gourd — Its Lesson

Then Jonah left the city, and on its east side he made a booth for himself and sat under it, until he might see what would become of the city. And the Lord prepared a gourd (a large leafy plant) and made it grow up to shade Jonah's head from the hot sun. The shade of the gourd gave Jonah great comfort. But at dawn the next day God prepared a worm which injured the gourd, so that it withered.

When the sun rose, God prepared a hot east wind; and the sun beat upon Jonah's head, so that he was faint and he begged that he might die, saying:

"It is better for me to die than to live."

God's gentle Humor and Counsel

Then God said to Jonah:

"Are you doing right in being angry about the gourd?"

He replied:

"I am right in being greatly angry!"

And the Lord said:

"You have pity on a gourd which has cost you no trouble and which you have not made grow; which came up in a night and perished in a night. Should I not have pity on the great city, Nineveh, in which there are more than one hundred and twenty thousand human beings so simple that they cannot distinguish their right hand from their left; and also much cattle?"

כְּתוּבִים

THE WRITINGS

תְּהִלִּים

PSALMS

HAVE you ever been lonesome and unhappy? Have you sometimes failed in your work and felt discouraged and depressed? Or, have you ever been so overjoyed that you could not find words adequate to express your feelings? Who has not done something wrong and been ashamed of it afterwards? There is not a person who has not felt fear, or lost confidence in himself, or yearned for someone in whom to confide and from whom he could get help. Everyone — whether young or old — has experienced these "moods of the soul." And throughout the ages poets have written about them.

The Book of Psalms is a collection of poems telling how the religious poets of Israel, whom we call psalmists, met sorrow or joy, fear or trust, dark sinning or righteous living. Every experience that men have faced is reflected in their shining words. And, furthermore, since they were Jews, they told also what they felt about Jewish life and experience.

In all that happened to them, the psalmists had one great help — their wonderful and unwavering faith in a loving God who never failed them. Thus, through a thousand years, in every circumstance of life, they felt that God was with them to strengthen and fortify them, and in all the poems they wrote they sang His praise.

The name of the Book of Psalms, if the Hebrew (*Tehillim*) were translated directly, would be "The Book of Praise-Songs." This name conveys immediately the spirit of its one hundred and fifty hymns, anthems and songs — the unending praise of God.

King David, according to ancient tradition, was the author of the Book of Psalms, and undoubtedly he wrote many of them. Seventy-three of the psalms have the superscription *le-David*, "to

421

David." Most of these psalms seem to deal with events in the life of David. Whether they were written by David himself has aroused much controversy. Even medieval Jewish commentators explained that *le-David* does not always mean "written by David," but at times means "concerning David." In the book itself, other names are mentioned as writers of psalms, such as Moses, Solomon, and Asaph, the sons of Korah, and Ethan, Heman and others. The Book of Psalms, therefore, is properly regarded as a collection of groups of religious poems written over many centuries by the religious poets of Israel.

The name, psalms, in English, comes from the Greek word *psalmos* which means the music of stringed instruments. This name was well chosen, for the psalms were originally sung to the accompaniment of musical instruments in the Temple service. At the beginning of many of the psalms is found a heading, called "the superscription," which tells by which instrument the psalm was to be accompanied, or the tune to which it was to be sung, and sometimes the circumstances in which it was composed.

Only a few of the song-poems can be brought here. But even these few convey the spirit of the psalms and contain the major ideas expressed in them. Here are songs about Nature and the God of Nature, the personal experiences of men, and some happy and tragic events in the history of Israel.

After reading these religious poems and others in the Book of Psalms, we can better understand why they were used in the Temple service in ancient Jerusalem and later as prayers in Israel's prayer book; indeed, how they became the religious inheritance of all mankind, so that from the rising of the sun even to its setting the name of God is praised in the praise-songs of the Jewish people.

The Book of Psalms is the first book of the third large division of the Bible, known as *Ketubim* or "The Writings," the other two being, as we have learned, *Torah*, "The Law," and *Nebi'im*, "The Prophets."

SWEET SINGER IN ISRAEL

King David* was not only a great warrior and ruler, and a statesman who brought prosperity, power and glory to his people, he was also an inspired poet who wrote some of the most beautiful religious songs and poems that have ever been written. Here are a few of the psalms which he wrote at various times. Like shining mirrors they reflect important experiences which deeply moved his spirit.

GOD, THE GOOD SHEPHERD

David had once been a shepherd who tended his sheep and loved them. He pictured God as a great good Shepherd who tenderly cared for His flock. The sheep who have faith in their shepherd are free from fear and worry; so, too, men who have faith in God.

A Psalm of David.

The Lord is my shepherd; I shall not want.
He maketh me to lie down in green pastures;
He leadeth me beside the still waters.
He restoreth my soul;
He guideth me in straight paths for His name's sake.
Yea, though I walk through the valley of the
        shadow of death,
I will fear no evil,
For Thou art with me;
Thy rod and Thy staff, they comfort me.
Thou preparest a table before me in the presence of
        my enemies;
Thou hast anointed my head with oil; my cup
        runneth over.
Surely goodness and mercy shall follow me
All the days of my life;
And I shall dwell in the house of the Lord for ever. (*Psalm 23*)

*For the story of King David's life, see the Books of Samuel, pages 203 ff. and the Books of Kings, pages 261 ff.

WHEN DAVID FLED FROM SAUL

When David fled from King Saul, he hid for a time in the Cave of Adullam. He was surrounded by enemies, and he feared for his very life. Just as the cave was a place of refuge for his body, so he believed God was a refuge for his spirit. Therefore, his heart was strong with courage.

A Psalm of David: when he fled from Saul, in the cave.

Be gracious unto me, O God, be gracious unto me,
For in Thee hath my soul taken refuge;
Yea, in the shadow of Thy wings will I take refuge,
Until calamities have passed by.

I will cry unto God, Most High;
Unto God who accomplisheth it for me.
He will send from heaven, and save me,
When he that would swallow me up taunteth.   Selah*

In the midst of lions that devour I must dwell,
Men whose teeth are spears and arrows,
And their tongue a sharp sword.
They have spread a net for my footsteps;
My soul is bowed down;
They have dug a pit before me,
But they themselves have fallen into it.   Selah

My heart is steadfast, O God,
My heart is steadfast.
I will sing, yes, I will sing praises.
I will give thanks unto Thee, O Lord, among the
        peoples;
I will sing praises to Thee among the nations.
For Thy mercy is great unto the heavens,
And Thy truth unto the skies.   (*Psalm 57*)

*A Musical term, marking a pause.

WHEN DAVID BROUGHT THE ARK
TO JERUSALEM

The happiest moment in David's life was the time when he captured Jerusalem and brought the Ark of the Covenant there. A great procession of priests and Levites sang as choruses answering each other, in celebration of the notable event. David describes the qualities that the true worshipper ought to have, when he comes into God's presence.

A Psalm of David.

First Choir:

> The earth is the Lord's and the fullness thereof;
> The world and they that dwell therein.

Second Choir:

> For He hath founded it upon the seas,
> And established it upon the floods.

First Choir:

> Who shall ascend the mountain of the Lord?
> And who shall stand in His holy place?

Second Choir:

> He that hath clean hands, and a pure heart;
> Who hath not taken My name in vain,
> And hath not sworn deceitfully.
> He shall receive a blessing from the Lord,
> And righteousness from the God of his salvation.

First Choir:

> Such is the generation of them that seek after Him,
> That seek Thy face, even Jacob. Selah

Chorus of Priests:

> Lift up your heads, O ye gates,
> And be ye lifted up, ye everlasting doors;
> That the King of glory may enter.

Chorus of Levites:
> Who is the King of glory?

First and Second Choirs:
> The Lord strong and mighty,
> The Lord mighty in battle.

Chorus of Priests:
> Lift up your heads, O ye gates,
> Yea, lift them up, ye everlasting doors;
> That the King of glory may enter.

Chorus of Levites:
> Who then is the King of glory?

First and Second Choirs:
> The Lord of Hosts;
> He is the King of glory!   Selah   *(Psalm 24)*

WHEN DAVID FLED FROM ABSALOM

The greatest sorrow that David ever suffered was caused by his son, Prince Absalom. Absalom had rebelled against his father, David, and sought to take his life. King David had to flee to the wilderness where he hid himself, a fugitive from the son whom he loved. His faith in God alone sustained him in those dark hours.

A Psalm of David, when he fled from Absalom his son.

How many are my foes, O Lord!
Many are they that rise up against me.
Many are they that say of my soul:
"There is no help for him in God."   Selah

But Thou, O Lord, art a shield about me,
My glory, and the one who lifts up my head.
With my voice I call unto the Lord,
And He answereth me out of His holy mountain.   Selah
I lay me down and I sleep;
I awake, for the Lord sustaineth me.
I am not afraid of ten thousands of people,
That have set themselves against me round about.

Arise, O Lord; save me, O my God;
Verily, Thou hast smitten all my enemies upon the
        cheek,
Thou hast broken the teeth of the wicked.
Salvation belongeth unto the Lord;
Thy blessing be upon Thy people.   Selah

(Psalm 3)

PSALMS ABOUT NATURE AND MAN

The psalmists loved the beauty, the majesty and the wonder of the world. They regarded the world as the garment with which God clothed Himself. The world they immediately knew was Palestine — its blue skies and warm sun, its bright stars and silver moon, its flowers, trees, hills and mountains, its deserts and rocky highlands, its little streams, its refreshing rains and angry thunderstorms, its hoar-frosts and fogs and snows, its wild beasts, its creeping things, its beautiful birds. All these the psalmists knew and loved and learned lessons from. Who created this marvelous world and its abundance? Who guided the planets in their courses? Who protected the beasts of field and jungle, and gave them their instincts and understanding? Who gave beauty and loveliness, as well as strength and majesty to all creation? God! And so the psalmists praised God — the Creator of the universe, its Guide and Protector. From this knowledge the psalmists drew strength and courage, faith hope and fortitude.

GOD, CREATOR OF THE WORLD

The psalmist speaks of God's grandeur in nature. He describes the creation of the world, following the story of creation as given in the first chapter of Genesis. In ancient times, the earth was thought of as a flat, plate-like mass resting upon an abyss of waters; the heavens were a vault covering the earth like a tent or "curtain," and the heavenly vault was also surrounded by water. God's abode, or "upper chambers," rested on the waters above the vault.

BLESS the Lord, O my soul.

O Lord my God, Thou art very great;
Thou art clothed with glory and majesty.
Thou coverest Thyself with light as with a garment;
Thou stretchest out the heavens like a curtain;

Thou layest the beams of Thine upper chambers in
    the waters;
Thou makest the clouds Thy chariot;
Thou walkest upon the wings of the wind;
Thou makest winds Thy messengers,
The flaming fire Thy ministers.

Thou didst establish the earth upon its foundations,
That it should not be moved for ever and ever;
Thou didst cover it with the deep as with a vesture;
The waters stood above the mountains.
At Thy rebuke they fled;
At the voice of Thy thunder they hastened away —
The mountains rose, the valleys sank down —
Unto the place which Thou hadst founded for them;
Thou didst set a bound which they should not pass over,
That they might not return to cover the earth.

Thou sendest forth springs into the valleys;
They run between the mountains;
They give drink to every beast of the field,
The wild asses quench their thirst.
Beside them dwell the fowl of the heaven,
From among the branches they sing.

Thou waterest the mountains from Thine upper chambers;
The earth is full of the fruit of Thy works.
Thou causest the grass to spring up for the cattle,
And herbs for the service of man;
To bring forth bread out of the earth,
And wine that maketh glad the heart of man,
And oil to make his face to shine,
And bread that strengtheneth man's heart.
The trees of the Lord are full of sap,
The cedars of Lebanon, which He hath planted,
Wherein the birds make their nests;
As for the stork, the fir-trees are her house.
The high mountains are for the wild goats;
The rocks are a refuge for the conies (rabbits).

Thou appointest the moon for seasons;
The sun knoweth his going down.
Thou makest darkness, and it is night,
Wherein all the beasts of the forest do creep forth.
The young lions roar after their prey,
And seek their food from God.
The sun ariseth, they slink away,
And lay themselves down in their dens.
Man goeth forth unto his work
And to his labor until the evening.

How manifold are Thy works, O Lord!
In wisdom hast Thou made them all;
The earth is full of Thy creatures.
Yonder sea, great and wide,
Therein are creeping things innumerable,
Living creatures, both small and great.
There go the ships;'
There is leviathan (sea monster), whom Thou hast
    formed to sport therein.

All of them wait for Thee,
That Thou mayest give them their food in due season.
Thou givest it unto them, they gather it;
Thou openest Thy hand, they are satisfied with good.
Thou hidest Thy face, they vanish;
Thou withdrawest their breath, they perish,
And return to their dust.
Thou sendest forth Thy spirit, they are created;
And Thou renewest the face of the earth.
May the glory of the Lord endure for ever;
Let the Lord rejoice in His works!
He toucheth the mountains, and they smoke.
I will sing unto the Lord as long as I live;
I will sing praise to my God while I have my being.
Let my musing be sweet unto Him;

As for me, I will rejoice in the Lord.
Let sinners cease out of the earth,
And let the wicked be no more.

Bless the Lord, O my soul.
Hallelujah.*   (*Psalm 104*)

MAN'S PLACE IN GOD'S WORLD

The psalmist says that, although God is the Creator of the universe, He has given man, though physically weak, mastery over the world he lives in.

For the Leader**; upon the Gittith.***   A Psalm of David.

O Lord, our Lord,
How glorious is Thy name in all the earth!
Thy majesty is revealed above in the heavens.
Out of the mouth of babes and sucklings hast
      Thou founded strength,
Because of Thine adversaries,
That Thou mightest crush the enemy and the avenger.

When I behold Thy heavens, the work of Thy fingers,
The moon and the stars, which Thou hast established,
What is man, that Thou art mindful of him?
And the son of man, that Thou thinkest of him?
Yet Thou hast made him but little lower than the angels,
And hast crowned him with glory and honor.
Thou hast put all things into his power:
The fowl of the air, and the fish of the sea,
Whatsoever passeth through the paths of the seas.

O Lord, our Lord,
How glorious is Thy name in all the earth!   (*Psalm 8*)

*Praise ye the Lord.
**Chief Musician, or Conductor of the Temple Choir.
***Musical instrument, or the melody to which this psalm was sung.

GOD IN NATURE AND IN LAW

The psalmist tells how God reveals Himself to men through the glory of nature and in the moral Law, with its precepts and commandments. Thus, God is not only the Creator of nature, He is also the power that makes for righteousness among men.

For the Leader. A Psalm of David.

The heavens declare the glory of God,
And the firmament showeth His handiwork;
Day unto day uttereth speech,
And night unto night revealeth knowledge.

There is no speech, there are no words,
Neither is their voice heard,
Yet their message goes out through all the earth,
And their words to the end of the world.

In the heavens hath He set a tent for the sun,
Which is like a bridegroom coming out of his chamber,
And rejoiceth as a strong man to run his course.
His going forth is from the end of the heaven,
And his circuit unto the ends of it;
And there is nothing hid from the heat thereof.

The Law of the Lord is perfect,
       restoring the soul;
The testimony of the Lord is sure,
       making wise the simple.
The precepts of the Lord are right,
       rejoicing the heart;
The commandment of the Lord is pure,
       enlightening the eyes.
The fear of the Lord is clean,
       enduring for ever;

The ordinances of the Lord are true,
 they are righteous altogether;
More to be desired are they than gold,
 yea, than much fine gold,
Sweeter also than honey and the honeycomb.
Moreover, by them is Thy servant warned;
In keeping of them there is great reward . . .

Let the words of my mouth and the meditation
 of my heart be acceptable before Thee,
O Lord, my Rock, and my Redeemer.   (*Psalm 19*)

PSALMS ABOUT MAN'S PILGRIMAGE THROUGH LIFE

The psalmists pictured the world to be like a vast palace which God has built and in which He reigns as supreme King. All the powers of nature are His courtiers, His messengers or angels, and they carry out what God decrees. Men share this magnificent palace with God, but God has laid down certain rules or laws for them. If men obey them, they can make for themselves a rich and happy life. But men ofttimes yield to wrongdoing and evil, and then they suffer for their foolishness and disobedience. The psalmists, therefore, sang of the rewards stored up for the righteous and warned of the misfortunes that awaited the wicked. But the wicked need not despair. If they change their conduct, God will forgive them and show them kindness and love. Therefore, men can go on their earthly pilgrimage confident that God will give them help in their misfortune, peace and strength in their sorrow and trouble, and forgiveness when they do wrong but repent.

TWO WAYS OF LIFE

The psalmist holds that a man may find happiness by avoiding the counsel of wicked men and by always seeking to understand the Law of God. Only what is right is permanent and grows and brings happiness, says the psalmist; but what is evil destroys itself and passes away.

Happy is the man that hath not walked in
    the counsel of the wicked,
Nor stood in the way of sinners,
Nor sat in the seat of the scornful.
But his delight is in the Law of the Lord;
And in His Law doth he meditate day and night.
And he shall be like a tree planted by streams of water,
That bringeth forth its fruit in its season,
And whose leaf doth not wither;
And in whatsoever he doeth he shall prosper.

Not so the wicked;
But they are like the chaff which the wind driveth away.
Therefore the wicked shall not stand, when judgments come,
Nor sinners in the congregation of the righteous;
For the Lord loveth the way of the righteous;
But the way of the wicked shall perish.   (*Psalm 1*)

THE MAN GOD LOVES

This psalm describes the character of the truly religious
man, the man worthy to come into the very presence of God.

A Psalm of David.

Lord, who shall sojourn in Thy tabernacle?
Who shall dwell upon Thy holy mountain?

God's Answer

He that walketh uprightly, and worketh righteousness,
And speaketh truth in his heart;
That hath no slander upon his tongue,
Nor doeth evil to his fellow,
Nor maketh a false charge against his neighbor;
In whose eyes a vile person is despised,
But he honoreth them that fear the Lord;
He that keepeth his promise at all costs, and changeth not;
He that lendeth not his money on interest,
Nor taketh a bribe to injure the innocent.

He that doeth these things shall never be moved.   (*Psalm 15*)

GOD'S PROTECTING CARE

The psalmist knows that men must always face peril and misfortune in life. However, he says that confidence and trust in God's goodness will fortify men when they face these difficulties.

He that dwelleth in the secret place of the Most High,
And abideth under the shadow of the Almighty,
Says of the Lord, "He is my refuge and my fortress,
My God, in whom I trust."
Surely He shall deliver thee from the snare of the fowler,
And from the deadly pestilence . . . .
Thou shalt not be afraid of the terror by night,
Nor of the arrow that flieth by day;
Of the pestilence that walketh in darkness,
Nor of the destruction that wasteth at noonday . . . .
For He will give His angels charge over thee,
To keep thee in all thy ways.

God speaks

"Because he hath set his love upon Me,
    therefore will I deliver him;
I will set him on high, because he hath known My name.
He shall call upon Me, and I will answer him;
I will be with him in time of trouble;
I will rescue him, and bring him to honor.
With long life will I satisfy him,
And make him to behold My salvation." *(Psalm 91)*

GOD — SOURCE OF OUR HELP

This psalmist, perhaps, was a pilgrim to Jerusalem. He saw the mighty fortress of Zion, and heard his companions express confidence in its mighty defenses. But he trusted in God as the source of his help rather than in man-made citadels and nature's rocky mountains.

A Song of Ascents.*

I will lift up mine eyes unto the mountains:
From whence shall my help come?
My help cometh from the Lord,
Who made heaven and earth.
He will not suffer thy foot to be moved;
He that keepeth thee will not slumber.
Behold, He that keepeth Israel
Doth neither slumber nor sleep.

The Lord is thy keeper;
The Lord is thy shade upon thy right hand.
The sun shall not smite thee by day,
Nor the moon by night.
The Lord shall keep thee from all evil;
He shall keep thy soul.
The Lord shall guard thy going out and thy coming in,
From this time forth and for ever. (*Psalm 121*)

*Fifteen psalms (*Psalms 120–134*) have this superscription. It is generally believed that these psalms were sung by pilgrims as they came up to Jerusalem for the festival celebrations. Zion was in the highlands, and the pilgrims went *up* (ascended) to Jerusalem. Some, however, believe that there were fifteen steps (ascents) in the Temple, corresponding to these fifteen Songs of Ascents, and the Levites stood on each step with musical instruments, and chanted these psalms.

IN THE DEPTHS OF DESPAIR

This is a psalm of repentance, or a penitential psalm. It tells how the psalmist was guilty of some sin for which he is now sorry. But he knows that God is kind and, therefore, that He will forgive him.

A Song of Ascents.

Out of the depths have I called Thee, O Lord.
Lord, hearken unto my voice;
Let Thine ears be attentive
To the voice of my supplications.
If Thou, Lord, shouldst record iniquities,
O Lord, who could stand?
But with Thee there is forgiveness,
That Thou mayest be feared.

I wait for the Lord, my soul doth wait,
And in His word do I hope.
My soul waiteth for the Lord
More eagerly than watchmen for the morning;
Yea, more than watchmen for the morning.

O Israel, hope in the Lord;
For with the Lord there is mercy,
And with Him is plenteous redemption.
And He will redeem Israel from all their iniquities.   *(Psalm 130)*

GOD IS EVERYWHERE

The psalmist feels that God is so near him that He knows his every thought; yet God is everywhere in the universe, so that the righteous man need never feel that God is far from him. This thought brings him confidence and quiet strength.

For the Leader. A Psalm of David.

O Lord, Thou hast searched me, and known me.
Thou knowest my downsitting and mine uprising,
Thou understandest my thought afar off . . .

For there is not a word in my tongue,
But, lo, O Lord, Thou knowest it altogether.
Thou hast hemmed me in behind and before,
And laid Thy hand upon me . . .

Whither shall I go from Thy spirit?
Or whither shall I flee from Thy presence?
If I ascend up into heaven, Thou art there;
'f I make my bed in the nether-world, behold, Thou
    art there.
If I take the wings of the morning,
And dwell in the uttermost parts of the sea,
Even there would Thy hand lead me,
And Thy right hand would hold me.
And if I say: "Surely the darkness shall envelop me,
And the light about me shall be night,"
Even the darkness hideth nothing from Thee,
But the night shineth as the day;
The darkness and the light are both alike to Thee . . .

Wonderful are Thy works;
And that my soul knoweth full well.   (*Psalm 139*)

AT LIFE'S END

This psalm contrasts the everlastingness of God and the
shortness of man's life. From this contrast, the psalmist draws
the lesson that we should hold each day precious. He expresses
the hope that God will give men joy in their brief life, and that
He will make their work permanent in the world.

A Prayer of Moses, the Man of God.

Lord, Thou hast been our dwelling-place
        in all generations.
Before the mountains were brought forth,
Or ever Thou hadst formed the earth and the world,
Even from everlasting to everlasting Thou art God.

Thou turnest man to dust,
And sayest: "Return, ye children of men."
For a thousand years in Thy sight
Are but as yesterday when it is past,
And as a watch in the night . . .

In the morning they are like grass which groweth up.
In the morning it flourisheth, and groweth up;
In the evening it is cut down, and withereth . . .
We bring our years to an end as a tale that is told.

The days of our years are threescore years and ten,
Or if, by reason of strength, they be fourscore years,
Yet is their pride but travail and vanity;
For it is speedily gone, and we fly away . . .

So teach us to number our days,
That we may get us a heart of wisdom . . .
O satisfy us in the morning with Thy mercy;
That we may rejoice and be glad all our days . . .

And let the graciousness of the Lord our God
      be upon us;
Establish Thou also for us the work
      of our hands;
Yea, the work of our hands establish Thou it.   (*Psalm 90*)

PSALMS ABOUT ISRAEL AND ZION

The psalmists loved their people Israel. They joined in the pilgrim processions on the holydays, singing their songs as they marched on the dusty roads to worship in the Temple of their God. They brought their sacrifices to His altar, though like the prophets they believed that God preferred right conduct to sacrifices of goats and oxen. The psalmists were proud of Israel's glorious past and sang songs of Israel's future. They rejoiced when Israel was victorious in battle; they wept when Israel suffered defeat. They grew thoughtful when their people endured shame and oppression and exile. Like the wise men of Israel, they wanted to know why their God turned His face from them. They believed that God loved Israel, though He punished them for their sins, as a father punishes his children. But also like a father, God gave them pity and tender sympathy and forgiveness when they suffered. The psalmists sang of repentance as the way back to God's presence. They hoped for a happier future for Israel and all mankind, and a great age of justice and peace. And out of their hearts they sang songs of praise to the God of Israel and all the world.

LONGING FOR GOD

The psalmist, perhaps a Levite, longs for the day when he can again come to the Temple of God. He seems to be far away from Jerusalem, and in his memory relives the joyous pilgrimages he used to make in the past.

For the Leader; Maschil* of the sons of Korah.

As the hart panteth after the water brooks,
So panteth my soul after Thee, O God.
My soul thirsteth for God, for the living God:
"When shall I come and appear before God?"
My tears have been my food day and night,
While they say unto me all the day: "Where is
    thy God?"

*A musical term meaning, perhaps, a skillful accompaniment.

These things I remember, and pour out my soul
within me,
How I passed on with the throng, and led them
to the house of God,
With the voice of joy and praise,
a multitude keeping holyday.
Why art thou cast down, O my soul?
And why moanest thou within me?
Hope thou in God; for I shall yet praise Him
For the saving help of His countenance. (*Psalm 42*)

ON PILGRIMAGE TO ZION

The psalmist describes the feelings of a pilgrim who has
reached the gates of Jerusalem. He recalls the city's former
glory when it was the seat of the government. He prays for the
prosperity of Jerusalem.

A Song of Ascents; of David.

I rejoiced when they said to me:
"Let us go unto the house of the Lord."
Our feet are standing
Within thy gates, O Jerusalem;
Jerusalem, that art builded
As a city that is solid and unbroken;
Whither the tribes went up, even the tribes of the Lord,
As a testimony unto Israel,
To give thanks unto the name of the Lord.
For there were set thrones for judgment,
The thrones of the house of David.

Pray for the peace of Jerusalem;
May they prosper that love thee.
Peace be within thy walls,
And prosperity within thy palaces.
For my brethren and companions' sakes,
I will now say: "Peace be within thee."
For the sake of the house of the Lord our God
I will seek thy good. (*Psalm 122*)

WITHIN THE TEMPLE COURTS

The psalmist compares the Temple he loves to the nest of a bird. As the bird finds there peace and safety, so he finds happiness in God's house, away from the evil buffetings and storms of the world.

For the Leader; upon the Gittith.* A Psalm of the
      sons of Korah.

How lovely are Thy tabernacles, O Lord of hosts!
My soul yearneth, yea, even pineth for the courts
      of the Lord;
My heart and my flesh sing for joy unto
      the living God.

Yea, the sparrow hath found a house,
And the swallow a nest for herself,
Where she may lay her young;
Thine altars, O Lord of hosts,
My King, and my God — shall be mine.

Happy are they that dwell in Thy house,
They are ever praising Thee. Selah
For a day in Thy courts is better than
      a thousand elsewhere;
I had rather stand at the threshold of the
      house of my God,
Than to dwell in the tents of wickedness.

O Lord of hosts,
Happy is the man that trusteth in Thee.   *(Psalm 84)*

*Musical instrument or melody to which this psalm was sung.

GOD IN THE MIDST OF ZION

The psalmist declares that Israel need have no fear, even
in a time of world calamity, if they trust in God. For God
destroys mighty armies. He will make wars to cease on the
earth. And He will cause justice to rule among men.

For the Leader; a Psalm of the sons of Korah; upon
      Alamoth.* A Song.

God is our refuge and strength,
A very present help in trouble.
Therefore will we not fear, though the earth be removed,
And though the mountains be carried into the heart
      of the seas;
Though the waters thereof roar and foam,
Though the mountains shake with the swelling thereof.
      Selah

There is a river, the streams whereof make glad
      the city of God (Zion, Jerusalem),
The holiest dwelling-place of the Most High.
God is in the midst of her, she shall not be moved;
God shall help her, and that right early.
Nations were in tumult, and kingdoms tottered;
He uttered His voice, the earth melted.

The Lord of hosts is with us;
The God of Jacob is our refuge. Selah

Come, behold the works of the Lord,
Who hath made desolations in the earth.
He maketh wars to cease unto the end of the earth;
He breaketh the bow, and cutteth the spear in sunder;
He burneth the chariots in the fire.
"Be still, and know that I am God;
I will be exalted among the nations,
I will be exalted on the earth."

The Lord of hosts is with us;
The God of Jacob is our refuge. Selah   *(Psalm 46)*

*Musical instrument.

SORROWS OF EXILE

This psalm describes how the exiled Israelites felt in Babylonia, their anguish and despair, their longing for Zion, and how they pledged everlasting loyalty to the land they loved.

By the rivers of Babylon,
There we sat down, yea, we wept,
When we remembered Zion.
Upon the willows in the midst thereof
We hanged up our harps.
For there they that led us captive
       asked of us words of song,
And our tormentors asked of us mirth:
"Sing us one of the songs of Zion."

How shall we sing the Lord's song
In a foreign land?
If I forget thee, O Jerusalem,
Let my right hand forget her cunning.
Let my tongue cleave to the roof of my mouth,
If I remember thee not;
If I set not Jerusalem
Above my chiefest joy.   *(Psalm 137)*

JOYFUL RETURN TO ZION

The psalmist recalls how the Israelites, on returning from the Babylonian exile, rejoiced, and he expresses the hope that God will enlarge the restored community.

A Song of Ascents.

When the Lord brought back those that returned to Zion,
We were like unto them that dream.
Then was our mouth filled with laughter,
And our tongue with singing;
Then said they among the nations:

"The Lord hath done great things with these."
The Lord hath done great things with us;
We are rejoiced.

Bring back the rest of our exiles, O Lord,
To fill us up, like streams in the dry south.
They that sow in tears
Shall reap in joy.
Though he goeth on his way weeping
    that beareth the measure of seed,
He shall come home with joy, bearing his sheaves.   *(Psalm 126)*

מִשְׁלֵי

PROVERBS

D O you remember what King Solomon chose when he was
asked in a dream what he desired most in the world? He
wanted "a wise and understanding heart." God granted him his
wish. And Jewish tradition, because of his reputation for great
wisdom, considered King Solomon the author of the Book of
Proverbs which is a book of wisdom and a collection of the sayings
of the wise. In this book itself, however, we find that others —
Agur, King Lemuel, the men of Hezekiah — also wrote and col-
lected many wise sayings. Indeed, there have always been wise
men in Israel, and the Jewish people has always highly esteemed
wisdom.

The Book of Proverbs answers some most difficult and important questions: How shall a person practice his religion in his
daily activities at home, at school, in the market-place? How
shall he fulfill his duties towards children, parents and neighbors?
How shall he overcome the temptations found in everyday life?
The wise men of Israel believed that wisdom came from God, to
help men choose between right and wrong conduct. Through
the choice of right conduct, men could attain a happy and prosperous life. These sages cast their ideals and principles of conduct in the crisp form of proverbs that sometimes grew into
delightful little essays.

A proverb is a convenient package of wisdom, neatly tied up
in attractive language, telling much in a few words. "A stitch in
time saves nine" is a well known proverb. It would take many
sentences to explain its rich, practical wisdom. The Book of
Proverbs is crammed full of instructive sayings written by the
wise men of Israel over many centuries of time.

These wise men were keen observers of life. In their proverbs
they used humor and kindly criticism. They liked to contrast

447

the wise and the foolish, the rich and the poor, the lazy and the diligent. They condemned pride, anger, envy, hatred, selfishness and greed. They praised trust in God, obedience to parents, the curbing of one's tongue, charity, honesty and good character.

Folly, the very opposite of Wisdom to these teachers in Israel, was bad because it led men to ungodliness, unhappiness, even to death. Wisdom, on the other hand, was good because it helped men to be better children and parents, kindly neighbors and friends, responsible citizens of the community, lovers of knowledge, and men of thoughtfulness and understanding.

The proverbs found here are but a handful out of many hundreds. These have been arranged about such large ideas as the love of wisdom, the duties we owe our families and those we live with in daily life, and the attitudes that a good citizen in the community ought to live by. But, in the Book of Proverbs itself, the proverbs are not arranged in this way. There, they are like heaps of glittering jewels in a treasure-chest, each one sparkling with its own beautiful light.

I.

INVITATION TO WISDOM

Wisdom is pictured as a gracious lady, pleading to all to come to her for help, guidance and understanding. Wisdom was the very first of God's creations and she was present at the creation of the world and of man. Wisdom can help man to get happiness and peace and contentment of mind.

THE proverbs of Solomon, the son of David, king in Israel:

The Foundation of Wisdom

The fear of the Lord (Religion) is the beginning of knowledge;
But the foolish despise wisdom and discipline.   (*1.7*)

Wisdom pleads with Men

Is not Wisdom calling,
And knowledge raising her voice?
At the head of the highways, on the road,
In the streets she takes her stand;
By the gates that enter the city,
At the doorways she cries aloud:
"O men, I am calling to you,
And my appeal is to the sons of men!
You simple ones, learn sense,
You foolish ones, learn wisdom!
Hear, for I shall speak excellent things,
And with right things my lips will open!
Receive my instruction, and not silver,
And knowledge rather than choice gold."   (*8.1–10*)

Wisdom at Creation

"The Lord formed me as the first of His works,
The beginning of His deeds of old;
In the earliest ages was I fashioned,
At the first when the earth began.
Before the hills was I brought forth,
While as yet He had not made the earth and the fields.
When He set the heavens up, I was there;
When He traced the vault over the face of the deep,

When He made firm the clouds far overhead,
When He fixed the fountain of the deep,
When He set for the sea its boundaries,
When He laid the foundations for the earth,
I was beside Him, His foster-child.
I was His delight day after day,
Playing in His presence constantly,
Playing here and there over His world,
Finding my delight in humankind.

Wisdom as Friend and Guide

"Now listen to me, children;
For happy are those who keep my ways.
Hear instruction and be wise,
And refuse it not!
For he who finds me, finds life;
But he who ignores me, wrongs himself." *(8.22–36)*

"Counsel is mine, and sound wisdom;
I am understanding; power is mine.
By me kings of earth reign,
And princes govern the earth.
I love those who love me,
And those who seek me earnestly shall find me." *(8.14–17)*

The Fruits of Wisdom

Happy is the man who finds wisdom,
And the man who obtains understanding.
For the merchandise of it is better than the merchandise of
    silver,
And the gain thereof than fine gold.
She is more precious than rubies;
No treasure can compare with her.
Long life is in her right hand;
In her left are riches and honor.
Her ways are ways of pleasantness,
And all her paths are peace.
She is a tree of life to those that lay hold upon her,
And happy is everyone who holds her fast. *(3.13–18)*

SOLOMON THE WISE

"Happy is the man who finds wisdom . . ."

(*Proverbs 3.13*)

see page 450

JOB, THE MAN OF FAITH

"... though He slay me, yet will I trust in Him."

(*Job 13.15*)

see page 471

II.

THE ART OF LIVING TOGETHER

We do not live alone. We are parts of the family and social life; we live together with neighbors; we want to have friends. Only as we learn the art of living together can we find life interesting and worth while.

The Duties of Parents

TRAIN up a child in the way he should go,
And even when he is old, he will not depart from it.   (*22.6*)

He who spares his rod hates his son;
But he who loves him chastens him betimes.   (*13.24*)

The rod of correction gives wisdom;
But a neglected child brings shame to his mother.   (*29.15*)

Correct your son, and he will give you peace of mind;
Yea, he will give delight to your heart.   (*29.17*)

The Duties of Children

Hear, my son, the instruction of your father,
And forsake not the teaching of your mother;
They shall be a crown of grace for your head,
And a necklace about your neck.   (*1.8, 9*)

Listen to your father who begot you,
And despise not your mother when she is old.   (*23.22*)

A foolish son brings grief to his father,
And bitter sorrow to her who bore him.   (*17.25*)

The father of a righteous man will greatly rejoice;
And he who has begotten a wise son will be glad of him.
Therefore, let your father and your mother be glad,
Let her who bore you rejoice.   (*23.24, 25*)

The pleasant Home

Through wisdom is a home built,
And by understanding it is established;
And by knowledge are its chambers filled
With all precious and pleasant riches. *(24.3, 4)*

House and riches are an inheritance from fathers;
But a sensible wife is a gift from the Lord. *(19.14)*

A continual dropping on a very rainy day
And a quarrelsome wife are alike. *(27.15)*

It is better to dwell in a desert land,
Than with a quarrelsome and nagging wife. *(21.19)*

He who finds a wife finds good fortune,
And wins a favor from the Lord. *(18.22)*

The ideal Wife

A good wife, who can find?
She is worth far more than rubies.
Her husband trusts her completely,
And he has no lack of gain.
She does him good and not harm
All the days of her life.
Strength and dignity are her clothing,
And she laughs at the time to come.
What she says is full of wisdom,
And on her tongue is kindly instruction.
She attends to the cares of her household;
She does not eat the bread of idleness.
Her children rise up and bless her,
And her husband praises her, saying:
"Many wives have done well,
But you excel them all."
Grace is deceitful, and beauty is vain;
But a woman who reveres the Lord, she shall be praised. *(31)*

The good Neighbor

Set your foot but seldom in your neighbor's house,
Lest he grow tired of you and dislike you.   (25.17)

Your own friend, and your father's friend, forsake not;
And in the day of your calamity, go not to your brother's house;
Better is a neighbor that is near than a brother far away.   (27.10)

Withhold not help from the needy,
When it is in your power to give it.
Say not to your neighbor: "Go, and come again,
Tomorrow I will give," when you have it beside you.
Plot no mischief against your neighbor,
When he lives in confidence beside you.   (3.27–29)

The blessed Friend

As oil and perfume gladden the heart,
So a man's counsel is sweet to his friend.   (27.9)

There are friends who play at friendship;
But there is a friend who sticks closer than a brother.   (18.24)

Wealth adds many friends;
But the poor man is estranged from his friend.   (19.4)

Sincere are the wounds of a friend;
But the kisses of an enemy are deceitful.   (27.6)

III.

SHARING THE BURDENS

Among ancient peoples the humbler forms of labor were despised; all work was done by slaves. But, the Jewish attitude towards labor was more generous and sensible. It was considered important to healthy living. Hence laziness was condemned, for the lazy man did not carry his share of the common burdens of life. The Jewish attitude towards wealth was that it was good, provided it was earned by honesty and diligence.

The lazy Man

I PASSED by the field of the sluggard,
And by the vineyard of the man without sense;
And lo! it was all overgrown with thistles,
Its surface was covered with nettles,
And its stone wall was broken down.
I looked, and reflected upon it;
I saw and learned a lesson. (24.30–32)

Go to the ant, you sluggard,
Study her ways, and learn wisdom;
For though she has no chief,
No officer, or ruler,
She provides her food in the summer,
And gathers her provisions in the harvest.
How long will you sleep, you sluggard?
When will you rise out of your sleep?
"A little more sleep, a little more slumber,
A little folding of the hands to sleep"—
So shall your poverty come upon you as a thief,
And your want like an armed man. (6.6–11)

Neither Poverty nor Riches

Better is a little with righteousness
Than great revenues with injustice. (16.8)

Better is a poor man who walks in honesty
Than he who is crooked in his ways, though he be rich.   (28.6)

Toil not to become rich;
Let your wisdom tell you to stop!
Scarcely have you set your eyes upon it,
When it is gone;
For riches make themselves wings,
Like an eagle that flies towards the heavens.   (23.4, 5)

Two things have I asked of Thee, O God,
Deny them not to me before I die:
Put falsehood and lying far from me;
Give me neither poverty nor riches;
Provide me with food sufficient for my needs;
Lest I be full, and deny Thee,
And say: "Who is the Lord?"
Or lest I be poor and steal,
And disgrace the name of my God.   (30.7–9)

IV.

THE GOOD CITIZEN

The good citizen is the man who lives among his fellow-men a life of temperance and self-control. He is a man of charity and good cheer. He is the man who loves his fellowman.

Temperance in Food and Drink

IF you find honey, eat no more than you need;
Lest you be filled with it, and vomit it.   *(25.16)*

Look not on the wine when it is red,
When it sparkles in the cup,
And glides down smoothly.
At the end it bites like a snake,
And stings like a basilisk.
Then your eyes shall see strange things,
And your mind shall utter confused things.
You shall be like someone sleeping at sea,
Like one that lies on the top of a mast.
"I have been struck, and I felt no pain;
I have been beaten, and I knew it not.
When shall I awake from my wine?
I will seek it yet again."   *(23.31–35)*

Controlling the Tongue

Death and life are in the power of the tongue;
They who are fond of using it shall eat its fruit.   *(18.21)*

A fool's mouth is his ruin;
And his lips are a snare to him.   *(18.7)*

He that is slow to anger is better than a warrior;
And he that rules his temper than he who takes a city.   *(16.32)*

A soft answer turns away wrath;
But a harsh word stirs up anger.   *(15.1)*

Even a fool is considered wise, if he keep silent —
Intelligent, if he close his lips.   *(17.28)*

Of Pride and Modesty

A man's pride shall bring him low;
But the humble shall attain honor.   *(29.23)*

Boast not yourself of tomorrow;
For you know not what the new day may bring forth.   *(27.1)*

Pride goes before destruction,
And a haughty spirit before a fall.   *(16.18)*

Of Charity

He who is kind to the poor lends to the Lord;
And He will repay him his good deed.   *(19.17)*

He who closes his ear against the cry of the poor
Shall himself also call, but shall not be answered.   *(21.13)*

Of Cheerfulness ›

A merry heart is a healing medicine;
But a broken spirit dries up the bones.   *(17.22)*

A merry heart makes a cheerful face;
But by sorrow of heart the spirit is broken.   *(15.13)*

Love against Hate ·

Hatred stirs up strife;
But love covers all transgressions.   *(10.12)*

Better a dinner of herbs where love is,
Than a fatted ox, and hatred with it.   *(15.17)*

Better a morsel of dry bread and peace with it,
Than a house full of feasting with strife.   *(17.1)*

V.

WHAT DELIGHTS THE LORD

Throughout the proverbs and interwoven with them is the belief that the wise man delights the Lord, for he combines piety with good conduct.

THE spirit of man is the lamp of the Lord,
Searching into his innermost soul.   (20.27)

There are six things that the Lord hates,
Yes, seven which are detestable to Him:
Haughty eyes and a lying tongue;
Hands that shed innocent blood;
A mind that plans wicked schemes;
Feet that make haste to do evil;
A false witness who utters lies;
And the man who sows discord among brothers.   (6.16–19)

The sacrifice of the wicked is hateful to the Lord;
But the prayer of the upright is His delight.   (15.8)

To do what is right and just
Is more acceptable to the Lord than sacrifice.   (21.3)

Righteousness exalts a nation;
But evil is a reproach to any people.   (14.34)

אִיוֹב

JOB

O NE of the serious questions we often ask is: Why do good people suffer misfortunes like sickness or poverty or the death of dear ones? Have you ever asked yourself why it is that good people you know are ofttimes unhappy? Do you sometimes wonder whether God is always fair and just?

People have always been troubled by such questions, and our ancestors, too, were puzzled by them. One of them, whose name we do not know, wrote the Book of Job to answer just such questions. Many consider it the most wonderful as well as the most beautifully written book in the Bible.

The Book of Job is a drama. It has a prologue; three cycles of acts, consisting of conversations about what happened to Job, its chief character; and an epilogue.

Its plot is simple. The opening scene takes place in heaven, before God's throne, where His messengers — the angels — report to Him what is happening throughout the world. Among the angels is Satan, who is like a prosecuting attorney. Satan is asked about a righteous and good man named Job. When he doubts that Job is really faithful to God, God grants Satan permission to put Job to the test to prove his steadfastness.

The scene of the drama then moves to the earth. Calamity after calamity befalls Job. His children die and he loses all his possessions. Yet he remains faithful to God. Then he himself is stricken with a painful and horrible disease. As he sits alone, forsaken, in anguish of body and mind, three friends — Eliphaz, Bildad and Zophar — who have heard about his misfortunes, visit him. They sit in silence before him for many days; then they begin to converse with Job.

During that long period of silence, Job has been brooding over his sickness, his suffering and his misfortunes. His self-control breaks down and he speaks first. He curses the day of his birth and prays for death to relieve him.

All through the play Job insists that he does not know why he is suffering, for he is innocent of having done anything wrong. His friends, however, are certain that he must have sinned, knowingly or unknowingly, for God is just and He would not make Job suffer if he were not guilty.

After much discussion back and forth, God Himself appears and speaks out of the whirlwind. Can men really understand these dark things, He asks? Suffering is as difficult to understand as the mysteries of Nature; like the heavens, or electricity, or life itself. What does man know of the meaning of the shining, blue expanse of the heavens? Do we understand the mystery of electricity? When we put a tiny seed in the earth and it grows into a tree, can we say that we really understand the secret of life and growth?

In a word, the whole world about us is a dark and strange and puzzling mystery. God created Nature — its heavens, its exhaustless energies, and its wonders of life and growth. From the little we know about them, we believe that God is good, for He created a useful and beautiful world for man to live in. There is much that we do not know and understand, but from what we do know and possess we should be grateful to Him, and we should have faith in His goodness and justice even in those matters that are beyond our understanding.

The Book of Job teaches us that God's ways are beyond the complete understanding of our little minds. Like Job, we must believe that God, who placed us in this world, knows what is best for us. Such faith in the goodness of God, even though we cannot altogether understand it, brings us strength and confidence to face our calamities, and sorrows and sufferings.

The Book of Job is one of the most profoundly religious books ever written by the hand of man.

CHARACTERS IN THE DRAMA

The Lord	Third Messenger
Satan	Job's Wife
The Sons of God	Eliphaz, the Temanite
Job, the Man of Uz	Bildad, the Shuhite
The First Messenger	Zophar, the Naamathite
Second Messenger	Elihu, the Youth

Voice out of the Whirlwind

PROLOGUE

Job was upright and prosperous

THERE was a man in the land of Uz whose name was Job; and he was blameless and upright; he feared God and shunned evil. He had seven sons and three daughters. His possessions also were seven thousand sheep, three thousand camels, five hundred yoke of oxen, five hundred donkeys; and he had many servants, so that he was the richest man among all the peoples of the east.

His sons used to hold a feast in the house of each one in turn; and they would send and invite their three sisters to eat and drink with them. When the days of feasting had gone round, Job would send and purify them, and he would get up early in the morning and offer sacrifices for them; for Job said:

"Perhaps my children have sinned, and offended God in their thoughts."

Thus would Job do always.

Job delivered to Satan

One day, when the sons of God came before the Lord, Satan came with them. The Lord said to Satan:

"From where do you come?"

Satan answered:

"From going to and fro on the earth, and from walking up and down on it."

The Lord said to Satan:

"Have you seen My servant Job? For there is no man like him on the earth, blameless and upright, who reveres God and avoids evil."

Satan answered:

"Is it for nothing that Job reveres God? Have You not Yourself made a fence all about him, about his household, and about all that he has? You have blessed whatever he does, and his possessions have greatly increased. Just put out Your hand now and take away all he has, and he certainly will curse You to Your face."

The Lord said to Satan:

"See, everything that he has is in your power; only do not lay hands on Job himself."

Then Satan left the presence of the Lord.

Calamities befall Job

One day, as Job's sons and daughters were eating and drinking in the oldest brother's house, a messenger came to Job and said:

"The oxen were plowing and the donkeys were grazing near them, when the Sabeans (a band of Bedouins) suddenly attacked and seized them. The servants were put to the sword, and I alone have escaped to tell you."

While he was still speaking, another messenger came and said:

"Lightning has fallen from heaven and has completely burned up the sheep and the servants. I alone have escaped to tell you."

While this man was still speaking, another messenger came and said:

"The Chaldeans, attacking in three bands, raided the camels and drove them away. The servants were put to the sword, and I alone have escaped to tell you."

While this one was still speaking, another came and said:

"Your sons and daughters were eating and drinking in their oldest brother's house, when a great wind came from across the wilderness, struck the four corners of the house, and it fell upon the young men and killed them. I alone have escaped to tell you."

*In spite of all, Job
blesses the Lord*

Then Job arose, tore his robe, shaved his head (as a sign of mourning), threw himself on the ground and worshipped, saying:

"The Lord gave, and the Lord hath taken away;
Blessed be the name of the Lord."

In all this Job did not sin nor blame God.

*Job meets the first Test, but
Satan is given greater Power
over him*

On another day when the sons of God came before the Lord, Satan came with them. And the Lord said to Satan:

"From where do you come?"

Satan answered:

"From going to and fro on the earth, and from walking up and down on it."

The Lord said to Satan:

"Have you seen My servant Job? For there is no man like him on the earth, blameless and upright, one who reveres God and avoids evil. He still is faithful, although you led Me to ruin him without cause."

Satan answered the Lord:

"Skin for skin! All that a man has he will give for his life. Just put out Your hand and touch his bone and his flesh. He will curse You to your face."

The Lord said to Satan:

"See, he is in your power. Only spare his life."

Job is stricken with Disease

So Satan left the presence of the Lord and afflicted Job, from the sole of his foot to the crown of his head, with leprosy so terrible that Job took a piece of broken pottery with which to scrape himself.

As he sat among the ashes, Job's wife said to him:

"Are you still holding to your faith in God? Curse God and die."

But he said to her:

"You speak like a senseless woman. Shall we receive good at the hand of God, and shall we not also receive evil?"

In all this Job said nothing that was wrong.

Thus, Job meets the second Test.
His three Friends now visit him.

When Job's three friends, Eliphaz the Temanite, Bildad the Shuhite, and Zophar the Naamathite, heard of all the troubles that had come upon him, they made an appointment to go together to express their sympathy for him and comfort him. But when they saw him in the distance, they did not at first know him. Then they all wept aloud and tore their robes and threw dust upon their heads. And they sat down with him on the ground seven days and seven nights, and none spoke a word to him; for they saw his grief was very great.   (*Job 1-2*)

I.

JOB'S COMPLAINT

Job is filled with bitterness and bewilderment as he broods
over the seemingly undeserved misfortunes and calamities which
he has suffered. For the first time in his life a cloud of doubt
has gathered over his faith in God's justice. The friends who
should have helped him, remain silent. Now Job breaks this
silence of seven days and nights, and in agony of spirit cries out,
and bewails his fate.

JOB began to speak and said:
   "Let the day perish when I was born,
     And the night when it was said: 'It is a boy!'
Why did I not die at birth,
And breathe my last when I was born?
I should now have lain still;
I should now have slept and been at peace,
With kings and statesmen of the world
Who built great monuments for themselves,
With princes rich in gold,
Who filled their palaces with silver.
There the wicked cease from troubling;
And there the weary are at rest.
Prisoners, too, lying quiet together,
Hear not the voice of the taskmaster.
The small and the great are there alike;
And the slave is free from his master.

"Why does God give light to him who is in misery,
And life to men in bitter despair,
Who long for death, and long in vain?
Sighs are my daily bread,
And groans pour from me like water.
I am not at ease, I get no rest,
I have no peace; for trouble keeps coming."   (*Job 3*)

II.

ELIPHAZ AND JOB

The first act of the drama begins. Eliphaz the Temanite tries to console Job and bring him hope. He speaks warmly and with great beauty. But his thoughts all come to one conclusion: God punishes the guilty. Job, however, is conscious of his innocence and refuses the comfort of Eliphaz. Job is irritated by his easy words. In his agony, his friends do not understand him. So that in the midst of his grief he feels utterly alone.

ELIPHAZ the Temanite answered and said:
    "Would you resent it, if we dared to speak?
But who can keep from speaking?
You have yourself instructed many,
And you have strengthened feeble souls;
Your words have kept men on their feet,
And you have supported the weak-kneed.
But now that trouble comes, you grow weary,
Now that it touches you, you lose courage.

"Is not your religion your confidence,
    Your upright life your hope?
Remember! What innocent man ever perished?
Or where were the upright ever destroyed?
Men reap the evil of what they plow,
And gather in the trouble that they sow.
Behold, happy is the man whom God corrects;
Therefore, despise not the discipline of the Almighty.
Then you shall come to the grave in a ripe age,
Like a sheaf borne home in the harvest."

Then Job answered:
"Friends should be kind to a despairing man,
    Even if he give up faith in the Almighty.
But my friends disappoint me like a stream,
    Like mountain brooks that overflow their banks,

Swollen and dark with ice, with melting snow,
Which vanish when they are scorched,
And disappear in the summer's heat.
Caravans turn to them, then turn away,
Take to the desert and then perish.
For their hopes are disappointed,
As I am in you.

"Show me where I have gone wrong;
Teach me, and I will keep silent.

"Therefore, I will not restrain myself any longer;
I will speak out, so bitter is my soul.
When I think my bed will ease me,
My couch will soothe my complaint,
Then Thou, O God, scarest me with dreams,
Thou frightenest me with nightmares,
Till I would rather be strangled;
I would prefer death to my pains.
Let me alone! For my days are like a breath.
Why dost Thou not forgive my sin?
Soon I shall lie down in the dust;
And when Thou searchest for me, I shall be no more."

(Job 4–7)

III.

BILDAD AND JOB

Bildad is the second of Job's friends, and his thoughts might well be considered the second act of this drama. Bildad is a man of firm and simple faith who believes in God's unfailing justice. He is shocked by Job's violent speech, but says nothing to help Job in his anguish. Job now challenges God's justice. This is his most daring utterance. He questions God's rule of the earth according to righteousness. It is the cry of a sorely afflicted human being caught in the net of a mystery he cannot understand.

THEN Bildad the Shuhite spoke:
  "How long will you talk like this,
For the words of your mouth are like a strong wind?
Is God a God of injustice?
Can the Almighty do any wrong?
If your children sinned against Him,
He has let them suffer the penalty.
If you are pure and upright,
He will surely answer your prayer,
And make your godly home prosperous."

Then Job answered:
"Yes, it is true; I know it;
But how is man to get his rights from God?
Even if God chose to argue,
You could not answer one of His thousand questions.
He is so wise, so mighty;
Who has ever defied Him and prospered?

"But I am innocent! never mind,
I despise my life; therefore I say:
He destroys the innocent and the wicked alike.
If it is not He, who then is it?
When He scourges us with sudden death,

He mocks at the despair of innocent men.
The earth is handed over to the wicked;
He makes the judges of men blind to justice!

"My days are few! Let me alone awhile,
That I may take comfort a little,
Before I go whence I shall not return,
To the land of darkness and gloom,
To a land dark as midnight, as darkness itself,
With no light but the shadows of death."   (*Job 8–10*)

IV.

ZOPHAR AND JOB

Zophar's speech begins the third act of the drama. Zophar is more outspoken and more brutally frank than Eliphaz and Bildad. He charges Job with wickedness and secret wrongdoing, and declares that Job has more than merited his sufferings. Job is now in complete despair of his friends. He turns from them and without fear questions God. Job demands to know why God persecutes him. He declares his unconquerable faith in God.

ZOPHAR the Naamathite then spoke:
"Is a crowd of words to go unanswered?
Is a glib talker to carry the day?
You say: 'My life is pure, I am clean in Thy sight.'
If God would only speak,
And open His lips against you,
Then you would learn that God does not remember
All your guilt against you!

"If you will turn your mind to God,
And stretch out your hands to Him (in prayer),
If you banish sin from your life,
And unrighteousness from your house,
Then you can face Him unashamed,
You can be steadfast and without fear.
You shall forget about your misery,
You shall remember it no more than floods gone by;
Your life shall be more radiant than the noonday,
Though there be darkness, it shall be as the morning.
You shall have hope and feel secure."

Then Job answered:

"No doubt you are the men who know!
And wisdom shall die with you!
But I have understanding as well as you;
Why, anyone knows all you say.
Does not a man's mind test what he is told,
As the palate tastes food for itself?
What you know I know, also;

I am not inferior to you.
You whitewash everything with lies,
You are physicians of no value, all of you.
If only you would hold your peace,
Then you might pass for wise men!

"Only — I would appeal to the Almighty,
It is with God that I desire to argue.
Silence! Let me alone that I may speak,
Let come on me what will! I will risk my very life!
Yes, though He slay me, yet will I trust in Him;
But I will maintain my innocence to His face.

"Spare me two things alone, O God,
And then I need not hide myself from Thee:
Lift off Thy heavy hand from me,
And scare me not with Thy terrors.
Tell me all I have done wrong,
Let me know what sin I am guilty of.
Why art Thou unfriendly to me?
Why treat me as Thine enemy!
Wilt Thou harass a poor driven leaf?
Wilt Thou pursue a withered straw?"

"Have pity on me, O my friends, have pity,
For the hand of God has struck me.
Why do you persecute me like God?
O that my defense were written in a book,
O that my words could be preserved in writing,
Cut with an iron pen on lead,
Or engraved on stone for ever!

"For I know that my Redeemer lives.
This body may crumble to dust, but even then
My soul shall have a sight of God.
O you who think to run me down,
To blame me for my sufferings,
Beware of your falsehoods!
Such slanders call for God's own sword,
To teach you impious men
What the Almighty is."

(*Job 11, 12, 13, 19*)

V.

ELIHU — THE BYSTANDER

Elihu's speech is an interruption in the main drama. Some think that it was put there later. But, Elihu does have his own explanation of why Job is suffering. He declares that it is God's way of warning him not to continue his wrongdoing. God is trying to prevent Job from further sinning. Elihu is a young man, and he seems to be somewhat pompous and vain.

THEN said Elihu, the son of Barakel, the Buzite:
   "I am young and you are very old;
So I held back, afraid to tell you my opinion.
But it is not always the aged who are wise,
Nor old men who understand.
No, I will offer my own opinion,
And speak my mind upon the matter.

"You, Job, argued in my hearing, for I heard you say:
'I am pure and sinless, innocent and guiltless;
But God picks a quarrel with me,
He treats me as His enemy.'
God speaks in one way;
Yes, and if man heeds it not, in another.

"In dreams, in visions of the night,
When deep sleep falls upon men,
As they slumber on their beds,
He reveals things to them,
And sends them awful warnings,
To draw them back from evil,
And make them give up pride,
To save their souls from death,
Their lives from rushing to destruction.
Or, man is chastened with pain upon his bed,
And his limbs are all benumbed,
Till his soul turns from even dainty food.

But, if an angel comes to his aid,
One of God's thousand angels,
To vouch for the man's uprightness,
And he prays to God and He accepts him,
Then his life may be saved from death.
Now God does all this over and again,
Twice, yes thrice, with a man,
To bring him back from death
Into the sunshine of life.

"So, tell God: 'Now that I have suffered,
I will offend no more;
Teach me what I have not known,
And, if I have sinned, I will not sin again.'

"Thus, God saves the sufferer by his suffering,
And by calamities He gets them to listen.
Supreme in power and rich in justice,
He does no unrighteousness.
For this men magnify His work,
And thoughtful men revere Him."   (*Job 32–37*)

VI.

GOD'S VOICE SPEAKS

The concluding scene of the drama is the majestic and magnificent discourse of God, coming out of the whirlwind. It is magnificent in language, stirring in grandeur. God shows the utter littleness of man in the presence of the mystery of creation. How then can such a being understand the meaning of human suffering? God bids Job to look away from his own darkness and see the wonderfully made world about him. Let Job renew his faith in the wisdom, goodness and justice of God, even though he cannot entirely understand them. Job is overwhelmed. His questions are still unanswered, but he has found a faith that helps him. And he is now satisfied and at peace.

OUT of the whirlwind the Lord answered Job:
　　"Who darkens My purpose
With a cloud of thoughtless words?
Stand before Me like a man,
And answer these questions.

"When I founded the earth, where were you then?
Answer Me that, if you have understanding.
Who measured out the earth? Do you know that?
Who stretched out the builder's line?
What were its foundations fastened on?
Who laid its corner-stone,
When the morning stars sang together,
And all the sons of God shouted for joy?

"What path leads to the dwelling-place of light,
And where does darkness dwell?
Have you found out the foundations of the sea?
Have you set foot on the depths of the ocean?
Have you grasped the earth in all its breadth?
How large is it? Tell Me, if you know that.
Surely you know! you, born when it was made,
You who have lived so long!

"Can you give orders to the clouds,
  For water in abundance to be yours?
  Can you send out the lightning on its mission?
  Does it say humbly to you, 'Here am I'?
  Who taught the feathery clouds, or trained the meteors?
  Who has the skill to mass the clouds,
  Or tilt the pitchers of the sky,
  When the soil runs into cakes of earth,
  And the clods stick fast together?

"Have you given the war-horse his strength,
  Or covered his neck with the tossing mane?
  Have you made him leap forward like a locust,
  Snorting terribly, furiously?
  He paws the valley proudly, facing the clash of arms;
  He mocks at fear, unterrified, he flies not from the
      sword;
  The quiver rattles against him, the glittering spear and
      javelin,
  But he charges in wild rage,
  Straight ahead, never swerving.
  When the trumpet sounds, 'Aha!' he cries,
  Scenting the battle afar off,
  Where captains thunder, amidst the shouts of war.

"Does your wisdom send the hawk to soar
  And spread her wings for the south?
  Does your word make the eagle mount
  To nest aloft among the hills?

"Will the fault-finder still dispute with the Almighty?
  To argue with God, first answer all these questions.
  Will you seek to discredit My justice?
  To justify yourself, will you condemn Me?"

  Then Job answered the Lord and said:
"How small I am! What shall I answer Thee?
  I lay my hand upon my mouth.

I spoke once, but will do so no more;
Yes, twice, but will go no further.
I know that Thou canst do all things,
And that nothing with Thee is impossible.
I spoke, therefore, without sense,
Of wonders beyond my knowledge.
I have heard of Thee but by hearsay,
But now my eye has seen Thee;
Therefore I despise my words, and repent,
Seeing I am but dust and ashes."   (*Job 38–42*)

EPILOGUE

Job restored; his Friends rebuked

After all this, the Lord said to Eliphaz the Temanite:

"My anger is kindled against you, and against your two friends; for unlike My servant Job, you have not told the truth about Me. But, out of regard for My servant Job, I will not bring destruction upon you for your impiety."

Then the Lord healed Job, and gave him twice as much as he had before. And the Lord blessed the latter part of Job's life more than the first part. And he had fourteen thousand sheep, six thousand camels, a thousand yoke of oxen, and a thousand donkeys. He also was given seven sons and three daughters.

Job lived a hundred and forty years; and he died, old, after a full life. (*Job 42*)   *(he lived two life times 70 70 140)*

7000
7000
14,000 sheep   *6000 camels*
                   1000 oxen
                   7000 clean beasts (all beasts of burden)
                   7000 donkies
{ 8,000 years we will meet G-d.
{ (on the 8th day we will see G-d)}

שִׁיר הַשִּׁירִים

THE SONG OF SONGS

THE Song of Songs, or "Canticles," or as it is also called "The Song of Solomon," is a collection of love lyrics of sheer beauty, tender and exquisite. We walk amidst country scenes where doves hide in the clefts of the rocks, gazelles leap over the hills, trees are clad in varied foliage, and flowers with bright colors and richly scented perfumes are everywhere. The golden sun of Palestine plays over the landscape, and the gentle breezes of spring blow across green meadows and fields.

There are two opinions about the Song of Songs.

One holds that it is a poetic drama which tells the story of a country maiden, betrothed to a handsome shepherd lad, who was led away by King Solomon to become the favorite of his palace in Jerusalem. The king was in love with her, and wooed her with warm feelings. But, the beautiful Shulammith rejected his love and remained faithful to her beloved. The king, unsuccessful in his wooing, restored her to her country lover. And, in the end, the two young lovers were united.

The other opinion considers the Song of Songs to be a collection of love and wedding songs sung during the seven-day marriage festivities customary among the ancient Israelites. Even today this custom is practiced by the Arabs of Palestine. The bride and bridegroom are seated upon a make-believe throne and are greeted as king and queen by singers and guests. The bridegroom is extravagantly praised for his manliness, the bride for her charm and beauty.

King Solomon, who had composed 1005 songs (*I Kings 5.12*), was, according to tradition, the author of the Song of Songs. He was the most magnificent of all kings. And the Shulammite woman, mentioned in *I Kings 1.3*, was the loveliest of maidens. Hence, all bridegrooms were compared to King Solomon, and all brides to Shulammith.

How did such a collection of poems in praise of human love win its way into the Bible? By being explained as an allegory, that is, a story whose language seems to represent one thing, but really means another.

The Beloved, in the Song of Songs, represents God, and Shulammith the bride, Israel. The King is the symbol of worldly temptation who sought to lure her away from her faithful Beloved, but unsuccessfully. Thus, the allegory tells of God's deep love for Israel, and of Israel's faithfulness to God, and praises the power of true love to resist the allurement of worldly splendor. Read in this way, we can understand why one of Israel's greatest sages said: "The whole world does not outweigh the day on which the Song of Songs was given to Israel; all writings are holy but the Song is holiest of them all."

As an allegory, the Song of Songs came to be read in Synagogue and at the *seder* table on Passover. All the more fitting is this because its description of spring, when Nature's awakening brings hope and cheer, symbolizes the spirit of the Festival of Freedom.

I.

LOVE IN SPRINGTIME

The beautiful Shulammith is unhappy in the palace of the King. She tells her companions about her beloved whom she vividly describes as coming for her in the springtime.

THE Song of Songs, which is Solomon's.

"Hark! my beloved!
See, here he comes,
Leaping over the mountains,
Skipping over the hills.
My beloved is like a gazelle,
Like a sturdy young stag.

"He stands now behind our wall,
He looks in through the windows,
He peers through the lattice!

"My beloved speaks, and says to me:
'Rise up now, my love,
My fair one, and come away!
For lo, the winter is past,
The rain is over and gone;
The flowers appear on the earth,
The time of singing has come,
And the voice of the turtle-dove
Is heard in our land.
The fig-tree is putting forth its green figs,
And the blossoming grapevines give forth fragrance.

'Rise up now, my love,
My fair one, come away!
O my dove in the clefts of the rocks,
In the recesses of the cliffs,
Let me see your face,
Let me hear your voice!
For your voice is sweet,
And your face is comely.' "   (*The Song of Songs 2.8–14*)

II.

IN PRAISE OF THE BRIDE

The beloved sings the praise of his young bride. He uses the images of the countryside with which he is familiar. Only once does he speak in military language to describe her lovely ornaments.

"BEHOLD you are fair, my love; behold, you are fair!
Your eyes are like doves behind your veil;
Your hair wavy like a flock of goats,
That trail down from Mount Gilead.
Your teeth are white like a flock of shorn ewes,
Fresh from washing,
All of them ranged in pairs, and not one lacking.
Your lips are like a thread of scarlet, your mouth is comely.
Like slices of pomegranate are your temples behind your veil.
Your neck is like the tower of David,
Built with turrets,
With a thousand shields (ornaments) hung upon it.
You are altogether fair, my love,
And there is no blemish in you.

"You have captured my heart, O my sister, my bride;
With one glance of your eyes, with one link of your necklace.
How fair is your love, my sister, my bride!
How much better your love than wine!
Your lips, O my bride, are laden with honey,

"Honey and milk are under your tongue;
And the fragrance of your garments is like the fragrance
of Lebanon.

"A garden shut up is my sister, my bride;
A spring shut up, a fountain sealed.
You are like a fountain of gardens, a well of living waters,
And flowing streams from Lebanon." (*The Song of Songs 4*)

III.

IN PRAISE OF THE BRIDEGROOM

The women of the palace ask Shulammith why she is so devoted to her beloved. Is he not like any other man? The maiden finds occasion to describe him, her bridegroom, in extravagant, Oriental imagery.

THE daughters of Jerusalem ask:

"What is your beloved more than another beloved,
O most beautiful of women?
What is your beloved more than another beloved,
That you so address us?"

Shulammith answers and praises her bridegroom:

"My beloved is fair and ruddy, chief among ten thousand;
His head is as the finest gold; his locks are curled and black as
    a raven.
His eyes are like doves besides the water-brooks,
Washed as with milk and fitly set.
His cheeks are as beds of spices, as banks of sweet herbs;
His lips are like lilies, dropping with flowing myrrh,
His hands are like rods of gold set in yellow jasper;
His body is like a column of polished ivory adorned with
        sapphires.
His legs are like marble pillars, set upon sockets of fine gold;
His appearance is like Lebanon, stately as the cedars.
His mouth is most sweet; he is altogether lovely.
This is my beloved, O daughters of Jerusalem;
    This is my friend."

(The Song of Songs 5.9–16)

IV.

THE LOVERS REUNITED

The king failed to win the love of the maiden, and he returns her to her beloved. The two lovers have proved faithful to each other. They are now permitted to go back to their simple, rustic home. On entering their home, the bride speaks to her beloved words of imperishable beauty.

"SET me as a seal upon your heart,
   As a seal upon your arm;
For love is strong as death,
And jealousy is cruel as the grave;
Its flashes are flashes of fire,
A very flame of the Lord.
Many waters cannot quench love,
Neither can the floods drown it.
Yet should a man give all his wealth for love,
He would surely be scorned."

The Beloved responds

"Solomon had a vineyard at Baal-hamon;
He rented the vineyard to keepers,
Each one for its fruit was to pay
A thousand pieces of silver.
O Solomon, I leave you your thousands,
And the fruit of the vines to their keepers!
My vineyard — my home — now lies before me!"

(*The Song of Songs 8.6, 7–11, 12*)

אֵיכָה

LAMENTATIONS

POWERFUL Babylonian armies swept down on Palestine in 586 B.C.E. and their commander, the Emperor Nebuchadnezzar, captured and sacked Jerusalem, sent the Temple up in flames, killed the flower of Jewish manhood, and carried off the rulers, priests, princes and leading citizens into what has come to be known as the Babylonian Captivity. Those left behind in the desolated land suffered terror, shame, starvation and death.

The Book of Lamentations consists of poems of grief and sorrow on the destruction of Jerusalem. These sad poems are called elegies, or dirges, or laments. The Book of Lamentations contains five such poems describing the misfortunes, calamities and sorrows that the Jewish people suffered when their Holy City was destroyed. Four of these poems are arranged acrostically, that is, each verse begins with a successive letter of the Hebrew alphabet.

Because Jeremiah was the last prophet in Judah, and spoke at the time of the destruction of the Jewish Commonwealth, Jewish tradition has held him to be the author of "Lamentations." Others maintain that its author is unknown. In either case, he was a profound lover of his people, as every word of this sad book testifies. His tears are hot upon its every page. He gave voice, too, to the eternal cry of faith in God, the confession of guilt, the call to repentance, and the prayer of hope that Israel might some day return to their ancestral inheritance.

The Book of Lamentations is read in Synagogue on the Ninth of Ab (*Tish'ah be-Ab*), the day on which, according to tradition, the First and Second Temples were destroyed.

483

L

DESOLATION AND MISERY

Jerusalem is compared to a widow in mourning. Her treasures and her glory have departed. Her leaders have been slain, and her children are in exile. Yet she acknowledges the righteousness of God. Later, Jerusalem herself speaks and bewails her condition.

HOW does the city sit solitary,
That was full of people!
How has she become as a widow!
She that was great among the nations,
And a princess among the cities,
How has she become a slave!

She weeps sore in the night,
And her tears are on her cheeks;
She has none to comfort her
Among all her lovers;
All her friends have dealt treacherously
　　　with her;
They have become her enemies.

Judah has gone into exile,
　　　to suffer and endure hard slavery.
She dwells among the nations;
She finds no rest.
All her pursuers have overtaken her
　　　in the midst of her distress.

The roads to Zion do mourn,
Because none come to the solemn assembly;
All her gates are desolate;
　　　her priests sigh.
Her maidens have been dragged off,
　　　and she herself is left in bitterness.

Her foes have now the upper hand,
Her enemies are at ease in triumph.
For the Lord has afflicted her
    for the multitude of her transgressions,
Her children have gone into captivity,
Captives before the oppressor.

Gone from the daughter of Zion
    is all her splendor.
Her princes have become like stags
    that can find no pasture,
And they flee exhausted
    before the hunter.

Jerusalem has grievously sinned,
Therefore she has become an unclean thing.
All that honored her, despise her,
Because they have seen her nakedness.
She herself is filled with sighs,
And turns her face backward.
The oppressor has laid his hand
    upon all her treasures;
And she has seen the nations
    enter her Sanctuary,
Those whom Thou, God, didst command
    not to enter Thy holy place.

*Jerusalem herself becomes
the Speaker*

"Ho, all you who pass along the road,
    look and see,
If there is any pain like my pain,
    which has been dealt to me,
With which the Lord has afflicted me
    in the day of His fierce anger.

"From above He has hurled fire;
    into my bones He has made it descend;
He has spread a net for my feet;
    He has tripped me up;
He has left me faint and forlorn,
    miserable all the time.

"The Lord is righteous,
    for I have rebelled against His word;
Yet hear, all you peoples,
    and look at my pain:
How my youths and maidens
    have gone into captivity.

"See, O Lord, how I am in distress,
    how my spirit is tortured;
How my heart is shaken within me,
    because I have been so rebellious.
On the streets the sword slays,
    and inside the plague."   (*Lamentations 1*)

II.

GOD'S CONSOLATIONS

In the midst of her dark sorrows, Israel finds ground for hope in God's mercy and kindness.

MY affliction and bitterness
　　are anguish and misery.
I think of them,
　　and I am crushed in spirit.
But this I recall to my mind,
　　and so I have hope:

The gracious deeds of the Lord never cease,
　　His compassion never fails;
They are new every morning;
　　great is His faithfulness.
"The Lord is my heritage," I said,
　　"therefore will I hope in Him."

The Lord is good to him who waits for Him,
　　to the one who seeks Him.
It is good that one should wait quietly
　　for help from the Lord;
It is good for a man,
　　that he should bear the yoke in his youth.
For the Lord for ever
　　will not spurn him.
Though He cause grief,
　　He has pity, so rich is His love;
He does not willingly cause pain,
　　nor grieve the children of men.

Let us search, and examine our ways,
　　and return to the Lord;
Let us lift up our hearts along with our hands
　　to God in the heavens.
The sin is ours, we have rebelled,
　　and Thou — Thou hast not pardoned.

I called on Thy name, O Lord,
  out of the lowest dungeon.
Thou didst hear my cry,
  close not Thine ear to my plea.
Thou didst answer my call,
  and saidst: "Fear not."

Hope of Deliverance

Thou, O Lord, art enthroned for ever;
Thy throne endures from generation to generation.
Why dost Thou forget us for ever,
And forsake us for so long a time?
Turn Thou us unto Thee, O Lord,
And we shall be turned;
Renew our days as of old! *(Lamentations 3.19–57, 5.19–21)*

קֹהֶלֶת

ECCLESIASTES

WHEN things do not turn out the way you think they should, and you are disappointed, it is very helpful sometimes to learn patience and to resolve to make the best of life's limited opportunities. So at least this wise Book of Ecclesiastes would teach us.

The Bible, for the most part, has a happy, joyous, hopeful attitude towards life. But, the Book of Ecclesiastes is sad and unhappy, and sometimes even gloomy. Its author was a gentle, kindly man who was greatly puzzled and disappointed by what he experienced. Like Job and many another man, he was perplexed by the mystery of life. Neither pleasure nor wealth nor wisdom brought him permanent satisfaction. He grew weary of everything. Nothing in the world seemed able to make him truly happy. And he summed up all his disappointment in words that have become immortal — "Vanity of vanities, all is vanity." That is, everything seems to be vain and empty of real value; nothing is truly worth while. As Ecclesiastes puts it, all man's effort is "only a striving after wind."

But Ecclesiastes was not an irreligious man. This kindly Jewish philosopher had wholesome advice to give his equally disappointed fellowmen. Therefore, our sages included his book in the Bible, although some of them wanted to keep it out. Ecclesiastes' advice to us briefly is: You may often be disappointed and even suffer by what you experience in life. Indeed, you may not understand what happens to you. But you must not become impatient and rebellious, nor be discouraged. You must enjoy life while you have it, for life is good and has many rewards. Moreover, if you do your duty as it comes to you, God will not fail you, for He is good. "Reverence God," he advises, "and keep His commandments; for this is the whole duty of man."

The Book of Ecclesiastes is known in Hebrew by the name *Koheleth*, which means "The Preacher." King Solomon is supposed to have written it in his old age.

"Ecclesiastes" is read in Synagogue on the Festival of Succot, the harvest festival of joy and happiness, as if to remind us, in the midst of our physical enjoyments, of the seriousness of life. Its reading, perhaps, was also suggested by the season of the year, for men are apt to feel a little melancholy when the gray, sad days of autumn have come, when leaves fall from the trees, the days grow short, and the year ages old and weary, soon to die in the white snows of winter. But, beyond those days, springtime will come again.

At such a time, it is good to remember Ecclesiastes' call to life and duty. For, as an English poet says:

> "If winter comes,
> Can spring be far behind?"

I.

NOTHING NEW UNDER THE SUN

Koheleth decided that life seems to be without purpose or meaning, for things are always the same, getting nowhere. Nothing new ever happens in Nature; everything repeats itself endlessly. Men are always wanting something, and when they get it, they are not satisfied. They feel disappointed, and their labor seems without profit and in vain.

THE words of Koheleth, the son of David, king in Jerusalem:

"Vanity of vanities," says Koheleth,
"Vanity of vanities, all is vanity.

"What profit has man of all his labor
In which he labors under the sun?
The generations come and the generations go,
And the earth remains for ever.
The sun also rises and the sun sets,
And hastens back to its rising place.
From south to north the wind blows round,
The wind turns as it blows,
Turning and returning on its track.
All the rivers run into the sea,
Yet the sea is never full;
To the place whither the rivers go
There they go again.

"All things toil to weariness;
Man cannot recount them:
The eye is never satisfied with seeing,
Nor the ear filled with hearing.
What has been, is what shall be,
What has been done, is what shall be done.
There is nothing new under the sun."   (*Ecclesiastes 1.1–9*)

II.

A KING'S SEARCH FOR HAPPINESS

Koheleth had the means to try such things as pleasures, learning, labor and wealth to find out whether they could bring him happiness. He found that these all disappointed him. They gave him no permanent satisfaction; instead he became convinced that there is no real difference between men and beasts.

I, KOHELETH, was king over Israel in Jerusalem. I set myself to study thoughtfully all that goes on under heaven. I have seen all the works that are done under the sun; and, behold, all is vanity and a striving after wind. I thought to myself thus: I have gained far more wisdom than any before me in Jerusalem. I have applied myself to wisdom and knowledge as well as to mad folly. And I find this also was a striving after wind.

The Search for Pleasure

I said to myself, "Come, let me try pleasure and enjoy myself."

I made myself great works. I built mansions for myself. I planted vineyards. I laid out gardens and parks, and I planted in them every kind of fruit tree. I made pools of water, to water a forest growing with trees. I bought slaves, male and female, though I already had a large household. I also had large herds and flocks, larger than any before me in Jerusalem. I gathered silver and gold, and the treasures of kings and provinces. I secured singers, both men and women, and all that gives pleasure to men.

Nothing I desired did I deny myself. But when I considered all I did, my labor and trouble, everything was vanity, and a striving after wind.

The Search for Wisdom

I then turned to understand wisdom and folly. Wisdom is better than folly, I saw, as light is better than darkness. For the wise man has eyes in his head; but the fool walks in darkness. But I also found that one event (death) happens to both.

So I said to myself, "The fate of the fool will also overtake me. Of what advantage then is my greater wisdom?" And I said to myself, "This, too, is vanity. The wise man is no more remembered than the fool; for in the days to come both alike will be forgotten. Alas! the wise man must die just like the fool!"

I hated life, because all that goes on under the sun seemed wrong to me; for all is vanity and a striving after wind.

The Search for Wealth

Now, when I considered wealth, I learned this: The man who loves money will never be satisfied with money; nor he who loves great fortune with gain. When wealth increases, they increase who share it. So what advantage then does the owner have except to see it with his eyes?

One of the great evils which I have seen in the world is wealth which the owner hoarded to his own pain. When his wealth is lost by bad business, he has nothing to leave his son. Naked was he born, and naked he must return; for all his toil he has nothing to take with him.

All this, too, is vanity and a striving after the wind.

Uselessness of Labor

I hated all that I toiled at under the sun, knowing that I must leave it to the man who follows me. And who knows whether he will be a wise man or a fool? Yet he will have it all in his own hands, all I have won by my toil and trouble and skill under the sun. This, too, is vanity.

What does a man get for all his labor and his carefully laid plans? All his days are full of pain and trouble, with no rest for his mind even at night. This, too, is vanity and a striving after wind.

Man is like the Beast

Once more I looked into the world, and I saw wrong done in the courts of justice. I said to myself, "God is showing what men are, to let them see they are no better than the beasts."

Man's fate is a beast's fate. The one dies like the other; the same breath is in them all. Man is no better than the beast; for all is vanity. All go to the same end; all are of the dust, and all return to dust. Who knows whether the spirit of man goes upward, while the spirit of a beast goes downward to the earth?

Again I looked into the world and there I saw that the race is not to the swift, nor the battle to the strong; the wise have no food, nor men of education wealth, nor the learned popular favor.

All alike are victims of time and chance.

All this is vanity, and a striving after the wind.

(Ecclesiastes 1.12–17, 2, 3, 5, 9.11)

III.

THE ADVICE OF THE SAGE

The sad but gentle Koheleth brings this advice to us: The enjoyment of life is itself God's gift. Let us therefore enjoy every minute of life. We must know that for everything there is a proper time. Take advantage of youth, while we have it. And, above all, reverence God and keep His commandments.

Life — God's own Gift

HERE is what I find right and good for man: To eat and to drink, and to be happy as he toils at his task on earth, during the few days God gives him to live. Such is his portion; yes, it is God's own gift when a man is given riches and wealth and has power to enjoy it all; to do his work and to enjoy himself as he toils. He should remember that the days of his life are few, and that God approves of his being happy.

A proper Time for Everything

For everything there is a season.
And a time for every purpose under the heavens:
A time to be born, and a time to die;
A time to plant, and a time to uproot;
A time to slay, and a time to heal;
A time to tear down, and a time to build up;
A time to weep, and a time to laugh;
A time to mourn, and a time to dance;
A time to keep quiet, and a time to talk;
A time to love, and a time to hate;
A time for war, and a time for peace.

Use your Time wisely

The light is sweet to the eyes,
And it is pleasant to see the sun.
If a man live many years,

Let him rejoice in them all,
And remember the days of darkness (death),
For they shall indeed be many.
Go your way, eat your food with joy,
And drink your wine with a merry heart.
Let your garments be always white.
Enjoy life with the wife you love
All the days of your fleeting life,
Which God has given you in the world.

And always be moderate!

Do not be righteous overmuch;
And do not make yourself overwise.
Why expose yourself to trouble?
Be not over-wicked, either,
Do not play the fool;
Why should you die before your time?
The best way is to take the one line,
And yet not avoid the other;
For he who stands in awe of God
Shall avoid both extremes.

Some Maxims for Success

A wise man's mind will keep him right;
But a fool's mind leads him wrong.
Indeed, when a fool walks on the road,
He proclaims to every one that he is a fool.

If a ruler's anger rises up against you,
Do not give up your post;
For calmness can overcome great offenses.

Here is an evil which I have seen on earth,
An error which is done by a ruler:
Folly is often enthroned on high,
And the rich sit in low places.

I have seen servants upon horses,
While princes walk on foot like servants.

He who digs a pit may fall into it;
And he who breaks through a fence,
A serpent may bite him.

He who quarries stones may be hurt by them;
And he who cuts wood may be endangered by it.

If the axe is blunt,
And a man does not whet the edge,
Then must he put more strength into the blow.

If the serpent bites before it is charmed,
Then the charmer's art has brought him no advantage.

The words of a wise man's mouth win favor,
But the lips of a fool lead him to ruin.
The beginning of his talk is foolishness;
And the end of his speech is grievous madness.

By slothfulness the roof sinks in;
And through idle hands the house leaks.

Curse not the king, not even in your thoughts,
And curse not the rich even in your bed-chamber;
For a bird of the air may carry your voice,
And a creature that has wings may reveal the matter.

The Enjoyment of Youth

Rejoice, O young man, in your youth;
And let your heart make merry while you are young.
Put away worry from your mind,
And remove evil from your body;
For youth and manhood will not always last.
Remember your Creator in the days of your youth,
Before the evil days (old age) come on,
Or the years draw near when you shall say,

"I find no pleasure in them;"
Before the sun grows dark,
And the light goes from moon and stars,
And the clouds gather after the rain;
And the dust returns to the earth as it was,
And the spirit returns to God who gave it.

"Vanity of vanities," says Koheleth;
"Vanity of vanities, all is vanity."

The End of the Matter

The conclusion of the matter, all having been heard is:

Fear God, and keep His commandments;
For this is the whole duty of man.

(*Ecclesiastes 5.17–19, 3.1–8, 11.7–8, 9.7–10,
7.16–18, 10.2–20, 11.9–12.8, 12.13*)

אֶסְתֵּר

ESTHER

YOU have heard, of course, of anti-semitism. It is a modern name for a very old, evil thing. Anti-semitism is prejudice against, and sometimes even hatred of, the Jews. It is so old that we find it in the pages of the Bible. It is described in the Book of Esther.

After the Babylonians had captured Jerusalem, they exiled the leaders, nobles, priests and a large part of the people of Judah to Babylonia. The people settled down in Babylonia, determined to be good citizens and loyal subjects of the king. Indeed, they received a letter from their great prophet Jeremiah advising them to do this.* They followed his wise counsel. They organized their little community and became law-abiding citizens. When Persia later conquered Babylonia, and the Jews became subjects of the new Empire, they gave their allegiance to their new king, the king of the Persians.

Years passed. The Jews of Persia lived in peace. But that peace came to an end in the reign of King Ahasuerus (Xerxes, 485–465 B. C. E.). An enemy named Haman, the Agagite, arose who hated the Jews and plotted to destroy them.

The Book of Esther tells of this plot, and how the Jews were saved from cruel destruction by the courage and loyalty of a beautiful Jewish maiden, Esther. Thankful to God for their deliverance, the Jewish people established the Feast of Purim. And on Purim the Book of Esther is read in Synagogue. This book is also called the *Megillah*, or "The Scroll of Esther."

In later times, when similar enemies plotted to destroy them, the Jews remembered their deliverance in the days of Esther and Mordecai; they placed their faith in God's help, and took new courage and hope.

*For Jeremiah's letter to the exiles see page 393.
499

While anti-semitism is prejudice against Jews, the Jews have not been the only victims of misunderstanding and hatred. Unfortunately, many men of different religions, races or nationalities at various times have been the innocent victims of these evils, but only partly because they happened to be different from the people about them. More often power-mad or money-hungry people have used hatred against the Jews and people of other groups to hide their own evil ambitions and schemes. The Book of Esther, therefore, has a message for all men as well as for Jews. It warns mankind against the terrible evil of prejudice which brings so much persecution, suffering and unhappiness into the world.

I.

THE KING'S BANQUET

In the third year of his reign, Ahasuerus, king of Persia, gave a feast for all his princes and servants. The commanders of the armies of Persia and Media, the nobles and governors of the provinces came before him. For one hundred and eighty days he showed them the riches of his glorious kingdom.

When these days were completed, the king made a seven-days' feast in the enclosed garden of the royal palace at Shushan. Vashti, the queen, also gave a feast for the women in the royal palace which belonged to King Ahasuerus.

Queen Vashti is dismissed; and
Esther becomes Queen in her Place

On the seventh day, when King Ahasuerus had been drinking wine, he commanded his seven court attendants to bring Vashti, the queen, before him with the royal crown on her head, to show the people and the princes her beauty, for she was very fair. But Queen Vashti refused to come as the king commanded. Therefore, the king was very angry.

In his anger the king said to his counselors:

"According to law what shall we do to Queen Vashti?"

Memuchan, one of his high officials, said before the king and his officers:

"Vashti, the queen, has done wrong not only to the king but also to all the nobles and to all the people in all the king's provinces. For the refusal of the queen will be reported to all the women so that they will disobey their husbands. If it seems best to the king, let him send out a royal command, and let it be written among the laws of Persia and Media, in order that it may not be changed, that Vashti may never again come before King Ahasuerus; and let the king give her place as queen to another who is better than she."

This plan pleased the king, and the king did as Memuchan advised.

Shortly after this, the king's pages who waited upon him said: "Let beautiful young maidens be sought for the king, and let them be gathered in the palace at Shushan. And let the maiden who pleases the king be queen instead of Vashti."

The plan pleased the king.

Now there was in the royal palace at Shushan a certain Jew named Mordecai, whose ancestors had been exiled from Jerusalem with the captives by Nebuchadnezzar, the king of Babylonia. He had adopted Esther, his uncle's daughter, for she had neither father nor mother. The maiden was very beautiful, and, after her father and mother died, Mordecai took Hadassah, that is Esther, as his own daughter.

When the king's command was made known, among the many maidens brought to the royal palace at Shushan, Esther also was taken and placed in charge of Hegai, who took care of the women. The girl pleased Hegai and won his favor, so that he moved her and her maids to the best place in the women's quarters.

Esther had not revealed who her people were or her family, for Mordecai had told her not to tell. Every day Mordecai used to walk in front of the court of the women's quarters to ask after Esther's welfare and what had been done with her.

When Esther's turn came to go in to the king, Ahasuerus loved her more than all the other women. She became his favorite and won his love, so that he placed the royal crown on her head and made her queen instead of Vashti. Then the king gave a great feast to all his princes and servants in honor of Esther.

Mordecai overhears a Plot

In those days, while Mordecai was sitting in the king's gate, two of the king's servants, who guarded the entrance of the palace, plotted to kill King Ahasuerus. Mordecai learned of the plot and told it to Queen Esther; and she told the king in Mordecai's name. When the truth was known, the men who plotted against the king were both hanged on a tree. And the incident was written down in the daily record of events that was kept before the king.

II.

HAMAN SCHEMES REVENGE

Now, King Ahasuerus promoted Haman, the Agagite, and gave him a place above all the princes who were with him. All the king's servants who were in the king's gate bowed down before Haman, for so the king had commanded. But Mordecai did not bow down before Haman.

Haman rises to Power and
becomes offended at Mordecai

The king's servants, who were in the king's gate, said to Mordecai:

"Why do you disobey the king's command?"

When they had thus cautioned him day after day without his paying heed to them, they told Haman, so as to find out whether Mordecai's acts would be permitted, for he had told them that he was a Jew. When Haman saw that Mordecai did not bow down before him, he was very angry. But, as they had told him that Mordecai was a Jew, he decided not to lay hands on him alone but to plot to destroy all the Jews in the kingdom of Ahasuerus.

Haman told King Ahasuerus:

"There is a certain people scattered among the peoples in all the provinces of your kingdom; and their laws differ from those of every other people; and they do not keep the king's laws. Therefore it is not right for the king to leave them alone. If it seems best to the king, let an order be given to destroy them, and I will pay ten thousand talents of silver into the royal treasury."

The king took off his ring and gave it to Haman, and said:

"The money is yours and the people also, to do with them as you wish."

Messages then were sent by men on horses to all the king's provinces, to destroy, to kill, and to put to an end all the Jews, young and old, little children and women, on the thirteenth day of the twelfth month, and to rob them of all that they had. Meanwhile the king and Haman sat down to drink, but the people of Shushan were troubled.

*Mordecai appeals to Esther to
plead with the King on behalf
of the Jews*

When Mordecai learned all that had been done, he tore his clothes and put on sackcloth, and he put ashes on his head (as a sign of mourning), and went out into the city and raised a loud and bitter cry of sorrow. He went as far as the king's gate, for no one could enter the gate clothed in sackcloth. In every province, wherever the king's command came, there was great mourning, fasting, weeping, and wailing among the Jews. And many of them sat in sackcloth and ashes.

When Esther's maids and servants told her about it, she was greatly troubled. She sent garments for Mordecai to put on, that he might take off his sackcloth. But he would not accept them. Esther then called Hatach, one of the king's servants whom he had appointed to wait on her. She ordered him to go to Mordecai to learn what this meant and how it had happened.

Hatach went to Mordecai at the city square in front of the king's gate. Mordecai told him all that had happened to him and the exact sum of money that Haman had promised to pay into the king's treasury. He also gave him a copy of the order to destroy the Jews, that had been given out in Shushan, to show to Esther that she might know about it. He also urged her to go to the king and ask his mercy and plead with him for her people.

When Hatach came and told Esther what Mordecai had said, she commanded Hatach to go and say to Mordecai:

"All the king's servants and the people of the king's provinces know that death is the punishment for any man or woman who goes to the king into the inner court without being called, except for the one to whom the king may hold out the golden scepter, which means that he may live. Now for thirty days I have not been called to go in to the king."

When Mordecai was told what Esther had said, he sent back this answer to Esther:

"Do not think that you alone of all the Jews will escape because you belong to the king's household. If you keep silent at this time, help will come to the Jews from somewhere else, but you and your family will perish. Who knows but that you have been raised to the throne for a time like this?"

Then Esther sent this message to Mordecai:

"Go, gather all the Jews in Shushan and fast for me. Do not eat or drink anything for three days and nights. I and my maids will fast also, and I will go in to the king, although it is against the law. And if I perish, I perish."

Mordecai went away and did as Esther directed.

III.

QUEEN ESTHER BEFORE THE KING

On the third day, Esther put on her royal robes and stood in the inner court of the royal palace opposite the king's house. The king was sitting on his throne in the palace, opposite the entrance. When he saw Queen Esther standing in the court, she won his favor, and he held out to her the golden scepter that was in his hand. Esther went up and touched the tip of the scepter. Then the king said to her:

"Whatever you wish, Queen Esther, and whatever you ask, it shall be granted, even to the half of my kingdom."

Esther replied:

"If it seems best to the king, let the king and Haman come today to the feast that I have prepared for him."

The king said:

"Bring Haman quickly, that Esther's wish may be granted."

So the king and Haman went to the feast that Esther had prepared. While they were drinking wine, the king said to Esther:

"Whatever you ask shall be granted, even to the half of my kingdom."

Esther answered:

"If I have won the king's favor and if it seems best to the king to grant what I ask, let the king and Haman come to the feast which I shall prepare for them; and tomorrow I will do as the king wishes."

Haman's Pride grows before his Fall

Haman went out that day joyful and happy; but when he saw Mordecai in the king's gate and noticed that he neither stood up nor moved for him, he was furiously angry with Mordecai. But Haman controlled his temper and went home. He called together his friends and Zeresh, his wife, and told them the greatness of his wealth, how many children he had, and all the ways in which the king had honored him, and how he had given him a place above the officials and the royal servants. And Haman continued:

"Queen Esther brought no one with the king to the feast which she had prepared but me, and tomorrow also I am invited by her along with the king. Yet all this does not satisfy me as long as I see Mordecai, the Jew, sitting at the king's gate."

Then Zeresh, his wife, and all his friends said to him:

"Let a gallows seventy-five feet high be built and in the morning speak to the king and let Mordecai be hanged on it. Then go merrily with the king to the feast."

This advice pleased Haman, and he had the gallows built.

The sleepless King learns of Mordecai's Loyalty

That night the king was unable to sleep. He gave orders to bring him the books that told of great deeds; and they were read before the king. And in them was written how Mordecai had told about the two servants of the king who had tried to kill King Ahasuerus. Then the king said:

"How has Mordecai been honored and rewarded for this?"

The king's courtiers replied:

"Nothing has been done for him."

The king demanded:

"Who is in the court?"

Now Haman had just entered the outer court of the king's house to speak to the king about hanging Mordecai on the gallows that he had prepared for him. So the king's courtiers said to him:

"Haman is standing there in the court."

The king commanded:

"Let him enter."

Haman entered, and the king asked him:

"What shall be done to the man whom the king delights to honor?"

Haman thought to himself, "Whom besides me does the king delight to honor?"

So Haman said to the king:

"To the man whom the king delights to honor, let a royal garment be brought, which the king has worn, and the horse on which the king has ridden and on whose head a royal crown has been placed. Then let the garment and the horse be placed in charge of one of the king's noble princes and let him clothe the man whom the king delights to honor and make him ride on the horse through the city square and proclaim before him: 'This is what is done to the man whom the king delights to honor.' "

Then the king said to Haman:

"Make haste and take the garment and the horse, as you have said, and do thus to Mordecai, the Jew, who sits in the king's gate. Do not fail to do all you have said."

So Haman took the garment and the horse and clothed Mordecai, and made him ride through the city square and proclaimed before him:

"This is what is done to the man whom the king delights to honor."

Haman's Fall from Power

Mordecai returned to the king's gate, but Haman hurried to his house, mourning, with his head covered. Haman told Zeresh, his wife, and all his friends everything that had happened to him. Then his friends and Zeresh, his wife, said to him:

"If Mordecai before whom you have already been disgraced is a Jew, you can do nothing against him, but you will surely fall before him."

While they were still talking with him, the king's servants came and escorted Haman to the feast that Esther had prepared. The king and Haman went to drink with Queen Esther. And the king said to Esther:

"Whatever you ask, Queen Esther, it shall be granted you, even to the half of my kingdom."

Queen Esther answered:

"If I have won favor, O king, and if it seems best to the king, let my life and my people be given me at my request; for I and my people have been sold to be destroyed, to be killed, and to perish!"

King Ahasuerus said to Queen Esther:

"Who is he and where is he who dares to do this?"

Esther answered:

QUEEN ESTHER

"... I and my people have been sold to be
destroyed ..."   (*Esther 7.4*)

see page 508

DANIEL INTERPRETS THE DREAM

"There is a God in heaven who interprets dreams . . ." *(Daniel 2.28)*

see page 518

"A foe, an enemy, this wicked Haman."

Haman shrank in terror before the king and the queen; and Harbonah, one of those who waited on the king, said:

"There, standing in the courtyard of Haman's house, are the gallows, seventy-five feet high, which Haman built for Mordecai."

The king said:

"Hang him on them."

So they hanged Haman on the gallows that he had prepared for Mordecai. And the wrath of the king was quieted.

IV.

THE JEWS' TRIUMPH

King Ahasuerus then gave the property of Haman, the Jews' enemy, to Queen Esther. And Mordecai was made one of the king's advisers, for Esther had told of his relationship to her. The king also drew off his signet-ring, which he had taken from Haman, and gave it to Mordecai; and Esther placed Mordecai in charge of Haman's property.

Then Esther came again before the king and fell at his feet and with tears begged him to prevent the evil that Haman had planned against the Jews. The king held out to her the royal scepter, and she arose and stood before him. Then King Ahasuerus said to Queen Esther and to Mordecai, the Jew:

"Write in behalf of the Jews as seems best to you, in the king's name, and seal it with the king's ring; for what is written in the king's name and sealed with the king's ring no one may disobey."

So Mordecai wrote in the name of King Ahasuerus and sealed it with the king's ring. And he sent by messengers, who rode the king's swift horses, mules, and camels, the king's command that the Jews who were in every city should gather together and protect their lives.

Mordecai's Letter

This was the letter that Mordecai wrote to all the Jews who were in all the provinces of King Ahasuerus, both near and far. He told them that they should keep the fourteenth day of the month of Adar, and the fifteenth day also, each year, the days on which the Jews were saved from their enemies, and the month which was turned for them from one of sorrow to gladness, and from mourning into a holiday; that they should make them days of feasting and gladness, and of sending presents to each other and gifts to the poor.

The Jews took it upon themselves to do as Mordecai had written them, because Haman the son of Hammedatha, the Agagite, the enemy of all the Jews, had conspired against them to destroy them, had not Esther come before the king and pleaded with him. He commanded that Haman's wicked scheme, which he had plotted against the Jews, should return upon his own head; and that he and his sons should be hanged upon the gallows.

Because of all that this letter said, and of all that they had seen concerning this matter, the Jews ordained and took it upon themselves and upon their descendants, and upon all who joined themselves to the Jews, that they would keep these two days according to what was written and according to the fixed time each year; and that these days should be remembered and observed throughout the generations, in every family, every province, and every city; and that these days of Purim should never disappear from among the Jews, nor the memory of them perish from among their descendants.

Queen Esther also writes

Then Queen Esther, the daughter of Abihail, also wrote a letter to confirm this in a second message about Purim. She sent letters to all the Jews, to the hundred and twenty-seven provinces of the kingdom of Ahasuerus, with words of peace and truth, to confirm these days of Purim in their fixed times, according as Mordecai the Jew had ordered, and as they had taken upon themselves and their descendants as commands concerning fasting and wailing. Queen Esther's letter confirmed in writing all the arrangements made for the observance of Purim.

The command was also given out in the royal palace at Shushan; and Mordecai went out from the presence of the king in royal garments of violet and white and with a great crown of gold and with a robe of fine linen and purple. The people of Shushan shouted and were glad. To the Jews there came light and gladness, joy and honor. And in every city and country, where the king's command came, there was gladness and joy among the Jews, and a holiday.

The Feast of Purim

On the fourteenth day of the month Adar,* the Jews rested and made it a day of feasting and rejoicing. Therefore the Jews

*About March.

who live in the country villages keep the fourteenth day of the month Adar as the day of rejoicing and feasting and a holiday, and as a day on which they send gifts to one another. But the Jews in Shushan rested on the fifteenth day of the same month and made it a day of feasting and rejoicing.

The Jews made it a custom for them, and for their children, and for all who should join them, so that it might not be changed, that they should observe these two days as feasts each year. For Haman had plotted to destroy the Jews completely, and he cast *Pur*, that is, lots, to destroy them. For this reason these days are called Purim.

דָּנִיֵּאל

DANIEL

ARE you sometimes called upon to make a sacrifice for your loyalty to Judaism? Have you always been willing to make this sacrifice? The Book of Daniel tells heroic tales of Jewish youths who were ready to make even the supreme sacrifice for what they as Jews believed in.

During their exile in Babylonia, the Jews were loyal citizens of their country, but they refused to give up their religion. Typical of these Jews were Daniel and his three friends. They were God's faithful who time and again had been put to severe tests, but each time proved their loyalty.

Later, in times of terrible persecutions, Jews read about Daniel and his friends, and they gained courage to endure their trials and to remain faithful to their religion. Indeed, some scholars believe that the Book of Daniel was written down, on the basis of an earlier text, during the days of the Maccabees (about 165 B.C.E.) to fortify the Jews against the cruelties of the madman, Antiochus IV.

The author, of course, had to write carefully, lest he be arrested or imprisoned or even put to death. Therefore, he used dreams and symbolic visions to convey his message about the downfall of tyrants and the coming of a better age of justice. He wrote as if he meant Babylonia and her king, but he really intended Antiochus and his Syrian kingdom. His book was read in secret gatherings among the persecuted Israelites, and from Daniel's loyalty they drew fortitude and devotion.

To courage the Book of Daniel added hope, for Daniel taught that God was the Ruler of all nations; He brought about their rise and fall; and He caused the wicked kingdoms to pass away. Daniel predicted that in due time God Himself would become

King over all the nations. Then Israel and all the world would enjoy justice and peace.

The author of the Book of Daniel wrote his thoughts about the future in the form of fantastic visions in which strange beasts played an important role, and voices were heard speaking from heaven. These visions and revelations are called "apocalypses." In them Daniel held out the hope that God would rescue Israel and bless those who remained steadfast in their faith in Him. With this hope in their hearts, the Jews were helped to find strength and courage, and fortified their determination to live.

I.

FOUR COURAGEOUS JEWISH YOUTHS

Daniel and his three friends were offered personal promotion in the court of Nebuchadnezzar, king of Babylonia. But this involved giving up the Jewish dietary laws. They refused and preferred to remain true to their religion, and insisted on keeping the ritual laws of food and drink.

NEBUCHADNEZZAR, king of Babylonia, commanded Ashpenaz, his chief officer, to bring to him certain of the Israelites who belonged to the royal family and the nobility. They were to be young men who were strong and handsome, well taught, quick to learn, and able to serve in the king's palace. And they were to be taught the learning and the language of the Chaldeans (Babylonians). The king, moreover, would give to them, each day, some of the king's food and of the wine which he drank. He also commanded that they should be taught for three years, and that at the end of that time they should enter the king's service.

Among these young men were Daniel, Hananiah, Mishael, and Azariah. The chief of the king's officers gave other names to them: To Daniel he gave the name Belteshazzar; to Hananiah, Shadrach; to Mishael, Meshach; and to Azariah, Abed-nego.

But Daniel made up his mind not to defile himself with the king's food nor with the wine which he drank. So he asked Ashpenaz not to make him defile himself. And God gave Daniel favor and kindness in the eyes of the chief of the king's officers, and he said to Daniel:

"I fear that my lord, the king, who has given you your food and your drink, will see that your faces are more haggard than those of young men who are your age, and so you will endanger my head with the king."

Daniel said to the steward whom Ashpenaz had put over Daniel, Hananiah, Mishael, and Azariah:

"Try your servants for ten days; and let them give us vegetables to eat and water to drink. Then compare the way we look with the appearance of the young men who eat the king's food. Then do to us as it seems best."

He did as they asked, and tried them ten days. At the end of ten days they looked better and they were stouter than all the young men who ate the king's food. So the steward took away their food and wine, and gave them vegetables.

To these four young men God gave knowledge, understanding and wisdom; and Daniel could interpret all kinds of visions and dreams.

At the end of the days which the king had fixed for bringing in all the candidates, Ashpenaz brought them before Nebuchad-nezzar, and the king talked with them. But not one of all the young men was found equal to Daniel, Hananiah, Mishael, and Azariah. So they began to serve the king. On every subject about which the king questioned them, and which called for understanding and wisdom, he found them ten times better qualified than all the wise men and magicians who were in his entire kingdom.

And Daniel retained his position till the first year of King Cyrus.   (*Daniel 1*)

II.

NEBUCHADNEZZAR'S DREAM

Daniel, like Joseph in Egypt, explained the king's strange dream. The huge image the king saw represented four great kingdoms: The head of gold was Babylonia; the breasts and arms of silver, Media; its body and thighs of brass, Persia; and its feet, part iron and part clay, part strong and part weak, Greece. The mighty image was shattered into pieces by a little stone, Israel. Daniel made the meaning of the dream clear. So far God had given the rule of the world to four different nations, each time taking it from the other. Soon He would give the rule to Israel.

IN THE second year of his reign, Nebuchadnezzar had dreams; and his mind was so troubled that he could not sleep. The king sent for the magicians and the wise men and those who studied the stars to tell him what his dreams meant. They came before the king, and he said to them:

"I have had a dream and my mind is troubled, for I want to know what the dream was and what it means."

They answered the king:

"There is not a man on earth who can do what the king asks; indeed, no king, however great and powerful, has ever asked such a thing of any wise man or magician, or of one who studies the stars. What the king asks is too hard. There is no one else who can tell it to the king, except the gods."

These words made the king very angry, and he commanded that all the wise men of Babylonia be put to death.

The command went forth, and the wise men were to be slain. And they sought Daniel and his friends that they too might be slain. Then Daniel spoke with discretion to Arioch, the captain of the king's guard, and said:

"Why is the king's command so harsh?"

When Arioch told Daniel about the king's dream, Daniel went to the king and asked that he give him time to tell him what the dream meant.

Then Daniel went to his house, and told these matters to Hananiah, Mishael, and Azariah, that they might ask the God of heaven to be kind to them and to tell Daniel the secret of the dream, so that they might not die with the rest of the wise men of Babylonia. The secret was revealed to Daniel in a vision of the night, and he praised the God of heaven.

Then Daniel went to Arioch and said to him:

"Do not destroy the wise men of Babylonia. Take me before the king, and I will tell him what his dream means."

Arioch quickly brought Daniel before the king and said to him:

"I have found a man among the captives of Judah who will tell you what your dream means."

The king said to Daniel:

"Can you make known to me the dream which I have had and what it means?"

Daniel answered:

"There is a God in heaven who interprets dreams, and He has revealed to King Nebuchadnezzar what shall come in the end of days (the future). Your dream and the visions which you had as you lay asleep are these:

"You, O king, had a vision in which you saw a great image. That image was large and it was exceedingly bright as it stood before you, and its appearance was terrible. The head of the image was of fine gold, its breast and its arms of silver, its body and its thighs of brass, its legs of iron, its feet part of iron and part of clay. You looked at it until a stone was cut out, not by the hands of men, which struck the image on its feet of iron and clay and broke them in pieces. Then the iron, the clay, the brass, the silver, and the gold were all broken in pieces and became like the chaff which blows from the summer threshing-floor, and the wind carried them away so that nothing was left. But the stone that struck the image became a great mountain and filled the whole earth.

"This is the dream, and we will tell the king what it means:

"O king, you are the king of kings to whom the God of heaven has given the kingdom, the power, and the strength, and the glory. The whole world He has given into your power — men, wild beasts and birds, and He has made you rule over them all. You are the head of gold.

"After you shall rise another kingdom inferior to you, and a third kingdom of brass, which shall rule over the whole earth. A fourth kingdom shall be strong as iron, for iron breaks in pieces and shatters all things; and, like iron which crushes, it shall break in pieces and shall crush all things. As you saw the feet and toes, part clay and part iron, it shall be a divided kingdom; but there shall be in it some of the strength of the iron, for you saw the iron mixed with clay. As the toes of the feet were part iron and part clay, so the kingdom shall be partly strong and partly weak. You saw the iron mixed with clay, for the rulers shall marry one another, but they shall not stick together, even as iron does not stick to clay.

"During the reigns of these kings, the God of heaven shall set up a kingdom which shall never be destroyed, nor shall the kingdom be left to another people; but it shall break in pieces and destroy all these kingdoms, and it shall stand for ever. This is shown by the fact that you saw a stone cut out of the mountain, but not with the hands of men. And it broke in pieces the iron, the brass, the clay, the silver, and the gold.

"The great God has made known to the king what shall come to pass hereafter; and the dream is real and this meaning true."

King Nebuchadnezzar then kneeled and worshipped; and he praised Daniel and said:

"Truly, your God is the God of gods and the Lord of kings, and a revealer of secrets to His servants, for you have been able to reveal this great secret."

Then the king promoted Daniel and gave him many costly gifts and made him ruler over the whole province of Babylonia and chief over all the wise men in Babylonia. (*Daniel 2*)

III.

IN THE FIERY FURNACE

The friends of Daniel — Shadrach, Meshach and Abed-nego — refused to worship the golden image of Nebuchad-nezzar, and they were thrown into a fiery furnace to die. But they were saved from the hostile flames, and escaped unsinged.

KING Nebuchadnezzar made a golden image ninety feet high and nine feet wide. He set it up in the plain of Dura, in the province of Babylonia. He sent for the officers, the governors, the judges, the treasurers, and all the rulers of the provinces to dedicate the image. They all came together and stood before the image that Nebuchadnezzar had set up.

The herald cried aloud:

"O peoples, nations, to you it is commanded that the moment you hear the sound of the trumpet, flute, lute, harp, bagpipe, and all kinds of musical instruments, you shall fall down and worship the golden image. Whoever does not fall down and wor-ship shall be thrown into a burning, fiery furnace."

When the sound of the trumpet, flute, lute, harp, bagpipe, and all kinds of musical instruments was heard, the peoples, nations and races fell down and worshipped the golden image that King Nebuchadnezzar had set up.

At that time certain Chaldeans came near to the king and made this charge against the Jews:

"O king, live forever! There are certain Jews — Shadrach, Meshach, and Abed-nego — whom you have placed in charge of the province of Babylonia. These men, O king, have not obeyed your command; they do not serve your gods nor worship the golden image which you have set up."

Nebuchadnezzar in his rage and fury gave command to bring in Shadrach, Meshach, and Abed-nego. When they were brought before the king, Nebuchadnezzar said to them:

"Is it true, O Shadrach, Meshach, and Abed-nego, that you do not serve my god nor worship the golden image which I have set up? If you do not worship, you shall at once be thrown into a burning, fiery furnace. Where is there a god who can deliver you out of my hands?"

They replied:

"O king, there is no need of our answering you about this. Our God whom we serve is able to save us from the burning, fiery furnace; He will save us out of your hand, O king. But if not, know, O king, that we will not serve your gods nor worship the golden image which you have set up."

Nebuchadnezzar was very angry at these words, and the appearance of his face changed against Shadrach, Meshach, and Abed-nego. He ordered that the furnace should be heated seven times hotter than usual. He also commanded some of the soldiers in his army to bind them, and throw them into the burning, fiery furnace. Shadrach, Meshach and Abed-nego were then bound in their cloaks, their tunics, their robes, and their other garments, and were cast into the midst of the burning, fiery furnace. As the furnace was exceedingly hot, the flames consumed the soldiers who had taken up Shadrach, Meshach, and Abed-nego. But Shadrach, Meshach, and Abed-nego themselves, fell down untouched by the flames into the midst of the burning, fiery furnace.

Nebuchadnezzar was so astonished at this sight that he said to his counsellors:

"Did we not throw three men, bound, into the midst of the fire?"

They answered:

"True, O king."

He said:

"Now I see four men, unbound, walking in the midst of the fire, and they are unhurt; and the fourth looks like a son of the gods (an angel)."

Nebuchadnezzar went near the door of the burning, fiery furnace and cried:

"Shadrach, Meshach, and Abed-nego, servants of the Most High God, come out!"

Shadrach, Meshach, and Abed-nego came out of the fire. The officers, governors, and counsellors who were there saw that the fire had no power over the bodies of these men, and that the hair of their heads was not singed and that their cloaks were not harmed, and that there was no smell of fire.

Nebuchadnezzar said:

"Blessed be the God of Shadrach, Meshach, and Abed-nego, who has sent His angel to save His servants who trusted in Him and refused to obey the king's command, and have offered their bodies that they might not serve nor worship any god except their own. Therefore, I command that every people, nation, and race that shall say anything against the God of Shadrach, Meshach, and Abed-nego shall be cut in pieces and their house shall be made an ash-heap, for there is no other god who is so able to save as is this one."

Then the king promoted Shadrach, Meshach, and Abed-nego in the province of Babylonia.   (*Daniel 3*)

IV.

THE HANDWRITING ON THE WALL

Belshazzar now ruled as king of Babylonia. Arrogant and boastful, Belshazzar dared to mock God by drinking from the sacred vessels of the Temple at one of his drunken banquets. Suddenly, a mysterious hand appeared and wrote the nation's doom on the wall. Daniel was called to explain it. Babylonia and her king had been found wanting. As with Babylonia, so with Syria; and as with Belshazzar, so with the mad Antiochus.

KING Belshazzar made a great feast to a thousand of his nobles, and drank wine before them. Under the influence of the wine, he commanded to bring the gold and silver vessels which Nebuchadnezzar, his father, had taken from the Temple at Jerusalem. They brought the golden vessels which had been taken from the Temple of God at Jerusalem. The king, his nobles, his wives, and the others of his household drank from them. They drank wine and praised the gods of gold, and of silver, of brass, of iron, of wood, and of stone.

At that moment the fingers of a man's hand appeared and wrote upon the plaster of the wall of the king's palace; and the king saw the palm of the hand that wrote.

The king grew pale. His thoughts frightened him, his legs trembled and his knees knocked together. The king called for the magicians and those who study the stars, and said to the wise men of Babylonia:

"Whoever shall read this writing and tell what it means shall be clothed with purple, and have a chain of gold about his neck, and shall rule as one of three in the kingdom."

All the king's wise men came in, but they could not read the writing nor tell the king what it meant. King Belshazzar was greatly frightened, and his face grew pale, and his nobles were thrown into confusion.

The queen, because of what the king and his nobles had said, came into the banquet-house, and said:

"O king, live for ever! Let not your thoughts frighten you, nor let yourself grow pale. There is a man in your kingdom in whom is the spirit of the holy gods; and in the days of Nebuchadnezzar, your father, he was found to have light and understanding and wisdom, like the wisdom of the gods. Let Daniel, whom the king named Belteshazzar, be called, and he will tell what it means."

Daniel was brought before the king, and the king said to him:

"Are you that Daniel, one of the men who were carried away captive, whom Nebuchadnezzar brought from Judah? I have heard that the spirit of the gods is in you, and that you have understanding and surpassing wisdom. The wise men and the magicians have been brought before me to read this writing and to tell me what it means; but they are not able. I have heard that you can tell what dreams mean and answer hard questions. Now if you can read the writing and tell what it means, you shall be clothed with purple, and have a chain of gold about your neck, and shall rule as one of the three in the kingdom."

Daniel answered the king:

"Keep your gifts, and give your rewards to another. Without them I will read the writing to the king, and tell what it means. O king, the Most High God gave Nebuchadnezzar, thy father, the kingdom and greatness, glory and majesty. Because of the greatness that He gave him, all peoples, nations, and races trembled and feared him. He killed or kept alive as he wished; and he raised up or put down whom he pleased. But when he became proud and haughty, he was made to come down from his kingly throne and his glory was taken from him, and he was driven away from men, and his mind became like that of the beasts, and he lived with the wild animals; he was fed with grass like oxen, and his body was wet with the dew of heaven, until he learned that the Most High God rules over the kingdom of men and that He sets up over it whom He will.

"But you, O Belshazzar, have not been humble, though you knew all this, but you raised yourself against the Lord of heaven, and have had the vessels of His Temple brought before you, and you, your nobles, your wives, and the others of your household have drunk wine from them. You have given praise to the gods of silver, of gold, of brass, of iron, of wood, and of stone, which cannot see nor hear nor know. And you have not praised the God in whose control are your very breath and all that you do."

Daniel continued:

"From Him then has the hand been sent and traced this writing:

MENE, MENE, TEKEL, UPHARSIN

"And this is the meaning of these words: MENE — God has numbered the days of your kingdom, and brought it to an end. TEKEL — You are weighed in the balances, and are found wanting. UPHARSIN — Your kingdom is divided, and given to the Medes and Persians."

Then Belshazzar commanded and Daniel was clothed with purple and a chain of gold was put about his neck, and he was proclaimed one of the three who ruled in the kingdom.

That night, Belshazzar, the king of Babylonia, was slain.

(Daniel 5)

V.

DANIEL'S FINAL FAITHFULNESS

Darius the Mede now ruled over Babylonia, and Daniel held a high place in his kingdom. But envious officials attacked Daniel on the ground that he prayed to his God and not to his king. Daniel faithfully and fearlessly continued to say his daily prayers. The officers stirred the king to anger so that he condemned Daniel to be thrown into a den of hungry lions. Daniel was wonderfully saved, and his courage and faith were honored.

IT pleased Darius to set over the kingdom a hundred and twenty satraps, who ruled the whole kingdom, and over them three chief officials, of whom Daniel was one; that these satraps might report to them and that the king should lose nothing. Daniel was better than the other chief officials and the satraps, for he showed a fine spirit; and the king intended to set him over the whole empire.

The chief officials and the satraps sought to find a way to accuse Daniel of not having done his duty; but they could not find anything against him, for he was faithful and was not guilty of any mistake or wrongdoing.

These men said:

"We shall not find any way to accuse this Daniel unless we find it in connection with the Law of his God."

So these chief officials and satraps went to the king, and said to him:

"King Darius, live for ever! All the chief officials of the kingdom, the counsellors and the satraps, the judges and the governors, have consulted together to have the king make a law and issue a strong command that whoever shall ask a petition of any god or man for thirty days, except of you, O king, shall be thrown into a den of lions. Now, O king, give the command and sign the law that, like the law of the Medes and the Persians, it may not be changed."

King Darius signed the law and issued the command.

Although Daniel knew that the law had been signed, he went into his house to pray. Its windows were open towards Jerusalem, and he knelt upon his knees three times a day and prayed, and gave thanks to his God as he had done before. These men rushed in and found Daniel praying and calling upon his God. They went before the king and reminded him about the royal command and said:

"That Daniel, who is one of the captives of Judah, pays no attention to you, O king, nor to the command that you have signed, but prays three times a day."

When the king heard these words, he was greatly displeased and set his heart on saving Daniel, and he worked until sunset to save him. Then these men all went to the king and said to him:

"Know, O king, that it is a law of the Medes and Persians, that no command nor law which the king gives may be changed."

The king then gave his command, and they brought Daniel and threw him into the den of the lions. But the king said to Daniel:

"May your God, whom you always serve, save you!"

Then a stone was brought and laid at the entrance to the den. And the king sealed it with his own seal-ring and with those of his nobles, that no change might be made so as to rescue Daniel. And the king went to his palace and passed the night fasting.

At dawn, as soon as it was light, the king rose and hurried to the den of lions. When he came near the den where Daniel was, he cried with a very sad voice:

"O Daniel, servant of the living God, has your God, whom you always serve, been able to save you from the lions?"

Daniel said to the king:

"O king, live for ever! My God has sent His angel and has closed the lions' mouths, and they have not hurt me, for I was innocent before Him; and also before you, O king, I have done no wrong."

The king was very glad and commanded that they should take Daniel out of the den. Daniel was taken out of the den, and it was found that he was not injured, for he had trusted in his God.

The king commanded that those men who had accused Daniel should be brought and thrown into the den of lions.

King Darius then wrote to all the peoples, nations, and races in his kingdom:

"May your peace be great! I make a law that throughout my kingdom all men shall reverence the God of Daniel; for He is the living God, and is the same for ever; and His kingdom shall not be destroyed and His rule shall be without end. He saves and rescues, and does wonderful things in heaven and earth. It is He who has saved Daniel from the power of the lions."

So Daniel was successful and happy during the reign of Darius and during the reign of Cyrus the Persian. (*Daniel 6*)

עֶזְרָא – נְחֶמְיָה

EZRA — NEHEMIAH

IS IT possible for a people to lose their land, live in exile for many
years, and then return to their country and become a nation
again?

Impossible as this may seem, it actually happened to the Jewish
people. The Books of Ezra and Nehemiah appear separately in
the Bible. Since they both deal with the same period, they have
here been combined. They tell how the Jewish people returned
to Palestine, how they faced innumerable difficulties there, how
they overcame powerful enemies, and how once again they
became a nation. Fortunately, great men arose at the right time,
and these leaders laid the foundations of what later came to be
known as the Second Jewish Commonwealth.

How did all this happen?

Fifty years had passed since Jerusalem had been destroyed,
and the Jews had gone into exile. During those years inspired
teachers and prophets, like Ezekiel* and Isaiah of the Exile,**
kept alive the hope that some day the Jews would return to Palestine, their ancestral land. But as the years passed, Jewish hopes
became dimmer and dimmer. Then, a great king named Cyrus
came to the throne of Persia. He conquered Babylonia and its
Empire. He then issued a proclamation, in 538 B.C.E., permitting
the Jews to return to Palestine, and he even helped them with
generous gifts. They were delirious with joy.***

Ezra and Nehemiah later became the leaders of the restored
Jewish Commonwealth in Palestine. The great work of rebuilding
the nation was aided by the prophets Haggai, Zechariah and
Malachi.

*See pages 399 ff. for the prophecies of Ezekiel.
**See pages 363 ff. for the prophecies of Isaiah of Babylonia.
***See page 445 f. for Psalm 126 which is supposed to have been written about
that time.

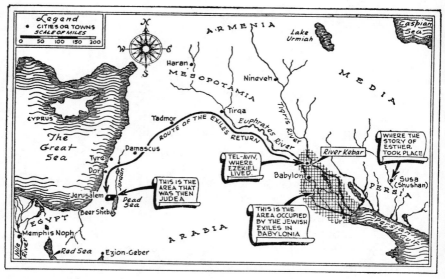

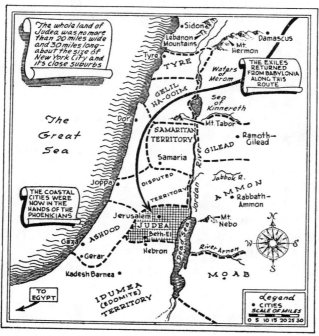

In the Days of the Restoration. Ezekiel, Esther, Daniel and Ezra and Nehemiah.

I

"PIONEERS, O PIONEERS"

King Cyrus issued his proclamation of freedom to the Jews, and about 43,000 returned to Palestine under the leadership of Zerubbabel, son of Shealtiel, and Joshua, son of Jozadak. Those early pioneers had to face terrible hardships — drought, failure of crops, and hostile neighbors. Of these, the Samaritans proved most troublesome. They were residents of Samaria, foreign settlers who had adopted the worship of the God of the Land of Israel. The Jews did not consider them to be true Jews, and rejected their offer to help rebuild the Temple. The Samaritans became furiously angry, and used every means in their power to hinder the work of rebuilding.

The Cyrus Declaration

IN THE first year of Cyrus, king of Persia,↓ the Lord moved Cyrus to issue a proclamation throughout all his realm, and he put it in writing:

"Thus says Cyrus, king of Persia:

The Lord, the God of Heavens, has given me all the kingdoms of the earth, and He has charged me to build Him a Temple in Jerusalem which is in Judea. Whosoever there is among you who belongs to His people (may his God be with him), let him go up to Jerusalem which is in Judea and build the Temple of the Lord, the God of Israel. And those who remain in the place where he dwells, let the men of that place help him with silver and gold and goods and beasts of burden as well as with free-will offerings for the Temple of the Lord in Jerusalem."

The Return to Palestine

The leaders of the tribes of Judah and Benjamin, and the priests and the Levites, whose spirits had been stirred by God, prepared to go up and build the Temple of the Lord in Jerusalem. All their neighbors helped them with silver, gold, goods and beasts of burden, and other valuables in addition to what was freely offered.

↓For archaeological note see Item 19, p. 555 in the back of the book.

King Cyrus also brought out the vessels of the Temple of the Lord which Nebuchadnezzar had removed from Jerusalem; and he put them in charge of Mithredath, the treasurer, and Sheshbazzar, the prince of Judah; and Sheshbazzar brought them back to Jerusalem, when the company of exiles returned from Babylonia to Jerusalem.

The Joy of Rebuilding

When the seventh month arrived, the Israelites in the cities gathered like one man to Jerusalem. Joshua, son of Jozadak, and his fellow-priests, and Zerubbabel, son of Shealtiel, with his kinsmen, began to build the altar of the God of Israel and to offer sacrifices on it, as it is written in the Law of Moses, the man of God.

The foundation of the Temple of the Lord was not yet laid, however. But, they hired masons and carpenters, and gave food and drink and oil to the men of Zidon and Tyre to bring cedar trees down from Lebanon by sea to Joppa, according to the permit granted by Cyrus, king of Persia.

In the second year of their return, when the builders had laid the foundation of the Temple of the Lord, Zerubbabel and Joshua appointed the priests in their official robes with trumpets, and the Levites with cymbals, to praise the Lord according to the direction of David, king of Israel. And they sang one to another:

"Give thanks unto the Lord, for He is good;
For His mercy to Israel endureth for ever."

And all the people raised a loud shout, when they praised the Lord, because the foundation of the Temple was laid.

Troubles and Discouragement

When the enemies of Judah and Benjamin — the Samaritans — heard that the exiles were building a Temple to the Lord, the God of Israel, they came to Zerubbabel and the leaders of the tribes and said to them:

"Let us build along with you, for we worship your God as you do; we have been sacrificing to Him ever since Esarhaddon, king of Assyria, brought us here."

Zerubbabel and Joshua and the rest of the leaders of Israel said
to them:

"You have nothing to do with us in building a Temple for
our God. We will build it ourselves for the Lord, the God of
Israel, as King Cyrus of Persia has ordered us."

Whereupon, the Samaritans hindered the people of Judea,
and caused them trouble as they were building; and they hired
agents against them to frustrate their purpose. They even wrote
letters to the king of Persia accusing the Jews of disloyalty.

The king thereupon sent orders to the Jews to stop their work.
Thus, the work of the house of the Lord which is in Jerusalem came
to an end, and it ceased for a long time.

Now the prophets, Haggai and Zechariah, the son of Iddo,
prophesied to the Jews who were in Judea and Jerusalem, in the
name of the God of Israel.   (*Ezra 1, 3–5.1*)

Haggai charges the People
with Selfishness

The Lord spoke by Haggai, the prophet, to Zerubbabel, governor of Judea, and to Joshua, the High Priest, saying:

"Thus speaks the Lord of hosts:

'This people declares: The time has not yet come to build
the house of the Lord!

'Is it a time for you to be living in panelled houses of your
own, while this house is lying in ruins?

'Give thought to your ways! Go up to the hill-country and
bring down timber to build the house, that I may take pleasure
in it and that I may be honored. You expected a rich harvest
and it came to little; even what you brought home I spoiled!
And why? Because of My house which still lies in ruins, while
each of you takes pleasure in his own house.' "   (*Haggai 1.2–9*)

Haggai encourages the
Leaders of the People

And the Lord spoke by Haggai, the prophet, to the leaders,
saying:

"Who is left among you that saw this house in its former

glory? What do you think of it now? You think nothing of it?

"Take courage, O Zerubbabel!

"Take courage, O Joshua!

"Take courage, all you people of the land!

"Courage! Do your work, for I am with you!

"A little while longer, and I will fill this house with glory. And greater shall be the glory of this house than of the former."

(Haggai 2.1–9)

Zechariah's Faith in Zion rebuilt

And this is the word of the Lord by the prophet Zechariah, to Zerubbabel:

"Not by might, nor by power, but by My spirit, saith the Lord of hosts." (*Zechariah 3.6*)

Thus says the Lord:

"I will bring My people, and they shall dwell in the midst of Jerusalem; and they shall be My people, and I will be their God, in truth and in righteousness.

"I will return to Zion, and I will dwell in the midst of Jerusalem;

"And Jerusalem shall be called 'The Faithful City,'

"And the mountain of the Lord of hosts, 'The Holy Mountain.'

"Old men and women shall again dwell in the streets of Jerusalem;

"And the broad places of the city shall be filled with boys and girls, playing in its streets.

"For I will sow prosperity; the vine shall yield its fruit, and the land shall yield its produce, and the heavens shall yield their dew; and I will make the remnant of this people possess all these things.

"And you, O house of Judah, shall become a blessing!

"Fear not! Let your hands be strong!" (*Zechariah 8.3–15*)

Thus the prophets Haggai and Zechariah preached to the Jews who were in Judea and Jerusalem in the name of the God of Israel. And Zerubbabel and Joshua began once again to rebuild the Temple of God which is at Jerusalem; and the prophets of God were with them, helping them.

And they completed the building as the God of Israel commanded, and as the king of Persia decreed. Then the Israelites, the priests, the Levites, and the rest of the returned exiles celebrated the dedication of this house of God with joy.

(Ezra 6)

II.

EZRA — RELIGIOUS LEADER

Ezra was a scribe, a writer. He was deeply religious, and loved the sacred writings of Israel's teachers. He traced his ancestry back to Aaron, the High Priest. Ezra went to Palestine to help his people there, for he had heard of their many difficulties. He arrived in Jerusalem in the summer of 458 B.C.E. He wanted to keep the Jewish people pure in blood and spirit. Ofttimes his eagerness for Jewish purity drove him to harsh measures. Some believe that the Book of Ruth, the story of the lovely Moabitess, was written in protest against Ezra's strict demands.* Ezra will always be regarded as a kind of second Moses who made the Torah the Constitution of the new Jewish Commonwealth.

Ezra gets the King's Permission

IN THE reign of King Artaxerxes of Persia, Ezra, a scribe skilled in the Law of Moses, went up from Babylonia to Palestine. For Ezra had set his heart to seek the Law of the Lord, and to do it, and to teach its statutes and commandments in Israel.

King Artaxerxes gave Ezra a letter which said:

"Any of the people of Israel in my kingdom, or any of their priests and Levites who choose to go up to Jerusalem, may go with you. Whatever is commanded by the God of the heavens, let it be carried out in full for the house of the Lord of the heavens."

Ezra writes his Diary

Ezra rejoiced in the words of the king, and he wrote these words in his book:

"Blessed be the Lord, the God of our fathers, who inspired the king to honor the Temple of the Lord in Jerusalem, and showed me kindness in the presence of the king and his advisers and all his great officers.

*For the Book of Ruth, see pages 193 ff.

"I was strengthened by the favor of the Lord my God, and I gathered leading men from Israel to accompany me.

"I gathered them together on the banks of the river Ahava, where we encamped for three days. I proclaimed a fast at the river Ahava, that we might humble ourselves before our God and obtain from Him a safe journey for ourselves, our children and our possessions. I was ashamed to ask the king for a guard of soldiers and horsemen to protect us against the enemy on the road, for we had told the king: 'God's favor is with all who seek Him, but His power and anger are against all who forsake Him.'

"We departed from the river Ahava on the twelfth day of the first month to go to Jerusalem.

"The favor of our God was with us and He kept us safe from the enemy and from any ambush on the road. We reached Jerusalem where we remained three days. We delivered the king's commission to the king's governor.

Ezra is shocked by the
Conditions he finds

"After this had been done, the leaders approached me and said: 'The people of Israel and the priests and the Levites have not separated themselves from the peoples of the land and from their evil practices. They have married their daughters, and have given their sons in marriage to their daughters. Indeed, the princes and the rulers have been foremost in this offense.'

"When I heard this, I tore my garment and my robe, I tore my hair and my beard as a sign of my grief, and I sat down appalled. I was joined by everyone who trembled at the word of the God of Israel, on account of the offense committed by the exiles. I sat appalled until the evening offering. After the evening offering I arose from my fast, I fell upon my knees and spread out my hands to the Lord my God in prayer:

'O my God, I am ashamed; I blush to lift up my face to Thee, my God, for our sins have risen higher than our heads and our guilt has reached the skies. After all that has come upon us for our misdeeds and our great guilt, and after Thou hast spared us this small remnant of Thy people, are we again to break Thy commands and intermarry with the peoples who practice abominable rites? Behold, we stand guilty before Thee, for none of us can face Thee in this plight.' "

Divorce of foreign Wives

While Ezra prayed and made confession, weeping and casting himself down before the house of God, he was joined by a very large assembly of men, women and children; and the crowd wept bitterly. Then Shechaniah, the son of Jehiel, spoke and said to Ezra:

"We have broken faith with our God and have married foreign women of the natives. Still there is some hope for Israel. Let us make a compact with our God to put away all these wives and their children, and follow the counsel of the Lord; let us act according to the Law. Arise, for it is your task, and we are with you. Be strong and take action!"

Ezra rose up and made the leading priests and the Levites and all Israel take an oath that they would carry out this plan.

(Ezra 7–10)

Malachi, the Prophet, appeals to the Priests to keep the religious Life pure

In those days, the Lord of hosts spoke by Malachi, the prophet, to the priests, saying:

"A son honors his father, and a servant his master. If I am a father, where is My honor? And if I am a master, where is My reverence?

"From the rising of the sun, even to its setting,
My name is great among the nations;
And in every place where an offering is made,
It is a pure offering;
But you are defiling it . . .

"The lips of the priest ought to treasure knowledge;
And men should seek instruction at his mouth;
For he is the messenger of the Lord of hosts."

(Malachi 1.6–11, 2.7)

III.

NEHEMIAH — NATION-BUILDER

Nehemiah was a man of affairs. He went to Palestine in 445 B.C.E. as the representative of the king. He built the wall about Jerusalem. He armed the workers to protect themselves against jealous and scheming enemies. Nehemiah kept a set of memoirs in which he recorded his thoughts and experiences. He proved himself a noble and unselfish leader. All through his memoirs, like a refrain, he repeated this prayer: "Remember me, O my God, for good!"

IN THE twentieth year of King Artaxerxes' reign, in the month of Kislev,* I, Nehemiah, was in Shushan, the royal palace, when Hanani, one of my brothers, and some men came from Judea. I asked them about Jerusalem and about the Jews who were left from the captivity. They told me:

"Those still living there in the province are in great trouble and disgrace. The wall of Jerusalem is broken down and its gates have been destroyed by fire."

When I heard these words I sat down and wept and mourned several days. I fasted and offered up prayer to the God of heaven.

Cupbearer to the King

I was cupbearer to the king, and in the month of Nisan,** in the twentieth year of the reign of King Artaxerxes, I had charge of the wine which was served to the king. Up to this time I had not been sad; so the king said to me:

"Why is your face sad, for you are not sick? This is nothing else but sorrow of heart."

I was greatly afraid, and I said to the king:

"May the king live for ever! Why should not my face be sad, when the city of my fathers' sepulchers is lying waste and its gates are ruined by fire?"

The king said to me:

*About December.
**March-April.

"What request have you to make?"

I prayed to the God of heaven, and said to the king:

"If it please the king and if your servant has won your favor, then send me to Judea, to the city where my fathers lie buried, that I may rebuild it."

The king said to me:

"How long will your journey take, and when will you return?"

I told him when I would return, and the king was willing to let me go.

Then I said to the king:

"If it pleases the king, let letters be given to me to the governors of the province west of the Euphrates, that they may let me pass through until I come to Judea, and a letter to Asaph, the keeper of the king's park, that he may give me timber to make beams for the gates of the castle which guards the Temple and for the wall of the city and for the house in which I shall live."

The king granted me all this, for my God kindly cared for me.

Nehemiah arrives in Jerusalem

I arrived in Jerusalem. After I had been there three days, I got up at night, together with a few of my followers. I told no one what God had put into my mind to do for Jerusalem, and I had no animal with me except the one on which I rode. I went out by night through the Valley Gate towards the Dragon's Well and to the Dung Gate. I examined carefully the walls of Jerusalem which had been broken down and the places where its gates had been destroyed by fire.

The rulers did not know where I went or what I did, for I had not as yet told my plans to the Jews or to the priests or to the nobles or to the rulers or to the others who did the work.

Then I said to the leaders:

"You see the bad condition in which we are, how Jerusalem lies in ruins and its gates are destroyed by fire. Come and let us rebuild the wall of Jerusalem, that we may no longer be in disgrace."

I also told them how God had kindly cared for me, and the words of the king to me. They said:

"Let us go to work and build."

So they took courage for the good work.

Israel's Enemies try again to prevent their Work

The king had sent with me officers and horsemen. When Sanballat, the Samaritan, and Tobiah, the Ammonite, heard all this, it troubled them greatly that one had come to look out for the welfare of the Israelites.

But we went on building the wall.

When Sanballat and Tobiah heard that the rebuilding of the wall was going on, they were very angry. They planned to come and fight against Jerusalem and frighten the people there. But we prayed to our God and appointed watchmen to protect us against them day and night.

The Workers are armed

From that time on, while half of my servants were at work, half of them held the spears, the shields, the bows and the coats of mail. And the rulers stood behind the people of Judah.

Those who built the wall and those who carried burdens were also armed, each using one of his hands for the work and ready with the other to grasp his spear. And each builder worked with his sword fastened at his side.

Neither I, nor any of my brothers, nor my servants, nor the men of the guard who accompanied me took off our clothes, but each kept his spear in his right hand.

After fifty-two days the wall was finished. (*Nehemiah 1–4*)

IV.

NEHEMIAH'S GREAT REFORMS

Nehemiah now proceeded to organize the inner life of the new Jewish community where serious abuses had arisen which threatened to destroy it. Nehemiah reformed Jewish life against the violation of the Sabbath and intermarriage with the heathen peoples of the land. He also sought to eliminate unjust financial practices that had sprung up among the people.

Sabbath Observance

IN those days I saw in Judea how some people treaded winepresses on the Sabbath, and how others brought into Jerusalem on the Sabbath day heaps of grain loaded on donkeys, and also wine, grapes, and figs, and all manner of burdens. And I protested on the day when they sold their provisions. Then I rebuked the authorities of Judea and said to them:

"What evil is this you are doing, profaning the Sabbath day? Did not your fathers do this, until our God brought all this misfortune upon us and upon this city? Yet, you bring more wrath upon Israel by profaning the Sabbath."

Accordingly, when darkness began to fall, before the Sabbath, I ordered the gates of Jerusalem to be shut; and I gave orders that they should not be opened till after the Sabbath. And I set some of my servants in charge of the gates to see that no burden should be brought in on the Sabbath day.

Intermarriage

In those days also I saw the Jews who had married women of Ashdod, of Ammon, and of Moab; and their children spoke half in the language of Ashdod, and could not speak in the Jews' language, but according to the language of each people.

And I rebuked them, and made them swear by God, saying: "You shall not give your daughters to their sons nor take their daughters as wives for your sons or for yourselves. Did not Solomon, king of Israel, sin by these things? Yet among many nations there was no king like him, and he was beloved by his God, and

God made him king over all Israel; nevertheless even him did the foreign women cause to sin. Shall we then permit you to do all this great evil, to break faith with our God in marrying foreign women?"

Thus I rid them of everything foreign.

Social Wrongs: Taking Interest

Now there arose a great outcry of the people and of their wives against their Jewish brethren. For there were those who said:

"We are giving our sons and daughters in pledge to secure grain that we may eat and live."

There were also those who said:

"We are giving our fields, our vineyards, and our houses in pledge that we may secure grain because of the famine."

There were others who cried:

"We have borrowed money for the king's tax. Indeed, we are compelled to bring our sons and daughters into bondage to be servants. And we cannot help it; for other men have our fields and our vineyards."

And I was very angry when I heard their cry and their words. I thought them over, and I rebuked the nobles and the rulers, and said to them:

"You are taking interest each of his own kinsmen."

And I held a great assembly against the wrongdoers; and I said to them:

"The thing that you are doing is not good. Ought you not to walk in the fear of our God, because of the reproach of the heathen, our enemies? Let us, I pray you, stop taking interest. Restore now to them at once their houses, the hundredth part of their money, the grain, the wine, and the oil that you exact of them."

Then they said:

"We will restore them, and will require nothing of them; we will do precisely as you say."

Then I called the priests, and made the wrongdoers take an oath to do as they had promised.

The unselfish Leader

Now, from the time that I was appointed to be governor in the land of Judea, that is, twelve years, neither I nor my kinsmen ate the food which was my right as governor.

I did not demand the food which was due me as governor, because the public work was a heavy burden on this people.

Remember unto me, O my God, for good, all that I have done for this people.　*(Nehemiah 13.15–30, 5.1–19)*

V.

THE TORAH — THE CONSTITUTION

Ezra and Nehemiah gave the Jewish people a constitution by which they could guide and govern the new Jewish community. This constitution was the Torah, the Law of Moses. It became the spiritual foundation of the Second Jewish Commonwealth. And once again in 445 B.C.E., at a public ceremony that recalled the giving of the Torah at Mount Sinai, Israel pledged their loyalty and faithfulness to the Covenant between themselves and God.

WHEN the seventh month drew near, the people gathered as one man in the broad place that was before the Water Gate; and they spoke to Ezra to bring the book of the Law of Moses, which the Lord had commanded to Israel.

Ezra brought the Law before the congregation, both men and women, and all that could hear with understanding. And Ezra stood on a raised wooden platform which they had made for the purpose. He opened the book in the sight of all the people — for he was above the people — and when he opened it, all the people stood up. And Ezra blessed the Lord.

And Ezra read in the book from early morning until midday; and the people listened carefully to the book of the Law. And the Levites instructed the people in the Law, and the people remained in their place. Thus, the Levites read in the book of the Law of God distinctly, and explained its meaning, and caused the people to understand the reading.

Then Nehemiah, the governor, and Ezra, the priest and the scribe, and the Levites who taught the people, said to all the people:

"This day is holy to the Lord your God; do not mourn or weep."

For all the people wept when they heard the words of the Law. Then Nehemiah said to them:

"Go your way, eat and drink, and send a portion to him for whom nothing is prepared, for this day is holy to the Lord. Do not be depressed, for the joy of the Lord is your strength."

When the people heard all these words, and how Ezra blessed the Lord, the great God, they lifted up their hands (in prayer) and bowed their heads, and worshipped the Lord.

And they all cried:

"Amen! Amen!" *(Nehemiah 8)*

ALONG THE PATHWAYS

YOU have now travelled on these pathways through the Bible. You have glimpsed in "The Torah" the beginnings of the world, mankind and Israel, as inspired Jewish writers have thought about them (*Genesis*). You have witnessed how Israel entered into the Covenant of the Law (*Exodus*) which laid upon them the duty to live a life of justice and righteousness (*Leviticus*), and how they struggled through the wilderness to the Promised Land (*Numbers, Deuteronomy*), where by example and teaching they might as a people bring blessing and hope to all mankind.

In "The Prophets" you have seen how Israel entered the Promised Land and conquered it (*Joshua, Judges*), and how they created there a great kingdom (*Samuel*), and how that kingdom grew, then became divided, and was finally destroyed (*Kings, Chronicles*). You have met the courageous prophets of Israel (*Amos, Hosea*) and Judah (*Isaiah, Micah, Jeremiah*) whose fiery words spoke to the conscience of the people and their rulers, appealing for righteous and just living, and those other prophets whose strong yet tender words about God's power, love and forgiveness (*Ezekiel, Isaiah of the Exile*) sustained the Jewish people in sorrow and exile until they returned to their land, overcame many difficulties, and built a new home and life for themselves again (*Jonah, Ezra-Nehemiah*).

And you have read the rich and varied abundance of "The Writings": the songs of religious poets (*Psalms, Lamentations*); the wise sayings of wise men (*Proverbs*); dramatic tales and love songs (*The Song of Songs*); the profound thoughts of men who sought answers to questions that perplexed their minds (*Job, Ecclesiastes*); short stories of faithful women who loved their people and their religion (*Ruth, Esther*); and the heroic episodes of valiant men who readily faced sacrifice and death for their Jewish way of life (*Daniel*).

We trust that you have had an interesting, enjoyable and enriching experience. Our purpose has been to help you become better acquainted with what the Bible has been saying to the Jewish people and to mankind throughout the ages.

We know that the Bible can and should be to you, as it has been to our forefathers, an inspiration for your daily tasks, a helpful companion on your life's pilgrimage, and an encouragement for you to live a worth-while life as a human being and as a Jew.

Therefore, we hope that this experience of the Bible will create in you the desire to read the full and complete story; for there is much more to read and enjoy.

You stand before a new adventure.

We believe that you are now better equipped to enter upon that adventure, and to travel into the wondrous realm of your people's Bible,

THE HOLY SCRIPTURES.

1. Stele of Merneptah, 13th century B.C.E.

It contains the first mention of Israel.
See Note 6, page 550.

2. Code of Hammurabi, about 1728 B.C.E.

The great ruler of Babylon issued
this Code of Laws.
See Note 7, page 551.

—*Courtesy of Oriental Institute,*
University of Chicago

3. King Solomon's Stables

One of King Solomon's
stables for horses was at
Megiddo. The ruins of the
stable indicate its large
size.

See Note 10, page 552.

4. King Solomon's Mines

—Courtesy of Dr. Nelson Glueck

Near Ezion-geber, Solomon's seaport on the
Red Sea, ore was mined for iron and copper.
A great smelting refinery was built around
the 10th century B.C.E.
See Note 10, page 552.

—Courtesy of Dr. Nelson Glueck

5. The Site of King Solomon's Mines

6. The Mesha Stone, 9th century B.C.E.

Now known as the Moabite Stone, it was
discovered at the Moabite capital, Dibon.
It tells how King Mesha successfully rebelled against King Joram of Judah.
See Note 11, page 552.

7. Black Obelisk of Shalmaneser III, about 858 B.C.E.

The first known pictures of Israelites are found here. In the second register from the top Jehu bows before the Emperor. A line of Israelites bearing tribute stands behind him. See Note 12, page 552.

8. Seal Signet Ring of Jotham, King of Judah

Two views of the ring.
See Note 17, page 554.

—Courtesy of Dr. Nelson Glueck

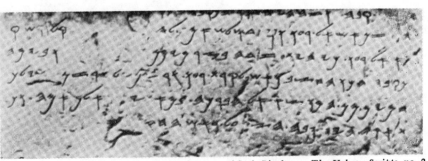

—Courtesy of S. A. Birnbaum, The Hebrew Scripts, no. 2

9. The Siloam Inscription

Found in the tunnel about 25 feet from the Siloam end. It has been the most important piece of monumental writing in ancient Palestine.

See Note 14, page 553.

10. Gezer Calendar

Provides us with an example of ancient Hebrew script during the 10th century. It describes the agricultural year and life of the ancient Israelite farmer. It may have been used by a schoolboy for his exercises.

ARCHAEOLOGICAL NOTES

1. Page 19   *"Ur of Chaldees"*

In Ur, near the Persian Gulf, archaeologists found remains of an unknown people called Sumerians after the name of their greatest city — Sumer. They lived about 3000 B.C.E. Ur, the birthplace of Abraham, was a large, thriving city, its inhabitants enjoying a high standard of civilization as seen from the ruins of their private homes. The archaeologists found there hundreds of clay tablets and traces of a ziggurat (a temple-tower) which may have suggested the story of the Tower of Babel. They also found signs of a terrible flood, and stories about it.

2. Page 28   *"Offer there a sacrifice"*

In the days of Abraham child sacrifice was practiced. Archaeologists have found skeletons of a newborn baby under a fireplace at Tell Abu Matar, a child buried as a foundation offering under a stone wall, and an infant stuffed into a jar and placed under the threshold of a house. The firstborn were often sacrificed to the gods so that the newly built house might be full of blessings. Abraham substituted an animal for the human being. It was a revolutionary change in mankind's religious thinking.

3. Page 43   *"Rachel stole the images"*
                                               The Nuzi Tablets

In the excavations of the town of Nuzi, the Hurrian city in Northern Mesopotamia, archaeologists found clay tablets which have thrown great light on the patriarchal period. They are dated about 1500–1300 B.C.E. and contain the ancient customs and laws of the Hurrians (called Horites in the Bible). Some of the incidents we find in our Bible reflect these customs and laws such as the sale of the birthright by Esau, death-bed blessings and wills, and the use of "household gods." Rachel's act, we now know, was prompted by an ancient legal custom of the Hurrians to make sure that her husband, Jacob, would be protected against the crafty schemes of Laban. Therefore, she carried off the household gods which represented her right to inherit her father's property, as well as her husband's rights in it.

4.   Page 46   *"In the Land of Canaan"*
                                                    The Mari Letters

We learn a great deal about the world of the Patriarchs from the many clay tablets found in Mari, a very important city on the Upper Euphrates in the 18th century B.C.E., and from a delightful story that was found in Egypt and elsewhere.

"The Story of Sinuhe"

The Story of Sinuhe, dated about 1900 B.C.E., tells of a high Egyptian official who fled to the "East" (Kedem), Canaan, land of the Patriarchs. There he met an Amorite chieftain very much like Abraham and Jacob who gave him his daughter in marriage. He tells of his varied experiences during his sojourn. His descriptions of places and customs correspond accurately with those we find in our Bible. And we also learn how close were the ties between Canaan and Egypt in those days.

The Ras Shamra (Ugarit) Tablets

Ugarit was located at the very crossroads of the ancient world, where many peoples and languages intermingled. Merchants, soldiers, priests and scribes lived there. Ras Shamra is the modern Arab name for ancient Ugarit. From the numerous tablets unearthed there, we learn about the Canaanitish myths, beliefs, and religious practices of the people. Their god's name was "El"; his wife's "Asherah" who was goddess of fertility; their son's name was "Baal" and he was god of vegetation. These names appear in our Bible many times. Later, the Israelites and especially the Hebrew prophets had to struggle against these religious beliefs and seek to uproot these pagan practices and all they implied.

5.   Page 49   *"Down to Egypt"*
                                                    The Age of the Hyksos

About 1700 B.C.E. a dark age seemed to settle over Egypt; it lasted about 150 years. Egypt had been invaded by Asiatics whom the Egyptians called Hyksos, that is, "rulers of foreign countries." Archaeologists have found remains and objects associated with them, and familiar names. It was during this time probably that Joseph rose to power, for some of the Hyksos were Semites. They were expelled under the Pharaoh Thutmose III (1490–1435 B.C.E.).

6.   Page 65   *Israel's First Mention out-*
                                                    side the Bible

One of the important finds of archaeology is a stele (a pillar of stone with an inscription) of the Pharaoh Merneptah who lived about 1220

B.C.E. The very first reference to Israel found in extra-biblical sources was made by this ruler. He boasted:

> "The people of Israel is desolate,
> it has no offspring;
> Palestine has become a widow
> for Egypt."

7.   Page 95   "*Their first Lawgiver*"
The Code of Hammurabi

In 1901 archaeologists unearthed in Susa, Babylonia, the now-famous monument on which had been written the great code of laws of King Hammurabi who lived about 1728–1686 B.C.E. Some resemble the laws in the Torah of Moses. This does not mean, however, that Moses took these laws from Hammurabi. On the contrary, there are profound differences between them. It does show, however, that our ancestors lived in a world where people faced the same problems, and tried to meet them with similar legal instruments. Before Hammurabi we know of the great King Ur-Nammu who 300 years earlier drew up a code for his people; this code influenced Hammurabi. Hammurabi was a contemporary of Abraham. The Torah, unlike the Code of Hammurabi, emphasizes the need for personal holiness, and never tires of pleading for justice to the poor and needy.

8.   Page 155   "*Across the Jordan*"
The Tell-el-Amarna Tablets

In 1887 a peasant woman discovered some tablets, written in cuneiform, at Tell-el-Amarna in Egypt. They proved to be letters sent from governors, rulers, officials, and individuals located in cities and villages on the east coast of the Mediterranean Sea, and from more distant places, to the Pharaoh pleading for help against invaders. In a number of passages from Jerusalem the ruler tells of his distress because of these people whom he calls "Habiru" or " 'Apiru." These letters come from the Library of Amenhotep IV (known as Akh-en-aton), 1370–1353 B.C.E. Some scholars believe that the Habiru-'Apiru refer to the Hebrews. Other scholars, however, question this whole theory.

9.   Page 247   "*At the Pool of Gibeon*"
An ancient town located

Between Joab and Abner a bitter struggle took place at Gibeon. But where was Gibeon? In 1838 an archaeologist chanced to be in a town in Palestine called el-Jib. He guessed that el-Jib might be the Arab name for Gibeon. Another archaeologist in 1956 began digging there. Among the debris of a large, rock-cut pool outside the city, he found two jar-handles inscribed with the name "Gibeon," in ancient Hebrew. In 1957 twenty-four more handles were found with "Gibeon" on them. This is how the archaeologists identified the city where the conflict between Joab's men and Abner's men took place. (II Samuel 2.13)

10.   Page 271   *"Chariot cities" and*
                                              "Ezion-geber near Eloth"

Archaeologists have unearthed ruins and remains from the time of King Solomon that cast brilliant light upon that great king. We now know that Megiddo and Lachish were government towns where Solomon established huge stables for horses and chariots used by his troops and by travelers. They were also trading centers for buying and selling horses and chariots to neighboring peoples. Excavations have revealed at Megiddo a site for 450 horses, the stalls fitted with channels for running water.

The Copper Mines of Solomon

Among the notable discoveries of archaeology the finding of Ezion-geber near where modern Elath is being built on the Gulf of Akabah, is most valuable. At ancient Ezion-geber Solomon berthed his ships that carried foreign trade (I Kings 9.26). The Queen of Sheba may have visited Solomon to regulate the trade between their two countries. More important, however, is the discovery that Solomon had built great refineries there for smelting copper out of the rich ore available nearby. These refineries are the largest ever found in the Near East. Green copper stains can still be seen on their crumbled walls. Undoubtedly Solomon set up this industrial center here where a natural wind tunnel is formed by the shape of the countryside, and close to a seaport.

11.   Page 299   *"Joram, the son of Ahab"*
                                              The Moabite Stone

On the death of King Ahab, his son Joram ascended the throne of Israel. The king of Moab rebelled successfully against him. King Mesha of Moab celebrated his victory by erecting a monument, since called by archaeologists "The Moabite Stone," on which he had inscribed,

"I have gained a victory over him, and over his house, and Israel is laid waste for ever."

12.   Page 303   *"Jehu"*
                                              The Black Obelisk

In an Assyrian palace, archaeologists have dug up a black limestone monument since called "The Black Obelisk" of Shalmaneser III (858–

824 B.C.E.) which he had erected to celebrate 31 military victories. Pictures at the very top show him seated on a throne receiving tribute from his conquered enemies and from nations that sought his help. In one panel we see the picture of Jehu, King of Israel, kneeling before him as his servants present rich tribute. He wrote,

"I received the tribute of Jehu, the Israelite, silver and gold . . ."

It is the first and only picture in existence of an ancient king of Israel.

13.   Page 305   *"End of the Northern Kingdom"*
                                      Tiglath-Pileser III

From a building inscription on clay we learn that Tiglath-Pileser III (744–727 B.C.E.) exacted tribute of King Menahem of Israel. "As for Menahem I overwhelmed him like a snowstorm . . . and imposed tribute upon him." He records that King Ahaz (Jehoahaz) of Judah paid him tribute. This is the first time that a Judean king is mentioned in archaeological records. He also boasts that, when Israel overthrew King Pekah, "I placed Hoshea as king over them."

Sargon II (721–705 B.C.E.)
The Fall of Samaria

Sargon II inscribed his name on many monuments. He referred to himself as "Conqueror of Samaria and of the entire country of Israel." He proudly recorded his victory over the Northern Kingdom thus,

"I besieged and conquered Samaria . . . I installed over them an officer of mine and imposed upon them the tribute of the former king."

14.   Page 310   *"Hezekiah also built a pool"*
                                      The Pool of Siloam

Anticipating the siege of Jerusalem by Sennacherib, King Hezekiah (715–687 B.C.E.) devised a brilliant means of getting water into the city. Archaeologists had long sought for this reservoir and at last found it. It was a great engineering feat. The Pool of Siloam inside the city was connected with the spring of Gihon on the outside. The event was celebrated with the so-called "Siloam Inscription" carved in the rock at the entrance. It reads in part,

"When the tunnel was driven through, And this was the way in which it was cut through . . . Each man toward his fellow, and while there were still three cubits to be cut through, (there was heard) the voice of a man calling to his fellow, axe against axe . . ."

15.   Page 318   *"Zedekiah, son of Josiah"*
                                      The Lachish Letters

About 25 years ago, during an excavation at the modern town of Tell ed-Duweir, ancient Lachish, a number of ostraca (potsherds on which messages were written in carbon ink) were discovered near a guard room at the gate of the city. These letters were sent by the commander of a small outpost north of the important city of Lachish to its military governor. They describe the conditions in Palestine during the Babylonian invasion. They are written in classical Hebrew prose and throw great light on the times of Jeremiah and portray the chaotic conditions in Judah during the last days of King Zedekiah. Jeremiah 34.7 echoes those tragic times.

16. Page 321   *"A King in exile"*
                                                             "Yaukin of Judah"

In 1939 information was published about 300 tablets which had been found earlier in the ruins of a building in Babylonia. These tablets, among other things, record the rations of grain and oil to prisoners of the King, captives and skilled workmen, who lived in Babylon during 595–570 B.C.E. One mentions "men of Judah," "sons of the King of Judah," and "Iaukin, king . . ." who was the King of Judah (Jehoiachin's name was transliterated Yaukin). This document indicates that King Jehoiachin, who headed the first captivity under Nebuchadnezzar II (605–562 B.C.E.), was being held as a hostage for the good behavior of the Judeans and that he was considered the true king.

Seals and Stamps

Further proof of King Jehoiachin's position comes from the discovery in Palestine of three stamped jar-handles which bear the words, "Belonging to Eliakim, steward of Yaukin."

Another stamp-seal from this time bears the following inscription, "To Gedaliah who is over the house." This is undoubtedly the same man whom Nebuchadnezzar appointed "over the people who remained in the land of Judah" after the fall of Jerusalem, and who was soon murdered. (II Kings 25.22-6 and Jeremiah 40.1)

17. Page 340   *Signet-ring of Jotham*

The only signet-ring of a King of Judah that has ever been found was picked up in the excavations of Ezion-geber. The signet-ring was hung on the belt of a prominent person and probably served to attest to his authority. The stone seal had figures engraved on it, and cut above in ancient Hebrew was the inscription — L Y T M where the letter "L" means "to" or "belonging to." Since no vowels are indicated, the consonants — Y T M — could only mean "YOTHAM" which is the proper name for "Jotham."

18.   Page 397 *"Captured Jerusalem"*
End of the Southern Kingdom
In 1956 archaeologists discovered four tablets in what has come to be known as "The Babylonian Chronicle." They tell about Nebuchadnezzar's capture of Jerusalem in 598–597 B.C.E. This was the first capture of Jerusalem when he took the King prisoner.

19.   Page 531 *The Cylinder of Cyrus*
When Cyrus conquered Babylonia, he prepared a baked cylinder of clay and wrote on it a full account of his achievements. He had a liberal policy towards conquered peoples. He "returned (to them) their habitations," rebuilt their sanctuaries. Under this policy, undoubtedly, Cyrus permitted the Judean exiles to return to Palestine. The declaration of Cyrus, about which we read in our Bible (Ezra 1.2-4; 6.3-5), gains new strength and significance in view of this Cylinder of Cyrus.

BIBLIOGRAPHY

In writing *Pathways Through the Bible*, many books too numerous to mention, have been consulted. The attention of readers and teachers is directed to the following volumes which they will find useful.

BIBLES

THE HOLY SCRIPTURES. A New Translation.
The Jewish Publication Society of America. 1917.
THE HOLY BIBLE. Revised Standard Version.
Thomas Nelson & Sons. 1952.

INTRODUCTIONS AND COMMENTARIES

THE PENTATEUCH AND HAFTORAHS. By Chief Rabbi Joseph H. Hertz.
Soncino Press. 1952.
PREFACE TO SCRIPTURE. By Solomon Freehof.
Union of American Hebrew Congregations. 1950.
INTRODUCTION TO THE OLD TESTAMENT. By Robert H. Pfeiffer.
Harper & Brothers. 1941.
THE INTERPRETER'S BIBLE. Volumes I to VI.
Abingdon-Cokesbury Press. 1952.

ARCHAEOLOGY AND THE BIBLE

THE JEWS. Edited by Louis Finkelstein.
Volume I, Chapter I, "The Biblical Period," by William Foxwell Albright.
The Jewish Publication Society of America. 1949.
THE ANCIENT NEAR EAST. An Anthology of Texts and Pictures.
Edited by James B. Pritchard.
Princeton University Press. 1958.
ARCHAEOLOGY AND THE OLD TESTAMENT. By James B. Pritchard.
Princeton University Press. 1958.
BIBLICAL ARCHAEOLOGY. By G. Ernest Wright.
The Westminster Press. 1957.

GENERAL REFERENCE BOOKS

ANCIENT ISRAEL. By Harry M. Orlinsky.
Cornell University Press. 1954.
OUTLINE OF JEWISH KNOWLEDGE. By Goldberg and Benderly.
Three Volumes. Bureau of Jewish Education. 1929.

EVERYDAY LIFE IN OLD TESTAMENT TIMES. By E. W. Heaton.
    Charles Scribner's Sons. 1956.
THE LEGENDS OF THE BIBLE. By Louis Ginzberg.
    The Jewish Publication Society of America. 1956.
THE WESTMINSTER HISTORICAL ATLAS TO THE BIBLE.
    Edited by G. E. Wright and T. V. Filson.
    The Westminster Press. 1946.